ALPINE LAKES WILDERNESS

ALPINE LAKES WILDERNESS

THE COMPLETE HIKING GUIDE

NATHAN BARNES & JEREMY BARNES

MOUNTAINEERS
BOOKS

TO ALL OUR CONSTANT TRAIL COMPANIONS, BOTH OLD AND NEW

 MOUNTAINEERS BOOKS is dedicated to
the exploration, preservation, and enjoyment of
outdoor and wilderness areas.

1001 SW Klickitat Way, Suite 201, Seattle, WA 98134
800-553-4453, www. mountaineersbooks. org

Printed in China
Distributed in the United Kingdom by Cordee, www. cordee. co. uk
First edition: first printing 2019, second printing 2021

Copyeditor: Kris Fulsaas
Cover and book design: Jen Grable
Cartographer: Lohnes+Wright
Cover photographs, front: *Isolation Lake gleams below Little Annapurna in the Upper Enchant-
ments (Hike 82)*; back, clockwise from top: *Big Heart Lake (Hike 66), balsam arrowroot along the
trail (Hike 62), marmot near the Chain Lakes Trail (Hike 74).*
Frontispiece: *Gem Lake from the High Lakes Trail en route to Wildcat Lakes (Hike 30)*
Last page: *Looking east from Putrid Pete's Peak (Hike 21) along the ridge to Mount Defiance*

The background maps for this book were produced using the online map viewer CalTopo. For
more information, visit caltopo.com.

Library of Congress Cataloging-in-Publication Data is available at https://lccn.loc.
gov/2018044987

Mountaineers Books titles may be purchased for corporate, educational, or other promotional
sales, and our authors are available for a wide range of events. For information on special
discounts or booking an author, contact our customer service at 800-553-4453 or
mbooks@mountaineersbooks.org.

Printed on FSC®-certified materials

ISBN (paperback): 978-1-68051-077-5
ISBN (ebook): 978-1-68051-078-2

An independent nonprofit publisher since 1960

CONTENTS

INTERSTATE 90

Snoqualmie River Basin

Central Snoqualmie Valley

Beyond Snoqualmie Pass

HIGHWAY 2

Skykomish

Icicle Creek Drainage and the Enchantments

EXTENDED BACKPACKS

HIKE FINDER

HIKE #	HIKE NAME	DISTANCE (MILES)	ELEVATION GAIN (IN/OUT, FEET)	HIGH POINT (FEET)	OVER-NIGHT	VIEWS	BEST SEASON	TRAIL TRAFFIC
	EASY							
2	CCC Road: West	5.4	400	1500			Year-round	Light
2	CCC Road: East	5.4	200	1500		Yes	Year-round	Light
5	Pratt River Trail	8.4	300	1300			Early summer to late fall	Moderate
6	Middle Fork Trail	11.4	300	1300	Yes		Year-round	Moderate
25	Talapus and Olallie Lakes	5.8	1200	3800	Yes		Late spring to late fall	Heavy
36	Gold Creek Pond	1.1	None	2550			Early spring to late fall	Moderate
46	Pete Lake	8.2	200	3000	Yes		Late spring to late fall	Moderate
48	Waptus Lake	16.9	900/300	3100	Yes		Early spring to late fall	Moderate to heavy
56	Hyas Lake and Little Hyas Lake	5.4	100	3500	Yes		Spring to late fall	Heavy
61	Red Top Lookout	3.0	350	5361		Yes	Early spring to late fall	Moderate
62	Ingalls Creek	6.0	900	2900	Yes		Late spring to late fall	Moderate
63	Lake Dorothy (shorter option)	3.0	900	3100	Yes		Late spring to late fall	Heavy
64	Evans Lake	1.0	50	3700	Yes		Late spring to late fall	Light
91	Icicle Creek Trail	10.0	500	3200	Yes		Late spring to fall	Moderate
	MODERATE							
1	Granite Lakes and Thompson Lake	12.2	3200/600	4100	Yes		Early summer to late fall	Light
3	Stegosaurus Butte	1.8	1000	2100		Yes	Late spring to early fall	Moderate
8	Otter Falls and Big Creek Falls	10.0	600	1700			Year-round	Moderate
9	Snoqualmie Lake	16.0	2100	3200	Yes		Late spring to early fall	Moderate
11	Tin Cup Joe Falls	4.2	600/100	2100			Late spring to early fall	Moderate
12	Myrtle Lake	9.8	2400	3800	Yes		Early summer to late fall	Moderate

HIKE #	HIKE NAME	DISTANCE (MILES)	ELEVATION GAIN (IN/OUT, FEET)	HIGH POINT (FEET)	OVER-NIGHT	VIEWS	BEST SEASON	TRAIL TRAFFIC
			MODERATE					
13	Hester Lake	10.4	2500	3900	Yes		Early summer to late fall	Light
14	Rock Creek	12.6	2700/100	4100	Yes		Late spring to early fall	Moderate
15	Goldmyer Hot Springs	10.9	700	2100	Yes		Early spring to late fall	Moderate
16	Loch Katrine	7.2	1500	3000			Early spring to late fall	Light
22	Mason Lake (shorter option)	6.8	2100	4300	Yes	Yes	Late spring to early fall	Heavy
23	Bandera Mountain	6.8	2900	5157		Yes	Early spring to early fall	Heavy
24	Island Lake	10.2	2500	4400	Yes		Late spring to early fall	Heavy
26	Pratt Lake via Pratt Lake Saddle	11.8	2300/750	4100	Yes	Yes	Spring to late fall	Moderate to light
28	Denny Creek and Melakwa Lake	8.5	2300	4600	Yes		Late spring to late fall	Heavy
29	Snow Lake and Source Lake Overlook	6.3	1300/400	4400	Yes	Yes	Late spring to late fall	Heavy
35	Kendall Peak Lakes	8.4	2100	4750		Yes	Late spring to late fall	Moderate
40	Margaret Lake	5.5	1600/300	5100	Yes		Early summer to early fall	Moderate to heavy
41	Rachel Lake	6.8	1900	4600	Yes		Late spring to early fall	Moderate to heavy
47	Diamond Lake via Polallie Ridge	8.0	2700	5100	Yes	Yes	Late spring to late fall	Moderate to heavy
50	Lake Ivanhoe	28.6	2600/300	4700	Yes	Yes	Early summer to fall	Moderate to heavy
54	Squaw Lake	5.4	1400	4800	Yes		Late spring to late fall	Moderate to heavy
55	Deep Lake (shorter option)	15.0	2200/1200	5600	Yes	Yes	Early summer to early fall	Moderate
58	Marmot Lake and Lake Clarice	8.6	1900/500	4900	Yes		Late spring to early fall	Heavy
59	Cathedral Rock and Deception Pass Loop	13.4	2800	5500	Yes	Yes	Summer to late fall	Moderate
60	Lake Ingalls	8.8	2100/100	6500	Yes	Yes	Early summer to late fall	Heavy
63	Bear, Deer, and Snoqualmie Lakes (longer option)	13.4	1600/700	3800	Yes		Late spring to late fall	Heavy

HIKE #	HIKE NAME	DISTANCE (MILES)	ELEVATION GAIN (IN/OUT, FEET)	HIGH POINT (FEET)	OVER-NIGHT	VIEWS	BEST SEASON	TRAIL TRAFFIC
			MODERATE					
68	Tonga Ridge and Fisher Lake	8.8	900/400	5200	Yes	Yes	Late spring to early fall	Moderate
69	Deception Creek to Deception Lakes	16.6	3100	5100	Yes		Early spring to late fall	Light
70	Surprise and Glacier Lakes	9.5	2700	4900	Yes		Late spring to early fall	Moderate
72	Hope and Mig Lakes	4.2	1500	4700	Yes		Late spring to early fall	Light to moderate
73	Josephine Lake	10.4	1500/800	5100	Yes	Yes	Late spring to early fall	Moderate
76	Wildhorse Creek	9.8	2100	4900	Yes	Yes	Early summer to late fall	Moderate
78	Larch Lake and Chiwaukum Lake	23.8	4300/100	6100	Yes		Late summer to late fall	Light
80	Icicle Ridge	4.6	1800	3000		Yes	Late spring to late fall	Heavy
83	Colchuck Lake	8.8	2300	5600	Yes		Late spring to late fall	Moderate to heavy
84	Lake Stuart	9.0	1600	5100	Yes		Late spring to early fall	Moderate to heavy
85	Eightmile Lake	7.8	1400	4700	Yes		Late spring to late fall	Moderate to heavy
88	Trout Lake	12.4	2000	4800	Yes		Late spring to late fall	Moderate
92	Klonaqua Lakes	18.2	2300	5100	Yes		Summer to fall	Light
93	Dutch Miller Gap and Williams Lake	34.3	4800	5900	Yes	Yes	Summer to early fall	Moderate
94	I-90 Lakes Tour	23.8	5300	5584	Yes	Yes	Late spring to late fall	Heavy
96	Trail Creek and Deep Lake Loop	31.5	5800	5600	Yes		Late spring to early fall	Moderate
97	Ingalls Creek to Lake Ingalls	31.0	4600	6500	Yes	Yes	Summer to early fall	Moderate
			HARD					
4	Rainy Lake	8.0	2900	3900	Yes		Late spring to early fall	Light
7	Marten Lake	8.4	1800	3000	Yes		Late spring to early fall	Moderate
10	Nordrum Lake	16.0	2700	3800	Yes		Late spring to early fall	Moderate
17	Sunday Lake	6.4	300	1900	Yes		Summer to early fall	Light

HIKE #	HIKE NAME	DISTANCE (MILES)	ELEVATION GAIN (IN/OUT, FEET)	HIGH POINT (FEET)	OVER-NIGHT	VIEWS	BEST SEASON	TRAIL TRAFFIC
			HARD					
18	Bare Mountain	8.2	3200	5353		Yes	Late spring to early fall	Light
19	Bear Basin Mines	6.0	2400	4200	Yes		Late spring to early fall	Light
20	Lennox Creek and Anderson Lake	10.2	2500/500	4600	Yes	Yes	Early summer to late fall	Very light
21	Putrid Pete's Peak	4.8	3000	5220		Yes	Late spring to late fall	Moderate
22	Mount Defiance (longer option)	10.4	3400	5584	Yes	Yes	Late spring to early fall	Heavy
27	Granite Mountain	8.6	3700	5629		Yes	Late spring to early fall	Heavy
30	Gem and Wildcat Lakes	13.8	2500/1300	4900	Yes	Yes	Early summer to fall	Heavy
31	Snoqualmie Mountain	3.0	3100	6278		Yes	Early summer to early fall	Moderate
32	Guye Peak	2.5	2000	5168		Yes	Late spring to early fall	Light
33	Commonwealth Basin to Red Pass	8.8	2400	5400		Yes	Late spring to early fall	Moderate
34	Kendall Peak and Kendall Katwalk	12.2	3000	5784		Yes	Early summer to early fall	Heavy
37	Alaska Lake	11.5	1700	4200	Yes		Late spring to early fall	Moderate
38	Rampart Lakes Backdoor	5.4	1700/300	5500	Yes	Yes	Early summer to early fall	Light
39	Lake Lillian and Mount Margaret	5.2	2000	5560	Yes	Yes	Early summer to fall	Light
42	Alta Mountain and Lila Lake	11.2	4000/200	6151	Yes	Yes	Early summer to early fall	Moderate to heavy
43	Hibox Mountain	7.0	3800	6547		Yes	Early summer to early fall	Moderate
44	Thorp Mountain	6.4	2300	5854		Yes	Late spring to late fall	Light
45	Mineral Creek	8.6	2500	4740	Yes		Early summer to late fall	Light to moderate
49	Spade and Venus Lakes	26.2	3600/300	5700	Yes	Yes	Early summer to fall	Moderate
51	Davis Peak	10.0	4000	6426		Yes	Late spring to early fall	Moderate
52	Sprite Lake via Paddy-Go-Easy Pass	6.6	2700	6100	Yes	Yes	Summer to late fall	Light

HIKE #	HIKE NAME	DISTANCE (MILES)	ELEVATION GAIN (IN/OUT, FEET)	HIGH POINT (FEET)	OVER-NIGHT	VIEWS	BEST SEASON	TRAIL TRAFFIC
			HARD					
53	Lake Michael	17.0	2500/800	5200	Yes	Yes	Early summer to late fall	Light to moderate
53	Lake Terence	20.2	3000/900	5600	Yes	Yes	Early summer to late fall	Light to moderate
55	Lake Vicente	19.0	3300/1200	5600	Yes	Yes	Early summer to early fall	Moderate
57	Tuck Lake and Robin Lakes	12.4	2900	6300	Yes	Yes	Late spring to early fall	Heavy
65	Rock Lake	4.4	1500/700	5300	Yes	Yes	Late spring to late fall	Very light
66	Foss Lakes	14.6	3300/300	4900	Yes		Early summer to late fall	Moderate to heavy
67	Necklace Valley	16.8	3200	4800	Yes		Early summer to late fall	Moderate to heavy
71	Trap Lake	9.2	2200/400	5400	Yes	Yes	Summer to early fall	Light
74	Chain Lakes and Doelle Lakes	22.2	3900/2200	6200	Yes	Yes	Early summer to early fall	Light to moderate
75	Whitepine Creek	12.0	1100	3900	Yes		Fall	Very light
77	Lake Ethel	9.1	3300/200	5700	Yes	Yes	Late spring to early fall	Moderate
79	Lake Augusta	14.8	4000	6800	Yes	Yes	Early summer to late fall	Light
81	Snow Lakes and Nada Lake	13.6	4200	5500	Yes	Yes	Late spring to early fall	Moderate
82	The Enchantments	25.2	6500	7800	Yes	Yes	Late summer to fall	Moderate
86	Lake Caroline	9.6	2500/100	6300	Yes	Yes	Late spring to fall	Moderate
87	Lake Edna and Cape Horn	11.2	4500/400	6750	Yes	Yes	Summer to early fall	Light
89	Cradle Lake	17.8	3400/100	6200	Yes	Yes	Summer to fall	Light
90	Bootjack Mountain	7.0	3900	6789		Yes	Summer to early fall	Very light
95	Pacific Crest Trail– Dutch Miller Gap Loop	57.6	11,400	5980	Yes	Yes	Summer to early fall	Heavy
98	Ladies Lakes Loop	21.8	5600	7100	Yes	Yes	Summer to fall	Moderate
99	The Cradle Loop	33.3	6400	6400	Yes	Yes	Late spring to fall	Moderate
100	PCT Through-Hike	67.6	14,200	5980	Yes	Yes	Summer to early fall	Moderate

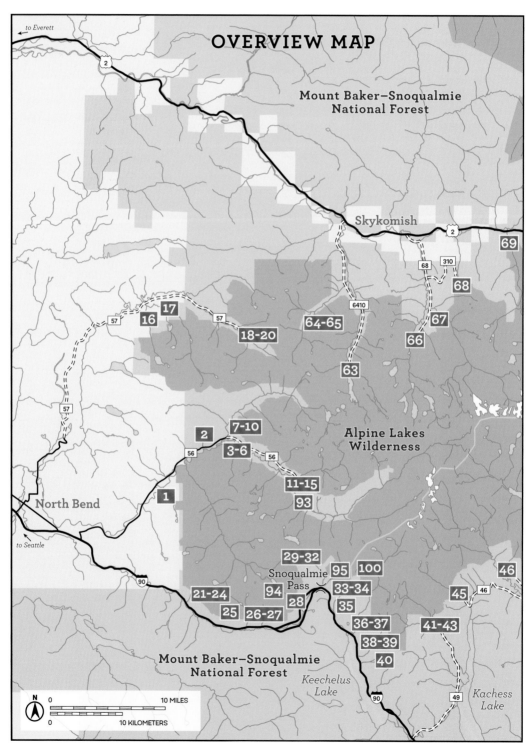

OVERVIEW MAP

to Everett

Mount Baker–Snoqualmie
National Forest

Skykomish

69

68

68   310

68

16 **17**

57

18-20

64-65

67

66

63

57

57

**Alpine Lakes
Wilderness**

7-10

2

3-6

56

56

11-15

93

1

North Bend

to Seattle

90

29-32

Snoqualmie
Pass

95 **100**

94

33-34

46

28

35

45

46

21-24

25 **26-27**

36-37

38-39

41-43

40

Mount Baker–Snoqualmie
National Forest

Keechelus
Lake

90

49

Kachess
Lake

N

0   10 MILES

0   10 KILOMETERS

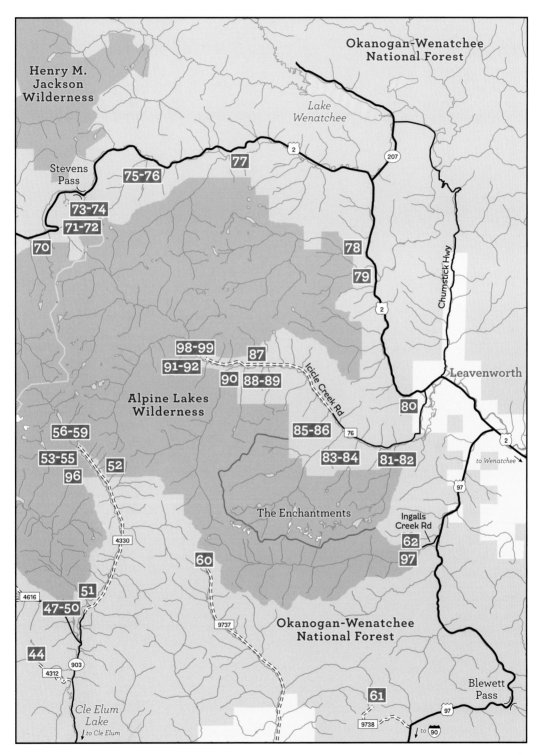

Okanogan-Wenatchee
National Forest

Henry M.
Jackson
Wilderness

Lake
Wenatchee

207

2

77

Stevens
Pass

75-76

73-74

71-72

70

78

79

Chumstick Hwy

2

98-99

91-92

87

Icicle Creek Rd

90

88-89

Leavenworth

Alpine Lakes
Wilderness

80

2

to Wenatchee

56-59

85-86

76

53-55

96

52

83-84

81-82

97

The Enchantments

4330

Ingalls
Creek Rd

62

60

97

51

4616

47-50

9737

Okanogan-Wenatchee
National Forest

44

903

4312

Blewett
Pass

61

97

Cle Elum
Lake

9738

to

90

to Cle Elum

INTRODUCTION

A sprawling, nearly 415,000-acre wonderland, the Alpine Lakes Wilderness encompasses old-growth forest, glacier-dredged creek valleys, and ice-sharpened peaks. Bounded on the north by Highway 2 and on the south by Interstate 90, the wilderness straddles the Cascade Crest, extending nearly to North Bend in the west and near Leavenworth in the east. It includes the section of the Pacific Crest National Scenic Trail (PCT) from Snoqualmie Pass to Stevens Pass, as well as the renowned Enchantments surrounding Mount Stuart.

Scattered throughout this wild and rugged landscape lie the glittering namesake alpine waters; more than seven hundred lakes, tarns, ponds, and pools are tucked in the wilderness. The stunning mountaintops and lakesides carved by geological forces and glaciation have drawn people for generations. The centuries of visitors, from indigenous peoples and prospectors to surveyors and PCT through-hikers, have left their mark: a system of trails has developed that today covers more than 600 miles.

The Alpine Lakes Wilderness includes a wide variety of flora and fauna, with stark differences between the wetter western side of the Cascades and the more arid portions on the eastern side of the mountain passes. Entire books are dedicated to this complex and diverse wilderness environment, exploring its climate, geology, wildlife, forests, and geography. Such books are fantastic resources for deepening visitors' understanding of the wilderness and digging into the finer details of what the wilderness holds (see the Bibliography at the end of this book). Thus, this guide intentionally avoids technical terms, scientific names, and extensive natural-history detail to focus instead on the experience of hiking the trails and the lore associated with them.

The trails and their stories are all connected by the overarching history of the Alpine Lakes Wilderness. Created in 1976, the area encompassed by the wilderness has not always enjoyed the protection and safeguards it has today. The scars left by mining, logging, and industry hint at how close this now-treasured wilderness came to becoming something much smaller and quite different. The gripping tale of how a scrappy group of conservationists, wilderness protectors, and trail stewards came together in 1968 to form what would become the Alpine Lakes Protection Society (ALPS) and spearhead the unlikely creation of the Alpine Lakes Wilderness is fascinating. Spurred by logging, road projects, and the prospect of a shrinking wilderness isolated to rocky islands above the tree line, ALPS spent years battling the US Forest Service, lobbying Congress, and standing up to opposing interest groups to protect this unique landscape.

While ALPS succeeded in creating the Alpine Lakes Wilderness, its work is ongoing and will never be complete. New challenges continue to arise, and the legacy of private ownership means that wilderness advocacy is still very much needed. Remember that the hikes in this guide and the majestic landscape

OPPOSITE: *Otter Falls tumbles down a natural granite spillway into Lipsy Lake (Hike 8).*

A yellow-pine chipmunk in the eastern Cascades

the trails travel through exist because of the tireless efforts of past protectors. When hiking these trails, treat the wilderness with respect, recognizing how hard people fought to preserve the opportunity for everyone to enjoy it. Better yet, find ways to connect with advocates and play a part in continuing the work of protecting wild places.

LAND MANAGERS

The Alpine Lakes Wilderness spans two separate national forests, divided more or less along the Cascade Crest: to the west is the Mount Baker–Snoqualmie National Forest, while to the east is the Okanogan-Wenatchee National Forest. The US Forest Service divides each of these national forests into two ranger districts each; for contact information for these four ranger districts, see the list at the back of this book. The Forest Service provides helpful pamphlets on wilderness regulations and guidelines that can be found on the Forest Service websites also listed in the back of this book. An overnight in the Enchantment Lakes area (Hikes 81–86) requires an additional permit process, outlined on the Forest Service website. The wilderness regulations and permit requirements

change frequently enough that it is not prudent to reproduce them here. While many guidebooks try to provide that information as a service to readers, they become quickly out of date, and bad information can ruin a carefully planned backpacking trip. Instead, hikers and backpackers should review the regulations and permit requirements every season to keep up with any changes.

It's also a good practice to check road and trail conditions before getting in the car and heading to the trailhead. Current road and trail conditions can be found on the Forest Service websites. The Washington Trails Association (www.wta.org) is also an excellent resource on trail conditions, as members of the organization often post recent trip reports that offer insight into the current conditions of a trail.

HIKING BEST PRACTICES

Hiking is perhaps the most approachable of outdoor activities. You do not need special equipment or training. The surroundings in which you undertake a walking journey from one destination to another are what distinguish a hike from a mere stroll. Your morning walk to your office, bus stop, or school or the daily trip down two flights of stairs to the office coffee machine are all walking journeys—but they are not hikes. Where the journey takes you and your reason for undertaking the journey are what make it a hike.

Perhaps because hiking appears so easy, many hikers do not put a trail into context before they start barreling down it. *Where* you're hiking matters, and not all hiking is the same. With one or two exceptions, every hike in this guide involves spending time in the Alpine Lakes Wilderness. Hiking in the wilderness is very different from sticking closer to civilization, and hikers should prepare accordingly.

This guide assumes that readers have some hiking experience and know they should approach trails with an abundance of caution. It cannot warn of every hazard that a hiker may encounter on any given trail, as trail conditions are constantly in flux. If you are new to hiking, round up some more-experienced friends to bring along. These broad guidelines—not intended as a primer on "How to Hike"—offer some topics to consider as you plan.

Be Aware

Although most hikers return from their trips without incident, hiking in the wilderness is filled with potential hazards. Loose trail surface, rotten snow, rockfall, lightning strikes, falling trees, fast-running icy creeks, snakebites, charging goats, and much more can be found along the trails in this book. At the same time, prepared hikers who pay attention to their surroundings can usually avoid these dangers. In short, be aware and do not assume that the wilderness is safe.

Be aware that trail routes and conditions may have changed significantly since the time of this writing. If a route ever seems unsafe, listen to your instincts. Always exercise caution and do not be afraid to turn around and hike another day, even when the rest of your group disagrees with your assessment. As beautiful and enjoyable as the wilderness is, it is also indifferent and unforgiving.

Check the Weather

It should go without saying that you should check the weather report before heading out to hike. Do that for every hike, regardless of where you're headed.

Hiking in the Alpine Lakes Wilderness requires some additional weather observation. Weather can change extremely rapidly in the wilderness, with unpredicted storms whipping up to blacken blue skies in a matter of hours. These storms can bring heavy rain, high wind, and snow. Do not get caught unprepared and have to take steps to avoid hypothermia. Even on the brightest, sunniest of summer days, carry lightweight raingear. For other times of year, warmer raingear might be more appropriate. Use your best judgment.

Bring the Right Gear

Pages upon pages could be filled describing the best equipment for any given hike, what is a must-have and what is superfluous. Backpackers and hikers spend endless hours arguing that the gear they use, the way they pack, and the methods they use on the trail are superior. The truth is that there really isn't any perfect answer for what gear you must bring into the Alpine Lakes Wilderness. It is all about context.

That said, always pack the Ten Essentials. If you do not know what they are, consider finding a more-experienced hiker to accompany you on your first trails in the Alpine Lakes Wilderness. The Ten Essentials can be grouped into two broad categories: to prevent and respond to emergencies (1–5) and to spend a night outside (6–10):

1. Navigation—map and compass
2. Headlamp or LED flashlight
3. Sun protection
4. First-aid kit
5. Knife
6. Fire—matches and firestarter
7. Shelter—emergency blanket
8. Extra food
9. Extra water—and/or water filtration system
10. Extra clothes

Lupine on Icicle Ridge above the town of Leavenworth (Hike 80)

Note that for several hikes we recommend that you bring an extra pair of lightweight shoes for fording major creeks or rivers, as well as hiking poles to aid in crossing. For other hikes with easier crossings, waterproof boots should work fine.

While there are few right answers to the question of what gear to bring, there are certainly wrong answers. When hiking in the Alpine Lakes Wilderness, avoid taking any of the following:

- Sandals or lightweight tennis shoes: These footwear choices unnecessarily increase the risk of foot injury and make it harder to navigate the trail. Wear lugged-sole hiking sneakers or, for rugged trails, waterproof or water-resistant hiking boots for ankle protection and traction on rocky terrain.
- Clothing that is restrictive, difficult to move in, or not functional: Don't wear something that will make it more difficult to survive a night in the wilderness if necessary.
- Food on overnight trips without a way to secure it from scavengers and bears: Always bring a bear can or a sturdy sack and a length of rope to hang up your food.

Leave No Trace and Have Zero Impact
The alpine high country is extremely fragile. Errant feet can cause damage that will take the

landscape many years to recover from. With so many people exploring the Alpine Lakes Wilderness every year, it is critical to treat these areas respectfully, lest they be loved and enjoyed right into oblivion.

Attempt a zero-impact approach when hiking through sensitive and fragile areas. Hike in small groups, stick to the trail and rocks, and use backcountry toilets where available. Camp only at existing sites, and practice Leave No Trace principles. If you are not familiar with Leave No Trace, take some time to review this philosophy on their website, https://lnt.org /learn/7-principles. The goal is to leave no indication of your time in the wilderness.

Follow Trail Etiquette

Hiking culture has its own etiquette, which includes certain practices that other hikers will assume you know, understand, and follow. Following this etiquette will help you better share the trail.

- Hikers headed downhill yield to hikers climbing uphill. Hikers working their way uphill are focused on that effort, while those going down are better positioned to step aside for those headed up.
- Don't cut switchbacks. This practice destabilizes the slope and makes it more likely that large sections of trail will be destroyed. There is never a need to take a shortcut; after all, spending time in the wild is the whole reason for hiking!
- Slower hikers yield to faster hikers. There is no wrong pace for a hike, but hikers taking the slow approach need to be aware of those coming up behind them to avoid creating a traffic jam on narrow trails.
- Unless a trail is flooded with people, it is customary to give a simple greeting to other hikers you encounter on the trail.
- Because sound carries a long, long way in the wilderness, be aware that your voice could cover a great distance and disturb wildlife and people you may not be able to see. You don't need to speak only in hushed, reverent whispers—speaking at normal tones and volume levels is just fine. Avoid shouting, especially around lakes or open areas where there are fewer trees to muffle the sound.
- Leave no trace. Pack out what you bring in. Don't carve your initials into logs, draw on rocks, cut down trees, create shortcuts on the trail, or otherwise mar the wilderness.

HAVE FUN

Hiking and backpacking through the Alpine Lakes Wilderness is an always rewarding, sometimes life-altering experience. Many of the routes outlined in this book pass through truly stunning landscapes and access remote areas where few boots have trodden. The path will be long and some part of your body will probably be aching by the end of the day, but you will also have a lot of fun. It's not every day that you can experience this wilderness. Our hope is that this guide will minimize the amount of time you spend planning your trip, giving you more hours to spend in awe of this majestic landscape.

HOW TO USE THIS GUIDE

Inside these pages you will find popular hikes and destinations within the Alpine Lakes Wilderness, as well as many lesser-known and less frequently traveled trails. This guide helps hikers, backpackers, wilderness explorers, and outdoor enthusiasts gain insight into the hundreds of miles of trails in and around the Alpine Lakes Wilderness.

It is organized to allow readers to quickly and easily find the information they are looking for. The bulk of the book broadly divides hikes into two geographical areas based on how the trailheads are accessed: along Interstate 90 and along Highway 2. Within these two parts, hikes are further organized into regional chapters based on the highways and forest roads that provide access to the trailheads. Within each part and chapter, hikes are presented in the order in which the reader will reach the trailheads when driving down the access road. The goal is to allow readers to quickly flip to hikes they want to consider. Generally speaking, within the first two parts, the higher the hike number, the farther east the hike is, and within each chapter, the higher the hike number, the farther down the access road it is. The third part, Extended Backpacks, includes longer hikes that are organized from west to east by trailhead (with the exception of Hike 100, which starts in the south and heads north).

There are 100 hikes in this guide, and each includes a description of what a hiker can expect to experience along the trail. An information summary provides trail data (such as elevation gain, high point, and hiking time). Following that are directions to the trailhead. Each hike write-up provides enough information to enable readers to choose a hike that will

work for their group, the time available to hike, and the current weather and trail conditions. Maps and route descriptions further aid hikers and backpackers in their adventures. The maps in this book are intended to help readers put a hike into the context of the surrounding landscape and give a general idea of where certain features are, but we recommend that you bring topographic USGS or Green Trails maps on the trail. Each hike concludes with suggestions for extending the hike and a brief history of the trail and its environs.

INFORMATION SUMMARIES

Each hike's summary includes key trail data, such as distance and elevation gain, plus information such as which topographic map covers the area and what permits are required.

Distance: All distances are given in miles, round-trip from the trailhead to the destination and back. They were calculated by comparing and cross-checking several different sources of information, including our firsthand experience, so as to be as accurate as possible. Additional text clarifies if the hike has more than one destination or any other ambiguity. The given mileages can, and often do, vary from the mileages seen on signs along the trail or in other sources. In many cases, this is due to trail routes changing over time and methods

OPPOSITE: *The snowy shores of Larch Lake (Hike 78)*

The boulder-strewn scramble to the summit of Little Annapurna (Hike 82), with Prusik Peak in the distance

for measuring trail distances varying, so subsequently those measurements are rounded into the nice, clean tenths of a mile that trail-goers expect.

Elevation Gain: The approximate amount of elevation hikers can expect to climb to the destination is given in feet, rounded to the nearest ten. If there is significant elevation gain on the return hike to the trailhead, this is also provided. In most cases, the gain is simply the difference between the starting elevation and the highest point on the trail. We do not account for situations in which elevation is lost and then regained farther down the trail. If hikers want to know that information, they can study a topographic map to discern a trail's ups and downs.

High Point: The highest point of elevation is provided in feet, to let hikers know how high they will be climbing. This approximate figure is useful in assessing whether a trail is above the snow line or likely has lingering snow in spring or even summer. If a hike ends at the top of an officially measured summit, the summit elevation is used.

Difficulty: Each hike is given a difficulty rating of easy, moderate, or hard. These subjective ratings are intended to give hikers a rough idea of how much effort is required to complete a hike. While the total elevation gain is a good indicator of how much climbing is involved,

some hikes spread that amount evenly along the trail, while others bunch it up in tight, steep bursts. Beyond elevation gain, other factors rolled into the difficulty rating include the quality of the trail, the difficulty of navigating obstacles, and the extent to which the trail is maintained. Depending on your fitness level and what you consider a reasonable amount of effort on a given hike, you may find that, for example, a hike rated "hard" is closer to "moderate" for you.

Hiking Time: The approximate number of hours it will take the average hiker to complete the hike is given, sometimes in a range. It is possible that some focused hikers will complete the hikes in less time and just as likely that some hikers will take more. This entry gives a general idea of the amount of time to set aside for enjoying the hike at a reasonable pace. Some longer hikes say "overnight" in addition to—or instead of—a time estimate, and the backpacking trips in Extended Backpacks give a range of days rather than hours.

The striking contrast between iron-rich rock and dark green forest is apparent from the saddle above Cradle Lake (Hike 99).

Backpackers working their way back down from Peggys Pond are rewarded with views of the still waters of Deep Lake (Hike 96).

Best Season: In general, the best season to hike in the Alpine Lakes Wilderness is mid-summer through the first half of fall. Some trails climb to heights where snow lingers later, and others are low enough that they can be hiked in the spring. For each hike, a range of seasons is given—not only for when the trail is most likely accessible, but also for when the trail conditions are best. These general guidelines may not hold from year to year: some years the snow melts weeks earlier than expected, and in others it holds on until August. Always check the most current trail conditions before heading to the trailhead.

Trail Traffic: This entry includes foot traffic, livestock traffic (mostly equestrian), and mountain bikers. Trail traffic is based on typical weekend traffic on the trail during summer. These subjective ratings, measured as light, moderate, or heavy, give hikers an idea of a trail's popularity with other users as well as hikers.

Permit: The permit or permits required to park at the trailhead are listed here. In most cases this will be either a Northwest Forest Pass, issued by the Forest Service, or a Discover Pass, issued by the State of Washington. All day hiking and backpacking in the Alpine Lakes Wilderness requires a permit that can be obtained at no cost at self-service kiosks at every wilderness trailhead. Spending the night in certain designated zones within the Enchantment Lakes area requires a fee and an additional permit. Currently, securing a permit requires entering a competitive lottery or grabbing one of the few first-come, first-served permits available on a daily basis from the Leavenworth Ranger Station. However, the requirements and process have changed many times over the years, so make sure to visit www.fs.usda.gov

/detail/okawen/passes-permits/recreation/ to find the most up-to-date information.

Maps: United States Geological Survey (USGS) and Green Trails maps are listed for each hike. USGS maps are excellent for hiking off-trail and orienting by compass, while Green Trails maps are a better resource for hiking on trails. While the 15-minute Green Trails map is generally listed for each hike, most hikers will find that purchasing just two maps—Green Trails Alpine Lakes West–Stevens Pass No. 176S and Green Trails Alpine Lakes East–Stuart Range No. 208SX—will be sufficient.

Trailhead GPS: The GPS coordinates (in decimal degrees) for the trailhead are intended to allow drivers with navigation systems to plug in the coordinates and have an easier time finding their way to the trailhead. Of course, consult the accompanying driving directions to make sure they generally align with where your navigation device is directing you. The coordinates were calculated based on the WGS 84 datum.

Notes: Some trails have significant obstacles or difficulties that hikers must be aware of before starting out. A common example is a creek ford; several hikes in this guide require wading across a creek or river, and hikers will need to come prepared for that crossing. Other considerations mentioned in this entry include crowded parking conditions, special permits, or road conditions that require high clearance or four-wheel drive.

GETTING THERE
Driving directions to the trailhead start from a major highway, such as Interstate 90 or Highway 2. All trailheads can be approached from either the west or the east side of the Cascades, so driving directions take that into account.

GOING FARTHER
There is almost always the possibility of adding a few extra miles to a day or a few extra destinations to a weekend in the wild. This section points hikers toward such possibilities, both

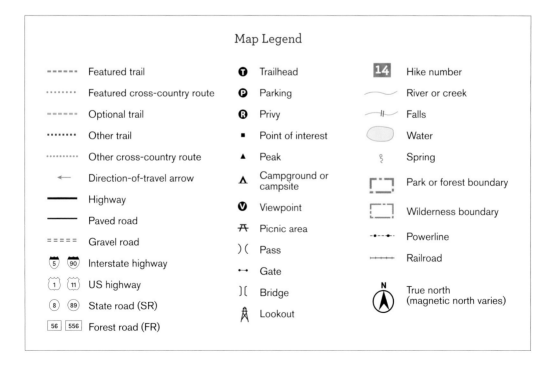

other hikes within the book and those that are not. These suggestions typically provide a broad description of the additional trail miles required to reach the destination; hikers should be sure to have a detailed map, consult other sources as necessary, and, in some instances, be comfortable traveling off-trail or along a faint path.

HISTORY

Every trail has a story to tell: a reason the trail was cut through the forest, blasted out of rock, or carved into a mountainside. Sometimes that reason is simply to get to a delightful alpine lake, but more often than not the trail follows in the footsteps of prospectors, lumberjacks, and fisherfolk. The jagged, ice-carved landscape of the Alpine Lakes Wilderness has drawn people for generations, and where there are people, there are stories. This section provides a window into that history and helps to connect trail users to the trail and the land. Humans are curious creatures, and knowing what came before can enhance your appreciation of a hike.

A NOTE ABOUT SAFETY

Safety is an important concern in all outdoor activities. No guidebook can alert you to every hazard or anticipate the limitations of every reader. Therefore, the descriptions of roads, trails, routes, and natural features in this book are not representations that a particular place or excursion will be safe for your party. When you follow any of the routes described in this book, you assume responsibility for your own safety. Under normal conditions, such excursions require the usual attention to traffic, road and trail conditions, weather, terrain, the capabilities of your party, and other factors. Keeping informed on current conditions and exercising common sense are the keys to a safe, enjoyable outing.

—Mountaineers Books

OPPOSITE: *Rachel Lake and Rampart Ridge seen from the route up to Alta Mountain (Hike 42)*

INTERSTATE 90

View from the 5353-foot summit of Bare Mountain (Hike 18)

1   GRANITE LAKES AND THOMPSON LAKE

DISTANCE: 12.2 miles to Thompson Lake; add
1.2 miles for round-trip to Granite Lakes
ELEVATION GAIN: 3200 feet in to Thompson Lake;
600 feet out from Thompson Lake
HIGH POINT: 4100 feet
DIFFICULTY: Moderate
HIKING TIME: 6 to 8 hours

BEST SEASON: Early summer to late fall
TRAIL TRAFFIC: Light foot traffic
PERMIT: Discover Pass
MAPS: USGS Lake Philippa, USGS Bandera;
Green Trails Middle Fork Snoqualmie No. 174SX
TRAILHEAD GPS: 47.4926°N, 121.6398°W

GETTING THERE: Take I-90 to Exit 34 near North Bend. At 468th Avenue just off the freeway, eastbound turn left, westbound turn right. Follow the road past the truck stop for about a half mile to SE Middle Fork Road (Forest Road 56). Turn right and follow this road for a few twists and turns, keeping left when the road splits. After 2.2 miles reach SE Lake Dorothy Road. Turn left, passing the Mailbox Peak Trailhead, and continue 3.6 miles to the Granite Creek Trailhead on the right just before crossing the Middle Fork Snoqualmie River. Privy available.

Rushing creeks, alpine lakes, and craggy mountaintops are all abundant on this hike along repurposed logging roads, complete with sections of newly constructed trail. Whether you're exploring Granite Lakes or spending the night at Thompson Lake, this hike is an excellent alternative to the crowds at Mailbox Peak. Overlooked for decades and now much more accessible, the Granite Creek Trail still does not see anything close to the traffic of its ever-popular neighbor. With more to see than can reasonably be enjoyed on a single visit, you're likely to need a few trips up into the Granite Creek valley to fully experience it.

From the Granite Creek Trailhead, follow a gravel trail into a young forest of alder, hemlock, and fir. The newly upgraded trail, in the Middle Fork Snoqualmie Natural Resources Conservation Area on the edge of the Alpine Lakes Wilderness, follows old roadbed steadily upward as it presses deeper into the creek valley. As you climb, openings in the canopy reveal the haystack of Mount Si just behind Mount Teneriffe and Green Mountain. Behind you, Rattlesnake Mountain eventually becomes visible, before the road takes you around the back of Mailbox Peak. At the same time, keep an eye out for mossy stumps with springboard notches cut into them, a lasting reminder of the area's timber history.

After 1.0 mile and a short-but-steep set of switchbacks, climb onto firm roadbed. This junction marks the connection with the old Granite Creek Trail route, now called the Granite Creek Connector Trail. If you were to head right and follow the connector trail downhill, it would take you to the old trailhead located on FR 56 near the Mailbox Peak parking lot. Instead, turn left at this junction, following the sounds of Granite Creek as it tumbles past the trail. Soon cross Granite Creek on a sturdy bridge, followed by a half dozen stream crossings of varying difficulty depending on the time of year. Most pose little challenge, but the largest may wet your boots when the water is high.

At 3.2 miles reach the signed junction for Thompson Lake. The Granite Creek Trail continues 0.6 mile down to both Granite Lakes, nestled beneath a craggy ridge that includes Mailbox Peak and Dirty Harry's Peak. The lakeshores offer sweeping views of the valley: a veritable sea of snowcapped mountains dominates the northwestern horizon. There's plenty of room to settle in near these pleasant tree-lined lakes and enjoy the landscape.

Thompson Lake is another 2.3 miles up and over a substantial ridge to the water and the Alpine Lakes Wilderness boundary. The route to the top of the ridge continues to follow a logging road, steadily working its way up the mountainside at a reasonable grade. The road gives way to trail at the top, becoming the Thompson Lake Spur Trail #1009.3 as it descends to the lake. Here the skyline

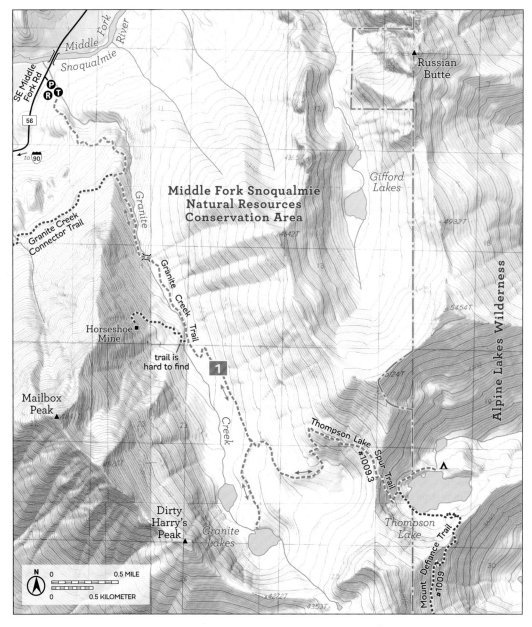

The forest is reflected in Upper Granite Lake below Dirty Harrys Peak, shrouded in the clouds above.

is dominated by Mount Defiance. For those spending the night, campsites are all along the lakeshore, with more-established sites near the lake outlet.

GOING FARTHER

For those interested in the area's mining history, the Horseshoe Mine on the slopes of Mailbox Peak is an interesting side trip. At 2.2 miles from the Granite Creek Trailhead, look for a slight dip in the trail indicating the long-overgrown road that once provided access to the mine. The otherwise unmarked trail requires a little bushwhacking to find a way across Granite Creek. The barely recognizable remains of the bridge that once spanned the creek can still be used, though nearby rocks and logs may prove easier to navigate. On the other side of the creek, the wide roadbed is easy to find, marked by the rusting remains of a 1941 Chevrolet Special Deluxe Coupe. Once across, follow the path uphill until it disappears, then use GPS to help guide you the last few thousand feet to the mine, whose location is marked on the map data of some GPS software.

From the west end of Thompson Lake, at the junction with the Mount Defiance Trail #1009, through-hikers can continue on, switchbacking steeply up the mountainside to the summit, then clambering down the rough and rooty trail to Mason Lake (Hike 22) and the Ira Spring Memorial Trail. Those looking for a few extra miles can return via the Granite Creek Connector Trail, which runs 2.8 miles to a small parking area on FR 56. From there it's another 3.5 miles along the Middle Fork Road back to the Granite Creek Trailhead.

HISTORY

Mining and logging have been a part of the Granite Creek drainage for more than a century, with various roads punched out to Granite Lakes and up into the surrounding ridges. While most logging activity deeper in the Middle Fork Snoqualmie Valley stopped many decades ago, the Washington Department of Natural Resources (DNR) has managed the area as a working forest, and as a result, the trees are younger and the signs of logging are much more apparent.

Less apparent is the mining activity that predates the timber industry. Back in 1904,

the Horse Shoe Mining Company was established in Seattle and eventually held eleven claims covering 220 acres in the Middle Fork Snoqualmie and Pratt River Valleys. One of the company's first claims, known as "Horse Shoe," was centered around a four-foot-wide vein of bornite ore. From this vein, now known as the Horseshoe Mine, miners used hand drills to follow the bornite a few hundred feet into Mailbox Peak. The bornite was then hauled out of the river valley to be smelted for copper. Sometime before 1909, the bornite ran out, and the company abandoned the claim.

Today, the remains of the mine slumber in the forests above Granite Creek. The DNR created the Middle Fork Snoqualmie Natural Resources Conservation Area in 2011 by setting aside 9000 acres, which has slowly grown over the last few years to nearly 11,000 acres encompassing Mailbox Peak, Granite Lakes, and Gifford Lakes.

2 CCC ROAD

DISTANCE: 5.4 miles heading west or east
ELEVATION GAIN: 400 feet heading west; 200 feet heading east
HIGH POINT: 1500 feet
DIFFICULTY: Easy
HIKING TIME: 3 to 4 hours
TRAIL TRAFFIC: Light foot traffic

BEST SEASON: Accessible year-round; best late summer to early fall
PERMIT: Northwest Forest Pass
MAPS: USGS Lake Philippa; Green Trails Middle Fork Snoqualmie No. 174SX
TRAILHEAD GPS: 47.5373°N, 121.5774°W

GETTING THERE: Take I-90 to Exit 34 near North Bend. At 468th Avenue just off the freeway, eastbound turn left, westbound turn right. Follow the road past the truck stop for about a half mile to SE Middle Fork Road (Forest Road 56). Turn right and follow this road for a few twists and turns, keeping left when the road splits. After 2.2 miles reach SE Lake Dorothy Road. Turn left, passing the Mailbox Peak Trailhead, and continue 8 miles to a pullout on the left side of the road.

Steeped in history and bursting with pocket views of the Middle Fork Snoqualmie Valley, this trail will delight hikers of any skill level. The road-trail known as the CCC Road stretches from the end of the Mount Si Road all the way to the Middle Fork Campground. The western portions wander down forest roads that property owners and loggers still use, whereas the portions east of Big Blowout Creek have been mostly reclaimed by Mother Nature. Varied forests, dozens of streams, and glimpses of mountaintops and the Middle Fork Snoqualmie River make a trip down this old roadbed an enjoyable introduction to the Middle Fork area while offering a preview of the trails found in the nearby Alpine Lakes Wilderness.

We suggest beginning from the CCC pullout just off the Middle Fork Road, a spot Harvey Manning affectionately referred to as the "Tall Moss Cliff." There is room here for five or so cars to fit comfortably near the cliff. Starting here, you can either head west toward Big Blowout Creek and Bessemer Road or turn east toward the Middle Fork Campground and a trek up to the Nordrum Lookout site.

West from Tall Moss Cliff: Start up the rocky roadbed into a heavily deciduous forest of alders and vine maples, sword ferns and salmonberry. Streams and rivulets often cut across the trail, sometimes with such ferocity that large chunks of the road have been obliterated, requiring some rock-hopping across boulders

and fallen timber. Keep an eye out for views of the valley below—Russian Butte can be particularly striking on a fall day, dusted with snow and framed by orange-red leaves. When views are shrouded behind the canopy, enjoy the thriving second-generation forests lining the trail. Rushing cascades and pools full of life are worth a pause, as are the big rock formations and occasional artifact found just off the trail.

Climb steadily but not very steeply through forest that has aggressively reclaimed most of the former road, which feels more like a trail with each passing year. At 2.7 miles, after occasionally skirting around a protruding ridge or high point, reach Big Blowout Creek. Just across the water, the trail connects with

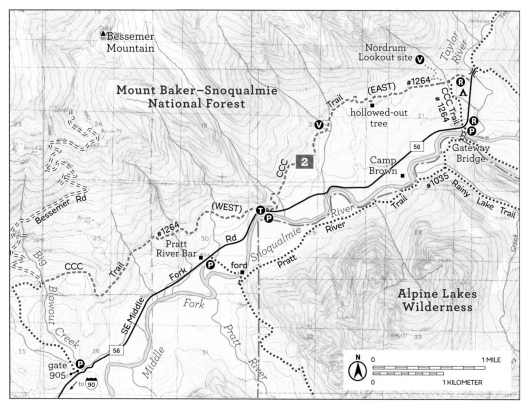

Springboard notches cut into mossy stumps are common in Middle Fork Snoqualmie River Valley, a legacy of the area's logging heyday.

Bessemer Road, abruptly leaving trail for a logging road. It's far better to stay among the trees and head back the way you came.

If you are looking for a loop, however, continue to the forest road, head downhill a few thousand feet to a junction, and then turn left to follow Bessemer Road to FR 56 and hike back along the road to the Tall Moss Cliff.

East from Tall Moss Cliff: From the parking area, head east down the Middle Fork Road a short distance to find a small sign marking the CCC Trail #1264. Climb up off the main road, following the path into a mossy mixed forest of alder, hemlock, and cedar. Streams and rivulets trickle across the trail, and occasionally the canopy opens up to reveal views of Garfield Mountain and Russian Butte. Unlike other sections of the CCC road-trail, here the CCC Trail often wanders away from the old roadbed,

crossing boardwalks and bridges over small streams and swamps. Volunteers work hard to keep this section of the trail in good shape—quite the contrast to other portions of the trail that are rocky, overgrown, and washed out.

At 1.2 miles, a washout creates a particularly good view of the surrounding landscape. Another 0.6 mile down the trail, find an enormous hollowed-out snag worth exploring. With little elevation change and smooth tread, this trail lets you focus on a quiet stroll through the forest. At the 2.6-mile mark reach a junction. Continue straight ahead to reach the Middle Fork Campground and a covered picnic shelter for lunch.

GOING FARTHER

Those looking for a little more adventure on the east end of the CCC road-trail can trek up to the site of the Nordrum Lookout, just a short bushwhack up from the CCC Trail along an abandoned trail that once led to the lookout tower. Although unsigned, the path is easily located: from the junction leading to the Middle Fork Trailhead or the Middle Fork Campground, head uphill following the faintest of paths through the ferns to the lookout site. It is a short 0.3-mile, 300-foot climb to stand on a little piece of history, though only a few cinder blocks and rusted cables remain.

On the other end of the CCC road-trail, ambitious hikers can continue west along the CCC Road beyond Big Blowout Creek, hiking past access to Bessemer Mountain and Green Mountain for 5.0 miles to the gated end of the Mount Si Road.

HISTORY

The Civilian Conservation Corps built the CCC Road in 1939, one of thousands of projects that put single young men to work doing public good during the Great Depression. The CCC built the road to facilitate access for timber and mining interests as well as increase recreation in the area. They had the lofty goal of punching a road all the way up to Highway 2, though they only got as far as the Taylor River when the end of the Great Depression and the start of World War II scrapped the project. The CCC Road, positioned higher on the mountainside above the Middle Fork Snoqualmie River, thrived as the most reliable access to the Middle Fork before more-modern iterations of the Middle Fork Road (FR 56) supplanted it. Much of the western end of the hike travels through areas that were clear-cut in the 1960s, as suggested by the still somewhat young third-generation forest that lines the trail.

The Nordrum Lookout began in the 1930s as a cabin on a recently logged hillock that suddenly found itself with an expansive view of the Middle Fork Snoqualmie Valley. By 1934 a tower was added, presumably to stay ahead of the rapidly recovering vegetation. The CCC boys added a garage in 1940, and the site enjoyed a short-lived career as a wartime plane lookout. By the 1950s, other lookouts on much taller perches made Nordrum obsolete, and the site was dismantled. Today, there is little more than a clearing with moss-covered foundation stones protruding with rusted metal.

3   STEGOSAURUS BUTTE

DISTANCE: 1.8 miles
ELEVATION GAIN: 1000 feet
HIGH POINT: 2100 feet
DIFFICULTY: Moderate
HIKING TIME: 2 to 4 hours
BEST SEASON: Late spring to early fall
TRAIL TRAFFIC: Moderate foot traffic; mountain bikes

PERMIT: Northwest Forest Pass
MAPS: USGS Lake Philippa; Green Trails Middle Fork Snoqualmie No. 174SX
TRAILHEAD GPS: 47.5479°N, 121.5372°W
NOTE: The Middle Fork Trail #1003 is open to mountain bikes on odd-numbered days from June through October.

GETTING THERE: Take I-90 to Exit 34 near North Bend. At 468th Avenue just off the freeway, eastbound turn left, westbound turn right. Follow the road past the truck stop for about a half mile until you reach SE Middle Fork Road (Forest Road 56). Turn right and follow this road for a few twists and turns, keeping left when the road splits. After 2.2 miles reach SE Lake Dorothy Road. Turn left, passing the Mailbox Peak Trailhead, and continue 9.4 miles to the well-signed Middle Fork Trailhead and ample parking area on the right. The trail to the Gateway Bridge is at the north end of the lot. Privy available.

This low-elevation, easily accessible prominence has long been a destination for those over-nighting at the Middle Fork Campground or anyone looking for a quick way to experience the valley. Although there are some good pocket views from the top, an official trail has never really materialized.

Begin by crossing the Gateway Bridge, constructed in 1993 in an effort to promote recreation in the Middle Fork area. Once across, head right onto the Pratt River Connector Trail (signed "Pratt River Trail #1035"), soon entering the Alpine Lakes Wilderness and enjoying the cheerful Middle Fork Snoqualmie River while noting any sandy beaches that may have emerged from the water: these beaches make a great spot for lunch on your return.

Tromp along the rocky riverbank for 0.25 mile to round the end of the butte. Shortly afterward, find an unmarked but well-trodden trail heading up the mountainside—this is the roughly hewn Stegosaurus Butte Trail. It has been slowly "under construction" for years:

portions are defined by logs and branches, with blowdowns cleared or circumvented. Although it's a work in progress, between the boot-trodden outline of the path and the trail markers, it is easy enough to follow.

However, much of the current route still forgoes niceties such as switchbacks—trailblazers instead opted to cut a leg-burning beeline straight to the top. Fortunately, the trail is short, and the almost brutal ascent is over quickly, yielding great views of the massive and imposing rock face of Garfield Mountain to the north and Preacher Mountain to the far south. Rainy Creek flows through the valley to the south, beneath a prominence unofficially known as the Pulpit. Settle down for a snack in

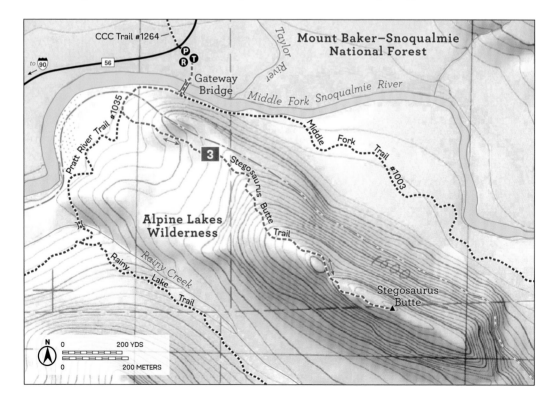

Stegosaurus Butte Trail winds under a canopy of second-growth forest.

the grassy open areas before breaking out the hiking poles to help navigate the steep descent back to the trailhead.

GOING FARTHER

The Rainy Lake Trail (Hike 4) can be reached by continuing another 0.3 mile down the Pratt River Connector Trail (Pratt River Trail #1035). Beyond the Rainy Lake Trail junction, you can continue on the Pratt River Trail (Hike 5) and create a big loop: ford the Middle Fork Snoqualmie River and hike along the Middle Fork Road (FR 56) back to the trailhead.

HISTORY

Over the years this little butte has had some colorful names. It's been dubbed Taylor Knob for its proximity to the Taylor River. Climbers familiar with the heights of Preacher Mountain and the Pulpit have called it Choirboy to bring it into the liturgical theme established by its neighboring peaks. Stegosaurus Butte is perhaps the best-known name, popularized by Harvey Manning and The Mountaineers for its resemblance to a slumbering stegosaurus when viewed from afar.

4 RAINY LAKE

DISTANCE: 8.0 miles
ELEVATION GAIN: 2900 feet
HIGH POINT: 3900 feet
DIFFICULTY: Hard
HIKING TIME: 5 to 8 hours
BEST SEASON: Late spring to early fall
TRAIL TRAFFIC: Light foot traffic; mountain bikes

PERMIT: Northwest Forest Pass
MAPS: USGS Lake Philippa; Green Trails Middle Fork Snoqualmie No. 174SX
TRAILHEAD GPS: 47.5479°N, 121.5372°W
NOTE: The Middle Fork Trail #1003 is open to mountain bikes on odd-numbered days from June through October.

GETTING THERE: Take I-90 to Exit 34 near North Bend. At 468th Avenue just off the freeway, eastbound turn left, westbound turn right. Follow the road past the truck stop for about a half mile until you reach SE Middle Fork Road (Forest Road 56). Turn right and follow this road for a few twists and turns, keeping left when the road splits. After 2.2 miles reach SE Lake Dorothy Road. Turn left, passing the Mailbox Peak Trailhead, and continue 9.4 miles to the well-signed Middle Fork Trailhead and ample parking area on the right. The trail to the Gateway Bridge is at the north end of the lot. Privy available.

Remote and somewhat challenging to reach, Rainy Lake is everything a wild alpine lake should be, with inviting wooded shores giving way to imposing granite cliffs. It's a long haul to this place of solace, and this difficult hike involves a lot of elevation gain on a rough route that's not for everyone. However, those willing to brave the trail can look forward to the quiet of this pristine alpine lake. Certainly, Rainy Lake would be a great base camp for those who want to summit Preacher Mountain or the Pulpit, but it is also a lovely and peaceful destination in itself. Whether you're looking for something a little different or just some solitude in the Alpine Lakes Wilderness, Rainy Lake is a great choice.

Starting from the Middle Fork Trailhead, cross the Gateway Bridge and veer right onto the newly upgraded Pratt River Connector Trail (signed "Pratt River Trail #1035"). As you leave the bridge, enter the Alpine Lakes Wilderness and follow the Pratt River Trail downstream toward Stegosaurus Butte (Hike 3). From the new trail, you can see the old riverside trail below, and after a 0.25-mile stroll you reach the junction with the Stegosaurus Butte Trail. Continue straight (southwest) on the mellow Pratt River Trail to the bridge spanning Rainy Creek. Cross the bridge, and a few dozen feet beyond is the unmarked junction with the Rainy Lake Trail. Head uphill, trading the wide trail for more-difficult terrain.

Follow the narrow boot path through lush forest and mossy undergrowth. Rainy Creek is

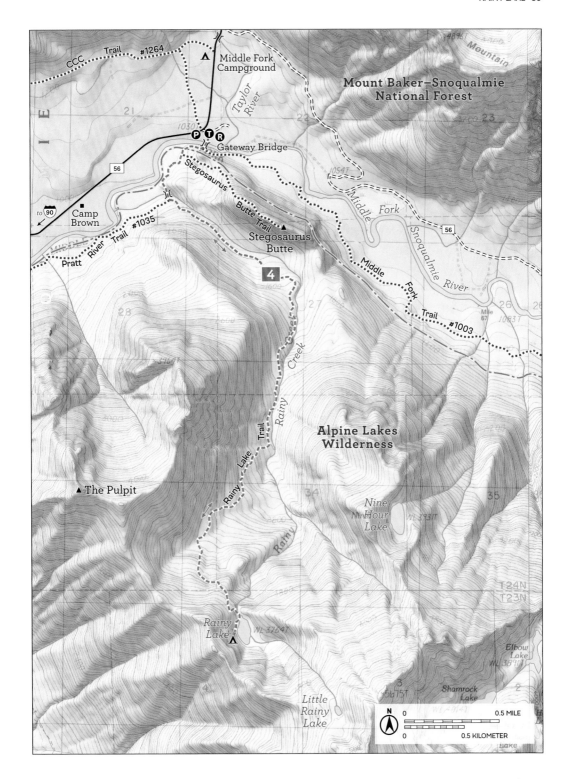

CCC Trail #1264

Middle Fork
Campground

Mount Baker–Snoqualmie
National Forest

Taylor
River

21

23

1030

P T R

Gateway Bridge

56

to 90

Camp
Brown

Pratt

River
Trail #1035

Stegosaurus

Butte Trail

Stegosaurus
Butte

1054T

Middle
Fork
Snoqualmie
River

56

Middle

Fork

Trail #1003

Mile
57 1083T

26

4

23

27

Creek

Rainy

Lake Trail

Rainy

Alpine Lakes
Wilderness

The Pulpit

Rainy

34

Nine
Hour
Lake   WL 3931T

35

T24N
T23N

Rainy
Lake   WL 3764T

Little
Rainy
Lake

Elbow
Lake
WL 3891T

Shamrock
Lake

N

0   0.5 MILE

0   0.5 KILOMETER

Rainy Lake and the talus-covered shoulders of Preacher Mountain

your merry companion for the first portion of your climb ever upward toward the lake. The path alternates between very steep inclines and occasional plateaus, traversing blowdowns and talus fields. While some portions are a bit overgrown, the trail is easy to follow, although mud and slick roots can make your ascent that much more challenging. Be prepared to occasionally use your hands for balance, and bring trekking poles to keep you steady as you work your way up the steep creek valley. Occasional views of Garfield Mountain are excellent, and the rugged trail lends a pleasant feeling of seclusion.

Eventually, after many scrambles over fallen logs and trickling streams, descend to the shores of Rainy Lake nestled beneath the exposed rock face of Preacher Mountain. A faint trail to the right as you reach the lake leads to decent campsites and a memorial plaque.

GOING FARTHER

A scramble route out to nearby Little Rainy Lake continues all the way up to the summit of Preacher Mountain, but it is very overgrown and

a struggle to navigate, more bushwhack than trail. Those with a little extra energy can add a quick climb up to Stegosaurus Butte (Hike 3) to round out the day. Find the unmarked trail at the foot of the butte where the trail bends up and away from the river.

HISTORY

Several areas in the Middle Fork area are named "rainy"—Rainy Creek, Rainy Lake, Rainy Mine. All appear to be named for the valley's above-average rainfall. Rainy Creek can be found on maps as far back as 1907 and likely lent its name to the lake. For decades, Rainy Lake was a destination for backwoods fisherfolk, who seem to be responsible for cutting the rough path to the shore. Trail Blazers like George Lewis hauled trout fry up this route to stock Rainy Lake (among many other lakes in the area).

To find a plaque near the lake honoring Lewis's efforts as a member of the Trail Blazers, follow the boot path around the west side of the lake. Over the years, the trail has been maintained mostly by users. The Forest Service may have been involved at some point, but the trail has long since been abandoned. Helpful hikers and anglers sometimes clear a little brush or reroute the trail around major blowdowns. While in recent years the underbrush has gotten the upper hand, there is some talk of reclaiming this trail to help make the lake a little more accessible.

5 PRATT RIVER TRAIL

DISTANCE: 8.4 miles
ELEVATION GAIN: 300 feet
HIGH POINT: 1300 feet
DIFFICULTY: Easy
HIKING TIME: 2 to 4 hours
BEST SEASON: Accessible year-round; best early summer to late fall
TRAIL TRAFFIC: Moderate foot traffic; mountain bikes

PERMIT: Northwest Forest Pass
MAPS: USGS Lake Philippa; Green Trails Mount Si No. 174, Green Trails Middle Fork Snoqualmie No. 174SX
TRAILHEAD GPS: 47.5479°N, 121.5372°W
NOTE: The Middle Fork Trail #1003 is open to mountain bikes on odd-numbered days from June through October.

GETTING THERE: Take I-90 to Exit 34 near North Bend. At 468th Avenue just off the freeway, eastbound turn left, westbound turn right. Follow the road past the truck stop for about a half mile to SE Middle Fork Road (Forest Road 56). Turn right and follow this road for a few twists and turns, keeping left when the road splits. After 2.2 miles reach SE Lake Dorothy Road. Turn left, passing the Mailbox Peak Trailhead, and continue 9.4 miles to the well-signed Middle Fork Trailhead and ample parking area on the right. The trail to the Gateway Bridge is at the north end of the lot. Privy available.

Those willing to ford the Middle Fork Snoqualmie River to cut out a few miles of trail can park at an established pullout 6.6 miles down the Middle Fork Road at the Pratt River Bar. See Going Farther for the route from there.

Some trails, like the Pratt River Trail, have a longer story to tell than others. While access has been limited in the last few decades, in recent years the US Forest Service and Washington Trails Association have made an effort to reconnect hikers to the Pratt River Valley. This forest hike can be as short or long as you like. There are no big views, but the Pratt River Valley is definitely worth a tour, especially for those looking for a bit of adventure.

From the Middle Fork Trailhead, cross the Gateway Bridge and veer right onto the newly upgraded Pratt River Connector Trail (signed "Pratt River Trail #1035"). Soon cross into the Alpine Lakes Wilderness and in 0.25 mile pass the junction with the Stegosaurus Butte Trail (Hike 3). Stroll along the smooth trail, enjoying the friendly sounds of the river and the bright riparian woods. At 0.6 mile, reach the bridge spanning Rainy Creek and the Rainy Lake Trail junction (Hike 4). Reserve that hike for another day and glide past, making good time along the nearly flat Pratt River Trail. Skip over a few streams and wander over sturdy boardwalks as the miles fly under your feet.

At 2.9 miles, which you reach surprisingly quickly, you'll find a campsite and access to the river at the Pratt River Bar, where some hikers ford the Middle Fork Snoqualmie River during the summer. That option not only shortens the hike by nearly 3 miles, it also follows a much older approach to the Pratt River Valley: this is the approximate location where bridges once provided more-direct access. Not far beyond, the trail reaches the Pratt River and turns up the river valley, along an old railroad grade.

The forest deepens, though it feels slightly off—a legacy of the logging practices of yesteryear: almost all the trees are Douglas fir of roughly the same age. Keep an eye out for artifacts such as rusting metal, old cables, and rotting railroad ties as you press deeper into the valley. After 1.0 mile of hiking up the valley, arrive at a junction signed simply "Big Trees"

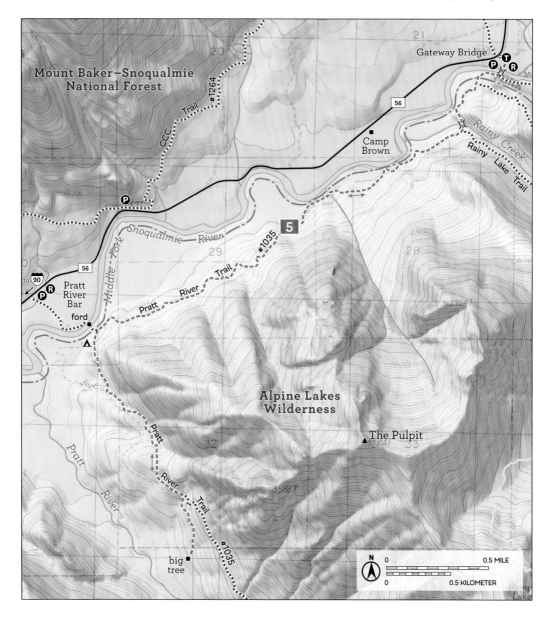

When the water is low, hikers can ford the Middle Fork Snoqualmie River at the Pratt River Bar.

and "Trail," with arrows directing hikers where to go. Veer to the right and downhill about 0.3 mile to find an enormous 250-foot-tall Douglas fir tree. After your trek out to the big tree, call it a day, enjoying the quiet solitude of this old trail.

GOING FARTHER

From the junction with the "Big Trees" trail, you can head left to continue on the Pratt River Trail's railroad grade until you've had your fill. It is possible for experienced hikers to make this a through-hike by bushwhacking all the way out to the Granite Mountain Trailhead via Pratt Lake (Hike 26).

If you wish to shorten the hike by starting with fording the Middle Fork, park at the pull-out at the Pratt River Bar. Cross a small creek and follow a meandering path through black-berries and cottonwood toward the sound of the river. At the river, head upstream a few hundred yards while looking across the water for a small trail leading up the opposite embankment. Once you locate it, ford the river and follow the trail a short distance up to the Pratt

River Connector Trail. For those looking for more mileage, the short trek up to Stegosaurus Butte (Hike 3) is an easy addition.

HISTORY

In 1887 prospectors staked mining claims in the vicinity of Chair Peak. Among them was George A. Pratt, who accessed his claims via the river valley that now bears his name and helped establish the first Pratt River Trail. During this era, a cabin was built at the conflu-ence of the Pratt and Middle Fork Snoqualmie Rivers that became known as the Halfway House for its location between North Bend and the Taylor River Ranger Station. The Halfway House provided shelter for those exploring the Pratt River Trail and appeared on USGS maps until the early 1920s, though nothing remains of the cabin today.

In 1934 the North Bend Timber Company acquired the rights to log the river valley and quickly constructed a logging railroad largely following the Pratt River Trail route. The com-pany completed a bridge across the Middle

Fork in 1936, and the railroad stretched the length of the valley by 1937. Over several years, the company logged the valley walls on either side of the tracks up to 300 feet, the farthest reach of the cables. By 1941 the easy timber had been harvested and the company pulled out the rails, leaving the wooden ties behind. Aside from some intermittent truck logging in the 1950s, this was the end of major logging along the Pratt.

Once the timber interests pulled out, more hikers and outdoor lovers started to explore the Middle Fork Snoqualmie Valley. Some followed the portion of the Pratt River Trail that leads up the Middle Fork toward Goldmyer Hot Springs (Hike 15), while others followed the railroad grade up the Pratt River Valley through a recovering forest out toward Melakwa Lake (Hike 28) or Talapus Lake (Hike 25). The Forest Service built up the trail, adding boardwalks and small bridges along the Middle Fork.

Eventually the railroad bridge washed out, and hikers replaced it in the 1970s with an improvised bridge anchored to stumps on either side of the river. That bridge also washed away, though you can still find the rusting anchoring cables along the river.

Without a bridge, trail use steadily declined and nature began to take back the trail. It wasn't until 1993, when the Gateway Bridge was built a few miles upstream, that hikers once again had access to the trail. In recent years, the Washington Trails Association has led an effort to restore the trail between the bridge and the Pratt River Trail. This section is now often referred to as the Pratt River Connector Trail, with some maps showing the Pratt River Trail beginning near the river confluence. Whatever the official name for this stretch of trail, it is now much easier to navigate, with large sections updated and improved with boardwalks, drains, and steps.

6 MIDDLE FORK TRAIL

DISTANCE: 11.4 miles
ELEVATION GAIN: 300 feet
HIGH POINT: 1300 feet
DIFFICULTY: Easy
HIKING TIME: 5 to 7 hours
BEST SEASON: Accessible year-round
TRAIL TRAFFIC: Moderate foot traffic, trail runners, and mountain bikes
PERMIT: Northwest Forest Pass

MAPS: USGS Lake Philippa, USGS Snoqualmie Lake; Green Trails Middle Fork Snoqualmie No. 174SX
TRAILHEAD GPS: 47.5479°N, 121.5372°W
NOTES: A mudslide closed this trail in 2018 and while there are plans to address it, the trail remains closed as of this printing; check with the Snoqualmie Ranger District for current status. Open to mountain bikes on odd-numbered days from June through October.

GETTING THERE: Take I-90 to Exit 34 near North Bend. At 468th Avenue just off the freeway, eastbound turn left, westbound turn right. Follow the road past the truck stop for about a half mile until you reach SE Middle Fork Road (Forest Road 56). Turn right and follow this road for a few twists and turns, keeping left when the road splits. After 2.2 miles reach SE Lake Dorothy Road. Turn left, passing the Mailbox Peak Trailhead, and continue 9.4 miles to the well-signed Middle Fork Trailhead and ample parking area on the right. The trail to the Gateway Bridge is at the north end of the lot. Privy available.

The Middle Fork River Valley's main arterial connects hikers to quite a few destinations along its 14.5-mile-long route that showcases the valley's enchanting landscapes. A classic and a must for any first-time visitor, this hike is perfect for any age or skill level: easily accessed, almost entirely flat, and enjoyable whether you hike a mile or the full length. From June through October the trail is open to mountain bikers on odd calendar days, and while there is plenty of room to share the trail, be aware of what could be coming down the trail. Although the hike outlined here never officially crosses into the Alpine Lakes Wilderness, this popular route skims so close to its edges that you will feel as if you've ventured into the wild.

From the Middle Fork Trailhead, cross the Gateway Bridge and turn to the left (southeast) to head upstream on the Middle Fork Trail #1003 alongside the wide, rushing river. To the right the Pratt River Connector Trail, leads out to Stegosaurus Butte (Hike 3), Rainy Lake (Hike 4), and the Pratt River Trail (Hike 5), adventures for another day. The effort that volunteers have put into this well-maintained trail is readily apparent from the extensive network of bridges and boardwalks. Although there are a few ups and downs, the fairly gentle trail generally follows the remnants of logging roads and railroad grades. Wander under

alders, hemlocks, and big-leaf maples, and take advantage of breaks in the canopy to see Garfield Mountain, the granite cliffs of Stegosaurus Butte, and Mount Thompson.

At just over a mile reach a large slide area that closed the trail; while it will undoubtedly be repaired, for now a rough path winds through downed trees and rough terrain. At 1.75 miles, reach the first stretch of wide railroad grade, a marked change from the riverside trail. Imagine the steam engines that pushed and pulled enormous old-growth logs through this area a century ago. Note the springboard-notched stumps in second-growth forest on the hills above the grade.

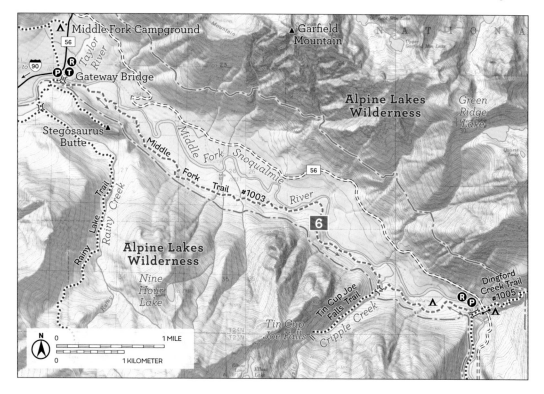

The towering walls of Garfield Mountain seen from the Middle Fork Trail

GOING FARTHER

One side trip is a mile-long scramble to Tin Cup Joe Falls (Hike 11), a spectacular set of cascades. Backpackers can push beyond the Dingford Creek Bridge for another 2.6 miles to the junction with the Rock Creek Trail (Hike 14) at 8.3 miles, which leads up to Snow Lake (Hike 29) and Snoqualmie Pass. At one time, the Rock Creek Trail was the preferred approach to Goldmyer Hot Springs (Hike 15), which can be reached in another 2.7 miles on the Middle Fork Trail. Beyond Goldmyer, the trail continues to follow the river, eventually crossing it and ending at the junction with FR 56 near Hardscrabble Creek and the Dutch Miller Gap Trail (Hike 93), 14.5 miles from the Gateway Bridge.

HISTORY

Around the turn of the last century, the demand for timber in booming Seattle continued to grow. In 1906 William C. Weeks and R. Webb Vinnedge formed the North Bend Lumber Company, focusing on timber claims along the Snoqualmie River that Weeks had held since the Great Seattle Fire in 1889. In 1911 the company opened a sawmill in the company town of Edgewick, near Rattlesnake Ridge. Named for the company's founders (Vinn*edge*, and Weeks became *wick*), the town flourished until a burst dam flooded and destroyed most of it in 1918, an event often called the Boxley Blowout, named after the creek that flooded.

By 1923 the company had recovered from the flood; Vinnedge bought out Weeks and focused exclusively on logging, renaming the company the North Bend Timber Company. That year, logging in the Middle Fork Snoqualmie Valley started in earnest. Roads were blazed and railroad tracks followed closely behind. By 1929 tracks extended past Camp Brown and the Taylor River, eventually reaching Goldmyer Hot Springs by 1936. Logging technology at the time limited activities to within a half mile of the tracks, and by 1941 most of the easy trees had been logged. The North Bend Timber Company pulled up most

At 3.0 miles, the trail drops off the grade and heads toward the river, only to rejoin the grade farther upstream. The reroute is due to a bridge washout hidden in the encroaching forest. Continue deeper into the river valley, enjoying the sounds of the river bumping up against the stillness of the mossy forest.

Work your way over roaring creeks, tumbling cascades, and the occasional washout, crossing the Cripple Creek Bridge at 4.5 miles. Push onward for a little more than a mile to reach the Dingford Creek Bridge, 5.7 miles from the trailhead and an excellent turnaround point for this long but not too strenuous day hike.

of its tracks in 1944, but the legacy of a few decades of intensive logging is still easy to spot—old pilings, long stretches of railroad grade, and rusting artifacts are plentiful.

Some logging activity continued until the early 1970s, around the time when a growing conservation movement began trying to protect areas like the Middle Fork. As industry left, some less savory recreation moved in, with drug labs, squatters, and weekend benders becoming somewhat common. The 1990s saw an effort to promote recreation in an area that had become difficult to access. In 1993 the Gateway Bridge was built, marking a renaissance for the river valley, and prompting a movement to pave the road and bring hikers, bikers, fisherfolk, and equestrians back to the Middle Fork.

7 MARTEN LAKE

DISTANCE: 8.4 miles
ELEVATION GAIN: 1800 feet
HIGH POINT: 3000 feet
DIFFICULTY: Hard
HIKING TIME: 6 to 8 hours
BEST SEASON: Late spring to early fall

TRAIL TRAFFIC: Moderate foot traffic
PERMIT: Northwest Forest Pass
MAPS: USGS Lake Philippa; Green Trails Middle Fork Snoqualmie No. 174SX
TRAILHEAD GPS: 47.5608°N, 121.5322°W

GETTING THERE: Take I-90 to Exit 34 near North Bend. At 468th Avenue just off the freeway, eastbound turn left, westbound turn right. Follow the road past the truck stop for about a half mile until you reach SE Middle Fork Road (Forest Road 56). Turn right and follow this road for a few twists and turns, keeping left when the road splits. After 2.2 miles reach SE Lake Dorothy Road. Turn left and continue 12 miles, crossing the Taylor River Bridge. Once across, soon reach the Garfield Ledges Trailhead where FR 56 (sometimes labeled FR 5620 or Dingford Creek Road at this point) veers sharply to the right and heads uphill. Privy available.

Many trails in the Alpine Lakes Wilderness owe their existence to those seeking a quiet place to cast a line into the water to catch their dinner. Hikers were usually not too far behind, expanding fishermen's paths and smoothing out the rough edges. Occasionally these buffed-out trails fall into disuse, slipping back toward the days when only fisherfolk trod the boot path. Such is the case of Marten Lake Trail #1006, a short, brushy trail out to a lovely alpine lake that is rough and difficult to follow. Still, the route offers good access to waterfalls along Marten Creek and the occasional view of Treen Peak and Garfield Mountain. The landscape is impressive—Marten Lake lies in a large cirque at the base of looming Rooster Mountain. This hike is perfect for escaping the crowds and finding something off the beaten path.

From the parking area, follow the road 0.4 mile to the Snoqualmie Lake Trailhead, cross a large bridge and follow the crumbling roadbed along the alder-lined Taylor River on Snoqualmie Lake Trail #1002. After 0.8 mile reach a junction with the Quartz Creek Road; keep right and continue to follow the river (learn more about the nearby cabin ruins in Hike 10, Nordrum Lake). As you progress, craggy Garfield Mountain makes an early appearance on

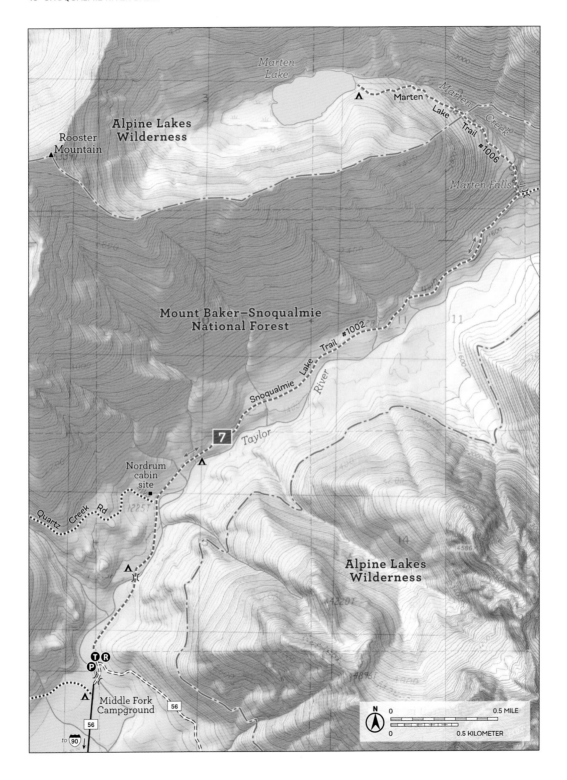

Marten Lake during the spring thaw with Rooster Mountain largely hidden in the fog

the opposite side of the river, eventually yielding the stage to Treen Peak.

At 3.1 miles reach Marten Creek and Marten Falls at a bridge over the creek. Small but pretty, this lovely little waterfall is worth a linger, particularly for the green and orange rocks in the pool below the falls. Here you will find the unmarked Marten Lake Trail #1006. Occasionally rock cairns or tags mark the trailhead, but these often disappear. Search about 150 feet before the Marten Creek bridge. A few faint paths branch up from the main trail here, each representing attempts to find the trail. If nothing is marked, take your best guess and head up, following the creek. The paths eventually reach the actual trail within 0.25 mile of the Taylor River.

The steep and narrow trail hugs Marten Creek through old-growth forest for about 0.5 mile before spilling out into an open, brush-filled canyon. The trail is fairly level, and if the weather is good, it's possible to catch glimpses of the Middle Fork landscape below. Rocky ridges line the creek valley as you press deeper and begin to climb higher.

Push on another brushy 0.5 mile to a steep set of switchbacks climbing up the mountainside before leveling off and dropping you to the shores of Marten Lake 4.2 miles from the trailhead. The best camping is by the outlet, but various smaller paths lead around the lakeshore to other appealing rocks and stopping points. Explore and find a good place for lunch and enjoy this quiet alpine setting.

GOING FARTHER

Otter Falls and Lipsy Lake (Hike 8) are another 1.5 miles farther down the Snoqualmie Lake Trail. Beyond that it's another 0.5 mile to the sturdy concrete bridge spanning Big Creek and a front-row seat to aptly named Big Creek Falls (Hike 8).

HISTORY

Marten Lake is named for the pine martens that were once prevalent in the area.

8 OTTER FALLS AND BIG CREEK FALLS

DISTANCE: 10.0 miles
ELEVATION GAIN: 600 feet
HIGH POINT: 1700 feet
DIFFICULTY: Moderate
HIKING TIME: 5 to 7 hours
TRAIL TRAFFIC: Moderate foot traffic

BEST SEASON: Accessible year-round; falls best
spring to early summer
PERMIT: Northwest Forest Pass
MAPS: USGS Lake Philippa, USGS Snoqualmie Lake;
Green Trails Middle Fork Snoqualmie No. 174SX
TRAILHEAD GPS: 47.5608°N, 121.5322°W

GETTING THERE: Take I-90 to Exit 34 near North Bend. At 468th Avenue just off the freeway, eastbound turn left, westbound turn right. Follow the road past the truck stop for about a half mile to SE Middle Fork Road (Forest Road 56). Turn right and follow this road for a few twists and turns, keeping left when the road splits. After 2.2 miles reach SE Lake Dorothy Road. Turn left and continue 12 miles, crossing the Taylor River Bridge. Once across, soon reach the Garfield Ledges Trailhead where FR 56 (sometimes labeled FR 5620 or Dingford Creek Road) veers sharply right and heads uphill. Privy available.

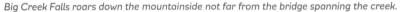

This riverside hike follows repurposed roadbed through a mixed forest, skirting the Alpine Lakes Wilderness as it leads out to impressive waterfalls with a minimum of elevation gain. The hike out to Big Creek Falls covers a few more miles than your average day hike, but most of that mileage is basically flat, ferrying hikers along at a good clip. Although the trail is fairly easy to access and relatively close to Seattle, the Taylor River Road feels remote and much farther from civilization.

Big Creek Falls roars down the mountainside not far from the bridge spanning the creek.

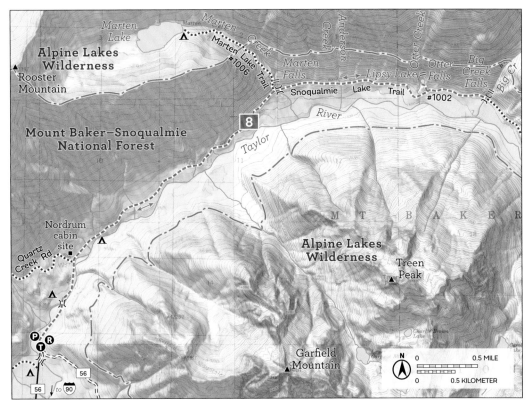

Begin from the parking area, following a forest road 0.4 mile to the Snoqualmie Lake trailhead. The Snoqualmie Lake Trail #1002 crosses the Taylor River on a sturdy concrete bridge, passing a few riverside campsites along a wide, rocky roadbed. With the river by your side, pass the Quartz Creek Road junction at 0.4 mile and continue straight ahead as the road slowly yields to trail. As you progress, enjoy views of the oft-snow-capped crags of Garfield Mountain and Treen Peak rising above the alder-lined Taylor River.

After a leisurely 3.1 miles, reach Marten Creek and what is known as Marten Falls. The bridge over the creek offers a front-row seat to this small but enchanting waterfall. Here too is the junction with the Marten Lake Trail #1006 (Hike 7). Pushing onward, hop over streams for 0.5 mile to Anderson Creek, which can be a little more challenging to cross depending on the season: when the water is low, it's easy to skip across the rocks, but during the spring

melt there is no way to cross without some very wet boots.

Reach Otter Creek at 4.5 miles, just after crossing a large culvert—big enough that you cannot possibly miss it. Keep an eye out for a cairn or other marking letting you know to head up. There isn't much of a formal trail but it's a short 0.1-mile climb to the falls, so just choose the path of least resistance. You can see Otter Falls once you reach the top—it's tempting to head straight for them, but instead veer right toward the falls for an easy place to cross the creek and avoid the brambles.

As impressive as the falls are from here, only the lower third of them are visible. Otter Creek slides almost half a mile down the exposed granite to cascade into tiny Lipsy Lake below. Because of the area's geology, Otter Falls is an almost entirely snow-driven waterfall without a lake above to keep it running throughout the summer. Visit before it runs dry in high summer.

Otter Falls makes for an idyllic, if sometimes popular, lunch spot, and if you've had your fill, it is also a fine turnaround point. If you want to continue, head back to the main trail and press onward to another waterfall waiting 0.5 mile farther up the trail. You'll hear it long before you reach the sturdy concrete bridge spanning Big Creek. The bridge is a remnant of the Lake Dorothy Highway project that never was. Supplied by both Dream Lake and Pothole Lake, Big Creek tumbles forcefully over the rocks just a few dozen feet from the bridge, keeping the concrete constantly mossy and slick with spray. It's quite a show: settle in on a nearby rocky perch and enjoy it.

GOING FARTHER

Backpackers can continue past Big Creek Falls onward and upward 3.0 miles to Snoqualmie Lake (Hike 9), though it is a 1500-foot climb. Another option is to add a side trip up to Marten Lake (Hike 7), which adds a little over 2 miles and a hefty dose of adventure.

HISTORY

Back around the turn of the last century, timber and mining interests had blazed the beginnings of what was to become the Taylor River Road out to Marten Creek. By the 1930s, timber companies had improved it enough to begin stripping the forests in earnest, steadily extending the road little by little every year.

In the late 1940s and early '50s, the Forest Service began sketching out a road project that became known as Lake Dorothy Road or Lake Dorothy Highway. The project aimed to improve the existing logging road and extend it up past Lake Dorothy to Highway 2, connecting North Bend and Skykomish. The primary goal of the project was timber extraction, though some thought was given to providing roadside access to the nearby alpine lakes. The disregard the Forest Service showed for the pristine wilderness was so brazen, it prompted a public outcry that led to the formation of the Alpine Lakes Protection Society (ALPS) and, in turn, the creation of the Alpine Lakes Wilderness. It took many years of effort, but the wilderness designation ultimately blocked the road project.

Also sometimes called Otter Slide Falls or Otter Creek Falls, Otter Falls is named for the granite slide that the falls tumble down, which looks like a natural feature an otter might enjoy playing on.

9   SNOQUALMIE LAKE

DISTANCE: 16.0 miles
ELEVATION GAIN: 2100 feet
HIGH POINT: 3200 feet
DIFFICULTY: Moderate
HIKING TIME: Overnight
BEST SEASON: Late spring to early fall

TRAIL TRAFFIC: Moderate foot traffic
PERMIT: Northwest Forest Pass
MAPS: USGS Lake Philippa, USGS Snoqualmie Lake; Green Trails Mount Si No. 174, Green Trails Skykomish No. 175
TRAILHEAD GPS: 47.5608°N, 121.5322°W

GETTING THERE: Take I-90 to Exit 34 near North Bend. At 468th Avenue just off the freeway, eastbound turn left, westbound turn right. Follow the road past the truck stop for about a half mile until you reach SE Middle Fork Road (Forest Road 56). Turn right and follow this road for a few twists and turns, keeping left when the road splits. After 2.2 miles reach SE Lake Dorothy Road. Turn left and continue 12 miles, crossing the Taylor River Bridge. Once across, reach the Garfield Ledges Trailhead where FR 56 (sometimes labeled FR 5620 or Dingford Creek Road) veers sharply right and heads uphill. Privy available.

Backpack out to a vast alpine lake that narrowly escaped extensive logging and life as a road-side recreational destination. Three-quarters of this hike is on decommissioned logging road as it follows the Taylor River nearly to its headwaters in the Alpine Lakes Wilderness, making it an approachable backpacking adventure for a wide range of skill levels.

From the parking area, hike 0.4 mile on a forest road to the Snoqualmie Lake trailhead. Here pick up the Snoqualmie Lake Trail #1002 Trailhead, crossing an oversized concrete bridge spanning the Taylor River and following the wide and rocky former Taylor River Road past a few campsites tucked under the trees along the river's edge. Pass the Quartz Creek Road junction at 0.4 mile, continuing upriver, the road becoming more traillike as you progress farther into the valley. Across the river, Garfield Mountain's spires, and later the top of Treen Peak, make appearances when the canopy thins or a creek cuts across the trail on its way to the Taylor.

Pass over Marten Creek and the Marten Lake Trail #1006 (Hike 7) at the 2.7-mile mark, taking a few minutes to enjoy Marten Falls merrily splashing into a deep and surprisingly colorful bowl. Push onward, and in 0.5 mile hop across Anderson Creek, one of the largest streams you'll navigate. Anderson Creek can run high during the spring melt or the rainy season, when crossing will likely result in wet boots.

From here the trail inclines slightly, passing Otter Creek at 4.1 miles and the trail up to Otter Falls (Hike 8). A short distance beyond, cross Big Creek and thundering Big Creek Falls at 4.6 miles. The falls demand a pause, before the hard work begins.

From the Big Creek Bridge, continue on what remains of the old roadbed through mixed forest for 1.0 mile to a junction and the farthest reaches of logging activities in the area, 5.6 miles from the trailhead. Note the broken sign referencing North Bend and Camp Brown, a legacy of the days when logging trucks and

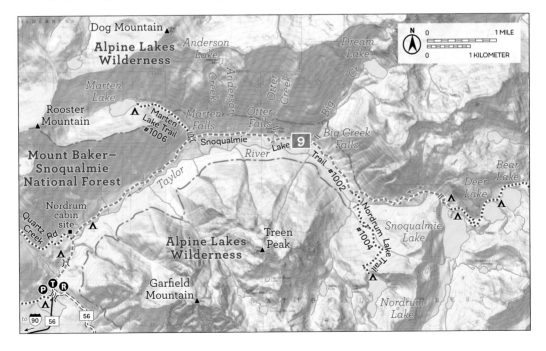

Snoqualmie Lake on a fall morning

four-wheel-drive vehicles could drive to this point. Continuing straight leads to the end of the road and the Nordrum Lake Trail #1004 (Hike 10). Instead, veer left onto a rocky trail that wastes no time climbing up to Snoqualmie Lake.

The change in the forest is abrupt—trade alders and young trees for moss-covered cedars as the old growth quickly closes in. It's a haul from the junction to the shores of Snoqualmie Lake—climbing more than 1300 feet in 2.0 miles. While quite a bit of old puncheon and other trail improvements help smooth out the climb, use caution when crossing them as they are often slick. Taylor River continues to guide you toward your destination, never too far away from the trail. A few large creek crossings require some rock-hopping and balancing on logs, but all that water creates a few waterfalls and robust cascades to see along the way. Climb up switchbacks and push through talus fields as you work your way steadily upward.

As you approach the lake, you will hear a large waterfall that isn't readily apparent from the trail. Snoqualmie Lake Falls, a wide and impressive waterfall, is easily found by following your ears. Past the falls are the first glimpses of Snoqualmie Lake—while there are a few campsites here, this is only one small arm of the lake. It makes for fine camping, but to take in the full extent of one of the largest alpine lakes in the Alpine Lakes Wilderness, push onward and upward, following the trail as it veers away from the lake and over a ridge, traversing the slopes above the lakeshore. There are a few choice campsites along the route as well as some excellent spots to take in this sprawling and gorgeous lake.

GOING FARTHER

Deer and Bear Lakes are a short 2.0-mile climb farther up the Snoqualmie Lake Trail. The trail switchbacks steeply to a low pass near Deer Lake. Find the water's edge and follow the trail along the shore. Bear Lake, just behind Deer

Lake, is well worth a visit. Beyond Bear Lake the trail becomes the Dorothy Lake Trail #1072 (Hike 63) and leads down to Lake Dorothy. It's not much farther but the trek requires dropping 600 feet to reach the water. Side trips such as Marten Lake (Hike 7), Otter Falls (Hike 8), or Nordrum Lake (Hike 10) can round out a longer stay in the Taylor River Valley.

HISTORY

In 1928 the North Bend Timber Company's railroad reached the Taylor River, and a logging camp was completed by 1929 on a gravel bar about 0.5 mile downstream from the present-day Middle Fork Trailhead. Camp Brown was named in honor of Robert Brown, a civil engineer killed by a locomotive while laying railroad track. During those years of intensive logging, Camp Brown housed dozens of lumberjacks and was served by water from Rainy Creek piped across the Middle Fork Snoqualmie in a large wooden pipe held together with wire banding. Remnants of the pipe can still be found today.

In 1937 the North Bend Timber Company abandoned Camp Brown and it was promptly taken over by the Civilian Conservation Corps, who named it a CCC Spike Camp. It sheltered the CCC boys who worked on the CCC Road (Hike 2) for a few years beginning in 1938 until they gave up on it.

In the 1950s and '60s, the Forest Service maintained a guard station in this location, which began as a cabin but was eventually replaced by a concrete slab that supported a trailer when the cabin needed to be torn down. By the 1980s, Camp Brown was left to return to nature, though it remained a popular spot for pitching a tent or spending the day on the river. Today Camp Brown has been reborn with bathrooms, picnic tables, and a 0.45-mile interpretive trail.

10 NORDRUM LAKE

DISTANCE: 16.0 miles
ELEVATION GAIN: 2700 feet
HIGH POINT: 3800 feet
DIFFICULTY: Hard due to trail conditions
HIKING TIME: Overnight
BEST SEASON: Late spring to early fall
PERMIT: Northwest Forest Pass

TRAIL TRAFFIC: Moderate foot traffic on main trail; very light to Nordrum Lake
MAPS: USGS Lake Philippa, USGS Snoqualmie Lake; Green Trails Mount Si No. 174, Green Trails Skykomish No. 175
TRAILHEAD GPS: 47.5608°N, 121.5322°W

GETTING THERE: Take I-90 to Exit 34 near North Bend. At 468th Avenue just off the freeway, eastbound turn left, westbound turn right. Follow the road past the truck stop for about a half mile to SE Middle Fork Road (Forest Road 56). Turn right and follow this road for a few twists and turns, keeping left when the road splits. After 2.2 miles reach SE Lake Dorothy Road. Turn left and continue 12 miles, crossing the Taylor River Bridge. Once across, soon reach the Garfield Ledges Trailhead where FR 56 (sometimes labeled FR 5620 or Dingford Creek Road) veers sharply right and heads uphill. Privy available.

Strap on your backpack and dive into the Taylor River Valley to an alpine lake seldom visited save for fishermen hauling fry to stock it for nearly three-quarters of a century. Well known in fishing circles, Nordrum Lake sees a steady stream of fisherfolk. While most of the trek is along pleasant decommissioned forest road, the last 2 miles are not well maintained. While certainly challenging, this backpack (or extended day hike) is a great option for experienced hikers comfortable with a little routefinding. Your reward is solitude, wilderness, and a picturesque alpine landscape.

Begin by trekking down 0.4 mile of forest road to the Snoqualmie Lake Trailhead. From here follow the former logging road across the Taylor River on a wide and sturdy bridge. A few campsites are hidden in the trees here, useful for anyone wanting to come up the night before to get an early start. The wide, rocky, and often watery road that is now the Snoqualmie Lake Trail #1002 follows the river through a young mixed forest of alder, vine maple, and hemlock rising above a thick, brushy understory. After a short 0.4 mile, pass the Quartz Creek Road junction, and just beyond keep an eye out for a clearing marking the site of Martin Nordrum's cabin. Little remains today beyond some cement foundations poking out of the grass, but Nordrum lived here for decades

and his name was given to a few features in the area, including this hike's destination.

As you progress, the forest slowly closes in, reclaiming the road that starts to feel a little more like a trail. The surrounding mountaintops make occasional appearances through the trees: the lofty heights of Garfield Mountain can be seen across the river early on, yielding later to Treen Peak. Along the way, the Taylor River is your constant merry companion, rushing along and guiding you deeper into the valley. At 2.7 miles cross Marten Creek and pause to admire Marten Falls tumbling down the rocks just off the trail. Note the unmarked junction with the Marten Lake Trail #1006 (Hike 7) before pushing onward.

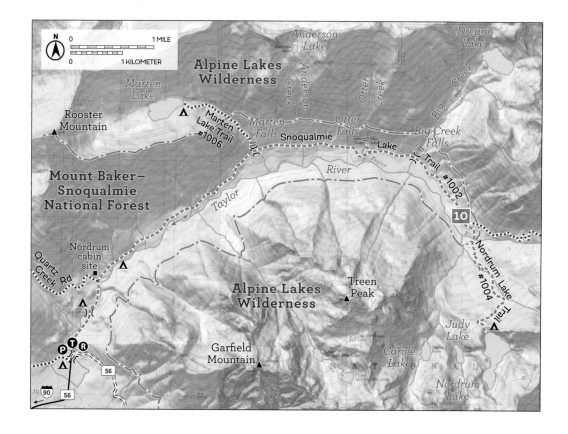

Beyond Marten Creek, skip across a number of small streams before reaching Anderson Creek at 3.2 miles. Depending on the water level, the creek can be a little challenging to cross: If you're hiking during the spring melt or after heavy rain, come prepared to get your boots wet. Otherwise it should not be difficult to hop across on rocks or logs. From here trail inclines slightly, though remains easy to navigate.

Reach Otter Creek at 4.1 miles, passing markers for Otter Falls (Hike 8) just after a large culvert. While it's a very short side trip, save it for your return—the real work of the hike is still to come. Push onward another 0.5 mile to the crashing sound of Big Creek Falls and the surprisingly substantial concrete bridge that spans the creek. Take a moment to enjoy the water show before wiping the spray off your face and heading deeper into the forest.

From the Big Creek Bridge, the road continues 1.0 mile to a small clearing and a trail junction. This marks the farthest extent of the logging activities and the beginning of rougher trail and wilder woods. The trail heading uphill and to the left leads to Snoqualmie Lake (Hike 9), but stay straight ahead to reach Nordrum Lake. Walk the last section of roadbed to the edge of the Taylor River, which may require a ford depending on the time of year.

Once across, enter the Alpine Lakes Wilderness and begin working your way through the challenges of this trail. Blowdowns are common along the unmaintained trail, with overgrown or washed-out sections too. The trail bed is rough, which makes steep sections all the more difficult. Persevere for 2.0 miles while climbing 1900 feet to reach Nordrum Lake. When you finally arrive, you're likely to find that you have the lake all to yourself. Settle in and enjoy this alpine gem.

GOING FARTHER
Side trips such as Marten Lake (Hike 7), Otter Falls (Hike 8), or Snoqualmie Lake (Hike 9) can round out a longer stay in the Taylor River Valley.

Hiking through mossy lowland forest on the old Taylor River road

HISTORY
In 1902 a pioneer named Martin Nordrum set up a homestead just past the Quartz Creek Road, building a cabin that stood until the 1960s. From 1910 to 1929, Nordrum did maintenance for the Forest Service and worked the fire patrol. When a fire lookout was built near the confluence of the Taylor and Middle Fork Snoqualmie Rivers in the early 1930s, it was named Nordrum Lookout in his honor. Over the years, Nordrum was a well-known and beloved presence in the valley, befriending any logger, hunter, fisherman, or outdoorsman who dropped by his cabin. Nordrum passed away in 1943 and his

cabin deteriorated in the following decades. Today a clearing marks the Nordrum cabin site just off the trail, with little more than some cement foundations and a few artifacts hidden among the grass.

Back in 1946 the Trail Blazers—a dedicated group of fisherfolk—pioneered a trail to Nordrum Lake. While the lake had visitors long before that time, the Trail Blazers wanted an official route to access a lakeside shelter they built in honor of William Simons, one of their members killed in World War II. The shelter stood until 1972 when it fell into such disrepair that it was burned down. Today the site can still be found near the lake outlet, and a plaque commemorates the Trail Blazers' efforts.

11 TIN CUP JOE FALLS

DISTANCE: 4.2 miles
ELEVATION GAIN: 600 feet in; 100 feet out
HIGH POINT: 2100 feet
DIFFICULTY: Moderate due to trail conditions
HIKING TIME: 4 to 6 hours
BEST SEASON: Late spring to early fall
TRAIL TRAFFIC: Moderate foot traffic; mountain bikes on Middle Fork Trail; very light foot traffic to falls
PERMIT: Northwest Forest Pass

MAPS: USGS Lake Philippa, USGS Snoqualmie Lake; Green Trails Middle Fork Snoqualmie No. 174SX
TRAILHEAD GPS: 47.5479°N, 121.5372°W
NOTES: A mudslide closed this trail in 2018 and while there are plans to address it, the trail remains closed as of this printing. The Middle Fork Trail #1003 is open to mountain bikes on odd-numbered days from June through October.

GETTING THERE: Take I-90 to Exit 34 near North Bend. At 468th Avenue just off the freeway, eastbound turn left, westbound turn right. Follow the road past the truck stop for about a half mile until you reach SE Middle Fork Road (Forest Road 56). Turn right and follow this road for a few twists and turns, keeping left when the road splits. After 2.2 miles reach SE Lake Dorothy Road. Turn left and continue 12 miles, crossing the Taylor River Bridge. After the bridge, keep right on FR 56, sometimes labeled FR 5620 or Dingford Creek Road at this point. Continue about 5 miles to the Dingford Creek Trailhead. Privy available.

While almost all of the approach to Tin Cup Joe Falls is an easy river walk, the last mile is a brushy climb alongside Cripple Creek that appeals more to hikers willing to endure a little extra challenge. There's no serious risk of getting lost with the creek as your guide, and the elevation gain is significant but not insurmountable. Most determined hikers should be able to make it to the falls if they're comfortable with a little bushwhacking and routefinding. And these falls are well worth it. Off the beaten path and seldom visited, this spectacular series of waterfalls may be a little difficult to reach, but they more than make up for it by the show they put on.

From the Dingford Creek Trailhead, drop down to the river, cross the Dingford Creek Bridge, and veer right onto the well-maintained and much-loved Middle Fork Trail #1003. The river is a lively companion as you wander beneath the heavy forest canopy. Remnants of old growth can be found among the mossy stumps still bearing notches from the timber harvests of the 1930s.

After a gentle 1.3 miles, reach a bridge crossing helpfully signed "Cripple Creek." A

The upper tiers of Tin Cup Joe Falls extend far beyond the small section shown here.

small cascade sometimes called Lower Cripple Creek Falls is here, splashing and crashing away during the melt. The path up to Tin Cup Joe Falls can be found on the west side of the bridge just after you cross. It's faint and unmarked, but it's not difficult to find once you look for it. Take a moment to tighten your laces and adjust your gear: the 0.8-mile climb is steep and the trail can be tricky to navigate.

As you climb, keep an eye out for the subtle signs of well-worn vegetation. At times, the trail may seem to completely disappear or take short detours around blowdowns. When in doubt, follow the creek and the path of least resistance. After some climbing and working your way through the brush, a distant roar will begin to grow. Through the trees, catch glimpses of the first set of falls cascading down from cliffs hundreds of feet above. Eventually, as you close in on the falls, the path works its way down to the creek, opening up your view to another set of falls just upstream and revealing another creek branch with two sets of waterfalls.

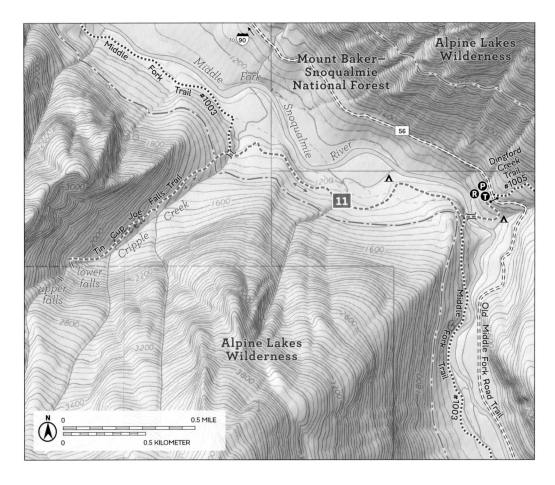

It is tempting to make a beeline to the horsetail falls ahead, but don't clamber across the creek just yet. Although these lower falls are impressive from creek level, push past them toward the upper set of Tin Cup Joe Falls. Circle wide and keep to the right, scrambling up the rocks above the short falls to a large rocky plateau. From here, water gushes off 200-foot cliffs from three separate channels unseen from the creek below. And what a show they put on: this little alcove of waterfalls has nearly 180 degrees of tumbling cascades in roaring surround sound, soaking viewers in a gentle mist. Superlatives seem lacking when you try to describe this rarity; it should be seen, not read about. Once you catch your breath, head back down to explore the lower falls, though they won't feel nearly as magical.

GOING FARTHER

The Middle Fork Trail continues downriver another 4.5 miles to the Gateway Bridge and the Middle Fork Trailhead (Hike 6). In the other direction from Cripple Creek, the trail plunges deeper into the river valley, passing the Rock Creek Trail #1013.1 (Hike 14) in 3.9 miles before reaching Goldmyer Hot Springs (Hike 15) in 6.1 miles. The trail then continues past the hot springs and ends when it connects to the Dutch Miller Gap Trail (Hike 93) at the 14.5-mile mark, 10.0 miles beyond Cripple Creek.

HISTORY

Tin Cup Joe Falls are found along Cripple Creek as it flows out of Derrick Lake toward the Middle Fork Snoqualmie River. It was known as Tin Cup Joe Creek back in the 1890s, during the Middle Fork Snoqualmie Valley's mining and prospecting heyday. Local miners named the creek in honor of a roving prospector.

12 MYRTLE LAKE

DISTANCE: 9.8 miles
ELEVATION GAIN: 2400 feet
HIGH POINT: 3800 feet
DIFFICULTY: Moderate
HIKING TIME: 7 to 9 hours or overnight
BEST SEASON: Early summer to late fall

TRAIL TRAFFIC: Moderate foot traffic
PERMIT: Northwest Forest Pass
MAPS: USGS Snoqualmie Lake; Green Trails
Middle Fork Snoqualmie No. 174SX
TRAILHEAD GPS: 47.5173°N, 121.4542°W

GETTING THERE: Take I-90 to Exit 34 near North Bend. At 468th Avenue just off the freeway, eastbound turn left, westbound turn right. Follow the road past the truck stop for about a half mile to reach SE Middle Fork Road (Forest Road 56). Turn right and follow this road for a few twists and turns, keeping left when the road splits. After 2.2 miles reach SE Lake Dorothy Road. Turn left and continue 12 miles, crossing the Taylor River Bridge. After the bridge, keep right on FR 56, sometimes labeled FR 5620 or Dingford Creek Road at this point. Continue for about 5 miles to the Dingford Creek Trailhead. Privy available.

Marsh-lined shores of Myrtle Lake in the summer

This hike to the slightly more popular of the two major lake destinations on the Dingford Creek Trail takes you through mossy forest, past gushing waterfalls, and up a rocky trail to lovely Myrtle Lake. Wild and relatively remote, this trail is frequented mostly by backpackers and fishermen, and because the trail doesn't see much traffic, it's a little rough and can be challenging. However, the surroundings—rushing waters, open valleys, deep forests—more than make up for it. While this hike works as a challenging day hike, its nearly 20 miles of forest roads to the trailhead and 2400 feet of elevation to the lake mean there isn't much daylight left to explore all the other nearby hidden vistas and lakes. With so much to see, this is an ideal overnight destination.

From the Dingford Creek Trailhead, begin steeply following the creek and Dingford Creek Trail #1005 up the mountainside. The first mile is filled with rocky switchbacks climbing through second-growth forest. At 0.7 mile, the trail enters the Alpine Lakes Wilderness, where the forest deepens and older stands of fir and cedar crowd the trail. As you progress, the trail crosses a couple of major streams flowing down from small lakes tucked into the hills above the creek basin. The most dramatic is Pumpkinseed Creek,

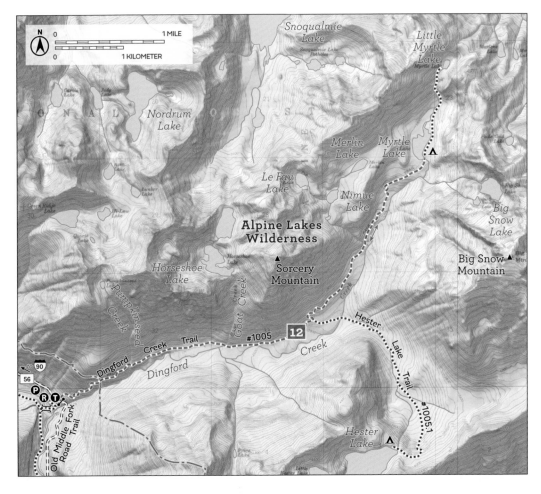

which creates a lovely little waterfall during the spring melt.

At 2.9 miles reach the junction with the Hester Lake Trail (Hike 13); veer left for Myrtle Lake. Past the junction, continue hopping creeks and climbing toward the lake. The grade eases as you approach Myrtle Lake, eventually depositing you on the shores of the shallow alpine lake at 4.9 miles. On a clear day, Big Snow Mountain looms above, an impressive backdrop. A couple of comfortable campsites nestle around the lake, making it an ideal base camp for exploring the sprawling lake country above.

GOING FARTHER

A faint path continues along the lakeshore and switchbacks up for about 1 mile to Little Myrtle Lake. For better views you can climb a little higher past Little Myrtle Lake to a pass to catch a glimpse of Lake Dorothy far below.

Alternatively, from Myrtle Lake you can head west cross-country to the Arthurian-inspired Merlin, Le Fay, and Nimue Lakes, collectively known as the Myrtle Lake Potholes, which rest beneath Sorcery Mountain. Nearby Big Snow Lake can also be reached with some difficulty by scrambling up a steep, talus-covered shoulder of Big Snow Mountain just south of Myrtle Lake. Another option is nearby Hester Lake (Hike 13), which adds a tough 4.6 miles to your day.

HISTORY

Myrtle Lake was named by Forest Supervisor Albert H. Sylvester sometime around 1918. By this time, his tradition of naming lakes after women was well entrenched (see Hike 87 for more detail), which means that "Myrtle" was likely a woman in the life of Sylvester or one of his rangers.

13 HESTER LAKE

DISTANCE: 10.4 miles
ELEVATION GAIN: 2500 feet
HIGH POINT: 3900 feet
DIFFICULTY: Moderate
HIKING TIME: 7 to 9 hours
BEST SEASON: Early summer to late fall

TRAIL TRAFFIC: Light foot traffic
PERMIT: Northwest Forest Pass
MAPS: USGS Snoqualmie Lake; Green Trails Middle Fork Snoqualmie No. 174SX
TRAILHEAD GPS: 47.5173°N, 121.4542°W

GETTING THERE: Take I-90 to Exit 34 near North Bend. At 468th Avenue just off the freeway, eastbound turn left, westbound turn right. Follow the road past the truck stop for about a half mile until you reach SE Middle Fork Road (Forest Road 56). Turn right and follow this road for a few twists and turns, keeping left when the road splits. After 2.2 miles reach SE Lake Dorothy Road. Turn left and continue 12 miles, crossing the Taylor River Bridge. After the bridge, keep right on FR 56, sometimes labeled FR 5620 or Dingford Creek Road at this point. Continue for about 5 miles to the Dingford Creek Trailhead. Privy available.

Most hikers and backpackers heading down the Dingford Creek Trail are aiming for Myrtle Lake, leaving Hester Lake to fisherfolk and serious lake baggers. The almost primitive spur trail out to Hester Lake is sporadically maintained, making it much more challenging than its few thousand feet of elevation gain would suggest. Yet this alpine lake offers wild solitude in the shadows of Mount Price, an appealing setting for those looking to explore some seldom-trodden trails.

From the Dingford Creek Trailhead, follow the steep Dingford Creek Trail #1005 as it ascends the mountainside. Enjoy mossy forest and splashing cascades as you tackle switchback after switchback, resisting the urge to linger too long on this pleasant stretch of trail. Cross into the Alpine Lakes Wilderness at 0.7 mile and trade young second-generation cedars for stands of ancient firs bearded with wispy moss. Push onward and upward through the old growth past Pumpkinseed Creek and Goat Creek.

At 2.9 miles, reach the junction with the Hester Lake Trail #1005.1, veering right for Hester Lake. The trail almost immediately becomes rougher, crossing Dingford Creek and then a series of three large creeks that cut across the trail. Depending on the time of year, these crossings may require some wading, so bring extra socks or an affection for hiking in soggy boots. Beyond the creeks, navigate an often-muddy section of trail still recovering from washouts in the recent past. Pay close attention to the trail as you navigate your way through the mud: it can be easy to lose the trail. Blowdowns are common on this trail and it is not cleared often, so expect to be climbing up, over, and around obstacles as you press deeper into the creek valley.

Soon you climb a steep series of switchbacks that eventually pass by two small ponds before delivering you to the shores of Hester Lake near the lake outlet. The lake rests below Mount Price and its surrounding ridges, with slopes more trees than rock. While a few avalanche chutes are evident, the trees dominating the shore explain the snag-clogged outlet. Some of the best views of the lake are from these logs, which tempt visitors with a wide view of the lake. For those spending the night, several campsites can be found nearby.

GOING FARTHER

Little Hester Lake is not far from end of the official trail; head around the north side of Hester Lake, picking your way through forest

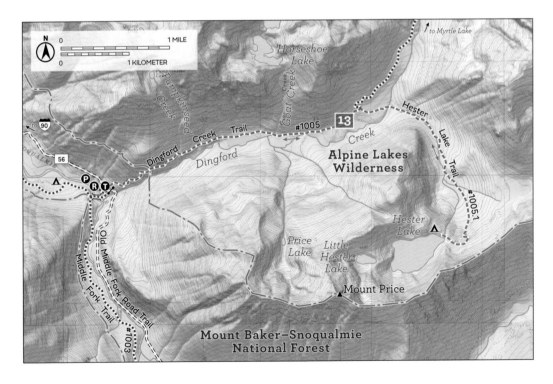

With few visitors, the quiet shores of Hester Lake are lovely but largely inaccessible.

and talus fields and following faint boot paths and game trails. Little Hester Lake is about 200 feet higher, so some scrambling may be required, depending on your route. More technically oriented climbers use Little Hester Lake as a jumping-off point to scale Mount Price and other nearby prominences. For a more significant addition to your day, you can add a climb to Myrtle Lake (Hike 12), 2.0 miles farther down the Dingford Creek Trail.

HISTORY

Hester Lake's history is tied up with that of nearby Myrtle Lake. Forest Supervisor Albert H. Sylvester very likely named Hester Lake around the same time he named Myrtle Lake. Although the 1932 edition of the USGS Skykomish quadrangle labels it "Lake Hessler," the name was soon replaced by "Hester Lake." When Sylvester named a feature, he would send the US Geological Survey a copy of the current map with his handwritten additions, which occasionally resulted in errors. Given that Sylvester was in the area and that Hester was a popular female name in the 1940s, it seems likely that he named it after a woman in his of one of his rangers' lives (see Hike 87 for more detail about this practice).

14 ROCK CREEK

DISTANCE: 12.6 miles
ELEVATION GAIN: 2700 feet in; 100 feet out
HIGH POINT: 4100 feet
DIFFICULTY: Moderate
HIKING TIME: 7 to 9 hours

BEST SEASON: Late spring to early fall
TRAIL TRAFFIC: Moderate foot traffic, mountain bikes
PERMIT: Northwest Forest Pass
TRAILHEAD GPS: 47.5173°N, 121.4542°W

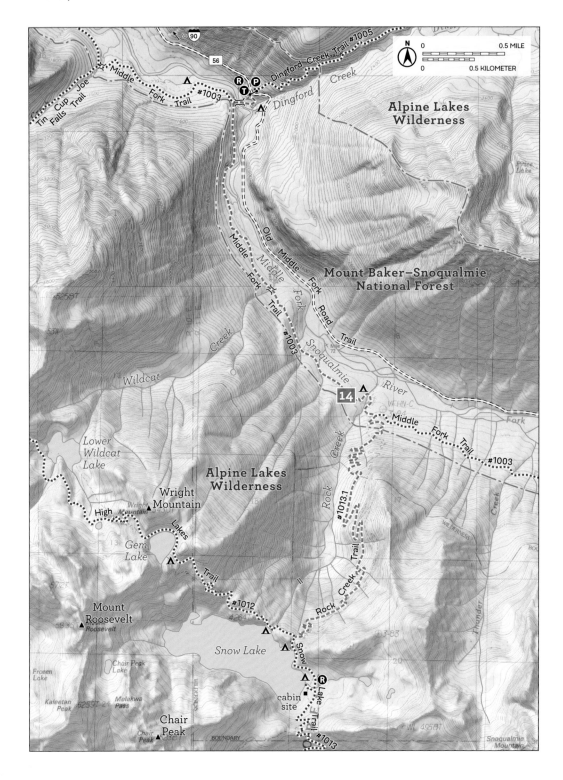

MAPS: USGS Snoqualmie Lake, USGS Snoqualmie Pass; Green Trails Skykomish No. 175, Green Trails Snoqualmie Pass No. 207
NOTES: A mudslide closed this trail in 2018 and while there are plans to address it, the trail remains closed as of this printing. The Middle Fork Trail #1003 is open to mountain bikes on odd-numbered days from June through October.

GETTING THERE: Take I-90 to Exit 34 near North Bend. At 468th Avenue just off the freeway, eastbound turn left, westbound turn right. Follow the road past the truck stop for about a half mile to reach SE Middle Fork Road (Forest Road 56). Turn right and follow this road for a few twists and turns, keeping left when the road splits. After 2.2 miles reach SE Lake Dorothy Road. Turn left and continue 12 miles, crossing the Taylor River Bridge. After the bridge, keep right on FR 56, sometimes labeled FR 5620 or Dingford Creek Road at this point. Continue for about 5 miles to the Dingford Creek Trailhead. Privy available.

This less-traveled trail leads to one of the largest waterfalls in the Alpine Lakes Wilderness. This is not an easy hike, though it is a great alternative approach to Snow Lake that exchanges the crowds for an impressive waterfall. But this route doesn't get a lot of traffic, and it shows—the trail is rough, narrow, and overgrown; you'll definitely want to bring the gaiters and hiking poles on this one. However, if solitude is what you're after, this trail comes highly recommended.

From the Dingford Creek Trailhead, drop down and cross the Middle Fork Snoqualmie River to join the Middle Fork Trail #1003. Keep left at the T-junction, following the river through pleasant second-growth forests, with only a few short bursts of elevation gain. At 1.6 miles, cross Wildcat Creek and soon connect with the old railroad grade, which you follow almost all the way to Rock Creek.

The grade over Rock Creek washed out long ago, forcing a short detour downstream to cross the creek and rejoin the grade on the other side. Here, at 2.8 miles, find the signed junction to the Rock Creek Trail #1013.1. The hike now begins in earnest.

The steep, rough, rocky trail steadily climbs the Rock Creek basin in a long series of tight switchbacks. As you gain elevation, the forest matures, slowly transitioning to old growth, complete with massive firs and hemlocks. Reach the Alpine Lakes Wilderness at 3.6 miles and soon cross mossy talus fields while taking in views of Garfield Mountain's sprawling granite faces. Hop across numerous streamlets cutting across your path as you continue your uphill battle through the wilderness.

Eventually you reach the impressive Rock Creek falls around the 5.0-mile mark. Watch the waters flowing out of Snow Lake and cascading almost 1200 feet down to the Middle Fork Snoqualmie Basin.

Not too much farther up the mountainside, the trail ends at 6.3 miles at the junction with the main Snow Lake Trail #1013 to the left and the High Lakes Trail #1012 to the right. Snow Lake (Hike 29) is just a few dozen feet from the end of the Rock Creek Trail, and its shores are an excellent lunch spot. Lakeshore campsites are available for those on longer journeys.

GOING FARTHER

While likely beyond the reach of most day hikers, Gem Lake (Hike 30) is another 1.3 miles up the High Lakes Trail. Alternatively, from the Rock Creek Trail junction you can continue on the Middle Fork Trail #1003 to reach Goldmyer Hot Springs (Hike 15). Those who arrange a shuttle can through-hike, following the Snow Lake Trail (Hike 29) out to Snoqualmie Pass.

The Rock Creek Trail ends on the north shore of Snow Lake with a view south to Chair Peak.

HISTORY

During the early twentieth century, the Rock Creek Trail linked the Snow Lake mining claims and the bustling timber industry of the Middle Fork Snoqualmie Valley. As the mines closed and the timber interests moved on, hikers and backpackers took their place. The Rock Creek Trail was once part of the Cascade Crest Trail (CCT), a regional predecessor of the Pacific Crest National Scenic Trail (PCT). When PCT trailblazers blasted a more efficient route into the side of a mountain—now known as the Kendall Katwalk—the Rock Creek route was largely abandoned. Today, the trail has become a road less traveled, with relatively few visitors every year.

15 GOLDMYER HOT SPRINGS

DISTANCE: 10.9 miles
ELEVATION GAIN: 700 feet
HIGH POINT: 2100 feet
DIFFICULTY: Moderate
HIKING TIME: 6 to 8 hours or overnight
BEST SEASON: Early spring to late fall
TRAIL TRAFFIC: Moderate foot traffic; mountain bikes
PERMIT: Northwest Forest Pass
TRAILHEAD GPS: 47.5173°N, 121.4542°W
MAPS: USGS Snoqualmie Lake, USGS Snoqualmie Pass; Green Trails Middle Fork Snoqualmie No. 174SX
NOTES: A mudslide closed this trail in 2018 and while there are plans to address it, the trail remains closed as of this printing. The full loop may require fording Burnboot Creek. The Middle Fork Trail #1003 is open to mountain bikes on odd-numbered days from June through October. If you want to use Goldmyer Hot Springs or spend the night, reservations are highly recommended; visit www.goldmyer.org for details.

GETTING THERE: Take I-90 to Exit 34 near North Bend. At 468th Avenue just off the freeway, eastbound turn left, westbound turn right. Follow the road past the truck stop for about a half mile to reach SE Middle Fork Road (Forest Road 56). Turn right and follow this road for a few twists and turns, keeping left when the road splits. After 2.2 miles reach SE Lake Dorothy Road. Turn left and continue 12 miles, crossing the Taylor River Bridge. After the bridge, keep right on FR 56, sometimes labeled FR 5620 or Dingford Creek Road at this point. Continue for about 5 miles to the Dingford Creek Trailhead. Privy available.

One of the best-known destinations in the Middle Fork Snoqualmie Valley, Goldmyer Hot Springs has been welcoming visitors for more than a century. While the route remains outside the Alpine Lakes Wilderness, the hike skirts the boundaries, and the springs are a stone's throw from the wild. Cross roaring creeks, tumbling cascades, and the occasional washout on this hike out to a well-earned soak. The ease of the trail and the comfortable destination make it easy to convince skeptics or beginners that backpacking is a lot of fun.

From the Dingford Creek Trailhead, wind down to the Middle Fork Snoqualmie River and the Dingford Creek Bridge. Take in the picturesque setting—water tumbling through the boulder-strewn riverbed, tree-lined riverbanks that light up during the autumn. Cross the bridge and veer left, following the Middle Fork Trail #1003 as it works its way up the river valley. The well-maintained trail is a dream, with a minimum of ups and downs. You soon reach Wildcat Creek at 1.6 miles, where the trail widens and follows the old railroad grade another 1.2 miles to Rock Creek.

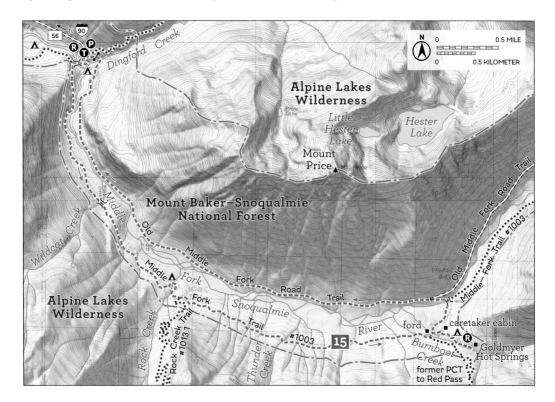

Outer cooling pool at Goldmyer Hot Springs

Pass the signed junction to the Rock Creek Trail #1013.1 (Hike 14) and campsite at 2.8 miles.

Continue wandering on the Middle Fork Trail under alders, hemlocks, and big-leaf maples, with breaks in the canopy showing Mount Price and the surrounding landscape. On this stretch the only real challenge is crossing Thunder Creek at 3.8 miles. The rock-hop is not too challenging during the summer, but when the water is high—during the spring melt or after a storm—the volume and force of water coming down are enough to make fording too dangerous. If you're headed to Goldmyer during this time of year, you can approach the hot springs by walking the forest road from Dingford Creek Trailhead—the walk is not as nice, but it is a lot safer.

Beyond Thunder Creek, it's 1.3 miles to Burnboot Creek aka Burntboot or Burnt, where hikers must ford the creek (until the log bridge is replaced) to reach the Goldmyer property at 5.1 miles. The tent sites are well groomed, the nearby river makes for easy access to water, and an enclosed outhouse borders on luxurious. The hot springs, a short 0.4-mile walk from the camp, are fairly small: no more than about ten people can fit in the various pools. Perhaps for this reason, camping is limited to twenty people a day, groups to no more than twelve.

To return, make a loop by following the Old Middle Fork Road (one of many names for this stretch of decommissioned forest road between Dingford Creek Trailhead and Hardscrabble Horse Camp). Simply follow the main trail out of the Goldmyer camping area to a bridge placed in 2007 to make access to the property a little easier. Cross the Middle Fork Snoqualmie and head left on the forest road, walking 4.7 miles back to the Dingford Creek Trailhead.

GOING FARTHER

Rather than driving to the Dingford Creek Trailhead, you can hike the Middle Fork Trail for some interesting side trips along the way. At 4.5 miles from the Middle Fork Snoqualmie Trailhead, you reach Cripple Creek and a 0.8-mile-long scramble up to Tin Cup Joe Falls (Hike 11). At just over 8 miles, the Middle Fork Trail intersects the Rock Creek Trail #1013.1 (Hike 14), which leads up to Snow Lake (Hike 29) and Snoqualmie Pass.

HISTORY

Goldmyer Hot Springs is named for William Goldmyer, an eccentric who settled in Seattle in 1868 and patented a mining claim at Goldmyer in the early 1900s. To firm up his claim, Goldmyer needed to make $500 worth of improvements to the land. He accomplished this, in part, by blasting open the cave where the hot springs are now located to gain better access to the hot water. He also built a cabin and a lodge for miners and outdoorsmen who ventured near the area, calling it Crystal Hot Springs Resort. Goldmyer died in 1924, and the property ended up in the hands of the Morrow family. "Big Bill" Morrow greatly expanded the resort, even building a hydropower plant. While his grand vision of a sprawling resort was never realized, the place was popular: enough visitors came that the timber railroad could not transport them all to the resort, prompting many visitors to access the property via the Snow Lake–Rock Creek Trail.

With the advent of World War II, attention shifted away from the hot springs, and floods in the 1960s destroyed a lot of the buildings and improvements. The Morrow family continued to own the property, but it was somewhat abandoned and fell into disrepair. By 1976 the Morrow family preserved the area by creating a nonprofit stewardship program called Northwest Wilderness Programs, which continues to manage Goldmyer Hot Springs today.

16 LOCH KATRINE

DISTANCE: 7.2 miles
ELEVATION GAIN: 1500 feet
HIGH POINT: 3000 feet
DIFFICULTY: Moderate
HIKING TIME: 3 to 4 hours
BEST SEASON: Early spring to late fall
TRAIL TRAFFIC: Light foot traffic; possible logging trucks

PERMIT: Campbell Global Permit at www.sqrecreation.com
MAPS: USGS Devils Slide, USGS Mt. Phelps; Green Trails Mount Si No. 174
TRAILHEAD GPS: 47.6495°N, 121.646°W
NOTE: A day pass is required to access Loch Katrine; visit www.sqrecreation.com for details.

GETTING THERE: Take I-90 to North Bend, taking Exit 31. Eastbound turn left around the traffic circle, following a sign pointing toward North Bend; westbound take a right onto unsigned State Route 202. After the outlet malls, take a right on North Bend Way and an almost immediate left onto Ballarat Street. After 4 miles, the road splits; veer left onto North Fork County Road (Forest Road 57). Continue on what soon becomes a bumpy gravel road for 12.6 miles to a large pullout across from a gated road.

This hike out to a lovely and lonely alpine lake is a study in stark contrast. If Loch Katrine were located elsewhere in the Alpine Lakes Wilderness, it would likely attract throngs of hikers to its charming shores. However, the approach to the lake is almost entirely through an active working forest, which requires a private permit to access, so few venture down the logging roads to reach it. While a stroll through recent timber harvests is not the most picturesque, there is a certain thrill to stepping off the end of a logging road and walking a few dozen yards to find what feels like a hidden slice of wilderness. It's also not too difficult a hike, making pretty Loch Katrine a bit more accessible than some other, more popular alpine lakes, and yet you're likely to get this big, beautiful lake all to yourself. The Washington Department of Fish and Wildlife stocks Loch Katrine and Upper Loch Katrine with more than one variety of fish, so pack your pole.

From the large pullout along FR 57, round the yellow gate and follow the logging road past a hillside of stumps. This is more or less what the majority of the hike is like: a trek up a largely denuded mountainside, with eventual views of the surrounding valley, much of which has also recently been logged. At 0.7 mile reach a junction; head left and angle upward to quickly put as much road behind you as possible.

Steadily climb the forest road on long switchbacks that cross small creek gullies, and eventually you gain enough elevation to see some interesting things. Spy Mount Phelps and Little Mount Phelps across the valley, and pick out the vibrant green of the Sunday Lake Trail marsh (Hike 17). Older maps suggest that a trail or old road once cut down to the Sunday Lake Trail, but nature or logging activities have erased all trace. At any remnant trail junctions, stay left.

Loch Katrine in the late spring from the logs near the lake outlet

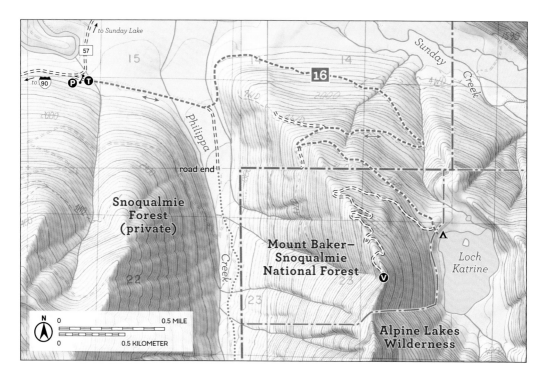

At about 2.9 miles, at a large hairpin turn, instead of switchbacking up the logging road, continue straight ahead into the Alpine Lakes Wilderness. Once you're in the trees, a boot path is readily apparent, dropping slightly toward the lakeshore. Within a few moments, reach Loch Katrine, which reveals itself like a lost world completely shielded from the logging activity left behind. There's even a charming little island near the outlet to complete the picture, and a campsite beckons those interested in a longer stay.

GOING FARTHER

For broad vistas and mountaintop views, return to the logging road and continue climbing up the mountainside on it. After a few switchbacks the road ends at a high point above Loch Katrine with partial views of Bare Mountain, Goat Mountain, and Lennox Mountain.

17 SUNDAY LAKE

DISTANCE: 6.4 miles
ELEVATION GAIN: 300 feet
HIGH POINT: 1900 feet
DIFFICULTY: Hard
HIKING TIME: 4 to 6 hours
BEST SEASON: Summer to early fall
TRAIL TRAFFIC: Light foot traffic
PERMIT: None

MAPS: USGS Mt. Phelps; Green Trails Mount Si No. 174
TRAILHEAD GPS: 47.66093°N, 121.6166°W
NOTE: Reaching Sunday Lake requires fording Sunday Creek, which should be avoided when the water is running high, such as during the spring melt or after significant precipitation.

GETTING THERE: Take I-90 to North Bend, taking Exit 31. Eastbound turn left around the traffic circle, following a sign pointing toward North Bend; westbound take a right onto unsigned State Route 202. After the outlet malls, take a right on North Bend Way and an almost immediate left onto Ballarat Street. After 4 miles, the road splits; veer left onto North Fork County Road (Forest Road 57). Continue on what soon becomes a bumpy gravel road for a total of 14.4 miles to a yellow gate labeled "Gate 30." Find an unobtrusive place to wedge your vehicle.

The trek out to Sunday Lake involves far more challenge and adventure than its mileage suggests. With little elevation gain on the 3.2-mile journey to the lakeshore, it may look perfect at first glance for fledgling hikers or a family outing, but an unmarked trailhead, difficult creek ford, and spotty trail maintenance limit visitors to Sunday Lake to the most ambitious hikers and anglers.

From the unmarked trailhead, start down the brush-lined logging road. In a few thousand feet, you'll pass a crumbling trail kiosk, and here the much-lamented and often-maligned Sunday Lake Trail #1000 begins. Continue 0.3 mile to the next obstacle: a marsh that has long since reclaimed the road. Over the years, volunteers and resourceful hikers have laid down

logs, rocks, and hunks of wood to help with the crossing. The water level varies throughout the year, but be prepared to get a little muddy as you try to tiptoe through the muck.

Once past the marsh, follow the trail past clear-cuts and into the sheltering forest, winding beneath rocky cliffs. At just over 1.0 mile, an overgrown junction leading off to the right once connected to the Loch Katrine trail (Hike 16), but you'll have no trouble staying to the left toward Sunday Creek.

At 1.5 miles reach the rocky creek bed and rushing Sunday Creek. Fording the creek is by far the most difficult aspect of this hike. Floods have long since washed away the bridge and portions of the trail along the riverside. Depending on the time of year, the crossing may be relatively easy, or waters may be running too high and fast to attempt it. If you have any doubt about the ford, end your hike here—the rocky riverbank makes for a great lunch spot.

If you ford the creek, you may need to do some backtracking to find the roadbed again. Cairns often mark the trail, making it relatively easy to find; when in doubt, follow the creek. Hike past the rusting remains of logging activity through the forest as it slowly changes into the older growth associated with the Alpine Lakes Wilderness, crossing the wilderness boundary at 2.1 miles.

As you push deeper into the valley, blowdowns and overgrowth are more of an issue,

Sunday Lake's shoreline can be marshy; hike toward the south end to find an opening in the trees.

though the trail does receive some maintenance from a few dedicated individuals engaged in a private war against the encroaching forest. The dense, fern-covered forest and stretches of mature trees are a sharp contrast to the young alders and maples on the other side of Sunday Creek.

After 2.8 miles, pass a large camping area and find the first indications that you are approaching the lake. These marshy sections are the beginnings of what will eventually become Sunday Lake. As you get closer to the lakeshore, the trail continues to worsen, becoming rockier and narrow with no real access to the water.

At 3.2 miles reach Sunday Lake's tree-covered shores. Getting a full view of the landscape is difficult, but a few big openings in the tree line let you take it all in. The snags and logs that clog the lake outlet where the marshes yield to open water offer a nice spot to have a snack and take in Sunday Lake as well as Goat Mountain rising above it.

GOING FARTHER

The trail continues along the lakeshore, and in better days it provided access up to Mowitch and Honey Lakes, but the old mining road is now overgrown and difficult to follow. Expect bushwhacking and a lot of routefinding.

HISTORY

Back in the 1890s, prospectors explored the river valleys that cut into the western slopes of the Cascades. The first claims on the North Fork Snoqualmie River Valley were made around 1896 near Lennox Mountain. The area was soon an organized mining district called Buena Vista, an extension of the Miller River and Money Creek mining districts. Ultimately most of the mining activity focused on Bear Basin at the upper end of the river valley, but not before more claims were made along the many creeks that fed the North Fork Snoqualmie, including Sunday Creek.

The trail to Sunday Lake appears on maps as far back as the 1920s, though it ends at the northern tip of the lake. In 1953 an 82-acre mining claim south of Sunday Lake, called the Lake Katrine Lodes, was patented by Nellie McMurray. Around this time, maps show the trail extending about a mile south of Sunday Lake, providing access to the claims along the creek where the waters from Honey Lake, Mowitch Lake, and Boomerang Lake merge. Here miners built roads, and lumbermen soon followed. Artifacts along the trail are a reminder of Sunday Creek's long-gone logging days.

18 BARE MOUNTAIN

DISTANCE: 8.2 miles
ELEVATION GAIN: 3200 feet
HIGH POINT: 5353 feet
DIFFICULTY: Hard
HIKING TIME: 4 to 6 hours
BEST SEASON: Late spring to early fall
TRAIL TRAFFIC: Light foot traffic

PERMIT: Northwest Forest Pass
MAPS: USGS Mount Phelps, USGS Grotto; Green Trails Mount Si No. 174, Green Trails Skykomish No. 175
TRAILHEAD GPS: 47.63975°N, 121.5287°W
NOTE: Use caution fording Bear Creek when the water is running high, during spring and fall.

GETTING THERE: Take I-90 to North Bend, taking Exit 31. Eastbound turn left around the traffic circle, following a sign pointing toward North Bend; westbound take a right onto unsigned State Route 202. After the outlet malls, take a right on North Bend Way and an almost immediate left onto Ballarat Street. After 4 miles, the road splits; veer left onto North Fork County Road (Forest Road 57). Continue on what soon becomes a bumpy gravel road for a little over 18 miles to a junction where FR 57 turns left across the North Fork Snoqualmie River. Almost immediately, at the next junction, follow FR 57 to the right for another 3 miles to the trailhead and small parking area.

A lookout site, a valley full of mining history, and panoramic views—most hikes do not include any of these things, much less all three. Bare Mountain and Bear Creek promise a day full of big views and exploration. This great hike has a singular drawback: the 21 miles to the trailhead. FR 57 is in decent shape but, like any forest road, it's riddled with potholes and rocks, which makes for a long, bumpy ride. The trail itself is approachable for just about anyone. The long switchbacks smooth out the elevation gain, all but eliminating "steep" portions of the trail. A little caution crossing Bear Creek and navigating the "fern-forest" is all that you need to enjoy the views at the top.

From the trailhead, begin by following the Bare Mountain Trail #1037 into a mixed forest of dominated by alder and hemlock. This section of former mining road is easy to navigate as it climbs gently, skipping over a few creeks the cut across the trail. At the 0.7-mile mark reach

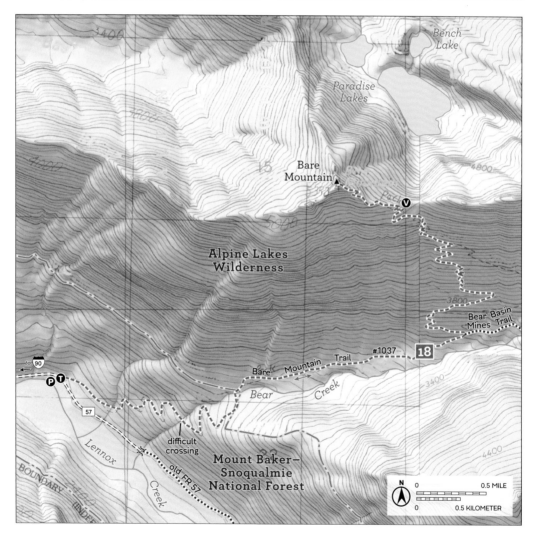

Paradise Lakes and Bench Lake from the summit of Bare Mountain

rushing Bear Creek, which can be tricky to cross when the water is running high. Hikers should use caution during the spring and fall. During the summer, the crossing is easy with the help of a rope railing that volunteers have maintained for many years and should not pose any problems. Beyond Bear Creek, at 1.1 miles, the trail crosses into the Alpine Lakes Wilderness and the open valley below the mountain.

Aside from the storied views at the summit, the hike is infamous for the "fern-forest" of bracken fern that encroaches on the lower reaches of the trail each year. Volunteers fight an endless battle against the vegetation, hacking wide swaths through the brush only to have it quickly return. The ferns also obscure the trail, hiding pits and potholes that can easily twist an ankle. Proceed with some caution through these sections. At a switchback at 2.0 miles, veer left to continue up switchbacks through the ferns, which slowly recede and give way to heather and endless patches of alpine blueberries.

As you approach the top, attain the ridgeline at about 3.8 miles and take a quick peek down to Bench Lake and Paradise Lakes. Then press on to the rocky summit, still clinging to the last remnants of the lookout that stood there for forty years. Here Mount Rainier dominates the skyline, and Glacier Peak and Mount Baker are both visible. In addition to the familiar Snoqualmie Pass peaks and a huge portion of the Alpine Lakes Wilderness, Mount Index and other Highway 2 peaks can also be seen. Settle in, break out your lunch, and enjoy the sweeping views.

GOING FARTHER

At around the 2.0-mile mark, where the trail to the summit abruptly switchbacks upward, the abandoned mining road continues straight ahead up the creek to Bear Basin (Hike 19).

HISTORY

The Bare Mountain Trail follows the remains of a road built to service the mines drilled into the mountainside above Bear Creek. Bare Mountain's summit hosted a fire lookout cabin from 1935 to 1973, when it was decommissioned.

19 BEAR BASIN MINES

DISTANCE: 6.0 miles
ELEVATION GAIN: 2400 feet
HIGH POINT: 4200 feet
DIFFICULTY: Hard
HIKING TIME: 4 to 5 hours, more if exploring
BEST SEASON: Late spring to early fall
TRAIL TRAFFIC: Light foot traffic
PERMIT: Northwest Forest Pass
TRAILHEAD GPS: 47.63975°N, 121.5287°W

MAPS: USGS Mount Phelps, USGS Grotto; Green Trails Mount Si No. 174, Green Trails Skykomish No. 175
NOTES: Use caution fording Bear Creek when the water is running high, during spring and fall. Use caution when exploring abandoned mining claims, and never enter a tunnel or adit without proper equipment and training. Unmaintained areas can be dangerous if unstable.

GETTING THERE: Take I-90 to North Bend, taking Exit 31. Eastbound turn left around the traffic circle, following a sign pointing toward North Bend; westbound take a right onto unsigned State Route 202. After the outlet malls, take a right on North Bend Way and an almost immediate left onto Ballarat Street. After 4 miles, the road splits; veer left onto North Fork County Road (Forest Road 57). Continue on what soon becomes a bumpy gravel road for a little over 18 miles to a junction where FR 57 turns left across the North Fork Snoqualmie River. Almost immediately, at the next junction, follow FR 57 to the right for another 3 miles to the trailhead.

Explore one hundred years of mining history on this splendid excursion into a remote creek basin. Clamber over rocks, peer into dark tunnels, and ponder rusting equipment as you spend the better part of a day climbing up and down the slopes of Bear Basin. Bring your sense of adventure and curiosity—there is a lot to see here. That this seldom-visited valley is thoroughly enjoyable to hike through makes it that much better.

From the Bare Mountain Trailhead, follow Bare Mountain Trail #1037 into a mixed forest. The well-graded trail is what remains of a long-abandoned mining road that once provided access to the claims in Bear Basin. As you gently climb, a number of creeks flow over the trail, eager to join Lennox Creek below, but pose no real challenge. At 0.7 mile, the trail crosses Bear Creek, which can be a little tricky when the water is high. While crossing is easy during the summer, use caution during the spring and fall. Once across—perhaps with the help of a rope railing that volunteers have maintained for many years—push onward into the trees, reaching the Alpine Lakes Wilderness at 1.1 miles. Soon enter the often-brushy open valley below Bare Mountain.

Part of the "bare" of Bare Mountain is a distinct lack of trees. Instead, the slopes are covered in large swaths of thick vegetation, primarily bracken fern. Unless trail maintenance crews or volunteers have come through to brush it out, it is likely to be a slow, wet march to the switchback at the 2.0-mile mark. Here, ignore the main trail switchbacking sharply up the mountainside. Instead, plunge into the brush, following the largely obscured roadbed as it parallels Bear Creek and leads you deeper into the basin.

Hop over the creeks that cut across the faint boot path, soon reaching a mossy and slick puncheon bridge at 2.3 miles. The creek tumbles over a short cascade here, the site of the small flotation mill the Snoqualmie Mining Company built to tease out the small amount of gold and silver they pulled out of the slopes above. The trail splits not far past the mill site, with both forks worth exploring. To the left, the trail veers toward the north slopes and Bear Lakes, the headwaters of Bear Creek.

Pass pieces of abandoned mining equipment, rusting so long in the elements that they have transformed from trash to artifact. Mixed in with the mining debris is what remains of a small airplane that crashed here a few decades ago, some of which has been repurposed in the nearby campsites—likely the same sites as the old mining camp that was once here. Push up the slope another 0.2 mile to reach an impressive steam donkey, set on its side at the bottom of the talus field it rolled down. Scramble up the talus field and keep left to find adits #6 and #7 of the Bear Basin Property. The wooden frame in the vicinity is a reminder of the tram that ferried ore down to the mill.

Back before the plane debris, another trail heads to the right, toward the south slopes of the basin before disappearing in 0.1 mile. From here it's a short scramble up to the mine: simply climb toward the obvious tailings to reach adit #3. After you've gotten your fill of the mine, take a moment to enjoy the view. Bear Basin looks like a rugged amphitheater, its

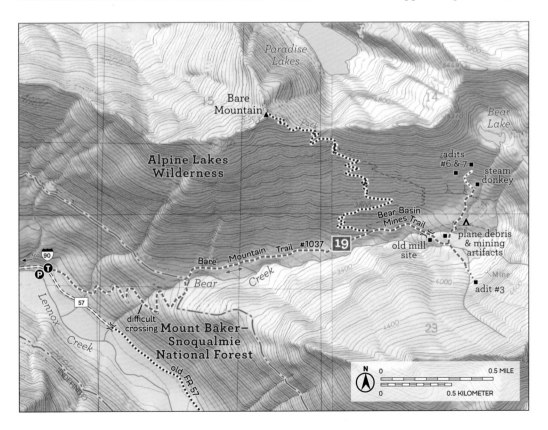

rocky slopes begging to be explored. You can discover and ponder an enormous amount of history and artifacts in and around the basin, more than enough for a full day of hiking.

GOING FARTHER

Of the eight adits that were drilled in the area, two have collapsed, you've just explored three, and that leaves another three to find for those looking for more adventure. A trip up Bare Mountain (Hike 18) adds a few more miles, big views, and a lot of extra work to the day.

HISTORY

The first organized exploration for minerals in the North Fork Snoqualmie River Valley began in 1896. Around then the area was broadly organized as the Buena Vista mining district. The Bear Basin Mines were one property in the area, with claims first laid in February 1905 by three prospectors: L. A. Nelson, Joseph Brown, and A. Loveless. Soon the Snoqualmie Mining Company was organized and began punching tunnels into the slopes above Bear Basin. Eventually, eight adits were dug, consisting of more than 2000 feet of tunnel. By 1917 the company had built a flotation mill on Bear Creek just below Bear Basin Camp—evidence of both can still be found on the trail. Some measurable amount of silver was mined between 1917 and 1922, but that proved to be the high-water mark for the property.

Along with the mill, the company built a 1500-foot-long two-bucket gravity tram to haul ore from adit #6 down to the mill. When the property was sold to a Mr. Anderson, he moved the tram to adit #3 on the opposite side of the basin. Unfortunately, the mill burned down in 1934 before the new tram went into operation.

Mining adit #6 is reached by scrambling up the talus field to the north. Look for the mine tailings, largely made up of processed gravel that does not match the rest of the boulder-covered mountainside.

By 1951 the property was in the hands of the Bear Basin Mining Company out of Spokane. Big plans to restart silver mining in the area never materialized. Today, nature is slowly reclaiming the area, with two of the eight adits already collapsed, but it will be many more decades before evidence of this history is completely wiped away.

20 LENNOX CREEK AND ANDERSON LAKE

DISTANCE: 10.2 miles
ELEVATION GAIN: 2500 feet in; 500 feet out

HIGH POINT: 4600 feet
DIFFICULTY: Hard

HIKING TIME: 5 to 7 hours

BEST SEASON: Early summer to late fall

TRAIL TRAFFIC: Very light foot traffic

PERMIT: None

MAPS: USGS Mt. Phelps, USGS Lake Philippa, USGS Snoqualmie Lake; Green Trails Mount Si No. 174, Green Trails Skykomish No. 175

TRAILHEAD GPS: 47.6364°N, 121.5233°W

GETTING THERE: Take I-90 to North Bend, taking Exit 31. Eastbound turn left around the traffic circle, following a sign pointing toward North Bend; westbound take a right onto unsigned State Route 202. After the outlet malls, take a right on North Bend Way and an almost immediate left onto Ballarat Street. After 4 miles, the road splits; veer left onto North Fork County Road (Forest Road 57). Continue a little over 18 miles to a junction where FR 57 turns left across the North Fork Snoqualmie River. Almost immediately at the next junction, follow FR 57 to the right for another 3 miles to the Bare Mountain Trailhead. Continue past the trailhead almost 0.2 mile to the washout and park here.

This lonely trail sits at the very end of more than 20 miles of bumpy forest road. Overlooked, barely maintained, and virtually abandoned, the Lennox Creek Trail is a difficult hike. Hard to reach and challenging to navigate, it understandably does not get a lot of foot traffic. But it rewards tenacious hikers with lovely subalpine meadows, broad vistas, and a pretty alpine lake. Trade a few scratches from the underbrush for solitude and the welcoming parklands on the slopes of Dog Mountain. Semiabandoned trails like Lennox Creek are perfect for hikers looking for a little more wilderness in their hike but wanting something short of a full routefinding bushwhack through the forest.

From the current end of FR 57, where Bear Creek washed out the forest road years ago, navigate your way across the creek to what remains of the decaying logging bridge and regain the roadbed. Follow the alder-lined old road deeper into the encroaching forest for nearly 2.0 miles, crossing Lennox Creek on another big logging bridge to reach the former Lennox Creek Trailhead. No signs mark the beginning of the Lennox Creek Trail #1001, but the transition from forest road to trail is clear.

The trail starts as more stream than path, and you'll clamber over rocks and roots and begin to climb in earnest, soon entering the Alpine Lakes Wilderness. Years of virtual abandonment can make the trail difficult to follow at times, as the narrow path is often overgrown or obscured, though a dedicated group of unofficial stewards occasionally clears out brushy sections. Old puncheon and trail improvements that mark the route are often slick or unstable and should be crossed with some caution. Pay extra attention to the route as you switchback up the shoulders of Dog Mountain and cross a few rushing creeks, as it can be easy to wander off the path. If you find that the trail has completely disappeared, you've likely missed a switchback and should retrace your steps.

The underbrush thins as you gain elevation, and the trail becomes easier to follow as the best portions begin. The route snakes beneath Dog Mountain through meadow parklands and large swaths of exposed granite. Look out across Lennox Creek far below to take in the rolling green ridges stretching northward. Enjoy the vistas of Bare Mountain and Lennox Mountain before working your way up to Anderson Pass, 4.7 miles from the trailhead.

Cross over the pass and soon find yourself in a talus field above Anderson Lake. No formal trail leads down to the lakeshore, though there are campsites on the far side of the lake. Find the path of least resistance down through the talus field to the lakeshore. Whether you

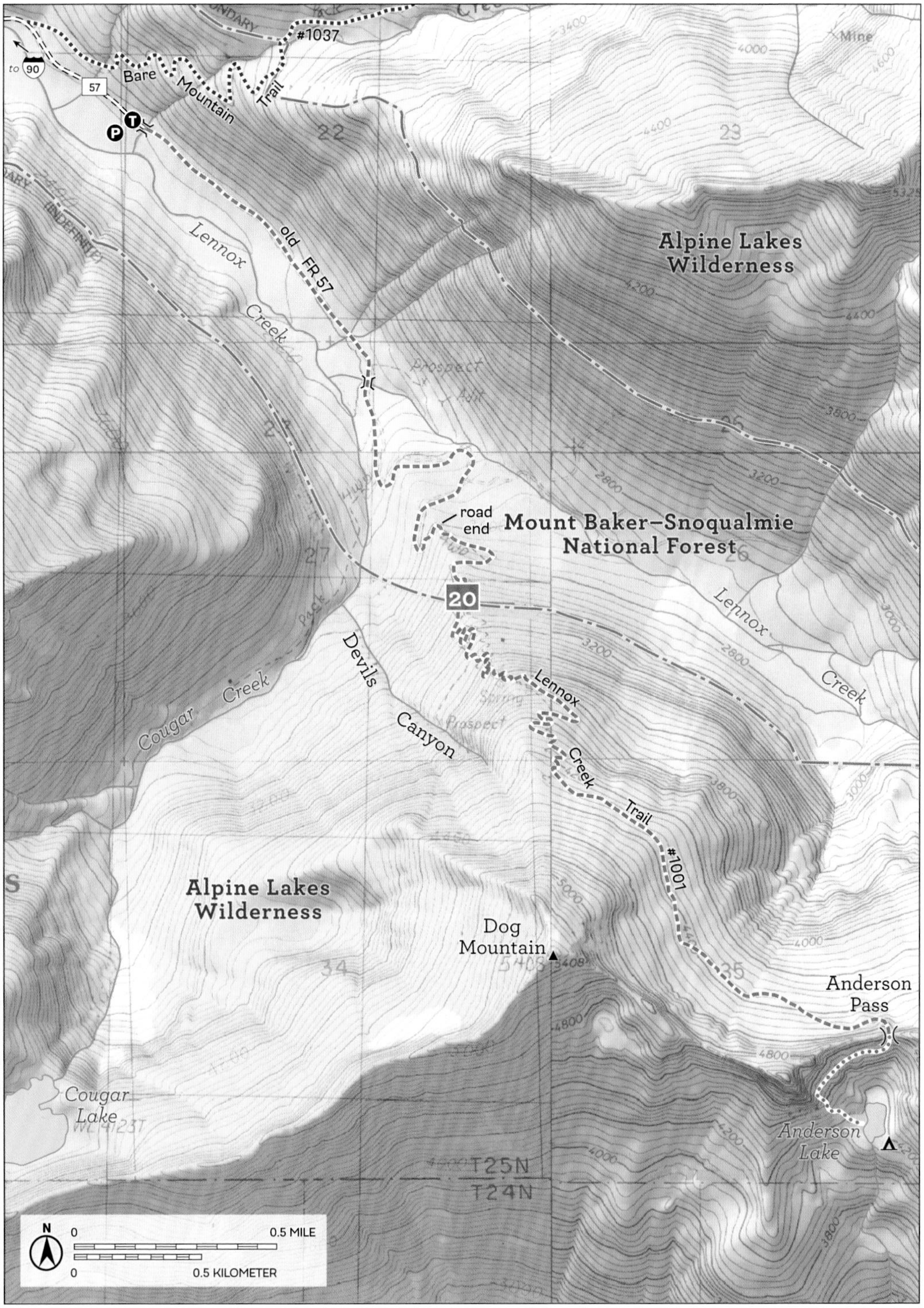

#1037

to 90

57

Bare Mountain Trail

P T

22

23

Mine

Alpine Lakes Wilderness

old FR 57

Lennox

Creek

Prospect

road end

Mount Baker–Snoqualmie National Forest

20

26

Lennox

Creek

27

Pack

Devils

Canyon

Spring

Prospect

Lennox

Creek

Trail

#1001

Cougar Creek

Alpine Lakes Wilderness

34

Dog Mountain 5408

35

Anderson Pass

Cougar Lake 4123

Anderson Lake

T25N
T24N

N

0   0.5 MILE

0   0.5 KILOMETER

Anderson Lake rests peacefully in a small bowl beneath Dog Mountain at the bottom of a talus field.

plan to overnight or not, bring your sense of adventure and a little extra stamina to tour this overlooked slice of the North Fork Snoqualmie Valley.

GOING FARTHER

Officially, Anderson Pass marks the end of the "maintained" portion of the Lennox Creek Trail #1001. Peak baggers, however, can follow a faint boot path from Anderson Pass up toward the summit of Dog Mountain, scrambling over exposed rock to reach panoramic views of the North Fork Snoqualmie landscape. Alternatively, explorers and bushwhackers can continue following the now-abandoned portion of the Lennox Creek Trail down toward the Taylor River. At one time, the trail connected with the Taylor River Trail, though those days are long past.

HISTORY

Like so much of the Snoqualmie Basin, Lennox Creek has a long history of mining and logging. The creek was officially named by The Mountaineers back in 1916, as the creek originates on the south slopes of Lennox Mountain. What is today FR 57 was once known as the Lennox Creek Road, which likely started as a mining road providing access to claims. One of those was the Devil's Canyon Mine in Devils Canyon, which the Lennox Creek Trail comes close to entering as it tightly switchbacks up Dog Mountain. The claim was first owned by V. M. Osterberg from 1912 to 1926 and later by Consolidated Molybdenum from 1948 to 1950. In the search for silver, tungsten, and molybdenum, a 160-foot adit was dug and a large cabin was built. Both the adit and now-crumbling cabin can still be found with a little exploration.

CENTRAL SNOQUALMIE VALLEY

The rocky points of Mount Roosevelt rise above Snow Lake (Hike 29).

21 PUTRID PETE'S PEAK

DISTANCE: 4.8 miles
ELEVATION GAIN: 3000 feet
HIGH POINT: 5220 feet
DIFFICULTY: Hard
HIKING TIME: 4 to 6 hours
BEST SEASON: Late spring to late fall
TRAIL TRAFFIC: Moderate foot traffic

PERMIT: Northwest Forest Pass
MAPS: USGS Bandera; Green Trails Bandera
No. 206
TRAILHEAD GPS: 47.42463°N, 121.5833°W
NOTE: Parking can be a challenge during summer.
Arrive early or be prepared to park up to 0.25
mile away on Forest Road 9031.

GETTING THERE: From I-90 between North Bend and Snoqualmie Pass, take Exit 45. Eastbound turn left to go under the freeway and join the westbound exit, following FR 9030 as it veers left and continues 0.9 mile to a fork. Veer left onto FR 9031 and follow it for 2.9 miles until the road terminates at the Ira Spring Trailhead. Privy available.

Why stick to only the most popular mountaintops and lakesides? Putrid Pete's Peak is a fun alternative to nearby Mason Lake and Bandera Mountain. Short and steep, this hike is a workout. The trail builders were much more interested in expedience than preserving your knees. Bring along some poles, especially for the descent, which can be tricky: many rocks are loose, making it easy to slip and lose your footing on the uneven ground or send boulders careening down the slopes. You're unlikely to find a great deal of company on this hike, but it affords many of the same views as other, more popular trails nearby.

From the trailhead, begin along the Ira Spring (Mason Lake) Trail #1038, which follows an abandoned roadbed for 0.2 mile. Here, where the Ira Spring Trail heads right to its first switchback up Mount Defiance, continue straight into the trees following a faint boot path. This unmarked trail is unofficial, though well maintained and easily followed once you're on it. Avoid paths that branch to the left and lead down the mountain. Some of these trails lead up to Dirty Harry's Peak, and others snake down to I-90.

Continue onward, upward, and always to the right, reaching an unsigned junction at 1.0 mile. The trail straight ahead leads to Dirty Harry's Balcony; instead, turn right, directly uphill, and begin climbing steeply, eventually breaking free of the trees into rocky meadows of bear grass and wildflowers in season. As

you leave the trees, the path becomes patchy and thin; keep heading up, and you'll soon find yourself on a minor ridge leading directly to your destination.

Clamber up the piles of rocks at the top of the peak and peer carefully over the edge; there's quite a drop into the bowl that cups Spider Lake below. Look west toward West Defiance (aka Web Mountain), Mount Washington, and Dirty Harry's Balcony just above I-90 as it disappears into the lowlands. To the north, the peaks of the Alpine Lakes Wilderness rise out of a vast blanket of green—and on good days, you can also pick out Mounts Adams and Baker and Glacier Peak. The view to the east is dominated by Mount Defiance, with Bandera Mountain close behind. And directly across the valley sits the unmistakable horn of McClellan Butte and its neighbors to the east,

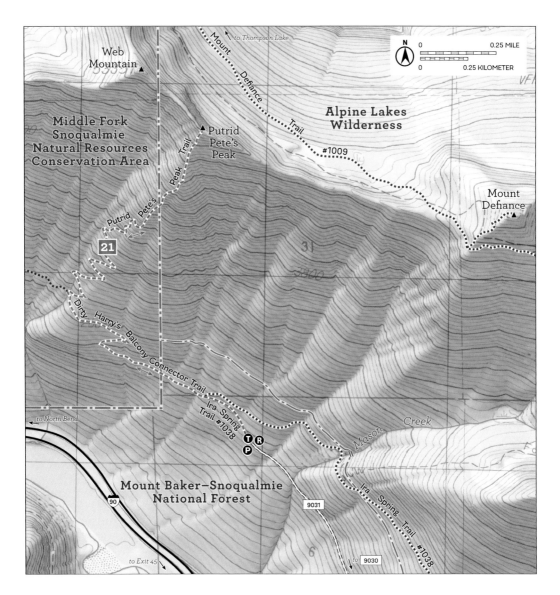

Mount Kent followed by Mount Gardner. Find a place out of the wind to soak up the views and add your name to the summit registry.

GOING FARTHER

A couple of well-worn unofficial paths lead down the mountainside toward I-90 to a short spur off Exit 42, a winter trailhead for the Ira Spring (Mason Lake) Trail when the main trailhead is snowed in. You can also continue on the trail at the 1.0-mile junction to head out to Dirty Harry's Peak, Dirty Harry's Balcony, and Web Mountain.

HISTORY

This little bump was named in honor of Pete Schoening, a Seattle-area mountaineer and outdoorsman who is most famous for his belay on

Looking north from the summit of Putrid Pete's Peak to Spider Lake and Pratt River Valley

K2 on August 10, 1953. On that day, Schoening managed to arrest the fall of all five members of his roped climbing party with nothing more than an ice axe, stopping them from plunging down the slopes of K2. In the mountaineering community, the legendary event is known simply as "The Belay." Schoening passed away in 2004, though it seems that Putrid Pete's Peak was christened sometime before his death by his friends Tom Hornbein and Bill Sumner. References to Putrid Pete begin around 2001,

which is probably when the registry was placed at the summit. Many thanks to the Schoening family for helping us piece this story together.

There is often some confusion regarding the names of the high points along this ridge. To clarify, Banana Ridge runs northwest from the top of Mount Defiance to another peak known as both West Defiance and Web Mountain. Putrid Pete's Peak, or P3, lies between the two ends of the ridge, and a few sources dubbed it Middle Defiance before 2001.

22 MASON LAKE AND MOUNT DEFIANCE

DISTANCE: 6.8 miles to Mason Lake; 10.4 miles to summit of Mount Defiance
ELEVATION GAIN: 2100 feet to Mason Lake; 3400 feet to Mount Defiance
HIGH POINT: 4300 feet Mason Lake; 5584 feet Mount Defiance
DIFFICULTY: Moderate to Mason Lake; hard to Mount Defiance
HIKING TIME: 6 to 7 hours for Mount Defiance
BEST SEASON: Late spring to early fall

TRAIL TRAFFIC: Heavy foot traffic to Mason Lake; moderate to Mount Defiance
PERMIT: Northwest Forest Pass
MAPS: USGS Bandera; Green Trails Bandera No. 206
TRAILHEAD GPS: 47.42463°N, 121.5833°W
NOTE: Parking can be a challenge during summer. Arrive early or be prepared to park up to 0.25 mile away on Forest Road 9031.

GETTING THERE: From I-90 between North Bend and Snoqualmie Pass, take Exit 45. Eastbound turn left to go under the freeway and join the westbound exit, following FR 9030 as it veers left and continues 0.9 mile to a fork. Veer left onto FR 9031 and follow it for 2.9 miles until the road terminates at the Ira Spring Trailhead. Privy available.

Accessible and not too challenging, Mason Lake is one of the more popular destinations in this region and a gateway to a number of other nearby destinations. Big and beautiful Mason Lake provides a window into the wilderness, inspiring hikers and would-be backpackers to delve deeper. Those who are thirsty for a vista can continue up to the summit of Mount Defiance, where you are richly rewarded with sprawling views of the Alpine Lakes Wilderness as well as a bird's-eye view of the Snoqualmie Valley below.

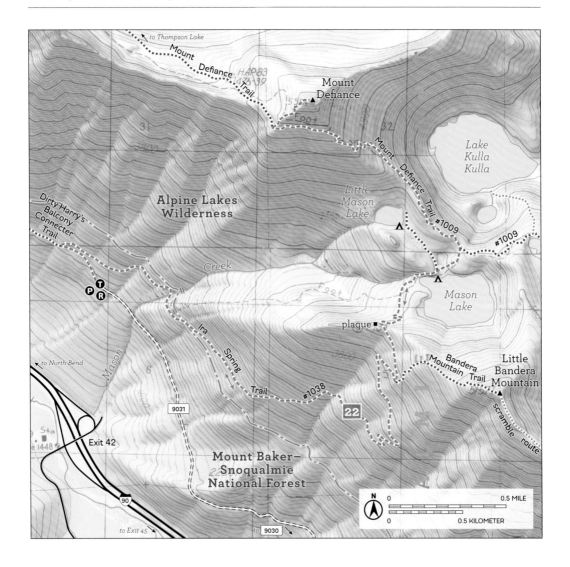

The Ira Spring Memorial Trail cuts through talus and fields of beargrass.

From the trailhead, the Ira Spring (Mason Lake) Trail #1038 begins on the bones of a repurposed fire road, with a grade suitable for conveying heavy machinery up a mountainside. You'll cross a few streams including Mason Creek, entering the Alpine Lakes Wilderness before 1.2 miles.

At 1.5 miles the trail leaves the young forest behind for a much steeper path up the mountain. The dusty trail moves beyond the evergreens for ever-larger glimpses of the valley below, and once the trail sheds the last of the trees, enormous views are your compensation for being fully exposed to the elements.

At 2.9 miles, reach the junction with the Bandera Mountain Trail (Hike 23) to the right. Stay left to continue upward to the west through subalpine meadows and talus fields, passing the Ira Spring Memorial plaque just before the short descent to Mason Lake, reached at 3.4

miles. The lakeshore offers an abundance of campsites and the possibility of a refreshing dip. This big lake has a lot of room, so keep walking to find a quiet spot to claim. This is a gorgeous place for picnicking or splashing in the water on a sunny summer afternoon.

Picturesque Mason Lake is a tempting place to stay, though there is plenty more to see. It's another 1.8 miles up to the summit of Mount Defiance, reached by following the trail around Mason Lake to the junction with the Mount Defiance Trail #1009. Veer left onto rougher trail, climbing through the trees over rocks and roots before eventually reaching the meadows of Mount Defiance, famously brimming with lush fields of wildflowers in the late spring and early summer. Watch for a small rock cairn at 5.0 miles marking the spur trail to the right to the summit. From here it's a short 0.2-mile climb to the top. On the best of days, you can see five volcanic peaks: Adams, Baker, Glacier, Rainier, and St. Helens. Lakes are liberally sprinkled throughout the bowl between Bandera and Defiance—Lake Kulla Kulla is the largest, with Blazer Lake and Rainbow Lake just to the east. Little Mason Lake is nestled below familiar Mason Lake. To the northeast you can make out a portion of Pratt Lake (Hike 26) resting at the base of Pratt Mountain.

GOING FARTHER

To beat the crowds at Mason Lake, consider a side trip up to Little Mason Lake, a short jaunt up from the main trail. There are also other nearby lakes found by following the Mount Defiance Trail east for 1.5 miles past Rainbow Lake to the Island Lake spur (Hike 24). Alternatively, you can reach Thompson Lake (Hike 1) from the top of Mount Defiance by following the Mount Defiance Trail as it continues northwest down the other side of the mountain, dropping 1400 feet over 2.8 miles.

HISTORY

Since it was first blazed in 1958, the trail known today as the Ira Spring (Mason Lake) Trail has had a reputation for being steep and dirty. Over the years, thousands of boots badly eroded the trail, and hikers were forced to negotiate long uphill stretches over rocks and boulders. At the urging of wilderness advocate Ira Spring, a new route was proposed to address the trail damage, the steep grade, and the rocky obstacle course. In 2003 and 2004, volunteers in coordination with the Forest Service made the new trail a reality. With Ira Spring's passing in 2003, the trail was dedicated the Ira Spring Memorial Trail.

23 BANDERA MOUNTAIN

DISTANCE: 6.8 miles
ELEVATION GAIN: 2900 feet
HIGH POINT: 5157 feet
DIFFICULTY: Moderate
HIKING TIME: 4 to 5 hours
BEST SEASON: Early spring to early fall
TRAIL TRAFFIC: Heavy foot traffic

PERMIT: Northwest Forest Pass
MAPS: USGS Bandera; Green Trails Bandera No. 206
TRAILHEAD GPS: 47.42463°N, 121.5833°W
NOTE: Parking can be a challenge during summer. Arrive early or be prepared to park up to 0.25 mile away on Forest Road 9031.

GETTING THERE: From I-90 between North Bend and Snoqualmie Pass, take Exit 45. Eastbound turn left to go under the freeway and join the westbound exit, following FR 9030 as it veers left and continues 0.9 mile to a fork. Veer left onto FR 9031 and follow it for 2.9 miles until the road terminates at the Ira Spring Trailhead. Privy available.

As prominences and high points go, Bandera Mountain is among the best, offering sprawling 360-degree views of the Alpine Lakes Wilderness and Snoqualmie Valley. Less popular than nearby summits that offer a little more space at the top, Bandera is a welcome challenge for those looking for new peaks to bag.

From the trailhead, follow the Ira Spring (Mason Lake) Trail #1038, which starts casually, following a repurposed logging road. Work your way through young forest, crossing a few streams before entering the Alpine Lakes Wilderness at 1.2 miles.

At 1.5 miles, leave the gentle logging road and begin the hike in earnest; the grade sharpens and begins a series of tight switchbacks. Whatever time of year, this section of the trail offers a front-row seat to an ever-expanding mountainous panorama, courtesy of the fires that have kept much of the mountainside free of trees.

At 2.9 miles reach a junction with the Bandera Mountain Trail #1038.1. Keep right here, continuing to traverse along the mountain's shoulders. Once you reach the ridgeline, peek over the edge at Mason Lake (Hike 22) tucked in a bowl beneath Mount Defiance. Follow the rocky path to the top of Little Bandera Mountain at 3.4 miles to find a sprawling vista. That's Island Lake below (Hike 24), and Mount Rainier presides over a sprawling landscape of lesser peaks. McClellan Butte and Mount Gardner are just across the snaking ribbon of I-90. You can make out the rocky outcroppings of Dirty Harry's Balcony just above I-90 to the

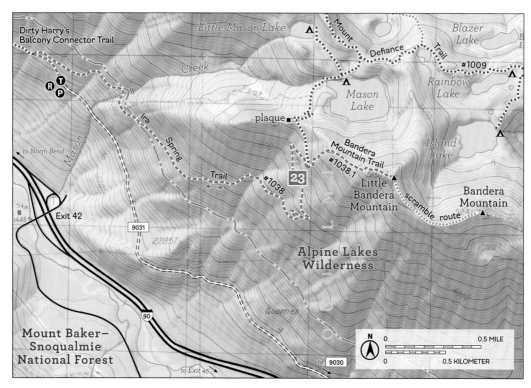

Looking west from the summit of Little Bandera toward with the sharp point of McClellan Butte above the freeway as it snakes toward North Bend

west. Find a rock and take in your hard-earned panorama.

GOING FARTHER

While Little Bandera is the usual stopping point, it's not the true summit. Reach the latter by scrambling east along the ridgeline as it drops slightly before working its way to the next prominence, about 100 feet higher than the first. From the true summit, there are better views of Granite Mountain (Hike 27) and Snoqualmie Pass.

After a long climb up to Bandera's upper reaches, a quick dip in Mason Lake (Hike 22), only 0.5 mile past the Ira Spring–Bandera junction, might be welcome.

HISTORY

Bandera has long been a name entwined with the history of Snoqualmie Pass. Though the mountain was officially recognized by the US Board on Geographic Names as Bandera Mountain only in 1920, a nearby train station along the Chicago, Milwaukee, St. Paul, and Pacific Railroad named "Bandera" had been operating since 1909 and continued service until 1980. In 1948, the Bandera Airstrip was dedicated, marking the first emergency airfield in the Snoqualmie Pass area; it is still actively used today. The original trail up the mountain was first blazed to provide access for crews fighting a large fire around Mason Lake in the summer of 1958 and was later popularized by the late Harvey Manning.

24 ISLAND LAKE

DISTANCE: 10.2 miles
ELEVATION GAIN: 2500 feet
HIGH POINT: 4400 feet
DIFFICULTY: Moderate
HIKING TIME: 5 to 8 hours
BEST SEASON: Late spring to early fall
TRAIL TRAFFIC: Heavy foot traffic to Mason Lake;
light foot traffic to Island Lake

PERMIT: Northwest Forest Pass
MAPS: USGS Bandera; Green Trails Bandera
No. 206
TRAILHEAD GPS: 47.42463°N, 121.5833°W
NOTE: Parking can be a challenge during summer.
Arrive early or be prepared to park up to 0.25
mile away on Forest Road 9031.

GETTING THERE: From I-90 between North Bend and Snoqualmie Pass, take Exit 45. Eastbound turn left
to go under the freeway and join the westbound exit. following FR 9030 as it veers left and continues
0.9 mile to a fork. Veer left onto FR 9031 and follow it for 2.9 miles until the road terminates at the Ira
Spring Trailhead. Privy available.

---

*Quiet and only a little deeper in the wilderness than Mason Lake, Island Lake offers a more
enchanting setting: little islands dot tranquil waters overshadowed by talus fields strewn down
the shoulders of Bandera Mountain (Hike 23). The hike to Island Lake is great if you're ready
to move beyond more popular and well-trodden trails. While the first two-thirds of the route
are likely to be crowded, as you push past the Bandera Mountain Trail junction and Mason*

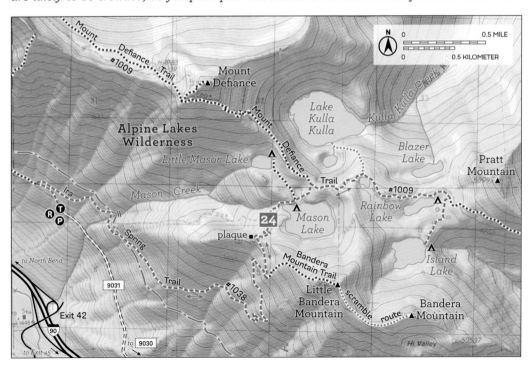

Lake, you'll soon find yourself almost entirely alone. Island Lake and Rainbow Lake also work as quick backpacking destinations, since you can be setting up camp on the quiet shores of a lovely alpine lake in fairly short order.

From the Ira Spring Trailhead, follow the Ira Spring (Mason Lake) Trail #1038 on an abandoned road as it wanders through a young forest still recovering from fires that ravaged the mountain as recently as 1958. The trail slowly works its way up the slopes, crossing Mason Creek and its waterfall before entering the Alpine Lakes Wilderness at 1.2 miles.

At 1.5 miles, the logging road is replaced by serious trail, exchanging the road's gentle grade for a steep, rocky path. After a short climb, the dusty trail moves beyond the conifers for ever-larger glimpses of the valley below. Once the trail sheds the last of the trees, enjoy the enormous views that come with traversing a grassy mountainside.

At 2.9 miles, reach the junction with the Bandera Mountain Trail to the right. Head left through subalpine meadows and talus fields, reaching the Ira Spring Memorial plaque just before the short descent to Mason Lake, at 3.4 miles. The lakeshore offers plenty of nooks to take in the sparkling waters, and it's tempting to remain here. But your destination lies beyond.

Push onward, following the trail along the lake and farther from the shore to reach the Mount Defiance Trail #1009 (Hike 22). Keep right and soon find yourself wandering through peaceful tree-lined meadows. Pass Rainbow Lake at 4.6 miles and reach the signed junction to Island Lake at 4.8 miles. From here it's just a 0.3-mile jaunt past a few tarns to sparkling Island Lake, resting quietly below Bandera Mountain. Find a cozy rock and enjoy a slice of tranquility.

GOING FARTHER

The Mount Defiance Trail continues eastward to connect with the Pratt Lake Trail #1007, providing access to Olallie Lake, Talapus Lake, and Pratt Lake (Hikes 25 and 26). These two trails also allow for a through-hike with a shuttle vehicle at the Pratt Lake/Granite Mountain Trailhead (Hikes 26 and 27).

Island Lake tempts swimmers during the summer heat.

HISTORY

Before the 1960s, the only way for hikers to reach Island Lake was to start at the Pratt Lake/Granite Mountain Trailhead and trek out to the Mount Defiance Trail junction. Named for the lake's small rocky island, Island Lake used to see many more visitors than it does today, and distant Mason Lake was a side trip for those heading to the top of Mount Defiance. That changed in 1958 when a large wildfire on the slopes of Bandera Mountain prompted crews to hastily build a fire road to

help fight the blaze. Not too long after, curious hikers explored the area and used it as a back door to Mason Lake and an approach to Bandera Mountain. Harvey Manning popularized the route, and soon the official Mason Lake Trail #1038 was born.

Much loved over the years, the trail was in desperate need of repairs by the turn of the twentieth century. Ira Spring advocated for a new route, which was built between 2003 and 2004 and renamed the Ira Spring Memorial Trail #1038 after his passing.

25 TALAPUS AND OLALLIE LAKES

DISTANCE: 5.8 miles
ELEVATION GAIN: 1200 feet
HIGH POINT: 3800 feet
DIFFICULTY: Easy
HIKING TIME: 3 to 4 hours
BEST SEASON: Late spring to late fall

TRAIL TRAFFIC: Heavy foot traffic
PERMIT: Northwest Forest Pass
MAPS: USGS Bandera; Green Trails Bandera No. 206
TRAILHEAD GPS: 47.4011°N, 121.5185°W

Talapus Lake from the log-clogged lake outlet

GETTING THERE: From I-90 between North Bend and Snoqualmie Pass, take Exit 45. Eastbound turn left to go under the freeway and join the westbound exit, following FR 9030 as it veers left and continues 0.9 mile to a signed junction with FR 9031 to the left. Keep right, following the sign to Talapus Lake. Continue for 2.3 miles to the trailhead parking lot. Privy available.

Talapus Lake and Olallie Lake deliver alpine lakes, waterfalls, and stretches of deep, mossy forest with minimal mileage. This hike is a popular summer choice with families and young backpackers, and a great introduction to the Alpine Lakes Wilderness, so you can expect a little company. Whatever time of year, the trail provides a tempting taste of the wilderness—stands of old growth, crystal-clear alpine lakes, and rugged landscapes make it easy to forget the relatively close trappings of civilization.

From the trailhead, follow Talapus Lake Trail #1039 on an old forest road into second-generation forest. Wander beneath stands of young trees before leaving the wide track for more-rugged trail. Soon after, at 0.3 mile, cross into the Alpine Lakes Wilderness.

As you climb, the trail cuts through marshy areas along an elaborate system of raised boardwalks and bridges. After navigating mild grades and walkways, the route soon reaches the banks of Talapus Creek. From here, the trail follows the creek to Talapus Lake, passing an impressive waterfall just off the trail at 1.3 miles. Look and listen for the cascade at a sharp bend in the trail just before it angles upward.

At 1.6 miles, reach Talapus Lake tucked in a bowl between Bandera Mountain (Hike 23) and Pratt Mountain. Explore the maze of boot paths snaking around the lake to a handful of campsites and inviting stopping points along the water—perfect for a snack or extended stay.

Once you've taken it all in, push onward toward Olallie Lake, following the trail as it meanders peacefully past mature cedars and firs. At the 2.3-mile mark, pass the Talapus Cutoff Trail #1039.1, which offers a quick connection with the Pratt Lake Trail #1007 and access to a number of nearby lakes and prominences.

From the junction, push on another 0.6 mile to reach the wooded shores of Olallie Lake, resting beneath the slopes of West Granite Mountain and Pratt Lake Saddle (Hike 26). Find a quiet spot and settle in to enjoy the solace.

GOING FARTHER

The Talapus Cutoff Trail #1039.1 offers access to nearby Pratt Lake (Hike 26) or Island Lake (Hike 24) via the Pratt Lake Trail. Hikers can also put together a longer through-hike by parking a shuttle vehicle at either the Granite Mountain Trailhead (Hike 27) or the Ira Spring Trailhead (Hike 22).

HISTORY

Like so many place names in the area, Talapus and Olallie Lakes bear the legacy of the early interaction of pioneers and American Indians. *Talapus* translates to "coyote" in Chinook Jargon, while *Olallie* roughly means "berry." Largely born through the necessity of trade, Chinook Jargon is an amalgamation of French, English, and Salishan languages native to the Pacific Northwest.

26 PRATT LAKE VIA PRATT LAKE SADDLE

DISTANCE: 11.8 miles
ELEVATION GAIN: 2300 feet in; 750 feet out
HIGH POINT: 4100 feet
DIFFICULTY: Moderate
HIKING TIME: 5 to 7 hours
BEST SEASON: Spring to late fall
TRAIL TRAFFIC: Moderate to light foot traffic

PERMIT: Northwest Forest Pass
MAPS: USGS Bandera; Green Trails Bandera No. 206
TRAILHEAD GPS: 47.39776°N, 121.4865°W
NOTE: Parking can be a challenge much of the year; arrive early to get a spot closer to the trailhead.

GETTING THERE: From I-90 between North Bend and Snoqualmie Pass, take Exit 47. If eastbound, turn left and cross over the freeway to a signed T intersection; if westbound, turn right to this T intersection. At the T, turn left and continue a short distance to the trailhead parking lot. Privy available.

The Pratt Lake Trail is one of the gateways into the Alpine Lakes Wilderness, providing access to many lakes and peaks. A trek out to Pratt Lake leads through dense forest, past dramatic views of Mount Rainier, and over Pratt Lake Saddle to the shores of a wooded alpine lake.

From the trailhead, the Pratt Lake Trail #1007 is well worn and wide, crossing small creeks and rivulets through pleasant stands of maturing firs and pines. Cross into the Alpine Lakes Wilderness at 0.8 mile, and shortly after, at 1.0 mile, reach the junction with the Granite Mountain Trail #1016 on the right. Stay left to continue on the Pratt Lake Trail for the first bit of real elevation gain, skirting the slopes of Granite Mountain (Hike 27) and occasionally catching glimpses of mountaintops through windows in the trees carved by streams and talus fields.

At 2.9 miles, the trail intersects the Talapus Lake Cutoff Trail #1039.1 to the left, which offers access to the shores of both Talapus and Olallie

False Solomon's seal, trillium, and bleeding heart line the trail above Pratt Lake.

Lakes (Hike 25). Continue straight ahead on the Pratt Lake Trail as it traverses the bowl above Olallie Lake, offering occasional glimpses of the water below. As you make your way around the end of the lake, the trees open up in a talus field to reveal a stunning view of Mount Rainier rising above the water, framed by Pratt Mountain on the right and Bandera Mountain (Hike 23) on the left. This is the best view on the hike, so take a few minutes to enjoy it.

Press on up to Pratt Lake Saddle at 4.0 miles, a low point on a shoulder of Pratt Mountain. Soon reach the junction with the Mount Defiance Trail #1009 (Hike 22) to the left; stay to the right to switchback somewhat steeply down through talus fields and sections of marsh and swamp into the Pratt Lake Basin. The trail breaks out of the trees and traverses the rocky slopes above the lake. Continue to the far end of the lake for the best campsites and lake views at 5.9 miles. Find a quiet spot to settle in and enjoy this pristine setting.

GOING FARTHER

The Pratt Lake Trail continues past the end of Pratt Lake for another 0.5 mile out to Lower Tuscohatchie Lake. From there, hikers can take the Kaleetan Lake Trail #1010 left up to its namesake lake or the Melakwa Lake Trail #1011 to the right to head up to Melakwa Lake (Hike 28).

Adventurous backpackers and throughhikers can follow the Old Pratt Lake Trail into the Pratt Valley, though this unmaintained section between Pratt Lake and the end of the Pratt River Trail #1035 (Hike 5) requires some bushwhacking and routefinding. Once you reach the Pratt River Trail, you can follow it all the way out to the Middle Fork Snoqualmie River.

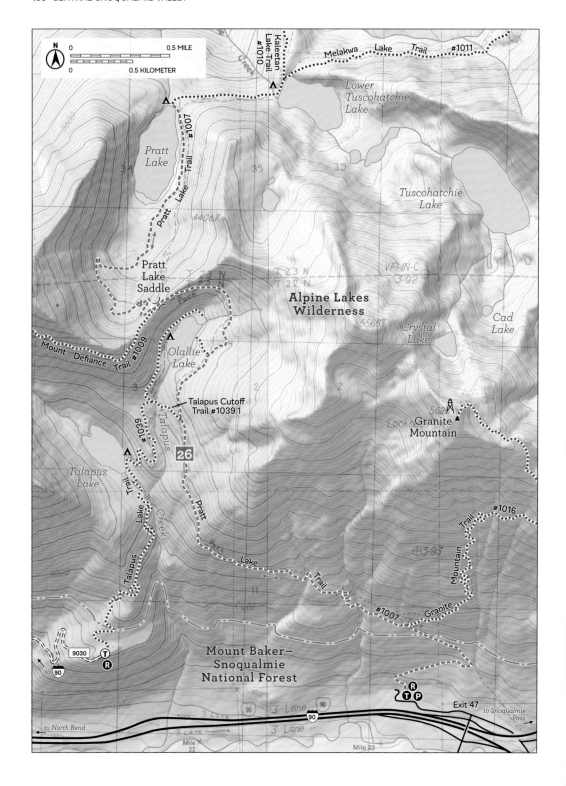

HISTORY

In 1897, a trail was blazed up the Pratt River Valley, past Pratt Lake and on to Melakwa Lake, to access mining claims on Chair Peak. Back then, the Pratt River was known as Tuscohatchie Creek, and Pratt Lake was labeled "Ollie Lake" on USGS maps. Sometime before 1916, The Mountaineers named the lake in honor of one of their own, John W. Pratt, and got the maps changed by 1917. Older maps show a "Twilight Camp" near Pratt Lake along the Pratt Lake Trail, most likely a long-gone mining camp. By the 1950s, the Pratt River Valley approach was largely abandoned, and hikers reached the lake by pushing past Olallie Lake and climbing over Pratt Lake Saddle.

27 GRANITE MOUNTAIN

DISTANCE: 8.6 miles
ELEVATION GAIN: 3700 feet
HIGH POINT: 5629 feet
DIFFICULTY: Hard; see note about avalanche hazard in trail description
HIKING TIME: 5 to 7 hours
BEST SEASON: Late spring to early fall
TRAIL TRAFFIC: Heavy foot traffic
PERMIT: Northwest Forest Pass

MAPS: USGS Snoqualmie Pass; Green Trails Snoqualmie Pass No. 207
TRAILHEAD GPS: 47.39776°N, 121.4865°W
NOTES: Parking can be a challenge much of the year at this popular trailhead; arrive early to get a spot closer to the trailhead. Spring avalanches have taken lives on Granite Mountain; use extra caution early in the season.

The sprawling view from the Granite Mountain Lookout includes Mount Rainier and a sea of other mountaintops.

GETTING THERE: From I-90 between North Bend and Snoqualmie Pass, take Exit 47. If eastbound, turn left and cross over the freeway to a signed T intersection; if westbound, turn right to this T intersection. At the T, turn left and continue a short distance to the trailhead parking lot. Privy available.

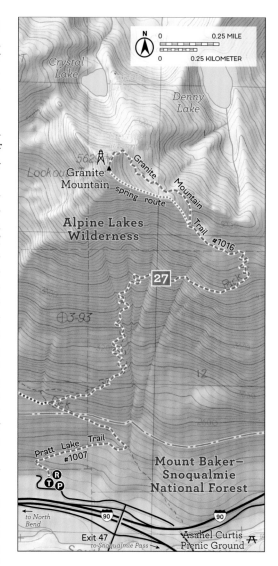

As the years pass and the lookout towers of a bygone era slowly disappear, the ones that remain draw hikers up steep mountainsides. They come not only to share the lookout's commanding views but also to connect to a time before satellites and aerial photography, when it was vitally important to maintain a small battalion of watchful eyes perched upon mountaintops, scanning the horizon for wildfire smoke. At 5629 feet, Granite Mountain is one of the most easily accessible and popular summits in the Snoqualmie Pass region. Still, this hike can be challenging. In summer, the sun beats down on exposed rocks and meadows, making the trail dusty without much available water once the snow melts. During the spring, avalanches have taken the lives of hikers on Granite, so use extra caution early in the season. The uphill trek to Granite's fire lookout tower makes for a long day, but the views from the top are more than ample reward.

From the trailhead, follow the Pratt Lake Trail #1007 as it rolls through lush forests of cedar and Douglas fir, frequently crossing creeks and streamlets along the way. Cross into the Alpine Lakes Wilderness at 0.8 mile and soon after, at 1.0 miles, reach the junction with the Granite Mountain Trail #1016. Turn right toward Granite Mountain.

Immediately the tenor of the trail shifts from an uphill amble to a thigh-burning workout. Navigate the rocky trail as it switchbacks through the increasingly dry terrain, and catch the occasional glimpse of your eventual goal high overhead. As you gain elevation, trees thin and become more diminutive while ferns yield to bear grass and mountain blueberry. Eventually you leave the trees entirely behind; the views are laid bare, breezes keep the bugs at bay during the summer, and the trail grade relents slightly as the fire lookout comes into view.

Climb, climb, and climb some more, working your way up to the base of the summit bluff. When snow is on the ground, follow the bootprints up the spine of the talus-covered ridge straight to the summit, avoiding most avalanche danger. As the snow recedes, the rocky ridge is less appealing than the formal trail that snakes beneath the ridge before zigzagging up the bluff the lookout resides upon. Whichever path you take, arrive at the boulder-strewn lookout at 4.3 miles from the trailhead.

The views that began hundreds of feet below culminate as you attain the lookout, snowy mountaintops spreading out with a mesmerizing immensity. Mount Rainier dominates the skyline, in every way demanding attention and dwarfing Mount Catherine and Humpback Mountain just across I-90 far below. If you can tear your eyes off Rainier, the beginnings of Keechelus Lake can be seen to the east, and Bandera Mountain (Hike 23) quietly neighbors to the west. Looking north, your eye is drawn to distinctive Kaleetan Peak, as well as Chair Peak and Mount Stuart far beyond, and just below, Crystal Lake and Tuscohatchie Lake gleam invitingly in the sunlight.

HISTORY

First established in 1920, Granite Mountain's fire lookout began as a flimsy cabin that was rebuilt and elevated in 1924. When the snow melts, the cement foundations of the 1924 cabin can still be seen near the current operational lookout tower, which was built in 1955 and is staffed by the Forest Service during the summer.

28 DENNY CREEK AND MELAKWA LAKE

DISTANCE: 8.5 miles
ELEVATION GAIN: 2300 feet
HIGH POINT: 4600 feet
DIFFICULTY: Moderate
HIKING TIME: 5 to 8 hours
BEST SEASON: Late spring to late fall
TRAIL TRAFFIC: Heavy foot traffic

PERMIT: Northwest Forest Pass
MAPS: USGS Snoqualmie Pass; Green Trails Snoqualmie Pass No. 207
TRAILHEAD GPS: 47.41525°N, 121.4433°W
NOTES: Parking is challenging during high season. The hike up to Melakwa Lake requires crossing Denny Creek; use caution during high water.

GETTING THERE: From I-90 between North Bend and Snoqualmie Pass, take Exit 47. If eastbound, turn left to cross over the freeway to a signed T intersection; if westbound, turn right to this T intersection. At the T, turn right, heading under the freeway for 0.25 mile to Forest Road 58. Turn left on FR 58 and follow it for 2.5 miles to Denny Creek Campground. Just past the entrance to the campground, turn left onto FR 5830 for 0.25 mile to the road-end trailhead and parking. Privy available.

Trek up to a secluded alpine lake, flanked by sentinels of craggy granite on this hike through talus, forest, and— if your timing is right—wildflower meadows. The trail also leads to the Denny Creek Waterslide, an area along the creek where the water flows over "slippery slabs" of granite to create a popular place for splashing and playing in the summer. The steep climb to charming Melakwa Lake doesn't dissuade thousands of hikers from visiting the lake every year. Though extra company does not diminish the beauty of the hike, plan an early start or a weekday venture to avoid the thickest crowds. On the plus side, all those boot steps keep the trail hardpacked and in decent shape, as do the volunteers who work hard to maintain this well-loved trail.

From the trailhead, follow the wide, well-trodden Denny Creek Trail #1014 through overarching trees into deep old-growth forest. Cross Denny Creek over a sturdy bridge and work toward the

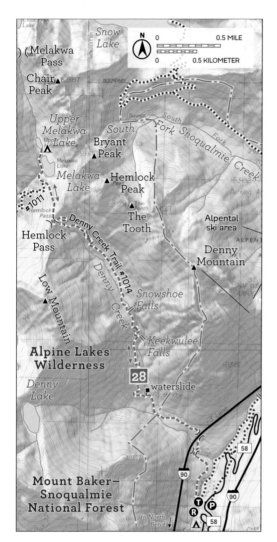

during the summer are treacherous to cross when icy water is blasting down the creek.

Across the creek, the trail continues through sheltering forest before leaving the trees for expansive meadows. At 1.7 miles, find lovely views of Keekwulee Falls dropping more than 140 feet into the basin below. Enjoy the waterfall and surrounding slopes splashed with swaths of verdant green before continuing onward, as the trail is about to become much steeper.

From the falls, the trail steeply switchbacks through talus and occasional patches of trees. As you climb, you may hear or catch a glimpse of Snowshoe Falls, the highest Denny Creek has to offer. These 150-foot falls are difficult to see from the trail itself and may require some off-trail effort to fully appreciate. The trail momentarily relents to cross Denny Creek once again on a log bridge before again switchbacking up to Hemlock Pass at 3.8 miles.

From the pass, drop slightly for another 0.4 mile to Melakwa Lake, passing a signed junction with the Melakwa Lake Trail #1011, which leads down to Lower Tuscohatchie Lake and Pratt Lake (Hike 26). Reach Melakwa Lake and cross the logjam of silver snags clogging the outlet to reach a heavily used camping area. The lake lies in a narrow cirque, nestled between the jagged mountaintops of Chair Peak and Bryant Peak on the eastern shore and Kaleetan Peak to the west. A thin band of trees clutches the shoreline, dividing the water from the vast talus fields that cover the slopes.

Just to the north, Upper Melakwa Lake hides behind a few trees and serves as the source of the Pratt River. Wander around the lakes to find a quiet spot to enjoy this quintessential alpine setting.

GOING FARTHER

A hike to Melakwa Lake all but requires a visit to Upper Melakwa Lake, which can be reached by following a boot path circling around the west side of the lake for 0.2 mile. From Upper Melakwa Lake, the adventuresome can scramble up to Melakwa Pass at the head of the

increasing din of I-90 as the trail approaches the elevated freeway. The roar of cars grows as you pass under the causeway at 0.5 mile and veer up into the creek valley, every step leaving the noise a little farther behind.

Before long, reunite with the creek at the wilderness boundary at 0.9 mile, followed soon after by the Denny Creek Waterslide 1.1 miles from the trailhead. There is no bridge here, though crossing during the summer should not pose much challenge. Heed the warning signs cautioning against a crossing during high water. The slabs that are such fun to slide down

Push past the busy day-use area to pretty Upper Melakwa Lake and views of Melakwa Pass.

cirque and from there continue a more technical scramble up to Kaleetan Peak. Another option is to continue to follow the Melakwa Lake Trail down to Lower Tuscohatchie Lake.

HISTORY

Most of the features in this area were named by The Mountaineers, and the names were officially submitted in 1916. They named the lake *Melakwa*, which means "mosquito" in Chinook Jargon, for reasons that become very obvious during the late spring and early summer. They also named one of the falls *Keekwulee*, which means "to fall down" or "low/below," both apt meanings. Denny Creek was named for David T. Denny, brother of Arthur Denny, who had claims along the creek in 1890. As The Mountaineers climbed, they may have been more focused on the hike than the names, since they christened Snowshoe Falls for the snowshoes they had on and Hemlock Pass for the trees growing there. A few years later, in 1924, The Mountaineers gave Bryant Peak its name honoring Sidney Bryant, a member of The Mountaineers who helped spearhead the construction of their Snoqualmie Lodge.

29 SNOW LAKE AND SOURCE LAKE OVERLOOK

DISTANCE: 6.3 miles
ELEVATION GAIN: 1300 feet in; 400 feet out
HIGH POINT: 4400 feet
DIFFICULTY: Moderate
HIKING TIME: 4 to 6 hours
BEST SEASON: Late spring to late fall

TRAIL TRAFFIC: Heavy foot traffic
PERMIT: Northwest Forest Pass
MAPS: USGS Snoqualmie Pass; Green Trails Snoqualmie Pass No. 207
TRAILHEAD GPS: 47.4454°N, 121.4235°W

GETTING THERE: Take I-90 to Snoqualmie Pass. Eastbound take Exit 52 and turn left onto Alpental Road for about 2 miles to a large gravel parking lot. Westbound take Exit 53, turning left under the freeway and soon reaching a T intersection. Turn right onto State Road 906, following the sign pointing toward Alpental. Continue 2.7 miles through the ski area to the parking area. The trailhead is across the road to the right. Privy available.

Snow Lake is one of the largest lakes in the Alpine Lakes Wilderness, as well as one of the most easily accessible. As a result, this enormously popular trail attracts hundreds of hikers every sunny weekend. While there is plenty of lake to accommodate the visitors, the short trip out to Source Lake provides a stretch of trail time that you are unlikely to have to share.

From the trailhead, Snow Lake Trail #1013 begins mildly, cutting a long swath through fields of bracken fern and salmonberry before entering a forest of hemlock and fir. As you slowly gain elevation, navigate your way across talus fields and cascading streams. Enjoy the well-trod path, beaten down by tens of thousands of boots every year that keep it clear of debris and encroaching brush.

At 1.7 miles, the trail meets up with Source Lake Trail #1013.2 signed "Source Lake Overlook Trail," which was the primary route to Snow Lake before washouts prompted building a more direct route over the cliffs. Stay to

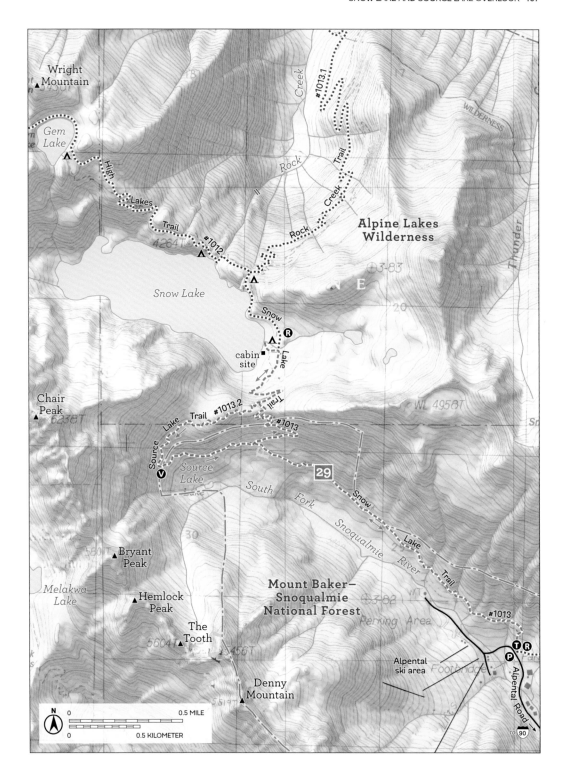

Wright
Mountain

Gem
Lake

High

Lakes

Trail

4264T

#1012

Snow Lake

Snow

cabin
site

Chair
Peak
6238T

Source

Lake

Trail

#1013.2

Source
Lake

#1013

Lake

Trail

Creek

#1013.1

Rock

Creek

Trail

Rock

Alpine Lakes
Wilderness

WL 4958T

29

Snow

Lake

Trail

#1013

Bryant
Peak
5801T

Melakwa
Lake

Hemlock
Peak

The
Tooth
5604T

Denny
Mountain

South

Fork

Snoqualmie

River

Mount Baker–
Snoqualmie
National Forest

Parking Area

Alpental
ski area

Footbridge

Alpental Road

to 90

N

0   0.5 MILE

0   0.5 KILOMETER

The climb up the Snow Creek headwall includes impressive views of Bryant Peak and other summits around Source Lake.

the right on the Snow Lake Trail, following the newer route to the lake.

Switchback steeply up the rocky ridge, crossing into the Alpine Lakes Wilderness and reaching the ridgetop at a saddle at 2.5 miles. At the saddle is another junction with the Source Lake Trail to the left; stay right on the Snow Lake Trail to descend to the shores of Snow Lake.

Stretching out over a mile, Snow Lake is large, its placid waters wrapping around Chair Peak, which obscures the lake's western reaches. The vegetation around the lake is riddled with footpaths, lingering evidence of the multitudes struggling to find their own private slice of solace near the water. At 2.8 miles, pass a short spur out to the water that leads to the foundations of the old Fenton family cabin. Designated campsites are just off the trail as it continues north around the lake.

On the hike back out, reach the junction at the saddle at the 3.3-mile mark. Here, follow the Source Lake Trail to the right to explore the Source Lake Overlook. Largely abandoned since the newer route opened, the trail is rough

and unmaintained, though easy to follow. It leads through small alpine meadows, past tiny lakelets, and under a small waterfall—and it is far less crowded than the main trail. By the time Source Lake is in view at 4.2 miles, the trail improves greatly, mostly thanks to adventurous mountaineers scrambling up to the Tooth and Chair Peak located nearby. Continue past the overlook another 0.4 mile to rejoin the Snow Lake Trail and return to the trailhead.

Snow Lake is not only beautiful, it's very accessible, drawing in thousands of hikers year after year. If solitude is your goal, this is not your trail. At the same time, this is a classic hike and one that every alpine lake lover should experience!

GOING FARTHER

From the cabin site, Gem Lake (Hike 30) is another 1.8 miles down the Snow Lake Trail and High Lakes Trail #1012. While it's a rocky climb, the tranquil setting is well worth the extra mileage. Alternatively, the junction with the Rock Creek Trail #1013.1 is 0.5 mile down the trail. It's a short-but-steep drop down to get a decent view of Rock Creek Falls (Hike 14).

HISTORY

Tucked on the slopes of Denny Mountain, the Alpental ski area is the most recent addition to this part of Snoqualmie Pass, having operated here since 1967. Various landlords held fleeting ownership long before, including the mountain's namesake, Arthur Denny, who staked mining claims in the area while prospecting for iron ore in 1869. Following in Denny's wake, mining claims proliferated throughout the valley, including along parts of Snow Lake. As the years passed, these claims were sold or abandoned, becoming either part of Alpental or what would become the Alpine Lakes Wilderness.

The cabin on the shores of Snow Lake was built in 1930 by Aldrich Fenton and a band of hired Norwegian carpenters. The private two-story cabin was built for the Fenton family to enjoy, as the family also owned several acres around the lake. After twenty years, the cabin roof collapsed under heavy snows in the winter of 1950, and times were changing. Tired of break-ins and vandalism, the family decided not to rebuild and eventually sold the land. The cabin slowly deteriorated over the years, with only the fireplace and a few sections of wall remaining today.

30 GEM AND WILDCAT LAKES

DISTANCE: 13.8 miles
ELEVATION GAIN: 2500 feet in; 1300 feet out
HIGH POINT: 4900 feet
DIFFICULTY: Hard
HIKING TIME: Overnight
BEST SEASON: Early summer to fall

TRAIL TRAFFIC: Heavy foot traffic to Snow Lake; moderate to light foot traffic on High Lakes Trail
PERMIT: Northwest Forest Pass
MAPS: USGS Snoqualmie Pass; Green Trails Snoqualmie Pass No. 207
TRAILHEAD GPS: 47.4454°N, 121.4235°W

GETTING THERE: Take I-90 to Snoqualmie Pass. Eastbound take Exit 52 and turn left onto Alpental Road for about 2 miles to a large gravel parking lot. Westbound take Exit 53, turning left under the freeway and soon reaching a T intersection. Turn right onto State Route 906, following the sign pointing toward Alpental. Continue 2.7 miles through the ski area to the parking area. The trailhead is across the road to the right. Privy available.

Spend a night on the shores of a lovely alpine lake, not too far from civilization but far enough to feel the solace of the wilderness. With three different lakes to choose from, each a little deeper into the wild, you have a lot of ways to enjoy this backpacking adventure.

From the trailhead, follow the Snow Lake Trail #1013 as it cuts through the underbrush and enters the forest. Slowly climb past firs, hemlocks, and cedars, eventually reaching fields of talus. The path is wide, well worn, and easy to navigate, thanks to the thousands of hikers who pound this trail bed every season. Skip across a few streams and, at 1.7 miles, pass the junction with the Source Lake Trail #1013.2, signed "Source Lake Overlook Trail," which served as the primary route to Snow Lake before washouts prompted the building of a more direct route over the cliffs. Keep right on the Snow Lake Trail.

Switchback steeply up the ridge, crossing into the Alpine Lakes Wilderness at 2.4 miles shortly before you crest the top of the ridge and reach the other end of the Source Lake Trail. Pause at the clearing at the top to catch your breath before descending to Snow Lake. It's a short 0.4-mile drop to the water, with lovely views of the lake sprawling out before you.

From the lakeshore, the first junction you reach leads to the water and the crumbling foundations of a cabin built in 1930 (see History for Hike 29). Explore the ruins and take in Snow Lake before pressing farther down the trail, circling the lake to reach a trail junction at 3.3 miles. Here, the Rock Creek Trail #1013.1 (Hike 14) to the right leads down to the Middle Fork Snoqualmie Valley, and the High Lakes

Trail #1012 begins to the left. Keep left, following the arrow toward Gem Lake, and begin your ascent.

And a climb it is; soon leave Snow Lake behind for narrow, rocky trail that goes up, up, up. Push through talus fields and pass moss-covered trees to eventually reach Gem Lake at 4.6 miles. Once you see the water, note the dozens of boot paths spiderwebbing up into the slopes around the lake and down to the shore. Some lead to campsites, others to quiet perches with views of Gem or Snow or both. Find a spot to rest, and when you're ready, push onward, following the widest trail around the north side of the lake and passing the boot path that climbs the flanks of Wright Mountain to its summit (the route is not

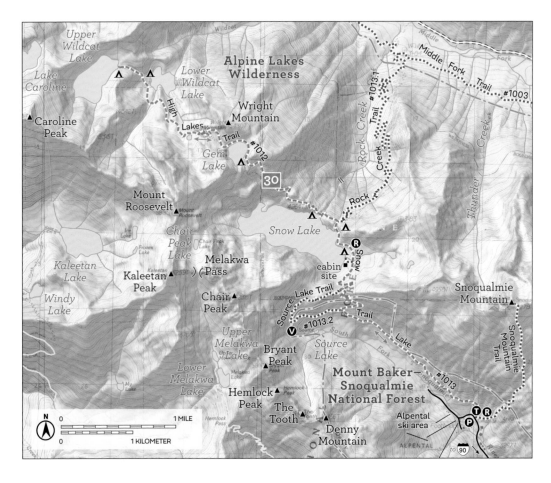

Gem Lake and Wright Mountain in the heart of summer

considered technical and the views from the top are excellent).

Beyond Gem Lake the trail climbs up a small ridge to a saddle before steeply dropping into Wildcat Basin, switchbacking first through talus and then forest all the way down to a creek. Work your way up the basin, gaining elevation and passing a number of ponds to a campsite and trail junction at 6.5 miles. The short path to the left leads down to Lower Wildcat Lake and another campsite. To the right the trail continues another 0.4 mile to Upper Wildcat Lake.

While the poorly maintained trail to it requires a bit more climbing, the upper lake is the more appealing of the two and worth the effort. Cross the logjam at the outlet to find campsites. Brushy boot paths lead around the lake, drawing you closer to its enchanting island. Above the lake, Caroline Peak rises

dramatically to the southwest. This truly is an alpine paradise.

GOING FARTHER

If a climb to the top of Wright Mountain near Gem Lake doesn't appeal, a side trip down to Rock Creek Falls (Hike 14) from Snow Lake is an easy addition. If time allows, add a swing out to Source Lake Overlook (Hike 29) to your journey as well.

HISTORY

Gem Lake is fairly small, less than fifteen acres. Perhaps its small size inspired The Mountaineers to give it a name suggesting a jewel set into the landscape. Wright Mountain's name is also a legacy of The Mountaineers, who named it in honor of George E. Wright, an early member who died in 1923.

31 SNOQUALMIE MOUNTAIN

DISTANCE: 3.0 miles
ELEVATION GAIN: 3100 feet
HIGH POINT: 6278 feet
DIFFICULTY: Hard
HIKING TIME: 4 to 6 hours
BEST SEASON: Early summer to early fall

TRAIL TRAFFIC: Moderate foot traffic
PERMIT: Northwest Forest Pass
MAPS: USGS Snoqualmie Pass; Green Trails
Snoqualmie Pass No. 207
TRAILHEAD GPS: 47.4452°N, 121.4234°W

GETTING THERE: Take I-90 to Snoqualmie Pass. Eastbound take Exit 52 and turn left onto Alpental Road for about 2 miles to a large gravel parking lot. Westbound take Exit 53, turning left under the freeway and soon reaching a T intersection. Turn right onto State Route 906, following the sign pointing toward Alpental. Continue 2.7 miles through the ski area to the parking area. The trail begins along an unsigned dirt road a few dozen feet south of the Snow Lake Trailhead. Privy available.

Climb to unmatched views from a perch high on the Cascade Crest, the tallest tip in the Snoqualmie Pass area. While this unimproved trail has all the challenges associated with a rough boot path, it leads to commanding views more than worth the brushy, sweaty climb.

Near the summit of Snoqualmie Mountain with Keechelus Lake and Guye Peak in the background

Start at an unsigned dirt road a few feet south of the Snow Lake Trailhead. At 0.1 mile, keep an eye out for a small side trail branching off to the right—if you reach a shed, you've gone too far. Buckle up for a rough ride on this first section of narrow trail. The route takes advantage of rocky stream beds that are sometimes brimming with bubbling water. Cut straight up the mountainside, pushing aside encroaching slide alder as you climb. Be mindful of loose rock as you navigate up talus slopes.

After a long 0.6-mile climb, reach a boulder-strewn saddle and a signed junction marking the routes to Snoqualmie Mountain to the left and Guye Peak to the right. Veer left over the rocks for Snoqualmie Mountain, and soon reach a stream crossing complete with a lovely waterfall. Push onward and ever upward, catching occasional pocket views of the ski slopes of Alpental and Snoqualmie Pass. Watch as the trail quickly trades thick underbrush for mountain forest before shedding the woods for alpine meadows spotted with wildflowers and a few trees. After the trail opens up, it begins a series of tight switchbacks up an exposed ridge, with views getting more impressive with every step.

It's a thigh-burning workout, but Snoqualmie Mountain dishes out a phenomenal panorama. On a clear day, Mount Rainier dominates the skyline. Looking clockwise from Rainer's snowy slopes, follow the long, craggy ridgeline that begins with Denny Mountain, becomes the Tooth, then extends to Hemlock Peak and Bryant Peak before culminating above Snow Lake (Hike 29) in a massive mountain that sprouts Chair Peak, Kaleetan Peak, and Mount Roosevelt. Swing past Snow Lake and check out the seemingly gentle ridges of the Middle Fork Snoqualmie Valley; on the best of days catch a glimpse of Glacier Peak in the distance. Nearby Lundin Peak and distinctive Red Mountain (Hike 33) sit almost directly opposite Rainier, along with Mount Thompson, Kendall Peak, and Alta Mountain (Hike 42). Cave Ridge and Guye Peak (Hike 32) sit to the southeast with Keechelus Lake beyond.

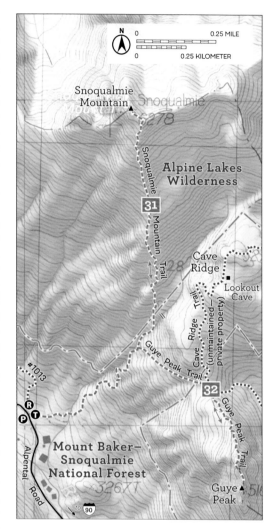

A trip to the top of Snoqualmie Mountain is not for everyone, but for those who persevere, there is plenty of room at the top to find a place to settle down, argue about the names of peaks, and enjoy a hard-earned lunch.

GOING FARTHER

A side trip out to Guye Peak (Hike 32) is available for those who still have the energy for more climbing. It's about 0.5 mile from the trail junction to the top, but it is somewhat of a technical scramble, so be sure your legs are up to the challenge before you venture out onto the rocks.

HISTORY

Snoqualmie Mountain rises quietly above the rest of the Snoqualmie Pass peaks, clocking in at 6278 feet. Despite being the highest peak in the pass, its broad, rounded slopes do not cut a dramatic profile. Snoqualmie Mountain and the surrounding area were already abuzz with activity by the time a USGS survey led by Albert H. Sylvester made the first recorded summit climb in 1898. While miners' boots originally pounded out most of the trails in the area, it was The Mountaineers who in the 1920s put Snoqualmie Mountain on their list of peaks to bag and kept the trail from being lost.

32 GUYE PEAK

DISTANCE: 2.5 miles
ELEVATION GAIN: 2000 feet
HIGH POINT: 5168 feet
DIFFICULTY: Hard
HIKING TIME: 3 to 5 hours
BEST SEASON: Late spring to early fall

TRAIL TRAFFIC: Light foot traffic
PERMIT: Northwest Forest Pass
MAPS: USGS Snoqualmie Pass; Green Trails
Snoqualmie Pass No. 207
TRAILHEAD GPS: 47.4452°N, 121.4234°W

GETTING THERE: Take I-90 to Snoqualmie Pass. Eastbound take Exit 52 and turn left onto Alpental Road for about 2 miles to a large gravel parking lot. Westbound take Exit 53, turning left under the freeway and soon reaching a T intersection. Turn right onto State Route 906, following the sign pointing toward Alpental. Continue 2.7 miles through the ski area to the parking area. The trail begins along an unsigned dirt road a few dozen feet south of the Snow Lake Trailhead. Privy available.

It's something of an exaggeration to call the route to the top of Guye Peak a trail, as it is more a series of scrambles over boulders and fallen trees connected by short boot-pounded paths through narrow bands of vegetation. The route aggressively attacks the elevation, conveying you up the slope with only an occasional begrudging switchback or two. The short trail distance and close proximity to I-90 mean easy access, making this route popular with both hikers and mountaineers year-round, but don't be fooled into thinking it is easy. Use caution near the top— quite a number of people have died on Guye Peak since the 1960s.

From an unsigned dirt road a few feet south of the Snow Lake Trailhead, begin heading up. Watch for a side trail branching off to the right at 0.1 mile; if you climb up to a shed, turn around and retrace your steps to find the trail. Battle up the mountainside, over streams, through brush, and across loose rock to the top of a talus field and a signed junction at 0.6 mile with the Snoqualmie Mountain Trail (Hike 31) to the left. Turn right for Guye Peak.

Here the trail levels out, and an unmarked spur trail leads off to the right (south), soon passing a seasonal pond. If you start to descend before finding the spur trail, you've passed the turnoff. Retrace your steps to find the path and begin the final push to the top. Leave the trees for exposed rock, navigating under granite overhangs and scrambling past big drop-offs to reach the windswept summit. Use caution in this section, as slick conditions can easily lead to a tumble or worse.

The Guye Peak Trail is never short on impressive views of the Snoqualmie Pass peaks.

Though the route up Guye Peak is short and brutal, the top pays dividends in spectacular views. Survey the ski slopes of Alpental and Snoqualmie Pass, as well as the whole of Commonwealth Basin. To the west lies Denny Mountain, supporting the slopes of Alpental and beginning a north-running ridgeline that includes the Tooth, Bryant Peak, and Chair Peak. Snoqualmie Mountain (Hike 31) dominates the view to the north, while Red Mountain (Hike 33) steals the show as you look east to take in Kendall Peak (Hike 34).

GOING FARTHER

A blistering climb to the top of Snoqualmie Mountain (Hike 31) is possible for those with a thirst for greater heights. Note that access to Cave Ridge can be found along this hike, but the Forest Service has asked that hikers avoid the area because parts of Cave Ridge are privately owned, and degrading trail conditions have created a hazard for hikers.

HISTORY

Largely exposed and bare, Guye Peak has a distinct look about it. Perhaps as a result of that look, it's had several names over the years. It was tentatively named Slate Mountain for a time, and the alternatives Mount Logan and Guye's Mountain were also considered. The Guye in question is Francis M. Guye, who, along with David Denny, staked out mining claims on both Guye Peak and Snoqualmie Mountain, all within what was then known as the Summit Mining District. Many of the rough paths that crisscross the mountains above Alpental have their origins in the mining activities of the late 1800s.

33 COMMONWEALTH BASIN TO RED PASS

DISTANCE: 8.8 miles
ELEVATION GAIN: 2400 feet
HIGH POINT: 5400 feet
DIFFICULTY: Hard
HIKING TIME: 6 to 8 hours
BEST SEASON: Late spring to early fall

TRAIL TRAFFIC: Moderate foot traffic
PERMIT: Northwest Forest Pass
MAPS: USGS Snoqualmie Pass; Green Trails
Snoqualmie Pass No. 207
TRAILHEAD GPS: 47.42787°N, 121.4134°W

GETTING THERE: Take I-90 to Snoqualmie Pass. Eastbound take Exit 52 and turn left under the freeway toward Alpental, and in a few thousand feet turn right onto a small spur road marked "Pacific Crest Trail." Westbound take Exit 53, turning left under the freeway, soon reaching a T intersection. Turn right onto State Route 906, following the sign pointing toward Alpental. Continue 0.7 mile through the ski area to a small spur road marked "Pacific Crest Trail." Follow the spur road to two large parking areas. The first is reserved for stock; hikers should continue to the farther parking lot and trailhead. Privy available.

This route leads out through a broad creek basin and up to a mountain pass with big views. Along the way enjoy chattering creeks, a lonely tarn, and, in the fall, mountainsides afire with oranges, reds, and yellows.

From the trailhead, begin down the Pacific Crest Trail #2000 (PCT) and in a short distance pass an unmarked but well-trodden trail branching off to your left. This is the old Cascade Crest Trail (CCT) route that is no longer maintained but is clearly still well loved. (If you're feeling adventurous, that trail also connects with the Commonwealth Basin Trail #1033, but it is a little more difficult to navigate.) Instead, continue straight ahead, sticking with the PCT.

Soon enter a mixed forest of fir and hemlock as the trail slowly climbs, crossing into the Alpine Lakes Wilderness at the 0.4-mile mark. Wide and well maintained, this section of trail breezes by. Skip over streams and cross long swaths of talus and meadowlands while finding increasingly better views of Commonwealth Basin and Snoqualmie Pass. Enjoy the wildflowers that dazzle during spring and summer as the trail steepens on long switchbacks and becomes increasingly rocky.

After 2.4 miles reach a connector trail on your left that leads a few hundred feet down to the Commonwealth Basin Trail. Veer down into the basin and follow the trail deeper into the valley. Enjoy the sounds of rushing water and occasional pocket views of the valley walls before reaching the end of the basin and beginning a sharp climb up the base of Red Mountain toward Red Pass. After a number of steep switchbacks, attain a level shoulder at 3.9 miles, where short spur trails lead down to Red Pond and up to the crown of Red Mountain. Decide here whether to brave the difficult scramble up Red Mountain, or take a quick jaunt down to Red Pond before pushing up to Red Pass.

Switchback upward, pressing toward the pass to find ever-better views of Commonwealth Basin stretching out below. Reach the pass at the 4.4-mile mark and note the junction signed "trail abandoned." This is the old PCT route leading down to the Middle Fork Snoqualmie and Goldmyer Hot Springs (Hike 15) that predates the Kendall Katwalk. While a few brave souls still try to follow this route, it's a long, unpleasant bushwhack best left abandoned.

Looking down from the trail at Red Pond's shallow waters and a snow-dusted Commonwealth Valley

The climb to the pass is well worth the effort: the views here are spectacular. The mountain simply drops away, providing you a perch at the top of a massive natural amphitheater. The horn of Mount Thompson steals the show, a fitting counterpoint to Mount Rainier to the south. Commonwealth Basin spreads out to Alpental in the distance. Red Mountain suddenly looks much craggier and more intimidating from this side. From here, Snoqualmie Mountain (Hike 31) and Guye Peak (Hike 32) seem less imposing than they usually do, and the rocky top of Lundin Peak is just ahead on the trail.

GOING FARTHER
Lundin East Peak is easily accessible from Red Pass. Simply follow the trail that continues along the ridge from the pass, ignoring signs that say the trail is abandoned. Take the left fork and head upward, sticking to the rough trail to the top. The views don't change much with the extra effort of pushing past the usual stopping point of Red Pass, but it's a cozy little spot to settle down and refuel.

HISTORY
The Commonwealth Basin Trail has its origins in the mining claims common in this

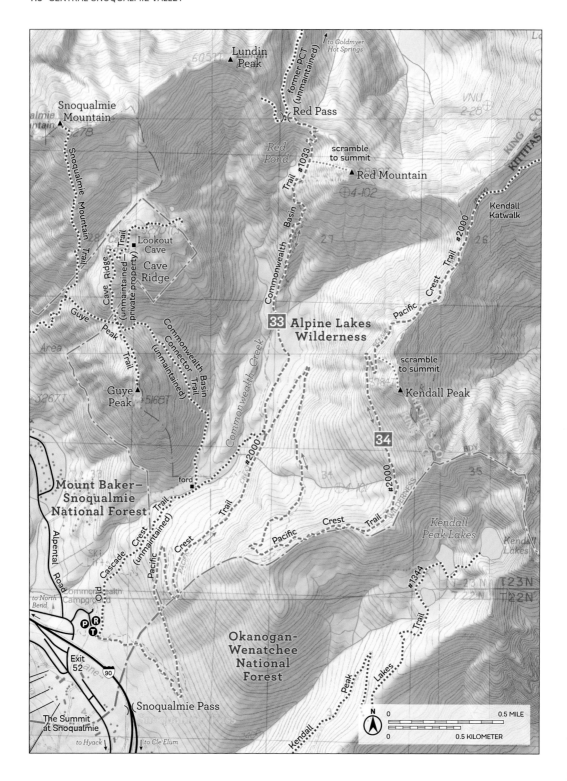

▲ Lundin Peak

to Goldmyer Hot Springs

former PCT (unmaintained)

Red Pass

Snoqualmie Mountain ▲

Red Pond

scramble to summit

▲ Red Mountain

Trail #1033

KING CO

KITTITAS

Kendall Katwalk

Snoqualmie Mountain Trail

Commonwealth Basin

Crest Trail #2000

Lookout Cave

Cave Ridge

Trail (unmaintained / private property)

Cave Ridge

Pacific

33 Alpine Lakes Wilderness

Guye

Peak Trail

Commonwealth Basin Connector Trail (unmaintained)

scramble to summit

▲ Kendall Peak

Guye Peak ▲

Commonwealth Creek

34

#2000

Mount Baker–Snoqualmie National Forest

ford

#2000

WILDERNESS

Kendall Peak Lakes

Kendall Lakes

Cascade Crest Trail (unmaintained)

Crest

Pacific

Crest

Trail

Pacific

Crest

Trail

Alpental Road

to North Bend

Commonwealth Campground

Okanogan-Wenatchee National Forest

#1344

Trail

123N

22N

122N

Exit 52

90

Snoqualmie Pass

Kendall

Peak

Lakes

The Summit at Snoqualmie

to Hyack

to Cle Elum

N

0   0.5 MILE

0   0.5 KILOMETER

area. The trail was originally built by prospectors around 1890 to access claims within the valley. In 1928 Fred Cleator, who was put in charge of the US Forest Service region encompassing Oregon and Washington, immediately pieced together a contiguous trail through his region that would eventually become the CCT. The old Commonwealth Basin route served as part of the CCT until the early 1960s, when the preferred CCT route shifted over to the Snow Lake–Rock Creek approach (Hikes 29 and 14).

34 KENDALL PEAK AND KENDALL KATWALK

DISTANCE: 12.2 miles to Kendall Katwalk
ELEVATION GAIN: 3000 feet
HIGH POINT: 5784 feet
DIFFICULTY: Hard
HIKING TIME: 6 to 8 hours
BEST SEASON: Early summer to early fall

TRAIL TRAFFIC: Heavy foot traffic
PERMIT: Northwest Forest Pass
MAPS: USGS Snoqualmie Pass; Green Trails Snoqualmie Pass No. 207
TRAILHEAD GPS: 47.42787°N, 121.4134°W

GETTING THERE: Take I-90 to Snoqualmie Pass. Eastbound take Exit 52 and turn left under the freeway toward Alpental. In a few thousand feet turn right onto a small spur road marked "Pacific Crest Trail." Westbound take Exit 53, turning left under the freeway, soon reaching a T intersection. Turn right onto State Route 906, following the sign pointing toward Alpental. Continue 0.7 mile through the ski area to a small spur road marked "Pacific Crest Trail". Follow the spur road to two large parking areas. The first is reserved for stock; hikers should continue to the farther parking lot and the trailhead. Privy available.

Something about the obvious intrusion of humankind onto a fairy-tale-like landscape has attracted hikers and backpackers for decades. "Kendall Katwalk" can summon thoughts of a vertigo-inducing shimmy across an exposed cliff face hundreds of feet in the air. In reality, this dynamite-blasted trail is not nearly so harrowing. It's a fun destination along this popular section of the Pacific Crest Trail, though the views from the Katwalk cannot compare to the stunning panorama from the top of Kendall Peak.

From the trailhead, begin by following the Pacific Crest Trail #2000 (PCT) into a forest of mixed fir and hemlock, soon passing an unmarked but obvious trail on the left that follows long-abandoned roadbed into young underbrush. This is the unmaintained but still loved Cascade Crest Trail (CCT) that can be used as an alternate approach to Red Pass (Hike 33). For now, press onward, watching as the trees quickly thin and give way to dense patches of huckleberry and salmonberry. At about 0.4 mile, cross into the Alpine Lakes Wilderness and follow long, lazy switchbacks up a mild grade, with the occasional rock and root to navigate around.

Eventually the trail steepens and begins a long traverse through talus fields and subalpine meadows, with accompanying open views of Snoqualmie Pass and the surrounding landscape. During spring and summer, the meadows fill with wildflowers, adding some much-needed color to an increasingly rocky trail. Pass the junction with the Commonwealth Basin Connector Trail (Hike 33) at 2.4 miles,

Drilled and dynamited in the 1970s, the Kendall Katwalk was carved directly into the mountainside.

continuing to navigate stretches of talus and ever-changing views of the basin below.

At about 5.0 miles, reach the shoulders of Kendall Peak, where the trail quickly switchbacks; just beyond, at 5.3 miles, look for an unmarked boot path straight up the mountainside to the summit. Though it's a bit of a scramble beset with loose rock, the path is fairly well defined and easy to follow. Quickly gain the narrow ridgeline and cautiously follow it to the top, keeping one eye on the rubble at the bottom of the cliffs hundreds of feet below.

The view is tremendous. The weather-worn spires and crags of the Alpine Lakes Wilderness fill the horizon like a sea of crumbling sand castles. Red Mountain catches the eye to the north, with Mount Thompson just beyond. Mount Rainier rises to the south, a dramatic backdrop for Mount Catherine and the Snoqualmie ski slopes. Guye Peak (Hike 32) is below, stoically keeping watch over Snoqualmie Pass. To the southeast are the shimmering waters of Keechelus Lake. Find a comfortable rock to sit down on—it's going to take a while to drink all this in. Before you head back down, look for the cast-iron tube containing a summit registry maintained by The Mountaineers, and add your name.

Scramble back to the PCT and continue another 0.8 mile to the Katwalk, which is farther down the trail than anyone expects. The Katwalk looks very much like it was blasted from the side of a mountain, and the rubble below is ample proof. Enjoy the view from this artificial balcony before packing up and heading back to the trailhead.

GOING FARTHER

The entire PCT route between Snoqualmie Pass and Stevens Pass, of which this hike is the first leg, encompasses a myriad of backpacking adventures outlined later in this book (Hike 100).

HISTORY

The PCT spent the better part of sixty years under construction. In the 1930s, a coalition of hiking and youth groups sketched out an approximate route for a Pacific coast counterpart to the Appalachian Trail. From the 1930s until 1968, the route was blazed and explored, receiving federal recognition under the 1968 National Trail System Act. Then various trail organizations, land management agencies, and an army of volunteers worked to link regional trails from Mexico to Canada to form the PCT. By the early 1970s, one of those regional trails—the CCT—was rerouted to meet the PCT's trail standards.

In 1938 the earliest CCT route went up Commonwealth Basin (Hike 33) and over Red Pass down to the Middle Fork Snoqualmie River Valley. By the 1960s, the preferred CCT route followed Rock Creek (Hike 14) down to the Middle Fork Snoqualmie and eventually up over Dutch Miller Gap (Hike 93). Both of those routes did not accommodate pack animals and, as a result, did not fully meet the trail standards set out by the 1968 Act.

By 1971, the Forest Service was trying to locate a better route and, after much consternation and a lot of pushback, decided on the Kendall Katwalk approach. Contractor Elmo Warren of Sagle, Idaho, won the bid to build it and quickly addressed a number of difficulties presented by the Forest Service. The problem of marking the route on the granite cliffs was solved by filling beer bottles with red paint and dropping them from a helicopter. The issue of how the trail would be carved out of the rock was solved by hauling eighty-pound gas-driven Pionjar drills to slowly chip away at whatever rock could not be blasted away by dynamite. Most of the initial clearing was done in 1976, and it was completed in 1977. The new section of the PCT that included Kendall Katwalk officially opened in 1979.

Mountain goats scamper across a snowfield above Upper Robin Lakes (Hike 57).

35 KENDALL PEAK LAKES

DISTANCE: 8.4 miles
ELEVATION GAIN: 2100 feet
HIGH POINT: 4750 feet
DIFFICULTY: Moderate
HIKING TIME: 5 to 6 hours
BEST SEASON: Late spring to late fall

TRAIL TRAFFIC: Moderate foot traffic
PERMIT: Sno-Park permit required in winter
MAPS: USGS Snoqualmie Pass, USGS Chikamin
Peak; Green Trails Snoqualmie Pass No. 207
TRAILHEAD GPS: 47.4019°N, 121.3929°W

GETTING THERE: Take I-90 to Hyak, Exit 54. Eastbound turn left under the freeway; westbound head right
to the parking area for the Gold Creek Sno-Park. The trailhead is 0.5 mile ahead on Forest Road 9090,
but a washout prevents vehicle access. Walking the road adds 1 mile to the hike distance.

*Ideal for hikers seeking a quick escape, this taste of the wilderness awaits just a few miles from
I-90. Its grade and distance make this route perfect for a wintertime romp through fresh powder,
especially on snowshoes.*

From the trailhead, Kendall Peak Lakes Trail #1344 is mostly decommissioned logging road, which makes for a leisurely stroll through alders and vine maples. Shrubbery quickly gives way to long views of stump-strewn clear-cuts, complete with young saplings struggling against low underbrush. The carefully carved slopes of the Snoqualmie ski area soon dominate the skyline, offering a contrast to the surrounding clear-cuts.

Recovering forest provides a view of Mount Rainier peeking over nearby mountaintops.

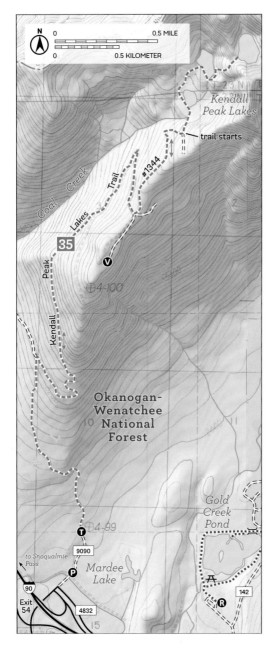

deeper into Coal Creek Valley while taking in even longer views of the Snoqualmie Valley.

At 3.0 miles, attain a ridgeline at a five-way intersection. Ignore the short spur roads leading straight ahead into the trees—they soon dead-end. The rightmost path leads out 0.25 mile to an overlook offering views of Keechelus Lake and the Gold Creek Valley, while the leftmost path continues up to Kendall Peak Lakes.

After the five-way intersection, the logging road begins to thin, and in 0.5 mile watch for a cairn indicating a boot path to the left leading to the lakes. Leave the logging road here and head toward the craggy mountaintops of the Alpine Lakes Wilderness on the roughly cut trail.

At 3.7 miles, reach the first meadow-bound lake. Really more pond than lake, these reed-lined waters are surrounded by marsh, so watch your step. Here the trail becomes more intermittent, with boot paths branching off in dozens of directions. Let whimsy be your guide and choose the path of most appeal as most of the paths eventually work their way around the water and lead to the next lake.

The middle child of the Kendall Peak Lakes sits at the 3.9-mile mark and makes for more of a destination, but it pales in comparison to the last lake. The trick is finding the trail to access it. The well-worn path is among the talus near the lake's inlet stream. When in doubt, follow your ears to find this shadowy path up the very steep mountainside. While the climb is tough enough to make it tempting to forgo this final climb, keep pressing upward; you will be well rewarded.

After slogging up about 200 feet, reach the shores of the last and largest of the Kendall Peak Lakes. Here at 4.2 miles from the trailhead, surrounded by steep cliffs and talus, the lake feels wild and remote, despite being less than a mile from the logging road. Unpack your lunch and enjoy.

HISTORY

Kendall Peak Lakes have always been seen more than visited. Couched in a cul-de-sac of

At 1.0 mile pass a junction with another logging road on the left, long ago decommissioned. Keep right and head up, staying on FR 9090 as it climbs a few switchbacks and then begins a long traverse, slowly pushing

mountain ridges, the three lakes were so often observed from the surrounding lofty heights that today we continue to refer to them as just that: lakes seen and accessed via Kendall Peak. Nowadays, extensive logging and the roads that go along with it have hewn a much easier route to Kendall Peak Lakes, though it was a high price to pay for ease of access, as the vast fields of clear-cut forest are still struggling to recover.

36 GOLD CREEK POND

DISTANCE: 1.1 miles
ELEVATION GAIN: None
HIGH POINT: 2550 feet
DIFFICULTY: Easy
HIKING TIME: 1 hour
BEST SEASON: Early spring to late fall
TRAILHEAD GPS: 47.3966°N, 121.3793°W
TRAIL TRAFFIC: Moderate foot traffic

PERMIT: Northwest Forest Pass ; Sno-Park permit in winter
MAPS: USGS Snoqualmie Pass; Green Trails Snoqualmie Pass No. 207
NOTE: This ADA-accessible trail works for strollers and wheelchairs, providing everyone a glimpse of the pond and surrounding landscape.

GETTING THERE: Take I-90 to Hyak, Exit 54. Eastbound turn left under the freeway; westbound head right, quickly reaching frontage road (Forest Road 4832). Turn right, following the road for approximately 1.5 miles to the signed Gold Creek Road (FR 142). Turn left and follow the road for 0.5 mile to the Gold Creek Pond parking lot and trailhead. Privy available.

The ADA-accessible Gold Creek Pond trails offers every hiker a taste of the wilderness.

Not every hike needs to be a multimile, hours-long trek deep into the wilderness. Sometimes a short walk to the edge of the wild is perfect, especially when it allows those in strollers and wheelchairs to get a taste of the lakes and rugged peaks that lie deep in the Alpine Lakes Wilderness. Gold Creek Pond is just that kind of walk: a short paved loop trail with satisfying views of the large pond and the craggy heights of Kendall Peak and Rampart Ridge.

From the trailhead, follow the Gold Creek Pond Trail #1250 a few hundred feet to the loop junction. Head right, following the trail alongside the pond's outlet creek for 0.4 mile to reach the signed junction with the Gold Creek Trail #1314 veering off to the right.

Keep to the pavement, continuing around the pond. Cross over a bridge and through wetlands while pausing to read interpretive signs. Paths lead down to the water and wider

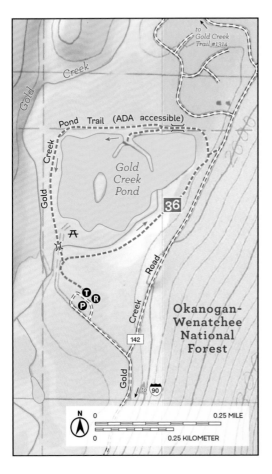

views of the landscape. Take a moment here to take in the tree-lined pond, which boasts several little islands and peninsulas that add to its appeal.

As you circle the water, enjoy the greenery dotted with wildflowers in the late spring as you cross creeks on sturdy boardwalk. Your circuit is nearly complete when you pass a large picnic area with several tables, benches, and open grills. Stop for a snack or to take in the scenery before heading back to the parking area.

This easy, accessible jaunt has ample opportunities for less-seasoned hikers to enjoy at a comfortable pace. Popular throughout the year, Gold Creek Pond is perfect for those looking for a first-time snowshoe or a summertime amble for the whole family.

GOING FARTHER

For a longer day hike, head down the Gold Creek Trail toward Alaska Lake (Hike 37), venturing into Lower Gold Creek Basin and crossing into the Alpine Lakes Wilderness in 2.5 miles. This is also a very popular snowshoe destination, as the wide, flat basin provides a lot of room to roam through the powder.

HISTORY

Before the 1960s, Gold Creek Pond could not be found on any map. There was no body of water at all until the mid-1960s when construction of I-90 was in full swing. Then a pond suddenly appeared on USGS maps, labeled "Gravel Pit." That is, in fact, what Gold Creek Pond is—a remnant of I-90's construction when it served as a sand and gravel mine. It wasn't until the 1980s that the area was repurposed for recreational use and developed into the destination we know today.

37 ALASKA LAKE

DISTANCE: 11.5 miles
ELEVATION GAIN: 1700 feet
HIGH POINT: 4200 feet
DIFFICULTY: Hard
HIKING TIME: 6 to 8 hours or overnight
BEST SEASON: Late spring to early fall
TRAIL TRAFFIC: Moderate foot traffic

PERMIT: Northwest Forest Pass
MAPS: USGS Chikamin Peak; Green Trails
Snoqualmie Pass No. 207
TRAILHEAD GPS: 47.3966°N, 121.3793°W
NOTES: Sections are not well maintained and can
be brushy in summer. Use caution when fording
the creeks in spring or after heavy rains.

GETTING THERE: Take I-90 to Hyak, Exit 54. Eastbound turn left under the freeway; westbound head right, quickly reaching frontage road (Forest Road 4832). Turn right, following the road for approximately 1.5 miles to the signed Gold Creek Road (FR 142). Turn left and follow the road for 0.5 mile to the Gold Creek Pond parking lot and trailhead. Privy available.

Alaska Lake in early July, still snowbound and ice-covered

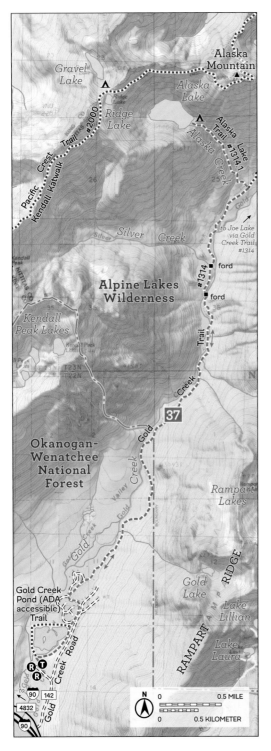

Hike out to a stunningly beautiful alpine lake along a trail that begins easily but becomes increasingly challenging as obstacles, degraded trail tread, and very steep elevation gain slow your progress. Aside from a creek crossing and an avalanche area, it is a pleasant stroll to the Alaska Lake junction, and turning around here makes for an easy 10-mile outing. The hike-scramble up to Alaska Lake is significantly more challenging, but ultimately rewarding and well worth the slog up the mountainside.

From the trailhead, begin along the Gold Creek Pond Trail #1250, an ADA-accessible, stroller-friendly asphalt loop around the pond. Head right at the loop junction. In 0.4 mile, signs direct you off the pavement and onto a series of private roads that meander for 1.4 miles before reaching the actual trail.

The Gold Creek Trail #1314 is fairly level and pleasant; the creek accompanies you through thimbleberry and vine maple, which slowly yield to hemlock and cedar. At 2.5 miles, just after you enter the Alpine Lakes Wilderness, you reach the 2002 avalanche area, an abrupt wasteland of rocks and fallen logs. On the plus side, the avalanche stripped the vegetation from the cliffs of Rampart Ridge above and exposed a few small waterfalls tumbling down to Gold Creek.

After you navigate the avalanche area, at 4.0 miles is a ford of Gold Creek. During the height of summer when the water is low, the crossing can be done without getting your feet wet. During the spring or after heavy rains, fording the creek can be treacherous, so use caution. Once across, you'll ford Silver Creek in 0.2 mile before continuing to the "end" of the trail at 5.0 miles, with a sign pointing you toward Alaska and Joe Lakes and glibly stating "trail not maintained beyond this point." This is an understatement. To reach Alaska Lake, veer left following the Alaska Lake Trail #1314.1 as it begins its ascent.

The rocky trek up to Alaska Lake is only 0.75 mile but demands 1000 feet of elevation gain. The boot path follows Alaska Creek through groves of slide alder and vine maple, alternating between climbing abandoned creek beds and clambering over talus fields. It is not an easy trek, but Alaska Creek is little more than one long waterfall cascade, and the views of the Gold Creek Valley and Alta Mountain are worth the attempt. Alaska Lake is a nice little destination tucked beneath Alaska Mountain and the Pacific Crest Trail, with a couple of pleasant campsites along the lakeshore.

GOING FARTHER

For the more adventurous, the Gold Creek Trail continues past the Alaska Lake junction another 2.0 miles up to Joe Lake, though some significant bushwhacking may be required depending on the time of year. A lighter addition might be a quick tour around the Gold Creek Pond Trail (Hike 36), which adds only 0.7 mile while providing some long views of Gold Creek Basin, Kendall Peak, and Rampart Ridge.

HISTORY

With names like Gold Creek and Silver Creek, it's not surprising to learn that the Gold Creek Trail started out in the 1880s as a prospecting trail following the creek to various claims in the valley. The trail soon became a well-graded road allowing mining companies easy access to the Snoqualmie Wagon Road and the Chicago, Milwaukee, St. Paul, and Pacific Railroad that opened in 1909. The wagon road crossed over Gold Creek near the north end of Keechelus Lake much as I-90 does today. Over a few decades, miners dug hundreds of feet of tunnel into mountainsides above Gold Creek Basin, though most have collapsed since the mining heyday ended in the 1930s.

As times changed and mining gave way to recreation, the trail deteriorated and all but disappeared. In the 1970s, the Forest Service rescued the route, and for the next thirty years, snowshoers and hikers enjoyed the gentle trip through the valley. In 2002 large swaths of the trail were destroyed by a massive avalanche that tumbled down the east side of the valley and splashed up the other side, leaving thousands of downed trees in its wake. Today, the Forest Service and volunteers have carved something of trail out of the debris, but portions remain a challenge to navigate.

38 RAMPART LAKES BACKDOOR

DISTANCE: 5.4 miles
ELEVATION GAIN: 1700 feet in; 300 feet out
HIGH POINT: 5500 feet
DIFFICULTY: Hard
HIKING TIME: 5 to 7 hours
BEST SEASON: Early summer to early fall
TRAIL TRAFFIC: Light foot traffic

PERMIT: None
MAPS: USGS Chikamin Peak; Green Trails Snoqualmie Pass No. 207
TRAILHEAD GPS: 47.3906°N, 121.3474°W
NOTE: Between the trailhead and the Lake Lillian Trail #1332, the trail is not well maintained.

GETTING THERE: Take I-90 to Hyak, Exit 54. Eastbound turn left under the freeway; westbound head right, quickly reaching frontage road (Forest Road 4832). Turn right, following the road for about 2.5 miles before it turns to gravel. Continue on FR 4832 for 1 mile or so to an intersection at the end of a switchback. Instead of turning uphill on FR 4832, head straight onto an unmarked road, labeled FR 136 on maps. Follow the increasingly overgrown FR 136 for about 2 miles to a major switchback and a small parking area.

Traditionally accessed from the Rachel Lake Trailhead via the Rachel Lake Trail, the Rampart Lakes can also be reached via this popular and semiofficial approach. It lacks some of the bells and whistles of the traditional approach, such as switchbacks and signage, but it provides a healthy dose of adventure. Perhaps unsurprisingly for a not-yet-fully maintained trail, portions of the route are rough and haphazardly scraped into the mountainside. Broad vistas, grassy meadows, and a number of sparkling alpine lakes are all found along the way.

From the parking area, the trail climbs steeply upward, following Rocky Run Creek through slide alders, devils club, and the occasional hemlock. The creek sports a couple of impressive, easily accessed cascades that offer a pause to catch your breath. After 0.6 mile of climbing, the trail briefly plateaus, and a spur trail to the left leads down a few hundred yards to sheltered little Lake Laura, well worth a quick visit. Access to the thickly wooded lakeshore is limited, but clambering down the rocks to the water offers one lonely campsite and a better view of the waterfall spilling into the lake, which can put on quite a show during the spring melt. What the

lake lacks in big views and majestic backdrops, it makes up for in privacy and tranquility—you're very unlikely to share Lake Laura with anyone.

The main trail continues up another 0.1 mile; the going can be tricky here, with loose rock and roots making it hard to find your footing. At 0.7 mile the trail ends at a junction with the Lake Lillian Trail #1332 on the right. Take the Lake Lillian Trail upward to placid Lake Lillian at 0.9 mile, which rests beneath Rampart Ridge and quietly fuels Rocky Run Creek. It's tempting to spend time in this tranquil setting, and tent sites welcome the stay, but the real prize is farther up the trail.

Climb an avalanche chute up from Lake Lillian to reach this view of Mount Rainier and your surroundings.

While not clearly marked, a path continues around the lake to the right, crossing exposed rock before dropping back down to the shore and working its way up a steep avalanche chute. Gain the ridgeline and soon leave the trees for captivating views of Mount Rainier rising over Lake Lillian with Lake Kachess in the distance (for an even better view, quick scrambles up the rocks reach easily accessed high points). Traverse the ridge through fields of wildflowers, bear grass, and huckleberry, angling slightly downward as you go. Keep right at an unsigned split in the trail at 1.8 miles and take in views of Hibox Mountain (Hike 43) and Alta Mountain (Hike 42) as the Rampart Lakes come into view.

Drop down through scree and talus to the lakeshore at 2.2 miles. A spiderweb of trails branches out around the lakes, each turn providing a view of yet another expanse of water. Stretching over 0.5 mile, these five rocky lakes have plenty of hidden nooks and crannies to discover. Take time to explore this fairy-tale landscape, whether you're staying for the afternoon or the night.

GOING FARTHER

Nearby Alta Mountain and Lake Lila (Hike 42), as well as Rachel Lake (Hike 41), are all within reach. Navigate the maze of trails by sticking to the widest path and heading toward the outlet creek. The Alta Mountain Trail leaves the Rampart Lakes, heads over a small rise, and soon reaches a signed junction with the Rachel Lake Trail. Continue straight ahead for Alta Mountain and Lake Lila or angle sharply downward for Rachel Lake.

HISTORY

Rampart Lakes take their name from the ridge they occupy, Rampart Ridge. Running from the shores of Keechelus Lake to the top of Alta Mountain, the ridge is named for the way it appears to block access through the mountains like a rampart. Early surveyors missed nearby Snoqualmie Pass in part because Rampart Ridge, Keechelus Ridge, and Box Ridge made it seem like there was no viable route here.

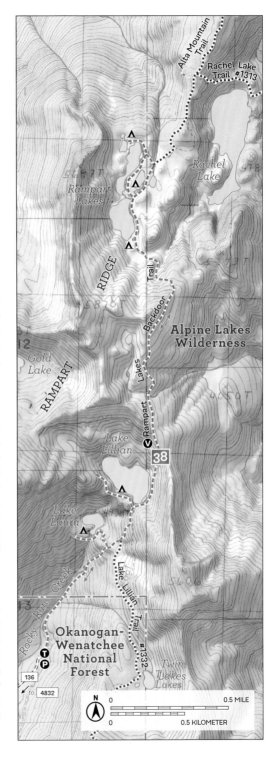

Lake Margaret and Stonesthrow Lake from the top of Mount Margaret

39 LAKE LILLIAN AND MOUNT MARGARET

DISTANCE: 5.2 miles

ELEVATION GAIN: 2000 feet

HIGH POINT: 5560 feet

DIFFICULTY: Hard

HIKING TIME: 4 to 6 hours

BEST SEASON: Early summer to fall, with spectacular fall color

TRAIL TRAFFIC: Light foot traffic

PERMIT: None

MAPS: USGS Chikamin Peak; Green Trails Snoqualmie Pass No. 207

TRAILHEAD GPS: 47.3906°N, 121.3474°W

NOTE: Between the trailhead and Lake Lillian Trail #1332, the trail is not well maintained.

GETTING THERE: Take I-90 to Hyak, Exit 54. Eastbound turn left under the freeway; westbound head right, quickly reaching frontage road (Forest Road 4832). Turn right, following the road for about 2.5 miles before it turns to gravel. Continue on FR 4832 for 1 mile or so to an intersection at the end of a switchback. Instead of turning uphill on FR 4832, head straight onto an unmarked road, labeled FR 136 on maps. Follow the increasingly overgrown FR 136 for about 2 miles to a major switchback and a small parking area.

Mount Margaret and Lake Lillian are more often approached from the Lake Lillian Trailhead, which begins on logging roads through old clear-cuts up Mount Margaret's shoulders and ends with a glittering alpine jewel. Instead, this route leads straight to Lake Lillian and then up to

the heights of Mount Margaret via a "back-door" approach. While this route isn't exactly smooth trail with carefully graded switchbacks, it wastes little time delivering hikers to alpine wilderness and broad vistas.

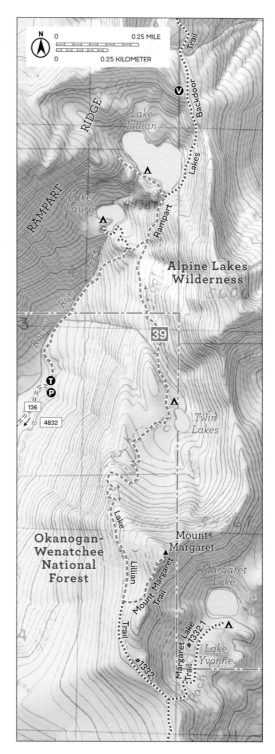

From the parking area, the trail immediately climbs straight up the slope alongside Rocky Run Creek. Work your way up through a brushy understory of slide alders, salmonberry, and devil's club punctuated with the occasional hemlock and fir. The trail is thin, rocky, and steep but it's easy to follow. In addition, a few small waterfalls provide ample reason to pause before climbing again. After ascending 0.6 mile, the trail briefly plateaus, and a trail branches off to the left, down to lonely Lake Laura, a worthy side trip (see Hike 38).

From the Lake Laura spur, it's another 0.1 mile to the Lake Lillian Trail #1332 junction. This short section is a little challenging to navigate, as you work your way up through loose rock and exposed roots, made more difficult when rain and melt partially transform the trail into stream bed. Reach the junction at 0.7 mile. Here, the hike to Mount Margaret continues to the right, but first head left to visit Lake Lillian.

It's 0.2 mile and a short climb to reach picturesque Lake Lillian. Rampart Ridge rises above the meadow-lined waters, while exposed rock and diminutive trees add to the alpine feel. The main trail circling around the lake to the left leads to the best campsites, while a boot path to the right leads up to Rampart Lakes (Hike 38). After visiting Lake Lillian's tranquil shores, double back and head down the Lake Lillian Trail, past the junction to where you parked and continue straight out toward Mount Margaret.

Cross a large talus field before working your way through big, dark stands of hemlock on rocky trail. Soon reach a series of tarns that culminate in the shallow waters of Twin Lakes at 1.7 miles. Side trails here lead around the lakes, offering a little more to explore. Push onward, climbing out of the Twin Lakes basin on the shoulders of Mount Margaret. Here are the beginnings of the view you'll soon enjoy from the mountaintop.

At 2.6 miles, reach the unsigned spur trail to the summit of Mount Margaret (the main trail continues to the Lake Lillian Trailhead, Hike 40). Veer left uphill for a steep, rocky, but short 0.2-mile climb to the top and take in the views from the wildflower-filled meadows. To the east

look down on Margaret Lake (Hike 40), Stonesthrow Lake, Swan Lake, Rock Rabbit Lake, and the green sea of mountaintops beyond. Settle in and enjoy the show.

GOING FARTHER

Beyond the all-but-mandatory side trip to Lake Lillian, a short trip down to Margaret Lake (Hike 40) is an easy addition.

40 MARGARET LAKE

DISTANCE: 5.5 miles
ELEVATION GAIN: 1600 feet in; 300 feet out
HIGH POINT: 5100 feet
DIFFICULTY: Moderate
HIKING TIME: 4 to 6 hours
BEST SEASON: Early summer to early fall

TRAIL TRAFFIC: Moderate to heavy foot traffic
PERMIT: Northwest Forest Pass
MAPS: USGS Chikamin Peak; Green Trails
Snoqualmie Pass Gateway No. 207S
TRAILHEAD GPS: 47.3641°N, 121.3585°W

GETTING THERE: Take I-90 to Hyak, Exit 54. Eastbound turn left under the freeway; westbound head right, quickly reaching frontage road (Forest Road 4832). Turn right, following the road for about 2.5 miles before it turns to gravel. Continue on FR 4832 for 1 mile or so to an intersection at the end of a switchback. Ignore an unmarked and slightly overgrown side road to the left that leads to the Rampart Lakes Backdoor (Hikes 38 and 39). Instead, continue up FR 4832, keeping left at the fork in a few hundred feet. Now on FR 4934, continue 0.4 mile to a parking lot labeled "Lake Margaret and Lake Lillian." The trailhead is a few hundred feet farther along the road.

Margaret Lake is everything a day hike should be: a simple jaunt out to a pretty alpine lake, accessible to most hikers nearly any time of year. Even better, this hike has lots of room to grow, with a scramble up to a summit and more lovely lakes nearby. One lake might seem like enough for one day, but after a few hours in the wilderness, you might be craving a little extra.

From the trailhead, the Lake Lillian Trail #1332 begins on a decommissioned logging road winding through vast acres of recovering clear-cut. This former road quickly gives way to an actual trail at 0.7 mile, albeit one that continues through the aftereffects of logging. Overall, the trail is fairly tame, and most of the elevation gain comes at the beginning. The clear-cuts burst with blue huckleberries during the season, adding fuel to your journey. Switchback up

the slope toward the shelter of mature Douglas fir and pine while noting the landscape as you ascend. If you're lucky, Mount Rainier will be headlining the horizon. Mount Catherine is the large isolated mound at the end of Keechelus Lake. In the middle distance you can make out the sharp point of Silver Peak.

Under the protection of the trees, you'll continue to gain elevation until you attain the ridge. At this plateau, reach a trail junction

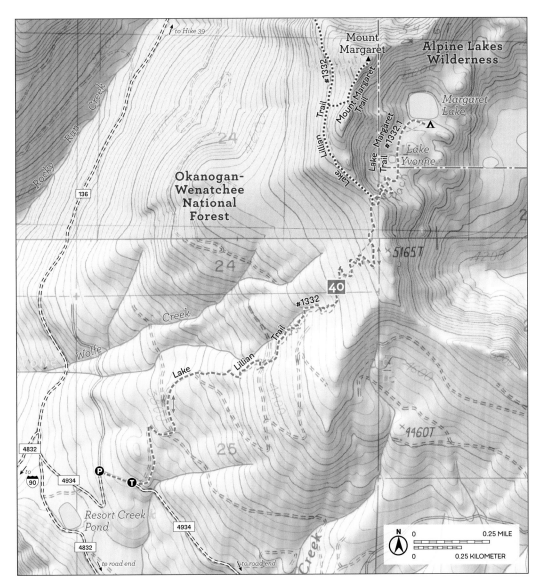

at 2.2 miles. The Lake Lillian Trail continues onward, but instead take a right to head down to Margaret Lake along the Lake Margaret Trail #1332.1 (the official trail name for some reason).

Almost immediately the trail descends into the bowl below Mount Margaret. Reach the Alpine Lakes Wilderness at 2.4 miles, and just beyond pass tiny Lake Yvonne—so tiny that it's not much more than a pond. As you progress, the trail opens up into meadows to reveal occasional openings in the trees and glimpses of what is to come. The trail around the lakes is also much muddier, so if it has rained recently, take extra care as the ground becomes very muddy and slick.

Reach Margaret Lake at just over 2.7 miles, set deep into the base of Mount Margaret. Find a quiet campsite and a few side trails to explore while taking in the heights of the mountain.

Hikers on forest road on early stretches of the trail on a foggy fall morning

This tranquil retreat is particularly impressive in the fall, when the slopes of Mount Margaret are afire with fall color. Settle in and enjoy the solitude.

GOING FARTHER

Lake Lillian (Hike 39) is a popular destination, and many hikers head that direction, reaching it just a few more miles down the trail. For a bird's-eye view of Margaret Lake, consider a climb up to the top of Mount Margaret (Hike 39), also found farther down the main trail. If you're up for doing some exploring, there are a number of other lakes right nearby—Stonesthrow Lake, Rock Rabbit Lake, and Swan Lake. Once accessed via long-lost trails, these are mostly visited by hikers comfortable with cross-country bushwhacks and armed with a well-connected GPS.

HISTORY

Like many in the Alpine Lakes Wilderness, the lakes in this area were likely named for the women in the lives of those who found these tarns. Lillian, Margaret, and Yvonne received names in the Albert H. Sylvester era of frenzied place naming, no doubt following his tradition of naming lakes he came upon for the wives, sisters, and girlfriends of the rangers who worked for him. The tradition began on his 1909 tour through the Ladies Lakes (Hike 98) when he named eight lakes he came across.

41 RACHEL LAKE

DISTANCE: 6.8 miles
ELEVATION GAIN: 1900 feet
HIGH POINT: 4600 feet
DIFFICULTY: Moderate

HIKING TIME: 4 to 6 hours
BEST SEASON: Late spring to early fall
TRAIL TRAFFIC: Moderate to heavy foot traffic
PERMIT: Northwest Forest Pass

MAPS: USGS Chikamin Peak; Green Trails Snoqualmie Pass No. 207

TRAILHEAD GPS: 47.40084°N, 121.2836°W

GETTING THERE: Take I-90 to Stampede Pass, Exit 62. Eastbound turn left under the freeway; westbound turn right onto unsigned Kachess Lake Road (Forest Road 49), following signs pointing toward Lake Kachess. Drive 5 miles to the Lake Kachess Campground and turn left onto Box Canyon Road (FR 4930). Continue for 4 miles and turn left into the Rachel Lake Trailhead parking area. Privy available.

Portions of the Rachel Lake Trail have always been a little rough. The trail bed is more rock and root than actual packed earth—a tangled mess with loose rock and unstable footing. Over the years many agencies have tried to find a better route to the lake, but thus far it has fallen to volunteer groups such as the Washington Trails Association to smooth out the path. Despite their admirable efforts, the trail remains a little challenging to navigate.

From the trailhead, the Rachel Lake Trail #1313 begins on a gentle grade, hugging Box Canyon Creek as it crosses into the Alpine Lakes Wilderness at 0.4 mile. The elevation gain remains fairly minimal as you cross numerous streams and cascades as well as dozens of creekside cul-de-sacs, perfect for taking a break and clambering around on the river rocks. Beneath a thin veneer of dust, stands of pine and cedar are surrounded by endless stretches of blue huckleberry, something of a contrast to the forests on the other side of Snoqualmie Pass. Alternate between clearings, talus fields, and thick forest, passing the Hibox Mountain Trail (Hike 43) on the right at 2.1 miles.

Reach a bridged creek at 2.3 miles. Out of eyesight, but well within earshot, is a lovely, rushing waterfall some refer to as Hibox Falls tucked into the mountainside. Push onward and start climbing. The trail packs most of the

Find ways to keep cool before tackling the final steep stretch up to Rachel Lake.

elevation gain into the last push to the lake, skirting around boulders and occasionally piggy-backing on stream beds. As you get closer to the lake, the trail begins to splinter, creating a network of interwoven side paths branching off to picnic nooks and secluded campsites along the lakeshore. Arrive at Rachel Lake at 3.4 miles.

The lake is dominated by Rampart Ridge, which lives up to its name and rises like a granite wall along the western edge of the lake. While tenacious trees have found small footholds on the ridge, the shores of Rachel Lake are more exposed granite than greenery. Trails and boot paths lead around both sides of the lake; wander until you find the perfect spot to settle in and enjoy.

GOING FARTHER

Continue your hiking day by climbing Rampart Ridge to reach either Rampart Lakes (Hike 38) to the left or Lila Lake or Alta Mountain (Hike 42) to the right. Or if you're looking for something closer to a scramble, consider adding a climb to the top of Hibox Mountain (Hike 43).

42 ALTA MOUNTAIN AND LILA LAKE

DISTANCE: 11.2 miles
ELEVATION GAIN: 4000 feet in; 200 feet out
HIGH POINT: 6151 feet
DIFFICULTY: Hard
HIKING TIME: 6 to 8 hours
BEST SEASON: Early summer to early fall

TRAIL TRAFFIC: Moderate to heavy foot traffic to Rachel Lake; light foot traffic beyond
PERMIT: Northwest Forest Pass
MAPS: USGS Chikamin Peak; Green Trails Snoqualmie Pass No. 207
TRAILHEAD GPS: 47.40084°N, 121.2836°W

GETTING THERE: Take I-90 to Stampede Pass, Exit 62. Eastbound turn left under the freeway; westbound turn right onto unsigned Kachess Lake Road (Forest Road 49), following signs pointing toward Lake Kachess. Drive 5 miles to the Lake Kachess Campground, and turn left onto Box Canyon Road (FR 4930). Continue for 4 miles and turn left into the Rachel Lake Trailhead parking area. Privy available.

Ascend to the heights of Alta Mountain for commanding views over a vast panorama of mountaintops, lakes, volcanoes, and river valleys. Spend the night beside petite Lake Lila, perched atop Rampart Ridge on a granite shelf overlooking Box Canyon and Rachel Lake. This alpine wonderland is sure to delight even the most jaded hiker.

From the trailhead, Rachel Lake Trail #1313 begins gently, following Box Canyon Creek into the valley and soon entering the Alpine Lakes Wilderness at 0.4 mile. Alternate roaming through wide wildflower meadows and open talus fields with short jaunts beneath canopies of pine, cedar, and fir. Crane your head to take in exposed Box Ridge jutting toward the sky above the trail. Huckleberries, common along the route in season, are a treat on the dusty trail. Streams and creeklets cut across the trail, rushing down to meet Box Canyon Creek, and plentiful pullouts along the water make for perfect rest stops or picnic areas. Younger hikers will enjoy splashing in water and clambering around on river rocks.

At 2.1 miles pass the unsigned junction with the Hibox Mountain Trail (Hike 43) and,

Lila Lake lies on a wide shelf below the trail with Hibox Mountain (Hike 43) dominating the skyline.

at 2.3 miles, reach a bridged creek. Out of eyesight but well within earshot is a lovely, rushing waterfall some refer to as Hibox Falls. As you push farther to the end of the valley, the trail becomes rougher and steeper, climbing through boulder fields and following rocky stream beds as it ascends the headwall. Take

your time and navigate with care, as sections of loose trail bed make it easy to lose your footing.

As you approach Rachel Lake, numerous side paths branch off the main trail and lead to campsites and lakeside access. Explore the shores and shimmering waters of Rachel Lake before continuing the climb up to the top of Rampart

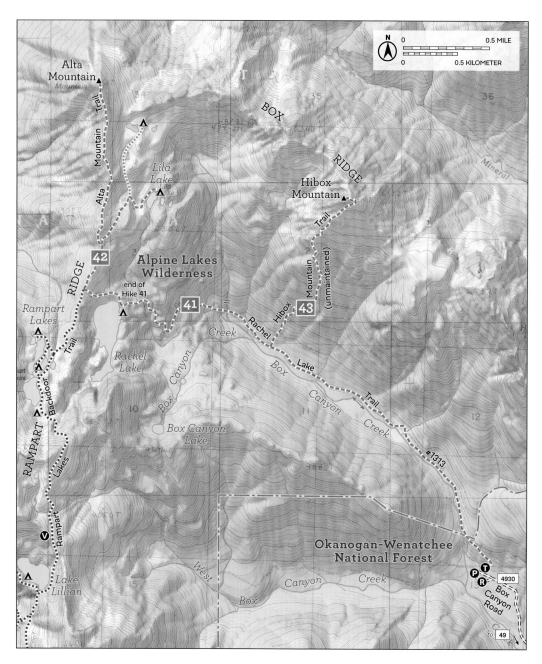

Ridge. When you're ready, find the "One Mile to Rampart Lakes" sign at 3.4 miles, which marks the main trail up the ridge toward Alta's summit.

As you climb, pause on the exposed cliffs to take in Rachel Lake, quietly nestled against Rampart Ridge, with Box Canyon stretching out into the distance. The short-but-steep 0.2-mile climb ends at a saddle, meeting up with the trail on Rampart Ridge, which spans the entire length of the ridge from Rampart Lakes up to the top of Alta Mountain. To reach Alta Mountain, veer to the right through brush and meadows to another intersection where the trail splits at 3.9 miles. To the left, the trail continues along the ridge up to Alta's summit, but first head down to the right out to Lila Lake—for a quick visit to a lovely alpine lake or to drop your pack if you're planning to spend the night.

The trail to Lila Lake drops down to a rocky shelf dotted with meadows and soon reaches a shallow tarn. The trail splits here, with the main route dropping 0.6 mile down to Lila Lake, which offers lovely campsites set against a rugged alpine landscape complete with views of Hibox Mountain and Box Canyon. Alternatively, hikers can continue north past the tarn for an optional 0.5 mile up to a set of unnamed lakes at the rubble-strewn base of Alta Mountain. After you've had your fill of exploring, head back up to the main trail and press on to the summit.

The last 1.1-mile stretch up Alta is fairly well defined at lower elevations, but as you trudge up the steep slope, the path gets muddled on exposed rock. False summits abound; time and again you will attain a ledge, only to find more mountain to climb. A gigantic cairn signals the real summit—and it is breathtaking. The landscape unfolds in all directions. Alaska and Lila Lakes are below to either side. The Rampart Lakes shimmer in the distance to the south, just below Mount Margaret. To the east the distinctive profile of Hibox Mountain grabs your attention. To the north Chikamin Peak, Four Brothers, and Mount Thompson are visible. As your eyes sweep west, Alaska Mountain stands above Alaska Lake (Hike 37), and Red Mountain peeks up over Kendall Peak. Snoqualmie Mountain is in the distance, with Denny Mountain just to the south. Unpack your lunch and see how many more mountaintops you can pick out.

GOING FARTHER
A visit to Rampart Lakes (Hike 38) is a fine addition to this adventure, though more likely for those spending the night at Lila Lake. Simply retrace your steps to the Rachel Lake Trail junction and continue to follow the ridge a few tenths of a mile to Rampart Lakes.

HISTORY
Back around the mid-1800s, Box Canyon was surveyed in an effort to find a suitable mountain pass through the Cascades. It is possible that some trails in the area may have been cut during these early explorations, but the trail to Rachel Lake was more likely blazed by adventurous fishermen who followed Box Creek looking for the next fishing hole. Over the years, the trail was improved and the fishing expanded by volunteers stocking a few of the Rampart Lakes. While the lakes brought in fishermen, Alta Mountain drew hikers hungry to bag another peak. The Mountaineers have records of a summit of the mountain as far back as 1902, and they maintained a summit register from 1929 to 1989 and from 1998 to 2000.

43 HIBOX MOUNTAIN

DISTANCE: 7.0 miles
ELEVATION GAIN: 3800 feet
HIGH POINT: 6547 feet
DIFFICULTY: Hard
HIKING TIME: 5 to 7 hours
BEST SEASON: Early summer to early fall
PERMIT: Northwest Forest Pass

TRAIL TRAFFIC: Moderate foot traffic to Hibox Mountain Trail; light foot traffic to Hibox Summit
MAPS: USGS Chikamin Peak; Green Trails Snoqualmie Pass No. 207
TRAILHEAD GPS: 47.40084°N, 121.2836°W
NOTE: The Hibox Mountain Trail is unmaintained, though volunteers often brush it out.

Looking north from Hibox Mountain to a dramatic landscape that includes Park Lakes and Chimney Rock

GETTING THERE: Take I-90 to Stampede Pass, Exit 62. Eastbound turn left under the freeway; westbound turn right onto unsigned Kachess Lake Road (Forest Road 49), following signs pointing toward Lake Kachess. Drive 5 miles to the Lake Kachess Campground, and turn left onto Box Canyon Road (FR 4930). Continue for 4 miles and turn left into the Rachel Lake Trailhead parking area. Privy available.

Hibox Mountain's massive, square-cut summit block draws the eye from the Rachel Lake Trail and from Rampart Ridge, just begging to be climbed. Perhaps for that reason, a scramble route leads up to this playground of boulders and talus. Climbing up to Hibox will challenge some hikers and is not recommend for everyone. Once you leave the Rachel Lake Trail, the trail is steep, rough, and easy to lose in the talus fields. On the upside, this route does not get a lot of traffic. If you've already explored Rampart Ridge and are hungry for more, Hibox is the perfect fit, as long as you're comfortable with a little routefinding and scrambling.

From the trailhead, follow the Rachel Lake Trail #1313 alongside Box Canyon Creek through small stands of pine and lush slide zones filled with bracken fern and salmonberry. The trail is relatively flat, with only small ups and downs and an occasional log to hop over. The creek also provides a couple of open areas that make for great rest stops. Cross into the Alpine Lakes Wilderness at 0.4 mile and as you progress, keep an eye out for the rocky finger of Hibox on the ridge. Your first glimpse is in a large slide area, and you get another at a second clearing at about 2.0 miles. Just after you cross the second clearing, at 2.1 miles, look in the trees for an unmarked but obvious trail heading toward the mountain.

From here, there is only one direction: up. Switchback up the shoulders of the ridge, for 1.4 miles, following a rough and narrow trail through the trees toward the summit block. Eventually the trees recede, replaced by talus and scree as the route veers to the right, under the cliffs that make up the mountaintop. Some sections of the trail are loose rock here, so tread carefully as you climb up to the ridgeline.

The final challenge is a short scramble to the top where 360-degree views await. From those heights you can easily pick out nearby Alta Mountain (Hike 42), Three Queens, and the Park Lakes to the north. Beyond find Chikamin Peak, Lemah Mountain, Chimney Rock, and Summit Chief Mountain. On a good day Glacier Peak makes an appearance. Turn east to find Mount Hinman, Mount Daniel, and Mount Stuart. To the south are Rampart Ridge (Hike 38) and Mount Rainier. Keep turning west to pick out Mount Thompson from among the Snoqualmie peaks. Settle in and enjoy the view from this hard-won vista.

GOING FARTHER

Those thirsty for more trail time can also visit Rachel Lake (Hike 41) by returning to the junction with the Rachel Lake Trail and continuing onward, adding 2.6 miles to the hike.

HISTORY

Back before Washington was a state, it was part of the Oregon Territory, and settlers carved out their lands on either side of the Washington Cascades. By 1853, Washington's population had grown enough that the decision was made to break away and create a separate Washington Territory. Almost immediately, the new government tackled the need to connect the eastern and western portions of the fledgling territory. Surveyors and explorers set about searching for suitable passage through the Cascades, eventually finding many routes, including Snoqualmie Pass. Box Canyon, named for the way Rampart Ridge and Keechelus Ridge "box" you in as you try to cross the Cascades, was explored during this time. Hibox (sometimes called "High Box") is the high point on Box Ridge, the inspiration for its name.

44 THORP MOUNTAIN

DISTANCE: 6.4 miles
ELEVATION GAIN: 2300 feet
HIGH POINT: 5854 feet
DIFFICULTY: Hard
HIKING TIME: 5 to 7 hours
BEST SEASON: Late spring to late fall
TRAIL TRAFFIC: Light foot traffic

PERMIT: None
MAPS: USGS Kachess Lake; Green Trails Kachess Lake No. 208
TRAILHEAD GPS: 47.3731°N, 121.1571°W
NOTE: Use caution fording Thorp Creek near the trailhead during spring melt.

GETTING THERE: Take I-90 to Roslyn, Exit 80. Eastbound turn left; westbound turn right, following Bullfrog Road 2.8 miles to the traffic circle junction with State Route 903. Follow SR 903 toward Roslyn for 13.2 miles through the town and along Cle Elum Lake to French Cabin Road (Forest Road 4308), just beyond the Cle Elum River Campground. Turn left onto FR 4308 and follow it a little over 3 miles to a signed intersection. Head right down FR 4312 for 1.5 miles to a gated spur veering to the right only, and find a spot to park here.

While a few miles shy of the wilderness boundary, Thorp Mountain Lookout offers a unique vantage point for surveying the Alpine Lakes Wilderness. The sweeping, panoramic views are so good that the US Geological Survey used it as a survey point in 1958; benchmarks from the survey are easy to spot from the lookout. Most hikers approach Thorp Mountain from the Knox Creek Trailhead, which is both shorter and easier than the Thorp Creek Trail, but this route offers a better chance of solitude. This longer, more difficult alternate approach is complicated by the absence of a bridge over Thorp Creek near the trailhead. The creek can be fast-flowing and ice-cold during the spring thaw—cross with caution.

Begin by following the spur road down to Thorp Creek and fording. Once across, start down the converted logging road, passing the junction with the Little Joe Lake Trail #1330.1 and continuing to follow the road as it parallels the creek through recovering clear-cuts. Slide alders and huckleberries line the trail, rising above the grass and brush that cannot quite disguise acres of bleached snags and stumps.

Continue on the gravel road to the 0.4-mile mark, where the Thorp Creek Trail #1316 begins, trading road for trail and quickly transitioning from mild switchbacks to steeper grades. As you climb, younger firs and pines eventually appear, making this area more attractive to

wildlife—don't be surprised if you stumble upon some elk and deer on your way up.

At 2.1 miles reach the junction with the Thorp Lake Trail #1316.1 to the left, which leads a short 0.25 mile down to Thorp Lake. Continue straight ahead to finish the rocky climb up to the lookout.

In another 0.3 mile, reach the junction with the Kachess Ridge Trail #1315, where the Thorp Creek Trail ends. Keep left and continue climbing and enjoying increasingly better views for another 0.5 mile.

Find the last trail junction at the 2.9-mile mark. Here, the short Thorp Mountain Trail #1315.2 spur leads up to the lookout. This last

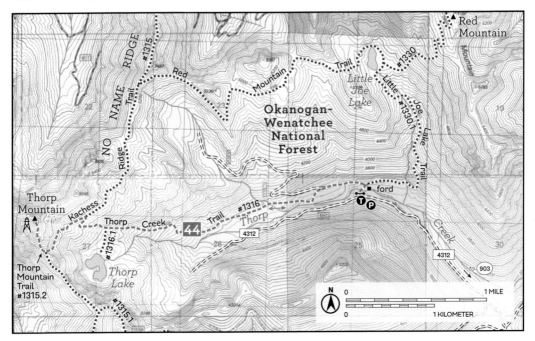

Thorp Mountain Lookout against a bluebird sky

stretch climbs steeply, a thin path scratched between the rocks, but any difficulties are soon forgotten as the expansive vistas come into view and command your full attention.

On a good day, Mount Rainier rises above the shimmering blue of Kachess Lake. Nearby Red Mountain is easy to pick out to the northeast. Below, Thorp Lake nestles among the trees. And beyond, the horizon is filled with hundreds of snow-topped peaks and the forests of the Alpine Lakes Wilderness. Climb onto the decks of the lookout to find your new favorite view.

While this approach is the hard way to reach this vista, the hike more than makes up for its challenges with a healthy dose of solitude—you're unlikely to meet too many fellow travelers willing to take on this lonely stretch of trail that climbs more than 2000 feet in a little over 3.0 miles. Come prepared for a workout!

GOING FARTHER

The short side trip down to Thorp Lake adds only 0.5 mile to the hike, while more adventurous hikers can climb up to Little Joe Lake via Little Joe Lake Trail #1330.1. It's a steep, somewhat brushy 1.5 miles to the lake and the Red Mountain Trail #1330. Those willing to endure some bushwhacking can make something of a loop by following the Kachess Ridge Trail #1315 north from the Thorp Creek Trail junction and traversing No Name Ridge for 1.2 miles to reach the Red Mountain Trail. Follow this trail down toward Little Joe Lake, navigating hard-to-follow brushy sections to reach the lake and the junction with Little Joe Lake Trail #1330.1. Follow this spur back to the Thorp Creek Trail to close the loop.

HISTORY

Like most things that bear the name Thorp, Thorp Mountain is named for Fielden Mortimer Thorp, a famed Yakima Valley pioneer who is often credited as being the first settler in that area, in 1860. The lookout was built between 1930 and 1931, a standard gabled L-4 tower cabin, 14 feet by 14 feet. Around the same time, lookouts were built on nearby Red Mountain and Jolly Mountain, though only the one on Thorp survives today. Extensive restoration of the lookout cabin was done in 2007 and 2008 to continue its legacy.

45 MINERAL CREEK

DISTANCE: 8.6 miles
ELEVATION GAIN: 2500 feet
HIGH POINT: 4740 feet
DIFFICULTY: Hard
HIKING TIME: 6 to 8 hours
BEST SEASON: Early summer to late fall
TRAIL TRAFFIC: Light to moderate foot traffic
PERMIT: Northwest Forest Pass

MAPS: USGS Polallie Ridge, USGS Chikamin Peak; Green Trails Kachess Lake No. 208, Green Trails Snoqualmie Pass No. 207
TRAILHEAD GPS: 47.4176°N, 121.2381°W
NOTES: Two creek crossings may require fording when waters are high. Some sections are unmaintained and can be brushy in summer.

GETTING THERE: Take I-90 to Roslyn, Exit 80. Eastbound turn left; westbound turn right, following Bullfrog Road 2.8 miles to the traffic circle junction with State Route 903. Follow SR 903 toward Roslyn for 15.5 miles through Roslyn and along Cle Elum Lake to reach the Cooper River Road (signed Forest Road 4600). Turn left onto the unpaved road and continue about 4.7 miles to the Cooper Lake turnoff. Stay on FR 46 and drive another 4.7 miles over Cooper Pass to the bottom of the valley and the signed trailhead.

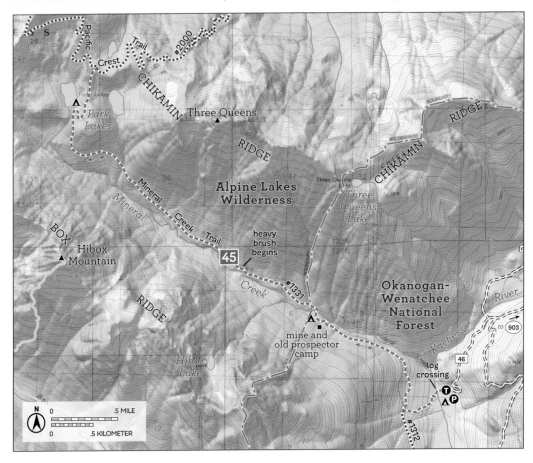

Hike down the century-old mining road that runs along the bottom of Mineral Creek's deep basin on your way to the gorgeous alpine Park Lakes. The rugged landscape and rocky precipices of Three Queens and Box Ridge offer a charming counterpoint to the creek fords and encroaching brush that give this trail a rough reputation. That reputation is partially deserved, but it also means you're likely to get a big slice of wilderness all to yourself.

From the trailhead, the Mineral Creek Trail #1331 wastes no time presenting you with its first challenge: a river ford. Logs spanning the Kachess River are usually easy to find, but when they are not, it's a short wade to the other side. Rejoin the trail and climb up the mountainside for 0.4 mile to the junction with the Little Kachess Trail #1312 to the left. Keep right on the Mineral Creek Trail, heading north and traversing into Mineral Creek Basin. Along these early stretches, the trail still hints that it was once a road, cutting a fairly gentle path above Mineral Creek.

Soon the granite points of Hibox Mountain and Three Queens appear, beckoning you deeper into the wilderness. At 1.6 miles, the trail reaches Mineral Creek. Here the curious can spend a little time investigating a nearby mine shaft at what remains of an old mining mill. This is also a good turnaround point for younger hikers.

The trail crosses Mineral Creek, which may require another dip in the water if no easy stepping stones are available. Enter the Alpine Lakes Wilderness shortly afterward and continue a somewhat leisurely stroll to 2.5 miles, where the truly brushy portion of the trail begins. Slide alder, thimbleberry, and bracken fern crowd the trail and slow your progress for the next mile. Sometimes volunteers brush this section out, but more often than not you'll need to push your way through the undergrowth. The trail remains easy to follow beneath the greenery; just take your time.

Soon reach the end of the basin, crossing yet another creek at 3.5 miles. Here the trail angles steeply uphill, leaving the brushy basin for mossy old-growth forest. Continue slogging up.

At 4.3 miles you reach Upper Park Lake, a gem set in the meadows of the Park Lakes Basin.

From the lakeshore the exposed granite of Peak 6300 dominates the landscape. Anchoring one end of Chikamin Ridge, it rises dramatically above the water. Look closely and you're likely to pick out hikers traversing the lower slopes following the Pacific Crest Trail #2000 (PCT) up to the pass. Follow one of the many boot paths that lead around the lake to find a slice of serenity.

GOING FARTHER

Another 0.5 mile farther, the Mineral Creek Trail connects with the PCT, 4.8 miles from the trailhead. Heading right on the PCT leads to an overlook of Lower Park Lake, past a number of unnamed tarns, and up to a windswept prominence above Spectacle Lake. The view here is spectacular, encompassing a number of lakes, waterfalls, and snowy mountaintops. The long drop down to Spectacle Lake from here is beyond the reach of most day hikers. Alternatively, head left on the PCT from the Mineral Creek Trail junction and climb up to the pass for more sprawling vistas filled with cliffs and peaks as well as Alaska Lake (Hike 37) and Joe Lake.

HISTORY

As its name suggests, Mineral Creek and the surrounding area have a long mining history. Prospecting began around 1900, but the major mining activity focused on copper extraction beginning in 1917. Back then Three Queens was known as "Mineral Mountain," a name it kept until most of the mining ceased.

The Mineral Creek Copper Company operated from 1917 to 1926, largely under the management of Charles and Ernest Durrwachter. By 1920 the first mill was operating near the major Copper Queen and Liberty Lode prospects. By this time, a road was completed to haul out the twenty-five tons of ore the mill could process in

Big boulders in Mineral Creek are perfect perches for soaking your feet on a hot summer day.

a day. At its height, the Durrwachters' total operations included more than 1000 feet of tunnels bored more than 450 feet into the ridges on both sides of Mineral Creek. A hydropowered rod mill, multiple Wilfley tables, and a concentrator all supported the mining effort.

By 1930, mining activity began to wane, and in 1951 the property was bought by the Cascade Gold Mining and Milling Company. Mining was largely abandoned by the 1960s, and the road, adits, and remaining buildings were left to nature.

46 PETE LAKE

DISTANCE: 8.2 miles
ELEVATION GAIN: 200 feet
HIGH POINT: 3000 feet
DIFFICULTY: Easy
HIKING TIME: 4 to 6 hours
BEST SEASON: Late spring to late fall

TRAIL TRAFFIC: Moderate foot and equestrian traffic; mountain bikes first 2 miles
PERMIT: Northwest Forest Pass
MAPS: USGS Polallie Ridge; Green Trails Kachess Lake No. 208
TRAILHEAD GPS: 47.4341°N, 121.1868°W

GETTING THERE: Take I-90 to Roslyn, Exit 80. Eastbound turn left; westbound turn right, following Bull-frog Road 2.8 miles to the traffic circle junction with State Route 903. Follow SR 903 toward Roslyn for 15.5 miles through Roslyn and along Cle Elum Lake to reach the Cooper River Road (signed Forest Road 4600). Turn left onto unpaved FR 46, crossing the bridge and continuing 4.7 miles to FR 4616. Turn right and continue 0.7 mile to a fork. Veer left onto spur FR 113 and continue 1 mile to the trailhead. Privy available.

Relatively flat with an easily accessed trailhead, the Pete Lake Trail is a popular day hike and often the first leg on a backpack out to Spectacle Lake or a longer foray along the Pacific Crest Trail. Approachable for hikers of all ages and skill levels, Pete Lake is perfect for an introduction to backpacking or a short jaunt through the woods. While there is a lot of traffic in the summer—from day hikers and backpackers to cyclists and pack animals—the shoulder seasons see far fewer feet, with the added bonus of abundant wildflowers or bright fall foliage, depending on the time of year.

From the trailhead, follow the Pete Lake Trail #1323 along the rushing Cooper River through a young forest of spruce, hemlock, and pine. Pass the junction with the Tired Creek Trail #1317 at 1.2 miles and press onward down the dusty trail.

At 2.2 miles the Pete Lake Tie Trail #1323.1 branches off to the right. The trail sign here points toward "Road No. 235," now shown as FR 4616 on modern maps. The short 0.5-mile Tie Trail is primarily used by mountain bikers to make a loop by cutting up to FR 4616 and following it back to the trailhead.

When you're ready, continue on the Pete Lake Trail and pick your way across a number of creeks and streams, occasionally emerging from the trees to cross pika-filled talus fields. In 0.3 mile cross into the Alpine Lakes Wilderness and older forest as you continue down the wide and well-trodden trail. Just before you reach the lake, pass the Waptus Pass Trail #1329 peeling off to the right. Keep left to reach the headwaters of the Cooper River and the shore of Pete Lake at 4.1 miles. From here, the trail continues around the lake, passing numerous shoreline campsites, each offering a slightly different expanse of water to enjoy.

The best views are the easiest to reach and can be found on the rocky beach near the lake's outlet. From here you can take in the full length of the lake with an imposing wall of mountains rising above the water. The sharp point of Chikamin Peak anchors the southern end of the wall, followed by Lemah Mountain, then the flanks of Chimney Rock. Directly south of the lake, the main show for most of the campsites is the more demure Island Mountain. Find a quiet spot to break out a snack and linger around this pristine alpine lake.

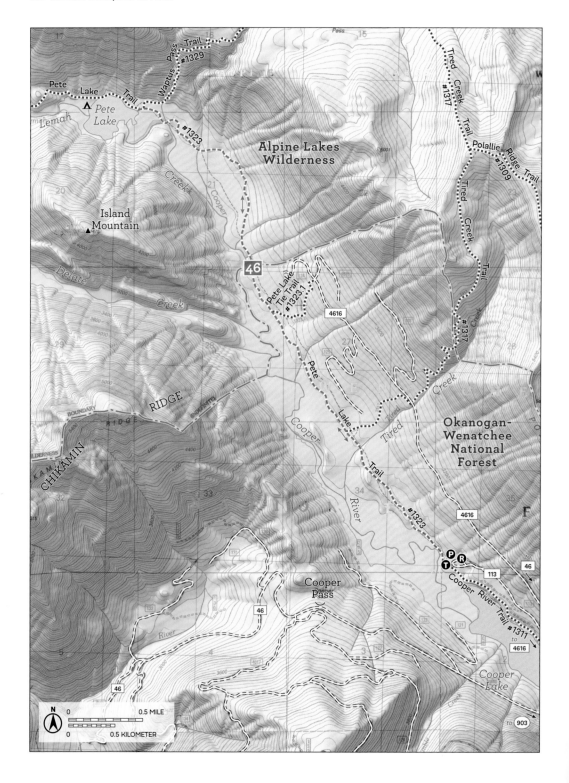

Lemah Mountain rises above still-as-glass Pete Lake.

GOING FARTHER

The Waptus Pass Trail offers a steep climb up to meadowy parklands before plunging back down to Waptus Lake (Hike 48). For those looking for more trail time, the Pete Lake Trail continues to hug the lakeshore before turning uphill and climbing through forest for 1.3 miles to the Lemah Meadow Trail #1232.2, which connects to the Pacific Crest Trail. Once there, hikers can push onward and upward to Spectacle Lake.

HISTORY

Pete Lake traces its name back to a US Forest Service packhorse that spent many a day plodding alongside the Cooper River, probably sometime around 1910. Until 1909, maps of the area leave the lake unnamed; only in 1916 does "Pete Lake" begin to appear. Before the 1960s, Pete Lake was a more remote backpacking destination, accessed via the Cooper River Trail #1311 that began at the Salmon La Sac Trailhead. Sometime in the mid-1960s the Forest Service finished building a road out to Cooper Lake, largely following the Cooper River Trail route. Today the Cooper River Trail still exists, and sharp-eyed travelers will note the trail signs found along FR 4616.

47 DIAMOND LAKE VIA POLALLIE RIDGE

DISTANCE: 8.0 miles
ELEVATION GAIN: 2700 feet
HIGH POINT: 5100 feet
DIFFICULTY: Moderate
HIKING TIME: 4 to 6 hours
BEST SEASON: Late spring to late fall

TRAIL TRAFFIC: Moderate to heavy foot traffic
PERMIT: Northwest Forest Pass
MAPS: USGS Davis Peak, USGS Polallie Ridge;
Green Trails Kachess Lake No. 208
TRAILHEAD GPS: 47.4096°N, 121.1067°W

GETTING THERE: Take I-90 to Roslyn, Exit 80. Eastbound turn left; westbound turn right, following Bullfrog Road 2.8 miles to the traffic circle junction with State Route 903. Follow SR 903 toward Roslyn for 16.6 miles through the town and along Cle Elum Lake to an intersection just beyond the Salmon La Sac guard station. Veer left across the bridge on Forest Road 4316 toward the Salmon La Sac Campground. Continue past the campground, keeping right on FR 4316-111 to the end of the road for the Salmon La Sac Trailhead. Privy available.

Climb up the flanks of this ridgeline along an old fire lookout access trail for sweeping views and a pretty alpine lake and—if you opt for the Going Farther option—the opportunity to visit a former lookout site.

From the trailhead, briefly follow the Cooper River Trail #1311 alongside the Cooper River for 0.1 mile to the junction with the Polallie Ridge Trail #1309. Head right, away from the river and almost immediately to the next junction with the Waptus River Trail #1310 (Hike 48). Here, stay left to begin your ascent up Polallie Ridge, following the rocky trail as it climbs through stands of pine and fir.

While some sections are steeper than others, the route is almost entirely an uphill battle. As you work your way along the ridge, the trees break for small meadows or talus fields that provide brief glimpses into the surrounding landscape. These are just hints of what is to come, as the first real views do not appear until you cross into the Alpine Lakes Wilderness at 2.8 miles. Here the trail briefly levels out and the trees thin enough to reveal Mount Daniel, Cone Mountain, Sasse Mountain, Jolly Mountain, and Hex Mountain, as well as the Waptus River Valley below.

Beyond the views, the trail returns to the trees and continues to climb another mile before dropping down to Diamond Lake at 4.0 miles. The tree-lined shore offers several campsites, as well as a number of spots to settle in and enjoy the stillness of this pretty alpine lake.

Less popular than other nearby trails, Polallie Ridge is a good alternative for those seeking relative solitude and a challenge. During the high summer, some hikers will want to avoid this steep, hot climb up a loose and rocky trail, but it's delightful when pocket meadows brim with wildflowers in late spring and early summer. For many, the long views are incentive enough to tackle this hike any time of year.

GOING FARTHER

Those looking for a longer day and more views can continue past Diamond Lake another 3.0 miles to the Polallie Mountain Lookout site.

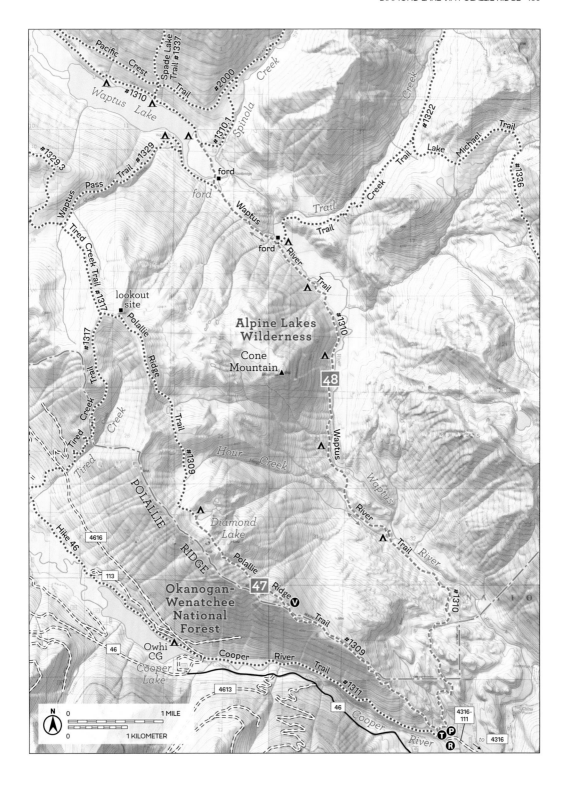

Diamond Lake's wooded shores are mirrored in its still waters.

HISTORY

Polallie means "dust" or "fine powder" in Chinook Jargon, and like so many of the trails in this area, the trail tends to be fairly dusty in high summer. Around 1921, a fire lookout cabin was built on the high point of Polallie Mountain. In 1936 the cabin was replaced by a 25-foot-tall tower that was in use only until 1947, when the site was abandoned. Faint traces of the former lookout remain today. Lookouts would have used the Polallie Ridge Trail to access the site and carry in supplies.

48 WAPTUS LAKE

DISTANCE: 16.9 miles
ELEVATION GAIN: 900 feet in; 300 feet out
HIGH POINT: 3100 feet
DIFFICULTY: Easy
HIKING TIME: Overnight
BEST SEASON: Early spring to late fall
PERMIT: Northwest Forest Pass

TRAIL TRAFFIC: Moderate to heavy foot traffic; equestrian traffic common
MAPS: USGS Davis Peak, USGS Polallie Ridge; Green Trails Kachess Lake No. 208
TRAILHEAD GPS: 47.4096°N, 121.1067°W
NOTE: This hike requires fording the Waptus River.

GETTING THERE: Take I-90 to Roslyn, Exit 80. Eastbound turn left; westbound turn right, following Bull-frog Road 2.8 miles to the traffic circle junction with State Route 903. Follow SR 903 toward Roslyn for 16.6 miles through the town and along Cle Elum Lake to an intersection just beyond the Salmon La Sac guard station. Veer left across the bridge on Forest Road 4316 toward the Salmon La Sac Campground. Continue past the campground, keeping right on FR 4316-111 to the end of the road for the Salmon La Sac Trailhead. Privy available.

Waptus Lake might be the quintessential Alpine Lakes Wilderness hike, complete with a big alpine lake, stunning landscape, and plenty of nearby destinations to explore. With easy trail-head access and minimal elevation to tackle, this classic hike has been popular with backpackers and horse campers for decades.

Situated on the banks of the Cooper River, the Salmon La Sac Trailhead is popular with campers staying at the Salmon La Sac Campground, who come here to enjoy the river on a hot day.

From here, begin along the Cooper River Trail #1311, passing a busy swimming hole on your way to the junction with the Polallie Ridge Trail #1309 at 0.1 mile. Head right, away from the river, and just beyond arrive at the next junction where the Waptus River Trail #1310 branches off to the right. Take this wide, tree-lined trail as it gently rises, leaving the river sounds behind and drawing you closer to the Alpine Lakes Wilderness.

Reach the wilderness boundary at 1.1 miles, where the trail becomes a bit more interesting as it crosses footbridges and streams, passes small meadows and tarns, and climbs rocky hillocks before reaching the edge of the 2006 Polallie Ridge Fire. The burn is extensive, though grass and wildflowers have returned to add some color to the sun-bleached trees that remain. With few trees to obscure your view, the skyline is largely dominated by the slopes of Davis Peak (Hike 51), parts of which were also burned in 2006. After working your way through the burn, return to the shelter of the pines and push onward to reach the Waptus River, your merry companion for most of the rest of the hike.

At 3.1 miles, the trail reaches the bridgeless Hour Creek, complete with campsite. Hour Creek can make for a wet crossing during the spring melt, though usually the water is low enough that you can work your way across without too much trouble. Around here, you start to catch glimpses of the exposed heights of Cone Mountain through gaps in the canopy.

As you progress, you climb across the lowest shoulders of the mountain and begin to swing away from the Waptus River. Push onward, past a variety of wildflowers including phlox and columbine, monkshood and tiger lily. Pass campsites at 4.4 miles, 5.1 miles, and 6.3 miles, each offering a quiet place to drop your pack and take a moment to enjoy the trees. Eventually, at the 6.9-mile mark, rejoin the river and reach the junction with the Trail Creek Trail #1322 to the right. This trail leads a short way down to the riverside if you need access to the water, but you'll need to ford the river to continue on this trail or reach the campsites, both of which are on the other side.

Press down the trail for nearly a mile to reach the junction with the Waptus Pass Trail #1329 at 7.8 miles. Here, signs state that the bridge across the Waptus River is out; it washed away in a flood in 2006 (it was a busy year!). Without a bridge, hikers and equestrians alike must now use the horse ford about 0.5 mile from the lake. Head left down the Waptus Pass Trail to the well-signed Waptus Horse Ford Trail #1329.1, taking it a short distance to the river. While there is some seasonal variation, the ford typically requires a 75-foot wade across swift-running, very cold water that is usually about 2 feet deep. If you wear waterproof footwear and

Bears Breast Mountain rises above the north end of Waptus Lake.

bring poles to help you navigate the river rocks, crossing should not pose much difficulty.

Once across, continue down the dusty trail to reconnect with the Waptus River Trail and reach the first campsites at the end of the lake at 8.4 miles from the trailhead. Head to the lakeshore to take in the full length of one of the largest lakes in the Alpine Lakes Wilderness. Water laps against tree-lined shores, while snowcapped Summit Chief Mountain to the west and more sharply pointed Bears Breast Mountain to the east rise like two sentinels guarding the wilderness beyond.

If you're spending the night, continue on the main trail to the far end of the lake for some excellent campsites, including one on an island and another on a secluded bluff above the lake. Both are just beyond the last horse camp before reaching the Pacific Crest Trail #2000 (PCT) at Spade Creek.

GOING FARTHER

Many lake-filled glacial troughs are hidden between the ridges above Waptus Lake, so it's no surprise that plenty of nearby trails have been built to access them, including the PCT. Destinations such as Lake Ivanhoe (Hike 50) and Spade and Venus Lakes (Hike 49) are both good day hikes if you're base camping at Waptus.

Backpackers can reach Deep Lake (Hike 55) and Spinola Meadows via the Spinola Creek Trail #1310.1 and the PCT, passing the junction for Lake Vicente along the way.

Pete Lake (Hike 46) can be reached either via the PCT or by backtracking, refording the Waptus River, and following the Waptus Pass Trail to Pete Lake while trekking past the trail to Escondido Lake along the way.

HISTORY

Waptus Lake's name comes from the Sahaptin word *wáptas*, meaning "feather." The language was spoken by American Indian tribes who lived along the Columbia River and its tributaries in southern Washington and northern Oregon. A lake as large and accessible as Waptus naturally attracted the attention of the tribes, and it was well known enough that oral traditions make mention of mythical creatures that dwelled in its waters.

More recently, in October 1968, this hike marked the first meeting of a group of outdoor enthusiasts and conservationists who eventually formed the Alpine Lakes Protection Society (ALPS) to spearhead the creation of the Alpine Lakes Wilderness. Since that time, the hike to the lake has continued to be popular with backpackers, though the lightning-sparked 2006 Polallie Ridge Fire radically altered a sizable stretch of the trail and consumed over 900 acres of forest.

49 SPADE AND VENUS LAKES

DISTANCE: 26.2 miles
ELEVATION GAIN: 3600 feet in; 300 feet out
HIGH POINT: 5700 feet
DIFFICULTY: Hard
HIKING TIME: 2 nights
BEST SEASON: Early summer to fall
PERMIT: Northwest Forest Pass
TRAIL TRAFFIC: Moderate foot traffic to Waptus Lake; light to Spade Lake
MAPS: USGS Davis Peak, USGS Polallie Ridge; Green Trails Kachess Lake No. 208
TRAILHEAD GPS: 47.4096°N, 121.1067°W
NOTE: Hike requires fording the Waptus River; see Hike 48 for details for first 16.9 miles

GETTING THERE: Take I-90 to Roslyn, Exit 80. Eastbound turn left; westbound turn right, following Bullfrog Road 2.8 miles to the traffic circle junction with State Route 903. Follow SR 903 toward Roslyn for 16.6 miles through the town and along Cle Elum Lake to an intersection just beyond the Salmon La Sac guard station. Veer left across the bridge on Forest Road 4316 toward the Salmon La Sac Campground. Continue past the campground, keeping right on FR 4316-111 to the end of the road for the Salmon La Sac Trailhead. Privy available.

This challenging backpack heads to a pair of rugged and remote alpine lakes nestled below the barren granite shoulders of Mount Daniel. They are tough to reach but offer the same dramatic vistas and lunar-like landscapes that the Enchantment Lakes are famous for—without the company. Spade Lake is a prime candidate for those looking to spend a night truly alone under the stars.

From the large camping area at the south end of Waptus Lake (see Hike 48), follow the Waptus River Trail #1310 north along the lakeshore for 0.6 mile to the junction with the Spade Lake Trail #1337. Turn right onto this trail and head uphill, following a creek up along a narrow trail through thick forest, crossing the Pacific Crest Trail #2000 (PCT) in 0.2 mile.

The trail steepens beyond the PCT, with breaks in the old-growth canopy offering ever-expanding views of Waptus Lake and the surrounding valley, soon followed by the top of Summit Chief Mountain and the jutting spire of Bears Breast Mountain. Press onward and upward until the switchbacks and near-constant climb give way around the 1.25-mile mark to a long traverse around the mountainside through meadowlands and smaller stands of hemlock and fir. During the spring, keep an eye out for fields of glacier lily and other wildflowers dotting the meadows. You're high enough here to catch your first glimpses of Mount Rainier and

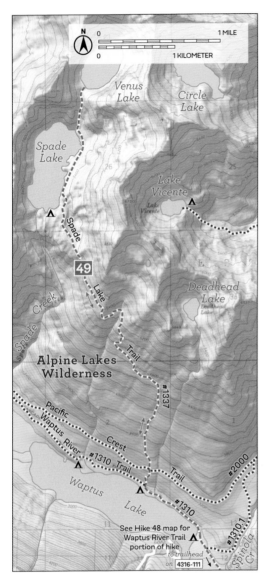

Enter the basin at the 3.6-mile mark, following a trail that soon splinters as you approach the lake, These boot paths lead off to various campsites and viewpoints, many of them worth exploring. Wander over the exposed washboard of granite slabs to find a suitable spot to take in Spade Lake's rocky shores. Make a beeline for the shore to find campsites in the bluffs, or circle around the east side of the lake, following boot paths to campsites deeper in the lake basin. Wherever you settle in, your eyes will be drawn to Mount Daniel's snowy crown dominating the horizon above the lake.

Venus Lake lies in a cirque another 1.1 miles up the trail. Your destination is easy to pick out from the shores of Spade Lake—Venus Lake lies just behind the lowest notch above the far end of the lake. Follow the sometimes-faint boot path around the east side of the water toward the stream that flows out of Venus and into Spade. There's no need to cross the stream; simply scramble up to the notch to reach steep-shored Venus Lake at 4.7 miles.

This is a challenging backpack. The approach to Waptus Lake (Hike 48) is long, the 2400-foot climb up to Spade Lake is grueling, and a visit to Venus Lake requires a scramble and some routefinding. Perhaps because the price of admission is so high, these lonely lakes feel special, like a little lost world. Whether you spend the night or just day trip up from Waptus Lake, allow extra time to linger—it is hard to pull yourself away.

GOING FARTHER

Spade and Venus are likely enough for a weekend of backpacking, but for those on a longer timeline, a day trip up to Lake Ivanhoe (Hike 50) or out to Deep Lake (Hike 55) are easy additions. There is a scramble route up to the summit of Mount Daniel from Venus Lake, but it is a very steep and challenging climb through talus and boulder fields to reach the top. If Mount Daniel is your goal, consider the easier Lynch Glacier approach from Peggys Pond (Hike 55) instead.

Mount Adams, which only get better as you continue to leave the trees behind.

Frequent rest stops are both much needed and easy to justify as you soon trade forest for talus and rugged bluffs. Continue your traverse, enjoying presiding views over the valley below. Within a mile of the lake, round a bend to find Spade Creek cascading down the steep cliffs below the lake, a sign that you'll soon reach the lake basin.

Find ample seating to take in the landscape on the large swaths of exposed granite surrounding Spade Lake.

HISTORY

Spade Lake gets its name from the vague resemblance its outline has to a garden spade, while Venus has no such apparent reasoning behind its name. Both of these lakes appear on maps dating back to 1902. The Mountaineers are widely credited with the first recorded ascent of Mount Daniel, in 1925, though it is likely they were following in the footsteps of previous climbers. While it generally appears as "Mt. Daniel" on USGS maps, The Mountaineers referred to it as "Mt. Daniels" for decades, and some maps label the mountain's five high points as "Daniels."

50 LAKE IVANHOE

DISTANCE: 28.6 miles
ELEVATION GAIN: 2600 feet in; 300 feet out
HIGH POINT: 4700 feet
DIFFICULTY: Moderate
HIKING TIME: 2 nights
BEST SEASON: Early summer to fall
TRAIL TRAFFIC: Moderate to heavy foot traffic, equestrian traffic common to Waptus Lake; light foot traffic to Lake Ivanhoe
PERMIT: Northwest Forest Pass

MAPS: USGS Davis Peak, USGS Polallie Ridge, USGS Big Snow Mountain; Green Trails Kachess Lake No. 208
TRAILHEAD GPS: 47.4096°N, 121.1067°W
NOTES: Hike requires fording the Waptus River; see Hike 48 for details for first 16.9 miles. The hike to Lake Ivanhoe requires at least two major creek fords; come prepared to wade through swiftly flowing water.

GETTING THERE: Take I-90 to Roslyn, Exit 80. Eastbound turn left; westbound turn right, following Bull-frog Road 2.8 miles to the traffic circle junction with State Route 903. Follow SR 903 toward Roslyn for 16.6 miles through the town and along Cle Elum Lake to an intersection just beyond the Salmon La Sac guard station. Veer left across the bridge on Forest Road 4316 toward the Salmon La Sac Campground. Continue past the campground, keeping right on FR 4316-111 to the end of the road for the Salmon La Sac Trailhead. Privy available.

Lake Ivanhoe sits quietly in the heart of the Alpine Lakes Wilderness, couched in a granite bowl between Summit Chief Mountain and Bears Breast Mountain. Accessed from either the Middle Fork Snoqualmie River Valley or the Waptus River Valley, it's beyond the reach of all but the most extreme day hikers. As a result, this remote alpine lake sees only a few visitors a year, making it an idyllic setting during the warm summer months.

From the large camping area at the south end of Waptus Lake (see Hike 48), follow the Waptus River Trail #1310 along the lakeshore, passing the junction with the Spade Lake Trail #1337

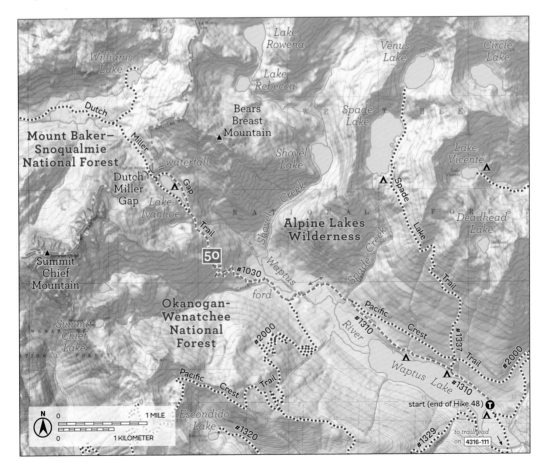

Nathan hops over a rushing creek near Lake Ivanhoe.

(Hike 49) after 0.6 mile. Push onward to the end of the Waptus River Trail, where it merges into the Pacific Crest Trail #2000 (PCT) at 2.1 miles.

Continue straight ahead over Spade Creek, enjoying the mixed forest and well-trodden PCT for a nearly a mile, and cross the Waptus River on a sturdy bridge before reaching the Dutch Miller Gap Trail #1362, signed for Lake Ivanhoe. Veer right onto the Dutch Miller Gap Trail. Cross a fairly flat area for 0.2 mile to reach Chief Creek, which will likely require fording. When waters are very low, it's possible to skip across on rocks, but most of the year expect to get your feet wet.

Beyond the creek the trail begins a long climb up forested slopes, switchbacking through sections of old growth interspersed with openings in the canopy that provide glimpses of the valley below. The views only get better as you climb and the trees recede. Eventually after 1.7 miles of climbing, the switchbacks end and you traverse around the mountainside and enter more-rugged territory, soon crossing an unnamed creek and its accompanying waterfall just shy of the lake.

From the falls, a short 0.1-mile climb brings you to Ivanhoe's outlet stream, rushing over what remains of the bridge that once provided easier access to the lake. The trail splits here and loops around the lake before heading up to Dutch Miller Gap. Keep right and in 0.4 mile reach a spectacular campsite on a bluff overlooking Lake Ivanhoe at 5.8 miles.

The setting is wild and pristine. Snow lingers late here, with white patches of ice clinging to the lakeshore most of the year, adding bright contrast to the lake's deep blue. Jagged cliffs rise high above either side of Ivanhoe, with rocky Dutch Miller Gap marking the low point in between. The rugged, steeply sloped shoreline can make access to the lakeshore a little challenging. Instead, continue around the lake a few thousand feet to reach a wide, stepped waterfall that makes for a perfect picnic spot.

GOING FARTHER

The Dutch Miller Gap Trail continues another 0.5 mile up and over Dutch Miller Gap before dropping into the Middle Fork Snoqualmie Valley and soon reaching Williams Lake (Hike 93).

HISTORY

Sometimes called Summit Lake, Lake Ivanhoe is named for Sir Walter Scott's Wilfred of Ivanhoe, the central character in *Ivanhoe*. Nearby Lake Rebecca and Lake Rowena, situated to the northeast on the other side of Bears Breast Mountain, are named for the two women Ivanhoe was torn between.

While Dutch Miller Gap was named for Andrew "Dutch" Miller, who discovered copper at La Bohn Gap in 1896, the miner probably did not make much use of his namesake gap to access his claims. Instead, foot traffic over Dutch Miller Gap was heaviest when it was one of the primary Cascade Crest Trail routes between the Middle Fork Snoqualmie and Snoqualmie Pass. When the Kendall Katwalk (Hike 34) opened in the late 1970s, hikers shifted to the new PCT route, leaving Lake Ivanhoe to become something of a backwater.

51 DAVIS PEAK

DISTANCE: 10.0 miles
ELEVATION GAIN: 4000 feet
HIGH POINT: 6426 feet
DIFFICULTY: Hard
HIKING TIME: 6 to 8 hours
BEST SEASON: Late spring to early fall

TRAIL TRAFFIC: Moderate foot traffic
PERMIT: Northwest Forest Pass
MAPS: USGS Davis Peak; Green Trails Kachess Lake No. 208
TRAILHEAD GPS: 47.41873°N, 121.0846°W

GETTING THERE: Take I-90 to Roslyn, Exit 80. Eastbound turn left; westbound turn right, following Bullfrog Road 2.8 miles to the traffic circle junction with State Route 903. Follow SR 903 toward Roslyn for 16.6 miles through the town and along Cle Elum Lake to just beyond the Salmon La Sac guard station, where the road splits. Keep right, continuing toward Tucquala Lake along Forest Road 4330 (aka Fish Lake Road or Cle Elum Valley Road) on dirt and gravel for 1.6 miles to the Paris Creek Trailhead. Park here if your car can't handle slightly rough gravel roads, and hike 0.25 mile to the trailhead; if your vehicle can handle the road, take FR 134 to the lower parking area and trailhead.

This is a fantastic hike with big summit views and a healthy dose of solitude, though the steep grade, tight switchbacks, and sun exposure can pose a challenge. Be prepared to log some extra trail hours working your way up to the summit of Davis Peak and taking your time on the descent. Though most of this hike lies outside the Alpine Lakes Wilderness, the trail ends at a windswept viewpoint just inside the wilderness boundary. From this rocky vantage point, you can survey a vast amount of this fabled lake country. Anyone attempting to grasp the magnitude of the Alpine Lakes Wilderness from a single point—short of breaking out the ice axe and crampons—would be hard pressed to find a better spot than this lonely prominence on Davis Peak. The tough climb intimidates a lot of hikers, and while reaching the top requires a hefty effort, you're likely to have the summit to yourself.

From the trailhead, the Davis Peak Trail #1324 begins with a short jaunt across a sturdy bridge spanning the Cle Elum River before beginning its long, steady ascent up the mountain. Well maintained and relatively free of rocks and roots, the trail climbs through a variety of landscapes: sections of old growth, meadows, recovering burn zones, and open ridgelines offering sneak peeks at the views to come.

As engaging as the trail is, it is almost overwhelmed by its defining characteristic: its seemingly endless series of tight switchbacks. The exact number depends on how you define a switchback, but the Davis Peak Trail racks up at least ninety as it ricochets up toward the

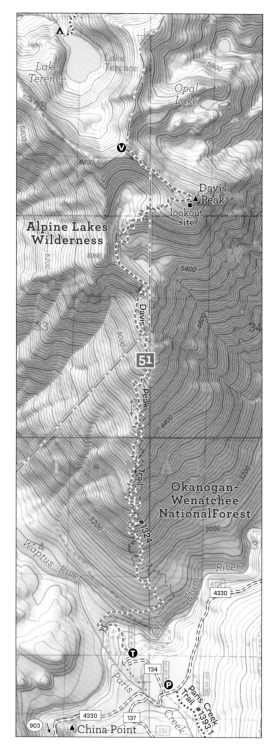

The fire-ravaged slopes of Davis Peak offer great views but little respite from the summer heat.

summit. Gaps in the tree line widen as you climb, with the occasional talus field framing views of nearby lakes and mountaintops. Around 2.0 miles you reach the edge of the burn zone and the last of the tree cover.

Continue onward and upward through rocky terrain to the first ridgeline. From here a false summit and lingering snow can lure hikers off the main trail. Keep an eye on the ground. If it suddenly turns into a rocky, upward scramble, you've gone too far. Backtrack to rejoin the main trail as it drops to the northeast, off the ridge and down into a bowl. The route traverses the bowl and crosses a snow-fed creek before switchbacking up to the next ridgeline.

The trail climbs through grassy slopes just before you crest the exposed ridge to reach the lookout site, now just an incomplete ring of piled stones. While it may not feel like it, this is the summit of Davis Peak—at least as labeled on most maps. Take a moment to soak up the expansive views, perhaps scanning the horizon for smoke like the lookouts who came

before you. After checking out what is left of the lookout's foundation, push up the last 0.5 mile of trail, following the ridgeline and clambering over rocks and boulders to reach a slightly higher overlook, 5.0 long miles from the trailhead.

From here the views are enormous. The two lakes below are Terence (Hike 53) and Opal. Facing north you'll see the other nearby prominences of Goat Mountain, Mount Daniel, and Mount Hinman. Over to the west Mount Stuart dominates the skyline, with nearby Hawkins Mountain rising underneath. Turning to the south, find Jolly Mountain and Sasse Mountain, with Cle Elum Lake and Mount Adams in the distance. Swing west to find Red Mountain, Lemah Mountain, and Chikamin Peak. Pull up a rock and enjoy the show.

HISTORY

Davis Peak is the southernmost prominence along a sprawling ridgeline known as Goat Mountain. Grover Burch, one of the first rangers in the US Forest Service, named the peak in 1926 when he became the Cle Elum District ranger. The peak was named to honor Louie Davis, a lookout worker who had recently died.

In 1934, a lookout cabin was constructed below the summit of Davis Peak and remained staffed until 1965 when the Forest Service shifted away from the lookout network as its primary means of fire detection. The lookout was removed in 1968. Today, all that remains of the lookout is a semi-circle of stones that were once part of the cabin's foundation.

In September 2006, a lightning-sparked fire known as the Polallie Ridge Fire burned large portions of the mountainside below Davis Peak, including areas traversed by the trail route. The fire eventually spread to over 900 acres and took more than two weeks to contain, closing the trail for months. Currently the trail wanders through large swaths of bleached and burnt trees, a legacy of that fire.

52 SPRITE LAKE VIA PADDY-GO-EASY PASS

DISTANCE: 6.6 miles
ELEVATION GAIN: 2700 feet
HIGH POINT: 6100 feet
DIFFICULTY: Hard
HIKING TIME: 4 to 5 hours
BEST SEASON: Summer to late fall
TRAIL TRAFFIC: Light foot traffic
PERMIT: Northwest Forest Pass

MAPS: USGS The Cradle; Green Trails Stevens Pass No. 176, Green Trails Alpine Lakes West–Stevens Pass No. 176S
TRAILHEAD GPS: 47.533°N, 121.0827°W
NOTE: Scatter Creek cuts across FR 4330 9.2 miles from the guard station, making the road impassable when the water is high.

GETTING THERE: Take I-90 to Roslyn, Exit 80. Eastbound turn left; westbound turn right, following Bull-frog Road 2.8 miles to the traffic circle junction with State Route 903. Follow SR 903 toward Roslyn for 16.6 miles through the town and along Cle Elum Lake to just beyond the Salmon La Sac guard station, where the road splits. Keep right, continuing toward Tucquala Lake along Forest Road 4330 (aka Fish Lake Road or Cle Elum Valley Road) on dirt and gravel for 11.3 miles to the Paddy-Go-Easy Pass Trail-head on the right. The trailhead parking area is small, with room for only a few cars. Privy available 1 mile farther down FR 4330 at the Cathedral Pass Trailhead.

This steep climb up to Paddy-Go-Easy Pass offers sweeping views of a lush valley, sprawling hills, and craggy peaks, while tranquil Sprite Lake is a quiet picnic destination. Do not expect much in the way of company on this lonely hike, as it is usually passed over for more popular nearby destinations like Tuck and Robin Lakes (Hike 57). A trek up to Paddy-Go-Easy Pass and Sprite Lake isn't easy, but the views and solitude are well worth it.

From the trailhead, the Paddy-Go-Easy Pass Trail #1595.1 immediately enters a mixed for-est and begins a nearly relentless climb to the pass. The narrow trail crosses the Alpine Lakes Wilderness boundary at 0.6 mile and begins steeply switchbacking up through the trees, crossing small meadows dotted with phlox and paintbrush. Gaps in the canopy offer glimpses of Tucquala Lake (formerly known as Fish Lake) and the valley below.

Before long the trees begin to thin out, and soon the trail pushes into grassy hillsides with ever-better views of nearby Cathedral Rock, Mount Daniel, Mount Hinman, and Mount Rainier. Reach the pass at 2.7 miles, trading the grass and trees for an expanse of exposed rock and the Cle Elum River Valley for the French Creek drainage. The trail now officially becomes the French Creek Trail #1595. Take a moment to pick out some of the more prominent peaks—find the Cradle, Harding Mountain, and the French Ridge Peaks before settling on Dragontail Peak to the southeast.

When you've gotten your fill, veer left, following the trail as it traverses a rocky semi-plateau toward Sprite Lake. At 3.0 miles, as the trail begins to angle downward, look for a cairn marking a rough path leading up through a boulder field. Veer right off the trail and up through the rocks, soon finding yourself on top of a grass ridge looking down on Sprite Lake. The path gently switchbacks down to the shore at 3.3 miles, with plenty of space to settle in and relax. Take in the scree-covered shoulders of

Point 6566, sometimes called Paddy Go North, and enjoy this tranquil lake.

GOING FARTHER

Adventurous souls can follow a rough scramble route from the lakeshore that eventually works its way up the ridge to Point 6566. The path is easily located near Sprite Lake's outlet. For those spending a few nights in the area, return to the main trail and follow its descent into the French Creek Valley. From here, backpackers can reach a number of destinations, including Klonaqua Lakes (Hike 92) and Cradle Lake (Hike 89).

HISTORY

In 1883, a large area around the Cle Elum River Valley was organized as the Cle Elum Mining District, and miners filed hundreds of patents and claims over the decades. Traces of gold, silver, and nickel were found in the area, but despite a great deal of effort, the veins of precious metals were never quite big enough to be very profitable. The ridges around Sprite Lake and Paddy-Go-Easy were

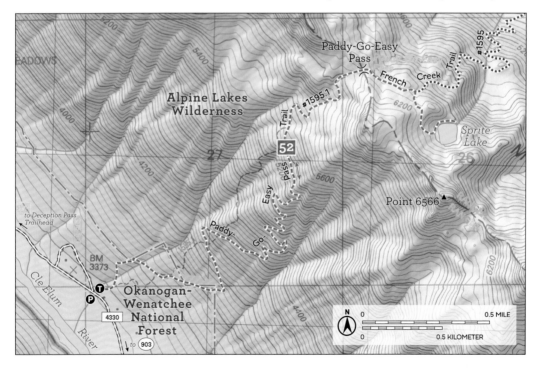

Sprite Lake through the haze of wildfire smoke

surveyed in 1910, and claims such as Mountain Sprite Lode No. 2 and Blue-Eyed Nellie were patented by the Aurora Mining and Tunnel Company in 1912. It's no surprise that all this mining activity left a mark on the area. Paddy-Go-Easy Pass is named for a miner's burro named Paddy, whose owner would tell the animal to "go easy" over rough portions of the trail. Perhaps that miner was John Lynch, who was involved in the Paddy-Go-Easy and Golden Rule Claims near the pass and owned a homestead near Fish Lake in 1919.

Miners and prospectors accessed their claims via a pack trail more or less where today's trail begins. Early maps show the pack trail had long switchbacks that made for a slow climb up to the pass. Today's trail is much more direct, but you can still find traces of the old route where the two trails cross. About 0.5 mile from the pass, you can follow a section of old trail out to the remains of an old mine, complete with rusting railroad ties, the last remains of a cabin, and a trickling stream. There are also a shaft and some tailings in the rocks above Sprite Lake, another legacy of those long-gone prospecting days.

53 LAKE MICHAEL AND LAKE TERENCE

DISTANCE: 17.0 miles to Lake Michael; 20.2 miles to Lake Terence
ELEVATION GAIN: 2500 feet in, 800 feet out to Lake Michael; 3000 feet in, 900 feet out to Lake Terence
HIGH POINT: 5200 feet (Lake Michael); 5600 feet (Lake Terence)
DIFFICULTY: Hard
HIKING TIME: Overnight
BEST SEASON: Early summer to late fall

TRAIL TRAFFIC: Light to moderate foot traffic
PERMIT: Northwest Forest Pass
MAPS: USGS Davis Peak; Green Trails Kachess Lake No. 208
TRAILHEAD GPS: 47.54348°N, 121.0968°W
NOTES: Scatter Creek cuts across FR 4330 9.2 miles from the guard station, making the road impassable when the water is high. Parking is scarce on summer weekends.

GETTING THERE: Take I-90 to Roslyn, Exit 80. Eastbound turn left; westbound turn right, following Bullfrog Road 2.8 miles to the traffic circle junction with State Route 903. Follow SR 903 toward Roslyn for 16.6 miles through the town and along Cle Elum Lake to just beyond the Salmon La Sac guard station, where the road splits. Keep right, continuing toward Tucquala Lake along Forest Road 4330 (aka Fish Lake Road or Cle Elum Valley Road) on dirt and gravel for 12.3 miles to the Cathedral Pass Trailhead. Privy available.

Overlooked and undervisited, this hike out to a pair of remote alpine lakes offers quiet solitude and a little slice of adventure. Rugged landscapes, crystal-clear waters, and lonesome trail— this hike has all the hallmarks of a great alpine backpack.

From the trailhead at Tucquala Meadows, follow the Cathedral Pass Trail #1345 over the Cle Elum River and into the trees. At first the rocky trail is relatively flat as it works its way across the river valley, crossing a handful of small creeks before starting a series of long switchbacks that slowly ratchets up the mountainside. At 0.4 mile the trail enters the Alpine Lakes Wilderness, drawing you past brushy undergrowth and deeper into older forest of hemlock and fir.

The trail begins to flatten again and reaches the signed junction with the Trail Creek Trail #1322 to the left at 2.0 miles. Veer left, following the arrow pointing toward the Lake Michael Trail. Wide and well-worn, the Trail Creek Trail continues through the woods, passing above Squitch Lake hidden in the trees (an elusive boot path leads down to this lakelet). Stay on

the dusty trail as it angles gently downward, and before long you'll hear the trickle of the route's namesake waterway, Trail Creek.

Cut through a small marsh that acts as the creek's headwaters before returning to the trees and continuing down the sheltered trail. A single campsite at 3.6 miles breaks up the journey through the uniform and relatively young forest, a legacy of a century-old forest fire. Push onward to the 4.7-mile mark to reach the junction with the Lake Michael Trail #1336 and where the real adventure begins. Leave the gentle grades and wide trails behind to climb steeply up the shoulders of Goat Mountain. Gone are the wide switchbacks and well-worn tread, replaced now by a narrow, rocky path leading up through increasingly sparse forest.

After about a mile of climbing, the trail levels somewhat as you cross Goat Creek, beginning a traverse that undulates through wildflower-filled meadows and rocky creek beds. Not far beyond Goat Creek, just before you reach Moonshine Creek's rocky creek bed, pass an unmarked trail leading farther up the mountainside at the 6.4-mile mark. Note this path, as it is the Moonshine Lake Trail #1336.1, which snakes 0.5 mile up to shallow Moonshine Lake and a single campsite.

Continue your traverse, eventually dropping steeply down to Lake Michael's outlet creek. From here the trail follows the creek back to its source, finally climbing up to the lakeside, which you reach at 8.5 miles. Here, Goat Mountain rises high above the sparkling waters, nearly surrounding the lake in exposed crags and talus fields.

The trail forks on the lip of the lake basin. A boot path heads around the lake to the left, and the main trail continues to the right, crossing the outlet creek and heading upward to Lake Terence. If you're looking to spend the night at Lake Michael, the best tent site is a few dozen feet down the lake trail, though there is also a horse camp a short way down the trail toward Lake Terence. Another former horse camp on the far end of Lake Michael is mostly buried under a rockslide, though some flat dry spaces can still be found there.

From Lake Michael, the rough and slightly overgrown route climbs a steep ridgeline above the lake before skirting the upper edges of a creek valley, offering some expansive views of surrounding mountaintops poking out of a sea of trees. Climb another ridge before a steep drop down to Lake Terence, 1.6 miles from Lake Michael, in the next bowl over, at the base of Davis Peak (Hike 51). There is only one campsite here near the outlet, as the lake is lined with steep, rocky slopes.

GOING FARTHER

Climbers seeking the heights of Goat Mountain follow a scramble route from Lake Michael, while others prefer a route from Moonshine Lake. A quick trip up to

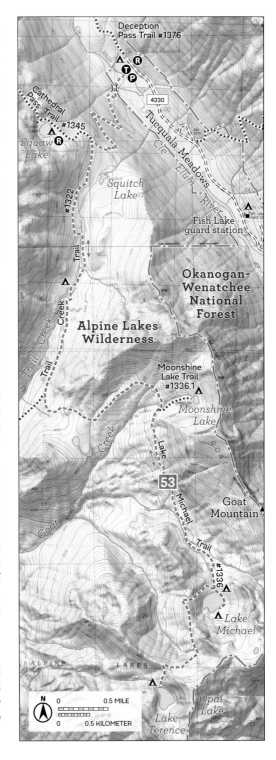

Lake Michael rests beneath the rocky heights of Goat Mountain.

Moonshine Lake outlined above is an easy addition to this hike, but the scramble routes are best left to those with the know-how for a more technical climb.

Backpackers looking to add some extra days can make a loop by returning to the Trail Creek Trail heading down to the Waptus River Trail #1310, connecting to the Pacific Crest Trail #2000 to go up past Deep Lake to the Cathedral Pass Trail #1345, and then returning to Tucquala Meadows (see Hike 96 for a more detailed description).

54 SQUAW LAKE

DISTANCE: 5.4 miles
ELEVATION GAIN: 1400 feet
HIGH POINT: 4800 feet
DIFFICULTY: Moderate
HIKING TIME: 3 to 4 hours
BEST SEASON: Late spring to late fall
TRAIL TRAFFIC: Moderate to heavy foot traffic
PERMIT: Northwest Forest Pass

MAPS: USGS The Cradle; Green Trails Stevens Pass No. 176
TRAILHEAD GPS: 47.54348°N, 121.0968°W
NOTES: Scatter Creek cuts across FR 4330 9.2 miles from the guard station, making the road impassable when the water is high. Parking is scarce on summer weekends.

GETTING THERE: Take I-90 to Roslyn, Exit 80. Eastbound turn left; westbound turn right, following Bullfrog Road 2.8 miles to the traffic circle junction with State Route 903. Follow SR 903 toward Roslyn for 16.6 miles through the town and along Cle Elum Lake to just beyond the Salmon La Sac guard station, where the road splits. Keep right, continuing toward Tucquala Lake along Forest Road 4330 (aka Fish Lake Road or Cle Elum Valley Road) on dirt and gravel for 12.3 miles to the Cathedral Pass Trailhead. Privy available.

Journey into the wilderness just far enough to picnic on a quiet beach next to a lovely alpine lake with plenty of lakeshore to explore. Nearby campsites have been used for generations, making Squaw Lake an excellent choice for a family backpacking adventure.

From the Cathedral Pass Trailhead (officially part of the Tucquala Meadows Trailhead), take a moment before you head down the trail to look up at the exposed heights of Cathedral Rock. That rocky summit presides over the valley and will be a constant, welcome presence throughout the entire hike. Begin by following the Cathedral Pass Trail #1345 over the Cle Elum River on a sturdy bridge, leaving the wildflower-filled meadows behind. March along roadbed for a short time before transitioning to trail and entering the Alpine Lakes Wilderness at 0.4 mile.

Brushy undergrowth thins as you climb long switchbacks, and the firs and hemlocks grow older and bigger. Cathedral Rock peeks through gaps in the canopy as you climb, and eventually the trail begins to level out near the junction with the Trail Creek Trail #1322 that branches off to the left at the 2.0-mile mark. Continue onward past the junction along the Cathedral Pass Trail.

The trail again steepens, climbing to reveal long views of the valley below. Reach the waters of Squaw Lake at 2.7 miles and find plenty of campsites and day-use areas just off the trail (a backcountry toilet is also available here). Drop your gear and take in this little lake. Squaw Lake is not the largest or most stunning alpine lake, but it has a certain charm. Gaze at the ridge across the water, with its layers of talus, underbrush, and trees. Follow boot paths around the lake and explore, or find a quiet spot and take in Cathedral Rock rising above it all.

Short day hikes in the Alpine Lakes Wilderness are few and far between. Those with enough elevation to feel like you've gotten a taste of the wild are even harder to find. Squaw Lake has a bit of Goldilocks' "just right" about it, providing almost any hiker with the opportunity to get a taste of what the Alpine Lakes Wilderness has to offer.

GOING FARTHER

Day trippers can push another 1.6 miles up to Cathedral Pass for closer look at Cathedral Rock and views of Deep Lake and the sprawling wilderness below. If you're lucky, you'll spot some mountain goats picking their way across Cathedral Rock's jagged outcroppings. Not far

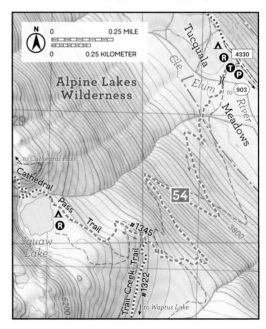

Multiple campsites along the shores of Squaw Lake make it a great option for first-time backpackers.

beyond the pass is the junction leading out to Peggys Pond, a rough 0.6-mile scramble out to a lovely tarn. Those overnighting at Squaw might consider a longer day hike down to Deep Lake (Hike 55) or a long haul out to Lake Michael (Hike 53).

HISTORY

While there has long been a trail up to Squaw Lake, the current route up to Cathedral Pass is relatively new, a product of trail reroutes and updates in the mid-1970s. Before that time, Squaw Lake was a destination unto itself, a side trip and favored rest stop along the Cascade Crest Trail that reached Deep Lake by heading down the Trail Creek Trail past Squitch Lake, then climbing steeply over the ridge to drop into the Spinola Creek Valley. The route then followed Spinola Creek up to Deep Lake, just as it does today.

55 DEEP LAKE AND LAKE VICENTE

DISTANCE: 15.0 miles to Deep Lake; 19.0 miles to Lake Vicente
ELEVATION GAIN: 2200 feet in, 1200 feet out to Deep Lake; 3300 feet in, 1200 feet out to Lake Vicente
HIGH POINT: 5600 feet
DIFFICULTY: Moderate; hard to Lake Vicente
HIKING TIME: 8 to 12 hours or overnight
BEST SEASON: Early summer to early fall
TRAIL TRAFFIC: Moderate foot traffic; light to Lake Vicente

PERMIT: Northwest Forest Pass
MAPS: USGS The Cradle, USGS Mount Daniel; Green Trails Stevens Pass No. 176
TRAILHEAD GPS: 47.54348°N, 121.0968°W
NOTES: Scatter Creek cuts across FR 4330 9.2 miles from the guard station, making the road impassable when the water is high. Parking is scarce on summer weekends. The final approach to Lake Vicente is a very steep scramble over indistinct trail and may require some routefinding; approach with caution.

GETTING THERE: Take I-90 to Roslyn, Exit 80. Eastbound turn left; westbound turn right, following Bullfrog Road 2.8 miles to the traffic circle junction with State Route 903. Follow SR 903 toward Roslyn for 16.6 miles through the town and along Cle Elum Lake to just beyond the Salmon La Sac guard station, where the road splits. Keep right, continuing toward Tucquala Lake along Forest Road 4330 (aka Fish Lake Road or Cle Elum Valley Road) on dirt and gravel for 12.3 miles to the Cathedral Pass Trailhead. Privy available.

This hike is a classic, offering some of the best the Alpine Lakes Wilderness has to offer: a pristine alpine lake, views of the surrounding rugged landscape, and the quiet solace of the wilderness. While strong hikers can tackle this trail as a day hike, the distance really lends itself better to an overnight or a multiday exploration of the area, as there are a number of destinations nearby, including a popular scramble route up Mount Daniel by way of Peggys Pond.

As you gear up for your hike, look up toward craggy Cathedral Rock jutting dramatically into the skyline, giving you a taste of what lies ahead. From the Cathedral Pass Trailhead (officially part of the Tucquala Meadows Trailhead), follow the rocky Cathedral Pass Trail #1345, crossing the Cle Elum River on a bridge, then a few creeks, before beginning a series of long switchbacks,

slowly ratcheting up the mountainside. At 0.4 mile the trail enters the Alpine Lakes Wilderness, drawing you past brushy undergrowth and deeper into dark stands of hemlock and fir.

Soon the trail begins to level out, and at 2.0 miles reach a junction where the Trail Creek Trail #1322 branches off to the left. Continue ahead on Cathedral Pass Trail for another 0.7

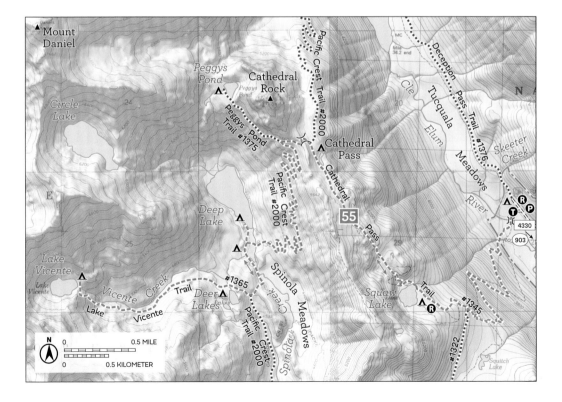

Cathedral Rock is reflected in the tranquil waters of Deep Lake.

mile to your first destination, Squaw Lake (Hike 54). A number of campsites around this little lake, as well as a backcountry toilet, make it a decent option for a quick overnight with the kids or base camp for exploring nearby trails.

From Squaw Lake, the trail begins a long, rocky traverse up toward Cathedral Pass, offering sporadic views of the Wenatchee Mountains just to the east, while skirting past the occasional tarn or campsite. Continue to push upward through thinning subalpine forest for 1.5 miles from the lake to the connection with the Pacific Crest Trail #2000 (PCT) at 4.2 miles. Cathedral Pass is only 0.1 mile up ahead, so climb the last few feet to the 5400-foot pass. Do not expect too much fanfare when you arrive at the pass—there is little in the way of big sweeping views. But take a moment to scan the cliffs for mountain goats before beginning the long descent into the Spinola Valley.

Over the pass, the trail is a breeze. Wide and almost smooth, it gently guides you down the mountainside. At the first big switchback is the junction with Peggys Pond Trail #1375—this lovely tarn is worth a visit, though the 0.6-mile trail to reach it is somewhat challenging to navigate. Most hikers continue down to Spinola Meadows and the shores of Deep Lake.

As you descend, enjoy a bird's-eye view of Deep Lake and the valley below as well as Circle Lake Falls cascading down the opposite side of the valley. Depending on the season, the waterfall can put on quite a show before the views disappear behind the trees as you reenter the forest. Eventually you reach the bottom where the old growth gives way to meadow. Here the barren cliffs of Cathedral Rock loom above Deep Lake, demanding your attention as you take in the panorama. At 7.4 miles find a spur trail leading toward the lakeshore. Take some time to explore before settling in—there are plenty of campsites around the lake for those planning to spend the night here, and you can afford to find the best vantage point to absorb this gorgeous alpine landscape.

Unless you're planning to overnight at Lake Vicente, stash your heavy gear at Deep Lake. When you're ready, push onward to the hike's final challenge: Lake Vicente. Reach it by continuing another 0.4 mile down the PCT to a junction with a trail leading up the mountainside. This is the Lake Vicente Trail #1365; veer right and follow it past Deer Lakes and its campsites in 0.3 mile and into an open creek valley. The trail becomes indistinct at this point, as past flooding and landslides have largely covered it. When in doubt, simply follow the creek, eventually reaching the end of the valley. Then climb, scramble, and pull your way up the steep headwall, following faint indications of the trail scratched into the rock. Vicente Creek tumbles loudly down the headwall as you clamber over talus and carefully cross often-slick granite slabs to reach the shores of lonesome Lake Vicente, 1.6 miles from the junction. Find one good campsite near the lake outlet and enjoy the lake's deep aquamarine waters. Do not expect company here, a distant 9.6 miles from the trailhead—you're very likely to get these rocky shores and rubble-strewn slopes all to yourself.

GOING FARTHER
Of course, a quick side trip out to Peggys Pond is worth the short semiscramble. The pond also serves as a base camp for those heading up Lynch Glacier to one of Mount Daniel's peaks.

HISTORY
In the late 1800s, prospectors and sheepherders were far more common in the Salmon La Sac area than hikers. One of these prospectors was a gold miner named James "Jimmy" Grieve, who was likely the first to scale Cathedral Rock. As a result, it was known both as Grieve's Peak and Jimmy's Jumpoff for years. The name did not sound regal enough for the Forest Service, however, so someone in the 1940s or '50s decided Cathedral Rock was a better fit. Grieve had several claims in the area and built a cabin near Peggys Pond that was a popular site for hikers to visit for decades, though it is little more than a pile of crumbling logs today.

The story behind other place names here is a bit murkier. Supposedly it was Spanish-speaking shepherds who inspired Albert H. Sylvester to give the Spinola Meadows and Vicente Creek and Lake their names. Deep Lake, unsurprisingly, was named for its depth, perhaps by the same folks who decided Grieve's Peak bore a striking resemblance to a cathedral.

56 HYAS LAKE AND LITTLE HYAS LAKE

DISTANCE: 5.4 miles
ELEVATION GAIN: 100 feet
HIGH POINT: 3500 feet
DIFFICULTY: Easy
HIKING TIME: 2 to 3 hours
BEST SEASON: Spring to late fall
TRAIL TRAFFIC: Heavy foot traffic; moderate
equestrian traffic

PERMIT: Northwest Forest Pass
MAPS: USGS The Cradle, USGS Mt. Daniel; Green
Trails Stevens Pass No. 176
TRAILHEAD GPS: 47.5451°N, 121.0977°W
NOTES: Scatter Creek cuts across FR 4330 9.2
miles from the guard station making the road
impassable when the water is high. Parking is
scarce on summer weekends.

GETTING THERE: Take I-90 to Roslyn, Exit 80. Eastbound turn left; westbound turn right, following Bull-frog Road 2.8 miles to the traffic circle junction with State Route 903. Follow SR 903 toward Roslyn for 16.6 miles through the town and along Cle Elum Lake to just beyond the Salmon La Sac guard station, where the road splits. Keep right, continuing toward Tucquala Lake along Forest Road 4330 (aka Fish Lake Road or Cle Elum Valley Road) on dirt and gravel for 12.3 miles to the end of the road and Deception Pass Trailhead (aka Tucquala Meadows Trailhead). Privy available.

Looking north from the shore of Hyas Lake toward the lower prominences of Mount Daniel

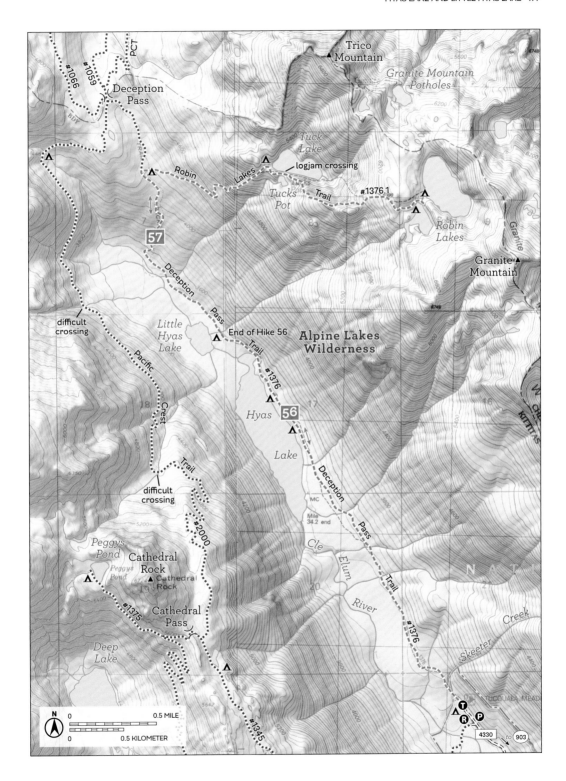

Trico Mountain

Granite Mountain Potholes

#1066 #1059 PCT

Deception Pass

Robin Lakes Trail

Tuck Lake

logjam crossing

Tucks Pot

#1376.1

Robin Lakes

57

Deception Pass

Granite Mountain

difficult crossing

Little Hyas Lake

End of Hike 56

Alpine Lakes Wilderness

Pacific Crest

#1376

Hyas 56

Lake

difficult crossing

Trail

#2000

Deception

MC

Mile 34.2 end

W CHE KITTITAS

Peggys Pond

Cathedral Rock

Peggys Pond

▲ Cathedral Rock

Cle Elum River

Pass

Trail

N A T

#1375

Cathedral Pass

Deep Lake

#1376

Skeeter Creek

TUCQUALA MEAD

▲ T R P

N

0   0.5 MILE

0   0.5 KILOMETER

#1345

4330   to 903

Short, sweet, and easily accessible Hyas Lake is both a popular day hike and a well-worn base camp for backpackers seeking (or returning from) adventures in the farther reaches of the Alpine Lakes Wilderness. Set dramatically beneath Cathedral Rock, this sprawling shallow lake offers engaging views and plenty of room to find your own secluded spot along the shore.

From the Tucquala Meadows Trailhead, follow Deception Pass Trail #1376 as it enters the Alpine Lakes Wilderness in 0.1 mile and glides up through second-generation mixed forest on a slight incline. The boot-pounded, wide trail is easy to navigate and filled with bright clearings that become a sea of green awash with color when wildflowers and flowering brush are in bloom. The incline quickly settles into a nearly flat trail, threading through trees and meadows and crossing a couple of large streams rushing down the mountainside to the Cle Elum River below. The exposed cliffs of Cathedral Rock peek through the trees, putting on the occasional show when the canopy opens up.

After a quick 2.0 miles, arrive at campsites and your first access to the lake. Hyas Lake is long. It's another 0.7 mile to Little Hyas Lake, a small lake just far enough beyond the end of Hyas Lake to perhaps be considered a distinct body of water, yet close enough that when water levels are particularly high, it can seem like they're both one slightly bigger lake. Some maps don't bother to differentiate between the two.

As you follow the lakeshore, find ample opportunities to trek down to the water and pop your head out of the trees for a view of Cathedral Rock and Mount Daniel—but, arguably, the better perspectives are down near

Little Hyas, at 2.7 miles. The campsites here are a good turnaround point for day hikers.

The hike to Hyas Lake is ideal for little boots and burgeoning backpackers. Even the most reluctant hiker cannot object to the ease of the trail. Abundant wildflowers in the spring and early summer are a great reason to hit this trail early in the season before the mosquitos and high-season crowds arrive.

GOING FARTHER

Beyond Little Hyas Lake, the trail switchbacks up the valley wall, steeply climbing past the junction to Tuck and Robin Lakes (Hike 57) to reach Deception Pass; the junction with the Lake Clarice Trail #1066 (Hike 58); and the Pacific Crest Trail #2000 (PCT), which can be followed for the Cathedral Rock and Deception Pass Loop (Hike 59).

HISTORY

Hyas is Chinook Jargon for "big" or "great." Many hikers and fishermen refer to Hyas Lake as "Big Lake," though that name never appears on official maps of the area. It was here at Hyas Lake over a long weekend of backpacking in the 1970s that the Alpine Lakes Protection Society (ALPS) was conceived and formed, a group that was later instrumental in creating the Alpine Lakes Wilderness.

57 TUCK LAKE AND ROBIN LAKES

DISTANCE: 12.4 miles
ELEVATION GAIN: 2900 feet
HIGH POINT: 6300 feet
DIFFICULTY: Hard
HIKING TIME: Overnight

BEST SEASON: Late spring to early fall
TRAIL TRAFFIC: Heavy foot traffic, moderate equestrian traffic to Hyas Lake; moderate to heavy foot traffic to Tuck and Robin Lakes
PERMIT: Northwest Forest Pass

Pause on your climb to Tuck Lake to take in views of Hyas Lake, Mount Daniel, and Cathedral Rock.

MAPS: USGS The Cradle, USGS Mt. Daniel; Green Trails Stevens Pass No. 176

TRAILHEAD GPS: 47.5451°N, 121.0977°W

NOTES: Scatter Creek cuts across FR 4330 9.2 miles from the guard station making the road impassable when the water is high. Parking is scarce on summer weekends.

GETTING THERE: Take I-90 to Roslyn, Exit 80. Eastbound turn left; westbound turn right, following Bullfrog Road 2.8 miles to the traffic circle junction with State Route 903. Follow SR 903 toward Roslyn for 16.6 miles through the town and along Cle Elum Lake to just beyond the Salmon La Sac guard station, where the road splits. Keep right, continuing toward Tucquala Lake along Forest Road 4330 (aka Fish Lake Road or Cle Elum Valley Road) on dirt and gravel for 12.3 miles to the end of the road and Deception Pass Trailhead (aka Tucquala Meadows Trailhead). Privy available.

Remote and famously challenging, the hike up to Tuck and Robin Lakes is something of a rite of passage for many hikers. Despite the rough ascent and a trail that is difficult to follow in places, the rugged skylines, captivating views, and jaw-dropping lakes are not to be missed. Depending on snow levels, aim for late spring or late fall to minimize the crowds that flock to these fabled lakes. Arrive early if you're planning an overnight up at Robin Lakes, as sites along the water fill up quickly. Mosquitos are also abundant in midsummer so come prepared.

From the trailhead, follow the Deception Pass Trail #1376 as it begins easily, gliding through mixed forest and frequent clearings that burst with wildflowers and flowering brush during the spring and summer. Almost entirely flat, the first 2.0 miles quickly disappear, and you find yourself standing on the quiet shores of Hyas Lake (Hike 56), taking in the contours of Cathedral Rock as it looms above the water. Continue onward, passing a number of campsites along the lakeshore. These are a great option for a quick backpack or a waypoint on a longer excursion into the wilderness.

Once you reach the end of Little Hyas Lake at 2.7 miles, the trail begins to climb toward Deception Pass, switchbacking up the mountainside for 1.3 miles to the signed junction with the Robin Lakes Trail #1376.1. Turn right onto the Robin Lakes Trail, which initially feels very similar, wandering pleasantly over streams and through dense forest.

Within a few tenths of a mile, the trail becomes serious, steeply climbing up a narrow trail increasingly made of roots and loose rock. The mile up to Tuck Lake gains 1000 feet, most of it by plowing straight up the mountain. Fortunately, frequent gaps in the tree line provide ever-grander views of Mount Daniel and Cathedral Rock, a welcome distraction during frequent stops to give your legs a rest.

Once the trail begins to level out, Tuck Lake is not far away. Crest the lake basin at 5.0 miles and make your way to the water to take in the rugged landscape. Rocky bluffs and cliffs rise high above the lake, spotted with trees and vegetation clinging to the steep slopes. Regroup here, but do not be tempted to set up camp. Robin Lakes is well worth the extra effort.

The trickiest part is here, as trails seem to snake off in many different directions, making the route difficult to follow. Cairns can be a helpful guide, though even these stake out competing routes. Work your way along Tuck's lakeshore,

aiming for the stream between Tuck and Tucks Pot. This approach will require you to climb up rocky bluffs and drop back down again, crossing the mass of logs piled at the lake's outlet. Once you're across, there will be a series of ups and downs for about 0.1 mile until you leave Tuck Lake behind, and the trail begins its steep ascent.

This section of trail is even steeper than the approach to Tuck Lake, but firmer footing helps make your next mile of relentless climbing a little easier. As you approach your destination, leave the last of the diminutive alpine trees behind and climb straight up exposed granite, eventually traversing your way toward Robin Lakes. The trail leads to a barren prominence above the lakes, and here you can see why some hikers refer to this area as the "Little Enchantments." To your right, Mount Daniel stands massively, taking up a good chunk of the horizon. To your left, the Robin Lakes sit in bowls of granite, a lunar landscape sparsely dotted with a few trees, 6.2 miles into the wild. Head down to the lakes to explore, finding campsites along the shore and hidden upslope. Make sure to visit the farthest lake, as the view of Mount Daniel rising above the waters is stunning.

This is a challenging hike, largely due to the rough and difficult-to-follow trail. Despite the difficulty, the otherworldly terrain makes it an extremely popular destination during the summer months. Keep an eye out for the mountain goats that often frolic in the lingering snows here, and marmots and pika are not uncommon. It's easy to spend hours exploring this alpine wonderland set against an enchanting backdrop.

GOING FARTHER

There are a number of scrambling options from Robin Lakes, including climbing to the top of Granite Mountain and Trico Mountain, both of which are usually well marked by cairns. The Granite Mountain Potholes are another popular destination just a few tenths of a mile beyond Robin Lakes.

58 MARMOT LAKE AND LAKE CLARICE

DISTANCE: 18.6 miles
ELEVATION GAIN: 1900 feet in; 500 feet out
HIGH POINT: 4900 feet
DIFFICULTY: Moderate
HIKING TIME: Overnight
BEST SEASON: Late spring to early fall
TRAIL TRAFFIC: Heavy foot traffic, moderate
equestrian traffic to Hyas Lake; light foot traffic to
Marmot Lake

PERMIT: Northwest Forest Pass
MAPS: USGS The Cradle, USGS Mt. Daniel; Green
Trails Stevens Pass No. 176
TRAILHEAD GPS: 47.5451°N, 121.0977°W
NOTES: Scatter Creek cuts across FR 4330 9.2
miles from the guard station, making the road
impassable when the water is high. Parking is
scarce on summer weekends.

GETTING THERE: Take I-90 to Roslyn, Exit 80. Eastbound turn left; westbound turn right, following Bullfrog Road 2.8 miles to the traffic circle junction with State Route 903. Follow SR 903 toward Roslyn for
16.6 miles through the town and along Cle Elum Lake to just beyond the Salmon La Sac guard station,
where the road splits. Keep right, continuing toward Tucquala Lake along Forest Road 4330 (aka Fish
Lake Road or Cle Elum Valley Road) on dirt and gravel for 12.3 miles to the end of the road and Deception Pass Trailhead (aka Tucquala Meadows Trailhead). Privy available.

Marmot Lake from the scramble route up to Jade Lake

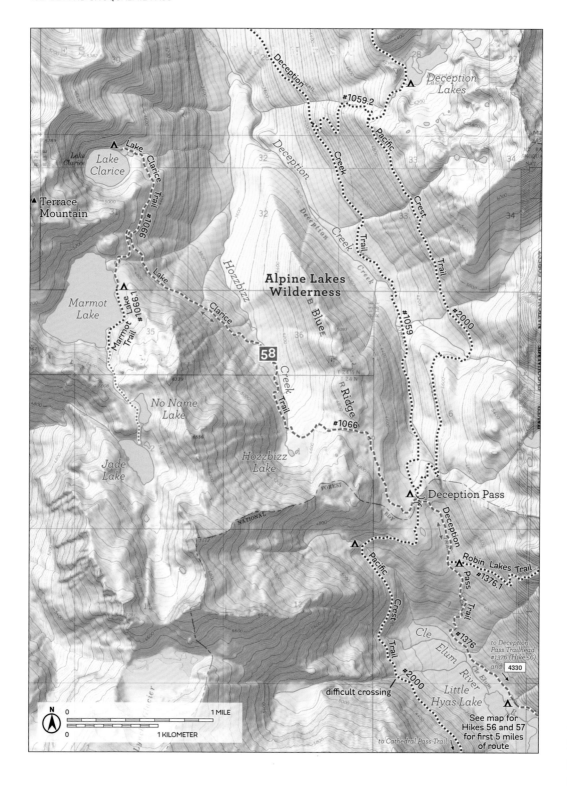

Deception Trail

#1059.2

Deception

Deception

Creek

Pacific

Crest

Trail

Deception Lakes

Lake Clarice

Lake Clarice Trail #1066

Lake Clarice

Terrace Mountain

Deception Creek Trail

Alpine Lakes Wilderness

Hozzbizz

#1059

#2000

Creek

Marmot Lake Trail #1066.1

Lake Clarice

Marmot Lake

Blue

58

No Name Lake

R Ridge

#1066

Hozzbizz Lake

Jade Lake

Creek Trail

NATIONAL

FOREST

Deception Pass

Deception

Pacific

Robin Lakes Trail

#1376.1

Pass

Crest

Trail

Cle

#1376

Elum

River

to Deception Pass Trailhead #1376 (Hike 56) and

4330

#2000

difficult crossing

Little Hyas Lake

See map for Hikes 56 and 57 for first 5 miles of route

to Cathedral Pass Trail

N

0   1 MILE

0   1 KILOMETER

Cradled in the arms of Terrace Mountain are two alpine beauties: Marmot Lake and Lake Cla-rice. Beyond the reach of all but the most dedicated day hikers and trail runners, these quiet lakes rest languidly in rocky bowls that are the soul of wilderness. Big brother Marmot Lake is the larger and more popular destination, while often-overlooked Lake Clarice offers a kind of solitude that is difficult to find in this area.

The first leg of your journey takes you out to Hyas Lake (Hike 56), following the gentle grade of the Deception Pass Trail #1376 from Tuc-quala Meadows 2.0 miles through flower-filled meadows and second-growth forest to the edge of the lake. Enjoy the view before pressing on to the end of the lake and the beginning of the 1900 feet of elevation gain to Marmot Lake. The route switchbacks with increasing steepness up the valley walls for 1.3 miles to the signed junc-tion with the Robin Lakes Trail #1376.1. Decep-tion Pass is another 0.5 mile up ahead.

Deception Pass is a crossroads for a num-ber of trails that merge in a wide hollow. Here the Deception Pass Trail ends as it connects to the Pacific Crest Trail #2000 (PCT). Taking the PCT south will lead back toward Tucquala Meadows via the highlands above Hyas Lake, eventually connecting with the Cathedral Pass Trail #1345. To the north, the PCT passes a junc-tion with the Deception Creek Trail #1059 a few hundred feet beyond the pass. Find the signed Lake Clarice Trail #1066 on the far side of the hollow to continue your journey.

Leave the pass behind and begin climbing past small tarns and through petite meadows as the trail makes its way over a small hump known as Blue Ridge before dropping down into a grassy, cliff-lined bowl 1.3 miles from Deception Pass. Here find the seasonal water-falls feeding marshy Hozzbizz Lake, easily accessed by a number of boot paths branch-ing off into the heather. The lake fuels Hozz-bizz Creek, your new trail companion as you cross the water and descend to the bottom of the valley and then immediately start to work your way back up again. Continue climbing, eventually crossing Marmot Lake's curiously unnamed outlet stream and reaching the junc-tion with the Marmot Lake Trail #1066.1 at the 7.9-mile mark. Veer left for Marmot Lake, another 0.4 mile up ahead; head right for Lake Clarice, 0.8 mile distant.

Marmot Lake is the better choice for over-night accommodations, as it has several sites, whereas Lake Clarice has only a single tent site to offer. Both lakes are lovely, though Lake Clarice is certainly the more dramatic, with tall exposed cliffs rising from half the shoreline. At the same time, the trail out to Lake Clarice does not get nearly the traffic that Marmot Lake does, so it often gets a little overgrown. Establish your base camp at Marmot Lake and visit both.

Whether it's a single overnight or part of a multiday trek, a visit to this pair of lakes is never disappointing. There are certainly more remote places to visit in the Alpine Lakes Wil-derness, but few offer the same flexibility of options for further exploration.

GOING FARTHER

The Marmot Lake Trail continues around Mar-mot Lake to a field of boulders and scree lead-ing straight up the mountainside. Cairns mark a steep scramble that leads up past stunning views of Marmot Lake below, then through the meadows around No Name Lake and eventu-ally to the prize of Jade Lake. Fed by Jade Gla-cier, the milky emerald waters are a sight to behold. This route is challenging and rough, but for those with enough endurance, it is a worthy adventure.

It is also possible (with a few more trail miles) to approach these lakes from the north via Decep-tion Creek or Surprise Lake (Hikes 69 and 70).

HISTORY

Marmot Lake is named for the abundance of marmots in the area.

59 CATHEDRAL ROCK AND DECEPTION PASS LOOP

DISTANCE: 13.4 miles
ELEVATION GAIN: 2800 feet
HIGH POINT: 5500 feet
DIFFICULTY: Moderate
HIKING TIME: Overnight
BEST SEASON: Summer to late fall
TRAIL TRAFFIC: Moderate foot and equestrian traffic
PERMIT: Northwest Forest Pass

MAPS: USGS Mt. Daniel, USGS The Cradle; Green Trails Stevens Pass No. 176
TRAILHEAD GPS: 47.54348°N, 121.0968°W
NOTES: Scatter Creek cuts across FR 4330 9.2 miles from the guard station, making the road impassable when the water is high. Parking is scarce on summer weekends. The hike requires multiple river fords and creek crossings that are easier to navigate later in the season.

GETTING THERE: Take I-90 to Roslyn, Exit 80. Eastbound turn left; westbound turn right, following Bullfrog Road 2.8 miles to the traffic circle junction with State Route 903. Follow SR 903 toward Roslyn for 16.6 miles through the town and along Cle Elum Lake to just beyond the Salmon La Sac guard station, where the road splits. Keep right, continuing toward Tucquala Lake along Forest Road 4330 (aka Fish Lake Road or Cle Elum Valley Road) on dirt and gravel for 12.3 miles to the Cathedral Pass Trailhead. Privy available.

This classic backpack route tours the Cle Elum Valley, from the heights of Cathedral Pass to the shores of Hyas Lake on the valley floor. Camp near alpine lakes, ford snowmelt-driven creeks, and wander through wildflower-filled meadowlands on this approachable and enjoyable wilderness adventure. While this loop can be done in either direction, the grade is steepest on the stretch of trail from Tucquala Meadows up to Cathedral Pass. By beginning along the Cathedral Pass Trail, you attack the elevation early and spend most of your hiking time gently descending back down to the meadows. Plus, by looping clockwise you can camp in the high country rather than spending the night somewhere along Hyas Lake.

Gear up with Cathedral Rock looming high above and dominating the horizon. The day's goal is to reach the base of that jutting rock a little over 4 miles distant. Begin by following the Cathedral Pass Trail #1345 as it leads away from the waving grasses of Tucquala Meadows over the Cle Elum River on a footbridge. Wide and nearly flat, the route heads straight for the ridge wall, where it transitions from old road bed to trail and begins to switchback up the slope. Cross into the Alpine Lakes Wilderness at 0.4 mile and continue pressing upward while the brushy understory soon thins, replaced by ever-larger trunks of fir and hemlock.

At 2.0 miles the trail briefly plateaus at the junction with the Trail Creek Trail #1322. Signs here point to Waptus Lake (Hike 48) and Lake Michael (Hike 53), both quite a few miles away. Save those lakes for another day and continue along the Cathedral Pass Trail as it again steepens.

The trail climbs another 0.7 mile before delivering you to Squaw Lake (Hike 54). Take a few minutes to pause and enjoy this pretty little lake. Paths snake around the lakeside and there is room to roam. There are excellent campsites here for hikers who are planning a multinight tour or are otherwise ready to camp.

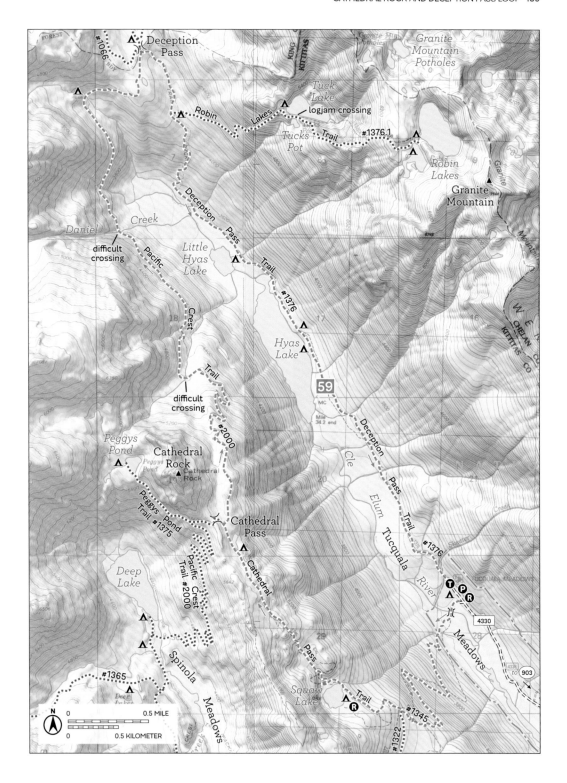

A backpacker pauses to admire Cathedral Rock.

The trail continues past the lake, beginning a long, rocky traverse up to Cathedral Pass. Along the way enjoy views of the Wenatchee Mountains just to the east and the vibrant greens of the river valley below. The trail snakes past the occasional tarn as it pushes up through subalpine forest for another 1.5 miles of widening views to reach the Pacific Crest Trail #2000 (PCT) at the 4.2-mile mark. While there is decent camping at the large unnamed tarn a few hundred feet before the PCT junction, complete with valley vistas just off the trail, there is an even better option less than a mile away: Peggys Pond. Those willing to add a little extra mileage and effort can reach it by continuing over 5400-foot Cathedral Pass

to the signed junction with the Peggys Pond Trail #1375. From there it's a somewhat difficult 0.6-mile traverse on primitive trail to the lake. Bunk down for the night in a gorgeous alpine landscape complete with a crystal-clear lake set beneath the towering heights of Cathedral Rock and the glacier-clad shoulders of Mount Daniel.

From the junction, the PCT wanders the high bluffs at the base of Cathedral Rock, beginning a long and very gradual descent toward Deception Pass. Views are plentiful, as is the potential to see some wildlife, whether it be mountain goats that frequent Cathedral Rock's ledges or marmots and pikas common along the talus slopes. Spot the rocky crowns of Granite Mountain and Trico Mountain rising above the sprawling Hyas Lakes below, a long swath of blue filling the bottom of the green valley. The oft-wildflower-lined trail is a breeze, the main challenge being the two creek fords you must navigate. Signs at either end of this stretch of trail warn that these fords can be dangerous and should be avoided when the waters are high. Reach the first creek at the 6.0-mile mark, and Daniel Creek at 7.2 miles. Of the two, Daniel Creek is deeper and swifter. Late in the season, these fords are unlikely to pose any real difficulty, but do not underestimate the strength of these waters barreling down the mountainside at breakneck speeds. When it doubt, retreat to hike another day.

Beyond Daniel Creek, cross through a few scree and talus fields before returning to the sheltering arms of mossy old-growth forest. Soon arrive at Deception Pass and the junction with the Deception Pass Trail #1376. Here find the Lake Clarice Trail #1066 leading out to Marmot Lake (Hike 58). Save that adventure for another day, and instead, veer off the PCT and follow the Deception Pass Trail as it heads down toward the Hyas Lakes and begins the long trek back to the trailhead.

In 0.5 mile, pass the Robin Lakes Trail #1376.1, and continue to descend through dense forest, ping-ponging down steep switchbacks before leveling out near the first campsite along Little Hyas Lake. From here the well-trodden trail glides through the trees, passing numerous opportunities to go out to the water to take in the landscape. Here again Cathedral Rock is the centerpiece, standing proudly over the sparkling waters of Hyas Lake. Pass more campsites as you progress, soon reaching the last lakeside campsite. From here the trail leaves the water for the last 2.0 miles through second-growth forest and wildflower-filled meadows to the parking area. Emerge from the trees into Tucquala Meadows to complete the loop and end your 13.4-mile journey.

GOING FARTHER

Aside from a trek out to Peggys Pond, a few side trips are well within reach for those planning an overnight. A trip down to Deep Lake (Hike 55) is an easy addition for those staying at Peggys Pond. While challenging, there is time to include a side trip up to Tuck and Robin Lakes (Hike 57), but rather than a rushed day trip, you are far better off budgeting an extra night in the wilderness to fully explore the "Little Enchantments."

60 LAKE INGALLS

DISTANCE: 8.8 miles
ELEVATION GAIN: 2100 feet in; 100 feet out
HIGH POINT: 6500 feet
DIFFICULTY: Moderate
HIKING TIME: 6 to 8 hours
BEST SEASON: Early summer to late fall

TRAIL TRAFFIC: Heavy foot traffic
PERMIT: Northwest Forest Pass
MAPS: USGS Mt. Stuart; Green Trails Mount Stuart No. 209
TRAILHEAD GPS: 47.4366°N, 120.937°W
NOTE: High-clearance vehicle recommended.

GETTING THERE: Take I-90 to Exit 85, following signs to State Route 970; merge onto SR 970 and continue 6.5 miles to Teanaway Road. Turn left and continue 13.1 miles, trading pavement for gravel to reach a fork just past 29 Pines Campground. Veer right onto Forest Road 9737 (North Fork Teanaway Road), following it 9.6 miles to the road end and the Esmeralda Trailhead. Note that additional forks branch off FR 9737 and could cause confusion. Once you're on FR 9737, always veer left when in doubt. Privy available.

Rock gardens and wildflower-filled creek basins, dusty trail and rugged vistas: the ever-popular hike out to Lake Ingalls is a delight. Teeming with mountain goats, the lake is a quintessential alpine lake, one that all hikers should have on their list of destinations.

From the Esmeralda Basin Trailhead, follow the Esmeralda Basin Trail #1394 on what remains of an old mining road up the hillside into the pines. Reach the Lake Ingalls Trail #1390 after a short 0.3 mile, and follow it as it veers right and begins to climb. The trail switchbacks up the mountainside, climbing steadily for 1.2 miles through open country.

At 1.5 miles, reach the junction with the Longs Pass Trail #1229. The views are almost immediately phenomenal. The Esmeralda Peaks are the nearest craggy, cliffy edifice, with dozens more mountaintops surrounding it. Alternate between savoring this engaging landscape and keeping an eye on the trail to avoid the loose stones that invariably find their way underfoot.

The rugged shore of Lake Ingalls with Mount Stuart in the distance

Continue past the Longs Pass junction, and begin a long upward traverse toward Ingalls Pass. Roll past boulders along the dusty trail, eyeing mesmerizing views. A few scattered trees crop up along the trail, but most of your sightline is unobstructed. Savor it all as you push up and over 6500-foot Ingalls Pass at 3.1 miles, entering the Alpine Lakes Wilderness as you do. The jagged Stuart Range now takes the stage, with Mount Stuart rising above the rest. Take in the Ingalls Creek Valley below Stuart. Look north to the heights of Ingalls Peak and below it, still hidden from view, Lake Ingalls.

Press onward into the Headlight Basin, named for Headlight Creek that flows through it—the name likely a legacy of the area's prospecting days. The trail splits shortly after the pass, the way to the right signed "Ingalls Way Alternate #1390.2." The main path heads left,

hugging the rim of the basin, while the alternate veers slightly right on a more direct route to the lake, plunging down into the basin, then climbing back out again on the other side. The main trail has more mileage, the alternate more elevation. Either route is a romp through patchy wildflower meadows, rock gardens, and trickling streams. Camping is prohibited at Lake Ingalls, so those overnighting should opt for the cross-basin approach, which passes a few more campsites en route.

Day hikers should keep left on the main trail, as it affords the best views. Press toward Ingalls Peak for an enjoyable mile-long tour of Headlight Basin, connecting with the alternate trail at a boulder field near the creek at 4.1 miles. It's a short but tough scramble up to the lake from here. Work your way up through the scree to reach the rocky, barren lakeside, likely populated by a goat or three. Find a quiet spot

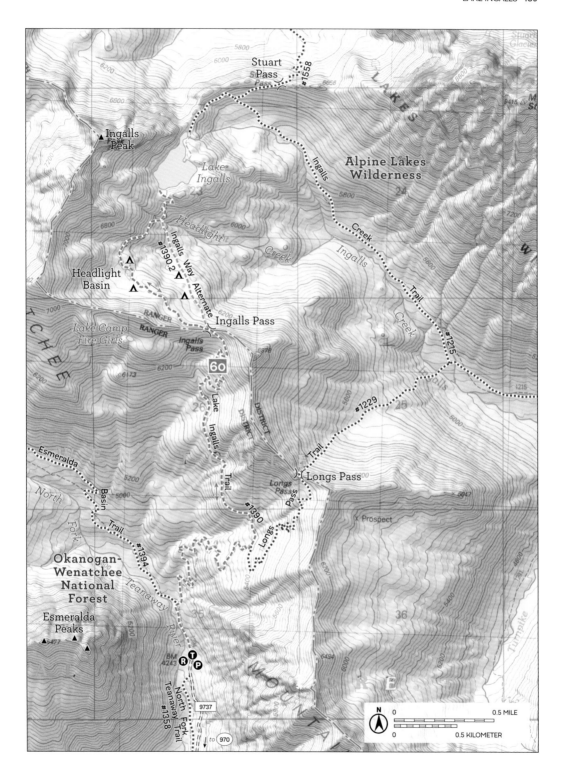

on a giant slab of rock and take in the stunning setting.

GOING FARTHER

From the lake it is not much farther to scramble up to Stuart Pass, following a faint boot path around the west side of the lake. Those planning a longer trip can then continue down from the pass along the Jack Creek Trail #1558 or the Ingalls Creek Trail #1215 (Hike 97).

HISTORY

There are a lot of Ingallses in the area—a peak, a lake, a creek, and a pass. All of them were named for and possibly by Captain Benjamin Ingalls, who led a survey expedition over the Wenatchee Mountains in 1855. He is credited with being the first prospector to discover gold in the area, though the gold find was not reported as part of the survey, and there has been a great deal of speculation over the years regarding exactly when and where Captain Ingalls made his discovery. We do know that Ingalls intended to return in 1861 to claim his riches—reportedly an alpine lake lined with gold quartz.

He never made it. A tree branch snagged on Ingalls's pack and whipped backward into the man behind him, causing the man to fire the fifty-caliber rifle he was carrying into Ingalls's back. As he lay dying on the banks of the Columbia River, Ingalls sketched out the location of his find before passing away two days later. The site he described was never found, becoming the stuff of legend. The quest to find the lake of gold drew fortune hunters to the area, and the legend and tragic end of Captain Ingalls led to the sprinkling of the Ingalls name over this section of wilderness.

Prospecting promoted by the legendary Ingalls gold lent the area names like Fortune Pass and Headlight Creek. Adits and shafts were dug in the area, and enough ore was pulled out of the nearby Tip Top prospect to prompt the building of a primitive mill. In the end, there was never enough mineral wealth found to prompt major mining work in the Ingalls Creek drainage.

61 RED TOP LOOKOUT

DISTANCE: 3.0 miles
ELEVATION GAIN: 350 feet
HIGH POINT: 5361 feet
DIFFICULTY: Easy
HIKING TIME: 2 to 3 hours
BEST SEASON: Early spring to late fall

TRAIL TRAFFIC: Moderate foot traffic
PERMIT: Northwest Forest Pass
MAPS: USGS Red Top Mountain; Green Trails
Mount Stuart No. 209, Green Trails Liberty No. 210
TRAILHEAD GPS: 47.2975°N, 120.7603°W

GETTING THERE: Take I-90 to Exit 85, following signs for State Route 970. Merge onto SR 970 and continue 16.6 miles, as SR 970 turns into Highway 97, to Forest Road 9738 on the left, just beyond the Mineral Creek Campground. Take FR 9738 for 2.6 winding miles to FR 9702, signed "Red Top Mountain." Turn left onto FR 9702 and continue another 4.5 miles to the trailhead parking area. Privy available.

This short loop hike has it all: incredible views, a restored fire lookout, and a tour of agate fields favored by rock hounds. The hike delivers big rewards without much strain, making it a popular choice for young families and those looking to stretch their legs while on their way to other destinations.

From the trailhead, follow old roadbed toward the lookout perched on a finger of granite just above the treetops. After 0.2 mile, reach the signed junction with the Red Top Trail #1364.1 and the Teanaway Ridge Trail #1364, which marks the beginning of the loop. The views and the lookout are to your left, as is the steepest grade. The agate fields are to the right, but head left first to get the work out of the way and enjoy the vistas earlier in the day. During the spring and early summer, wildflowers are common along this stretch of trail, splashing purples, yellows, and whites across the red-gray rocks.

The sign suggests it's 0.5 mile to the lookout, but it is not even half that distance; the steep trail delivers you to the top in about 0.2 mile. While the lookout cabin is staffed in the summer and they are happy to answer any questions you have, you're likely to be too distracted by the sweeping views. Snowy Mount Rainier dominates the southern skyline. The north is a sea of rocky spires, with Mount Stuart rising high along the Stuart Range. Swing east to cast your gaze over the dozens of prominences in the Chelan and Entiat Mountains. To the northwest find the Teanaway peaks.

Soak up the views and poke your head into the lookout to see the historic equipment they have, including a working Osborne Firefinder, before continuing along the trail as it descends the bluff. In 0.2 mile reach another junction, this time with the Teanaway Ridge Trail and the Blue Creek Trail #1364.2. On your return, you'll take the Teanaway Ridge Trail to the right to loop back to the trailhead. For now, ignore the Blue Creek Trail and veer left onto the Teanaway Ridge Trail to the agate fields, reaching them at the junction with the Indian Creek Trail #1364.3 at 0.9 mile from the trailhead. Interpretive signs provide information about the rocks found here.

Wander among the rocks until the 1.5-mile mark, when the trail starts to angle downward. It continues out to FR 9738-111 at 2.0 miles and after some forest-road walking regains the

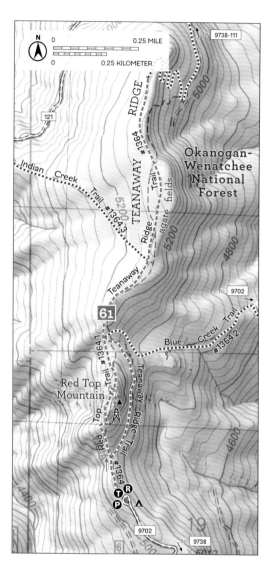

Teanaway Ridge Trail. Instead, turn around and work your way back down the trail, passing the junction with the Blue Creek Trail at 2.4 miles. Continue for another 0.6 mile, keeping close to the base of the lookout bluff as you progress, soon closing the loop and arriving back at the parking area.

HISTORY

In 1924 a fire lookout cabin was built on the red-tinted prominence then known as Redtop.

The Stuart Mountain Range dominates the northern horizon from the summit of Red Top Mountain.

The cabin was replaced in 1928 with a more standardized D-6 cupola cabin. Then in 1952, an L-4 tower cabin was added alongside the 1928 cabin on what was increasingly called "Red Top." The lookout was actively used for decades before it was largely abandoned sometime in the 1970s. Between 1996 and 1997, volunteers restored the Red Top Lookout and returned it to service, and the lookout is now staffed during the summer.

62 INGALLS CREEK

DISTANCE: 6.0 miles
ELEVATION GAIN: 900 feet
HIGH POINT: 2900 feet
DIFFICULTY: Easy
HIKING TIME: 3 to 4 hours
BEST SEASON: Late spring to late fall
PERMIT: Northwest Forest Pass

TRAIL TRAFFIC: Moderate foot and equestrian traffic
MAPS: USGS Blewett, USGS Enchantment Lakes; Green Trails Liberty No. 210, Green Trails Mount Stuart No. 209
TRAILHEAD GPS: 47.4629°N, 120.6733°W

GETTING THERE: Take I-90 to Exit 85, following signs to State Route 970. Merge onto SR 970 and continue 37.9 miles, as SR 970 turns into Highway 97, to Ingalls Creek Road on the left. Turn onto the road, cross the bridge, and keep left at the fork, continuing 1.2 miles to the road end and trailhead. Privy available.

Explore the Ingalls Creek Valley on this creekside hike through fields of wildflowers set beneath the towering granite buttress of the Stuart Range. Trek through swaths of burn from relatively recent fires, clamber over boulder fields, and glide through groves of sheltering trees in the company of the rushing waters of Ingalls Creek.

From the trailhead, the Ingalls Creek Trail #1215 begins gently, the wide and dusty trail ascending slightly as it enters the Alpine Lakes Wilderness at 0.3 mile. Wildflowers are abundant here, a wide variety blooming trailside from spring to midsummer. While the trail has long been known for its dazzling wildflower show, the 2014 wildfires have given the flowers more room to shine.

At 0.8 mile pass a swimming hole that tempts you to take off your boots and take a break from the dusty trail. Pass campsite after campsite as you progress, with a particularly good one at 1.0 mile that is perfect for a first backpack with a little one or a first-timer.

As you progress up the creek, cross streams tumbling down talus fields, hop across rocks, and peer up avalanche chutes at the sharp peaks above. Another good campsite is at 3.0 miles, where the terrain and trail begin to change. This is a good turnaround point for day hikers, as the trail becomes brushier ahead.

Settle in for lunch, enjoying your view of Three Brothers on the opposite side of Ingalls Creek.

Long trails like this offer a little something for everyone. They allow day hikers to get a taste of the trail while backpackers can cover a lot of distance without an enormous amount of elevation gain. With lovely views, varied landscapes, a wildflower bonanza, and ample space to stretch out, Ingalls Creek has enough to offer to keep you coming back again and again.

GOING FARTHER

The Ingalls Creek Trail extends 15.5 miles to Stuart Pass. Backpackers can push as far as they would like, with campsites fairly common along the route. But the trail itself is just the beginning. A half dozen trails branch off from Ingalls Creek, though many require fording the creek or balancing across it on a fallen log. Beginning around the 5.5-mile mark, reach the Falls Creek Trail #1216. Signs point across the water toward forested slopes and steep grades.

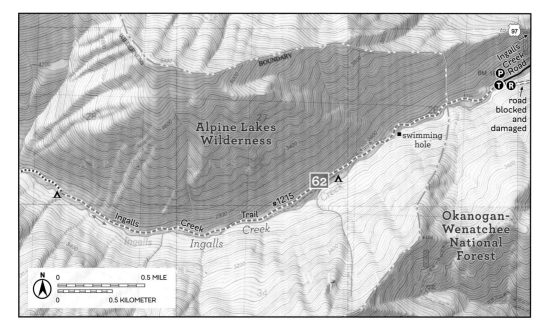

Ingalls Creek is your constant companion as you hike deeper into the valley.

Also in this area, find the grave of Fred Ericson, a man who owned a cabin nearby and was killed in an avalanche in 1928.

Beyond Falls Creek reach trails leading up various creek drainages including Cascade, Hardscrabble, Fourth, and Turnpike Creeks. If you prefer passes, you have the option of Longs Pass or Stuart Pass. See Hike 97 for ideas on farther-flung destinations.

HISTORY

In the 1910s, automobile touring was on the rise, and Washington's roadways were expanding and improving. The long-sought dream of a reliable roadway from Seattle through the Cascades was realized in 1915 with the dedication of the Sunset Highway, which ran from Spokane to Renton over Snoqualmie Pass. By 1922 it was routed to go over Blewett Pass.

As a result of the increased traffic through Blewett Pass, gas stations and accommodations popped up all along the route, including the Ingalls Creek Lodge, originally built in the 1920s where the Ingalls Creek Trailhead is today. Old pipes and a few crumbling foundations found here date back to that building. In 1942 the lodge was purchased by Edmond and Florence Archambault. In 1956 the Sunset Highway was expanded and rerouted, which required moving the lodge. The Archambaults moved it 1.3 miles to the other side of the new highway and operated it until 1973, when Florence passed away. The lodge continued to welcome visitors until it burned down around 1985. A replacement lodge was soon built, operating as Ingalls Creek Lodge until 2015, when it was purchased by the adjoining landowner.

OPPOSITE: *Big Heart Lake (Hike 66)*

HIGHWAY 2

SKYKOMISH

A golden larch at Larch Lake (Hike 78)

63 LAKE DOROTHY AND BEAR, DEER, AND SNOQUALMIE LAKES

DISTANCE: 3.0 miles to Lake Dorothy outlet; 13.4 miles to Snoqualmie Lake
ELEVATION GAIN: 900 feet to Lake Dorothy; 1600 feet in, 700 feet out to Snoqualmie Lake
HIGH POINT: 3100 feet (Lake Dorothy); 3800 feet (Snoqualmie Lake)
DIFFICULTY: Easy (Lake Dorothy); moderate (Snoqualmie Lake)

HIKING TIME: 4 to 8 hours or overnight
BEST SEASON: Late spring to late fall
TRAIL TRAFFIC: Heavy foot traffic to Lake Dorothy; moderate to light to Snoqualmie Lake
PERMIT: Northwest Forest Pass
MAPS: USGS Snoqualmie Lake, USGS Big Snow Mountain; Green Trails Skykomish No. 175
TRAILHEAD GPS: 47.6087°N, 121.386°W

GETTING THERE: Take Highway 2 to the Money Creek Campground between mileposts 45 and 46. Turn onto the Old Cascade Highway and follow it out toward the campground, crossing the railroad tracks and continuing for 1.0 mile, then turn right onto the Miller River Road (Forest Road 6410). Follow FR 6410 for 9.5 miles as it becomes FR 6412 until the road ends at the trailhead. Privy available.

Climb an elaborate series of boardwalks leading up into the wilderness on this extended hike out past one of the largest alpine lakes in the Alpine Lakes Wilderness. Short and rewarding, the hike to Lake Dorothy is very approachable for kids, families, and nonhiking friends, while the farther-flung Bear, Deer, and eventually Snoqualmie Lakes offer a longer, wilder trek into the woods. Rewards and lakeshores are plentiful along this heavily forested trail following a route that was once nearly a highway—a proposed road so controversial it helped spur the creation of the Alpine Lakes Wilderness.

The Dorothy Lake Trail #1072 begins easily, following the East Fork Miller River for a little over 0.4 mile before crossing into the Alpine Lakes Wilderness. Just beyond, reach Camp Robber Creek, and enjoy the rushing water at the bridge before plunging deeper into the old-growth forest. Across the bridge the trail steepens, but stairs, boardwalks, and countless volunteer hours have tamed the once-rocky trail. Thousands of boots also keep the trail wide and extremely well maintained.

At 1.5 miles, a junction with a very short spur trail points you to the log-filled Lake Dorothy outlet and a view of the narrow lake with Big Snow Mountain in the distance. After this side trip, the main trail then continues along the entire length of Lake Dorothy, passing numerous campsites and backcountry toilets along the way. Small islands dot the lake and private nooks and coves abound, making it easy to find a good place for a break or a campsite.

For additional trail time, continue around the far end of the lake. The company soon dwindles and you'll find yourself largely alone as you pass a large camping area at 3.0 miles. Cross a few creeks as you climb to the saddle between Lake Dorothy and Bear Lake at 4.7 miles, where the trail becomes the Snoqualmie Lake Trail #1002.

Continue to the quiet shores of Bear Lake at 5.0 miles. Campsites are located here, but press onward to Deer Lake 0.3 mile distant. Explore to find a hidden camp by a waterfall between the two lakes. The trail continues to the end

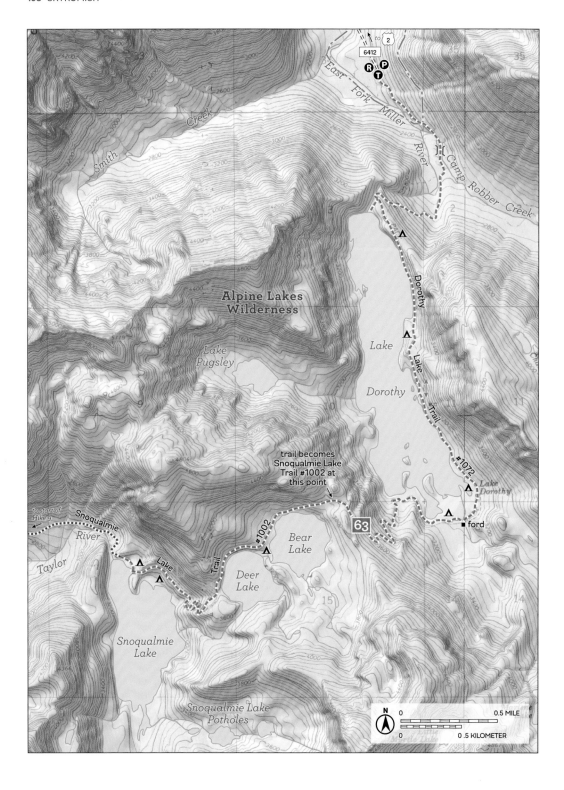

Smith Creek

2

6412

R P

T

East Fork Miller River

Camp Robber Creek

Alpine Lakes
Wilderness

Lake Pugsley

Lake Dorothy

Dorothy Lake Trail

#1072

Lake Dorothy

trail becomes
Snoqualmie Lake
Trail #1002 at
this point

63

ford

to start of
Hike 9

Snoqualmie River

Taylor

Lake

#1002

Trail

Bear Lake

Deer Lake

Snoqualmie Lake

Snoqualmie Lake
Potholes

N

0   0.5 MILE
0   .5 KILOMETER

of Deer Lake and then begins the precipitous descent to enormous Snoqualmie Lake.

The trail makes quite a drop in about a mile from Deer Lake, reaching the first decent campsites on Snoqualmie Lake at 6.3 miles. Continue west to the far northern end of the lake at 6.7 miles. Whether you're overnighting here or turning around at one of the lakes in between, the rich and lush old growth is a palpable presence. Knowing that all of this wilderness was on the chopping block in the late 1960s adds an air of wonder. Linger long and be thankful for those who worked so tirelessly to preserve this chain of subalpine lakes from the bulldozer and the saw.

GOING FARTHER

Through-hikers can continue beyond Snoqualmie Lake, following the Snoqualmie Lake Trail (Hike 9) down into the Middle Fork Snoqualmie Valley.

HISTORY

Lake Dorothy is one of dozens of lakes named after women, a tradition started by Forest Supervisor Albert H. Sylvester, who in 1909 began naming lakes he came across after wives, sisters, mothers, and daughters of forest service workers (see Hike 87 for more detail). Whether Sylvester or one of his many forest rangers named Lake Dorothy is not known, but we do know the lake has borne the name for more than one hundred years.

In the 1960s, forest managers proposed ramming a highway along the shores of Lake Dorothy, past Deer, Bear, and Snoqualmie Lakes, and beside the Taylor River down through the Middle Fork Snoqualmie Valley to North Bend. While roadside recreation was certainly incorporated into the proposal, the primary motivation was access to the rich old-growth timber that would have (temporarily) lined the route. There was already a growing wilderness movement at the time, and the proposal to cut a highway through a once-remote hiking area, in conjunction with a similar project near Cooper Lake, propelled activists

Often overlooked, Deer Lake has more than a few campsites tucked along its shores.

to form the Alpine Lakes Protection Society (ALPS) and ultimately led to the creation of the Alpine Lakes Wilderness. Still, plans progressed and the Washington State legislature even gave the proposed highway an official number, one that would never be used: Highway 29.

64 EVANS LAKE

DISTANCE: 1.0 mile
ELEVATION GAIN: 50 feet
HIGH POINT: 3700 feet
DIFFICULTY: Easy
HIKING TIME: 30 minutes to 1 hour
BEST SEASON: Late spring to late fall

TRAIL TRAFFIC: Light foot traffic
PERMIT: None
MAPS: USGS Skykomish; Green Trails Skykomish
No. 175
TRAILHEAD GPS: 47.6588°N, 121.3231°W

GETTING THERE: Take Highway 2 to the Foss River Road (Forest Road 68) near milepost 50. Turn onto FR 68 and continue for 4.7 miles as the road turns to gravel to a junction with FR 6840. Veer left to follow FR 6840 for 3.4 miles to the junction with FR 6846. Head left onto FR 6846 and drive 2.3 miles to the signed Evans Lake Trailhead.

On the marshy shore of Evans Lake on an overcast day

Often called the easiest hike in the Alpine Lakes Wilderness, Evans Lake is usually visited by only the most ardent alpine lake enthusiasts, but it makes an excellent excursion for introducing little backpackers, youngsters, and burgeoning families to the wilderness.

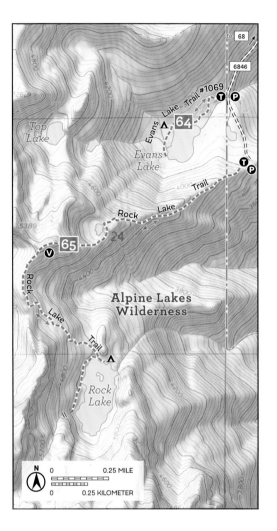

In less than 0.5 mile, the wide and well-trodden Evans Lake Trail #1069 snakes beneath thick stands of old growth and mossy understory to the shore of this quiet, tree-lined lake. It's wilderness with minimal effort and a pleasant alpine lake that is never far from the car—a trial run for bigger, better, and longer adventures.

There are a few campsites around the lake for those fledgling backpackers, though most hikers will find a secluded spot to settle in and soak up the serenity for an hour or two. With about 10 miles of unpaved forest road to navigate to reach the trailhead, you're unlikely to be sharing the lake with anyone else.

GOING FARTHER
Pair this hike with Rock Lake (Hike 65) to round out a day of hiking. Fisherfolk and adventuresome bushwhackers can follow a faint boot path near Evans Lake's inlet creek west up to Top Lake, though the path soon disappears as you progress up the hill.

65 ROCK LAKE

DISTANCE: 4.4 miles
ELEVATION GAIN: 1500 feet in; 700 feet out
HIGH POINT: 5300 feet
DIFFICULTY: Hard
HIKING TIME: 3 to 4 hours
BEST SEASON: Late spring to late fall

TRAIL TRAFFIC: Very light foot traffic
PERMIT: Northwest Forest Pass
MAPS: USGS Skykomish; Green Trails Skykomish No. 175
TRAILHEAD GPS: 47.6545°N, 121.3204°W

GETTING THERE: Take Highway 2 to the Foss River Road (Forest Road 68) near milepost 50. Turn onto FR 68 and continue for 4.7 miles as the road turns to gravel to a junction with FR 6840. Veer left to follow FR 6840

Catch a glimpse of Rock Lake and Malachite Peak on the descent to the lakeshore.

for another 3.4 miles to the junction with FR 6846. Head left onto FR 6846 and drive 2.6 miles, past the signed Evans Lake Trailhead, to the end of the road and the unofficial Rock Lake trailhead.

Sometimes the pseudosecret paths and unmarked trails are the most fun. The trail to Rock Lake is primitive but well-worn. It leads to a secluded alpine lake that requires some work to attain. Rock Lake is certainly a challenging trail that is reserved for experienced hikers comfortable with a little routefinding, but the solitude is well worth the climb. More likely than not, you won't meet a soul on this climb through the wilderness.

From the end of the road, backtrack a few dozen feet to a small unmarked path on the left (west) side of the road. Follow it into the brush and trees, ducking under branches as you pick your way up to a ridgeline where the path widens into something that more closely resembles a trail. Follow the ridge as it climbs straight up the mountainside, eschewing switchbacks for a more streamlined approach.

At 0.8 mile, the trail drops down to an unnamed tarn and skips across the outlet creek before beginning a tough and very steep scramble up above the tarn. The trail can fade or become lost under blowdowns, so when in doubt, head up, up, up to a rocky prominence that offers views of Evans Lake below.

From here the trail continues through the trees before descending to hidden Rock Lake, straddled by Malachite Peak's tall cliffs. A small island in the lake draws the eye, as does the large waterfall spilling down into the lake from the cliffs above. The landscape strikes an otherworldly scene and makes the lakeside feel far more remote than a mere 1.9 miles of trail would normally provide. If you're spending the night, there are a few campsites along the water near the outlet creek. If you're feeling adventurous, you can follow a faint trail 0.3 mile around the edge of the lake to the base of the waterfall.

GOING FARTHER

Evans Lake (Hike 64) is short, sweet, and worth the visit. It is also a useful base camp for those who are spending a day up at Rock Lake and don't want to haul tents and stoves up the difficult trail.

HISTORY

This unofficial trail has been an open secret for decades. Built entirely by fishermen determined to find a quiet place to enjoy their sport, the rough trail is perhaps difficult by design.

66 FOSS LAKES

DISTANCE: 14.6 miles
ELEVATION GAIN: 3300 feet in; 300 feet out
HIGH POINT: 4900 feet
DIFFICULTY: Hard
HIKING TIME: Overnight
BEST SEASON: Early summer to late fall

TRAIL TRAFFIC: Moderate to heavy foot traffic
PERMIT: Northwest Forest Pass
MAPS: USGS Skokomish, USGS Big Snow Mountain; Green Trails Skykomish No. 175
TRAILHEAD GPS: 47.6348°N, 121.3039°W

GETTING THERE: Take Highway 2 to the Foss River Road (Forest Road 68) near milepost 50. Turn onto FR 68 and continue for 4.7 miles as the road turns to gravel to a junction with FR 6835. Veer left to follow FR 6835 for just under 2 miles to the end of the road and the West Fork Foss Lakes Trailhead. Privy available.

Trek deep into the Foss River Valley, passing stunning alpine lakes, rushing waterfalls, and swaying marshlands. Expect wildflowers and shimmering shores, wilderness and ancient forest. Stacked nearly on top of one another, about a dozen named alpine lakes are packed into this long river valley, all reachable with varying degrees of effort—and all more than worth it. The length and difficulty of this trail means that crowds tend to thin as you push closer to Big Heart Lake, making it a great backpacking destination. Still, this lake is the most popular stopping point on this trail, very likely to host throngs of backpackers, fisherfolk, and even an enthusiastic alpine kayaker or two.

From the trailhead, the West Fork Foss Lakes Trail #1064 enters a mixed forest of alder, hemlock, and underbrush before crossing into the Alpine Lakes Wilderness. As you begin climbing, note the dry stream bed that parallels the trail—a legacy of the 2006 floods. At roughly 0.5 mile, cross the West Fork Foss River on a sturdy bridge spanning a small

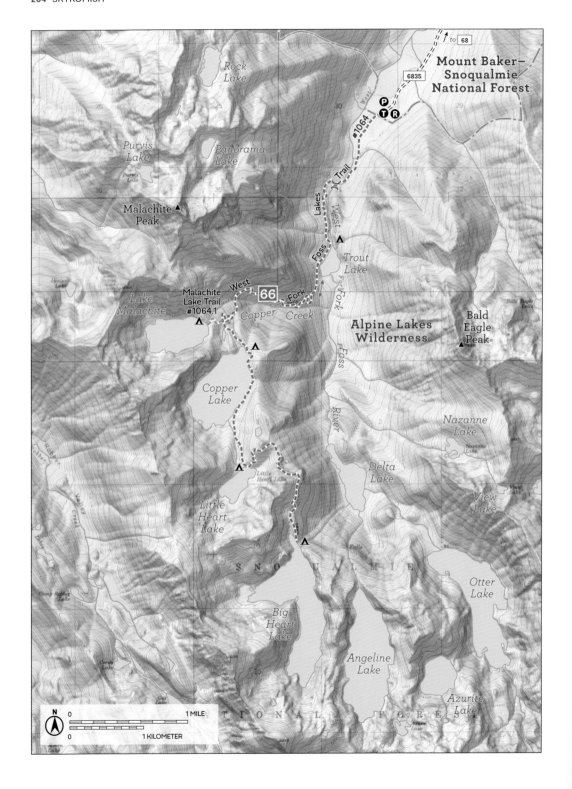

Rugged and wild alpine landscapes lure hundreds of backpackers to Big Heart Lake every year.

canyon carved by those same floods. Continue climbing through deepening forest for 1.0 mile to Trout Lake at 1.6 miles. Tucked beneath the rocky slopes and exposed cliff faces of Malachite Peak and Bald Eagle Peak, Trout Lake offers a taste of what is to come. With numerous campsites and plenty of room to fish, the lake is also a good option for backpacking with youngsters.

From Trout Lake the trail becomes steeper and rockier, switchbacking up the mountainside while following the outlet stream that many folks call Copper Creek. The sheer cliffs and steep drop-offs create a number of waterfalls, often collectively referred to as the Waterfalls of the West Fork River Valley. Water tumbles hundreds of feet down to the West Fork Foss River, much of which can be seen from the trail. Continue climbing up to the 1064.1 spur trail that leads out to Lake Malachite.

Push past the junction, crossing a bridge over the top of a waterfall, and then balance across a series of stepping stones to arrive at Copper Lake at just under the 4.0-mile mark. There is less camping at Copper Lake, though there are a few sites tucked in under the trees. Copper Lake is a worthy turnaround point for day trippers, and an ideal setting to drop your gear and take a hard-earned break.

Continue along the shore of Copper Lake, through rock slides and past occasional viewpoints, to the far end of the lake. Here the trail turns upward again, though the grade is more reasonable. After another few hundred feet of elevation gain, arrive at Little Heart Lake at 5.4 miles, nestled at the bottom of a rocky cirque. There is some camping here, but the real prize is still ahead, less than 2.0 miles down the trail.

This last section of trail from Little Heart Lake to Big Heart Lake is the most challenging portion of the route. Not only does it come late in the hike, but much of the steep ascent is along exposed rocky slopes that offer big views but little protection from the sun. The trail passes through talus fields and among a few small tarns as it relentlessly pushes upward. After a little over 1.0 mile of climbing, the trail crosses over a ridge and begins quickly switchbacking down toward the lakeshore.

Suddenly the trees thin and Big Heart Lake lies sparkling before you, its shores a tangle of gray rock, bleached driftwood, vibrant evergreens, and snowy ridgelines. Settle in to enjoy the view. When you're ready to set up camp, continue on the trail as it drops down to the water and crosses a wide expanse of driftwood at the lake's outlet before beginning to climb up a small hill. Here, at 7.3 miles from the trailhead, start looking for a campsite—there are quite a few spots scattered around the hillside.

GOING FARTHER

Aside from the 0.5-mile side trip to Lake Malachite, there are quite a few other alpine lakes hidden in the valleys and bowls surrounding Big Heart Lake. Angeline Lake, Azurite Lake, and Chetwoot Lake are all accessible via faint boot paths from Big Heart Lake or a little bushwhacking. If you're looking for solitude, check out the valleys and bowls surrounding Big Heart Lake.

HISTORY

Back around the turn of the last century, prospectors explored the Foss River Valley in search of mineral wealth. By 1906 the Foss River Consolidated Mining Company was formed out of various mining claims that had sprung up. Copper Lake and Lake Malachite are part of that era's legacy, as both were named for the presence of malachite copper ore found in the area.

Today's trail likely follows routes first cut by those early prospectors, and traces of abandoned boot paths that once connected mining claims can still be found throughout the river valley. In 2006 flooding caused considerable damage to the West Fork Foss Lakes Trail, washing out bridges and transforming portions of the trail to rocky stream bed. In 2010 the Washington Trails Association and the Ira Spring Trust repaired and rerouted the first half mile of trail.

67 NECKLACE VALLEY

DISTANCE: 16.8 miles
ELEVATION GAIN: 3200 feet
HIGH POINT: 4800 feet
DIFFICULTY: Hard
HIKING TIME: 12 hours or overnight
BEST SEASON: Early summer to late fall
TRAIL TRAFFIC: Moderate to heavy foot traffic
PERMIT: Northwest Forest Pass

MAPS: USGS Big Snow Mountain; Green Trails Skykomish No. 175, Green Trails Stevens Pass No. 176
TRAILHEAD GPS: 47.6649°N, 121.2883°W
NOTE: Crossing the East Fork Foss River is sometimes difficult when the water is high; use caution.

GETTING THERE: Take Highway 2 to the Foss River Road (Forest Road 68) near milepost 50. Turn onto FR 68 and continue for 4.2 miles as the road turns to gravel, to the Necklace Valley Trailhead and parking area on the left. Privy available.

This long and somewhat strenuous hike out to a lush meadowy valley filled with a half dozen alpine lakes certainly lights your imagination. There is plenty of room to camp along one of these remote but popular lakes and plenty of history to keep you interested.

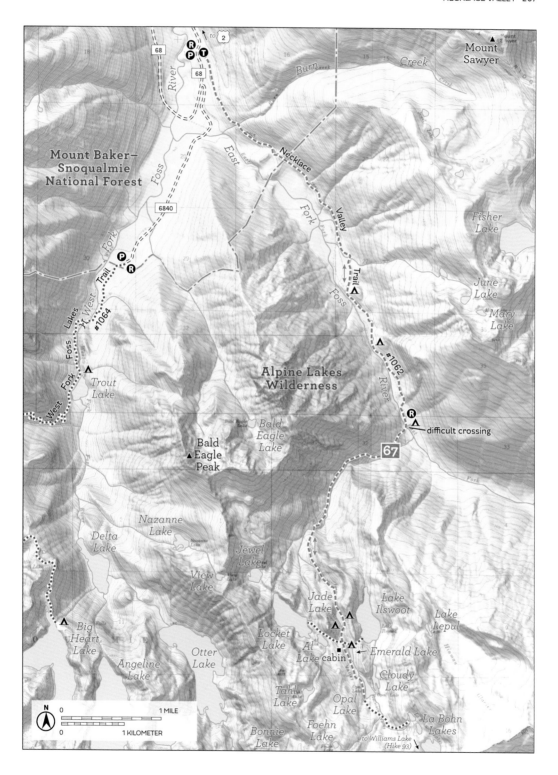

Enjoy an afternoon at Emerald Lake with Mount Hinman rising in the distance.

From the trailhead, the Necklace Valley Trail #1062 begins very gently, following long abandoned rail bed into the trees. Head up the valley through mature second-growth forest still bearing signs of the logging crew cut it took in the 1930s. Crumbling mossy stumps bearing springboard notches can be spied through the hemlocks as you hop across creeks, working your way toward the East Fork Foss River. Cross into the Alpine Lakes Wilderness at 1.5 miles.

Feel the valley walls close in, marveling as you glide over streams on aging puncheon bridges. Wildflowers are abundant, the sound of rushing water constant. After 3.3 miles reach a decent campsite, with another not far beyond at 3.8 miles. These are perfect for backpacking with a little one for the first time or just spending the night in the woods.

Push onward to the 4.6-mile mark and a sometimes-difficult crossing of the East Fork Foss River; use caution during times of high water. Campsites and a backcountry toilet make this a popular stopping point for more-casual backpackers or those wanting to tackle the next portion of the trail in the morning rather than the heat of the afternoon.

After the crossing, the trail leaves the bottom of the river valley to begin a rough-and-tumble climb up the ridge, following the Necklace Valley Lakes drainage creek. Ascend steeply, trading trees for open country dominated by talus fields, low brush, and the dancing creek. The granite crown of Bald Eagle Peak emerges from behind the ridge as you gain elevation, while the greenery of the East Fork Foss River Valley opens behind, framing the barren top of Shroud Mountain rising on the far side of the valley. Pause frequently along the well-maintained trail to enjoy the views and catch your breath as you slowly but surely draw closer to the meadow-filled lake basin ahead.

After more than 2.0 miles of hard climbing, reach Jade Lake, the first of the Necklace Valley Lakes. Here, after 7.4 miles of hiking, it's tempting to drop your pack, but the show is just beginning. Enjoy your first real sighting of Mount Hinman, the rocky precipice that presides grandly over Necklace Valley.

Press onward another 0.5 mile to a memorial cabin placed by the Trail Blazers in a rolling meadow just above Emerald Lake, at 7.9 miles. From here side trails branch out in many directions, but this route heads to the last Necklace

Valley lake, Opal, another 0.5 mile through the lush meadows.

Other trails lead down to Emerald Lake and beyond to Lake Ilswoot, where some of the best campsites lie hidden in the trees, and past Al Lake to Locket Lake. Tucked in Necklace Valley find Cloudy Lake and Jewel Lake. Farther up the scree-covered slopes are Tahl Lake, Tank Lakes, Foehn Lake, and La Bohn Lakes.

Spend some time exploring the glacier-carved valley, seeking out hidden alpine lakes, discovering enchanting campsites, and climbing to quiet overlooks. But remember that this is high-traffic high country, especially prone to long-term damage. Stick to the existing boot paths and side trails that have already created deep creases in the meadow to keep from damaging it even more. Camp at designated sites, and if a site isn't readily apparent, press onward. There are good sites at all the lakes.

GOING FARTHER

For those looking for adventure, a number of lakes and basins are accessible with a little cross-country roaming and ridge climbing. In addition to those mentioned above, Williams Lake (Hike 93) and the Chain Lakes are a short distance away.

From the Tank Lakes you can head cross-country to descend into the West Foss River Valley, passing Otter Lake or Big Heart Lake (Hike 66) to connect with the West Fork Foss Lakes Trail #1064 and loop back to FR 68, a mere 0.5 mile from the Necklace Valley Trailhead. There's a fair amount of route-finding along this big loop, but it sees enough traffic that faint boot paths can be followed.

HISTORY

Back around the early 1900s, miners and prospectors roamed the river valleys and mountain passes of the Cascades, hoping to strike it rich. Efforts by the Foss River Consolidated Copper Company resulted in many adits and prospects and even a railroad to haul out the ore and, later, timber. Over the years, the mining waned, as did the timber business, and the railroad tracks were pulled up, but the legacy remains. The first few flat miles of the Necklace Valley Trail follow the old rail bed, and rusting artifacts from mining and logging activities are plentiful along the trail and around the lakes.

The valley was named for the way the three main lakes seem to be strung together like jewels, connected by strands of stream. Jade, Emerald, and Opal are the principal lakes, though later Locket was added to align with the theme. Ilswoot was named for *itswoot*, the Chinook Jargon word for "black bear." Mount Hinman, which presides over the Necklace Valley, was named in 1934 for Dr. Harry B.

Hinman, founder of the Everett chapter of The Mountaineers.

The Necklace Valley cabin was built by the Trail Blazers between 1949 and 1951, inspired by the short-lived Mountain Cabin Memorial Association founded by Ome Daiber in 1947 as a way to honor outdoorsmen who were killed fighting in World War II. Their first attempt was destroyed by an avalanche, and the cabin site was moved to its current location. The cabin was then dedicated to Jack Streeter, who was killed in the final days of the war. Other memorial cabins were built at Nordrum Lake and Lower Tuscohatchie Lake, but the movement did not grow much beyond the initial handful of cabins.

68 TONGA RIDGE AND FISHER LAKE

DISTANCE: 8.8 miles
ELEVATION GAIN: 900 feet in; 400 feet out
HIGH POINT: 5200 feet
DIFFICULTY: Moderate
HIKING TIME: 5 to 8 hours
BEST SEASON: Late spring to early fall

TRAIL TRAFFIC: Moderate foot traffic
PERMIT: Northwest Forest Pass
MAPS: USGS Scenic; Green Trails Skykomish No. 175, Green Trails Stevens Pass No. 176
TRAILHEAD GPS: 47.6788°N, 121.2648°W

GETTING THERE: Take Highway 2 to the Foss River Road (Forest Road 68) near milepost 50. Turn onto FR 68 and continue for 3.5 miles as the road turns to gravel to a junction, turning left onto FR 6830 and following it for almost 7 miles to the signed FR 310 spur. Head right onto the spur and drive a little over 1 mile to the end of the road and the trailhead. Privy available.

While the trail to Fisher Lake is technically unofficial, decades of use have dulled most of its rough edges. What was once a faint path reserved for folks looking to spend a quiet weekend fishing is now a trail frequented by small bands of backpackers and hikers. Large and somewhat secluded, Fisher Lake sits in a tranquil bowl just waiting to be enjoyed.

The Tonga Ridge Trail #1058 begins by gently climbing through second-growth hemlock and fir. The well-maintained trail is largely free of rocks and roots, allowing you to quickly reach the Alpine Lakes Wilderness in 0.6 mile. The route traverses the ridgeline, ambling alternately through meadows and stands of evergreen, gliding over the ridge's ups and downs without much difficulty. The high meadowlands offer bright blasts of colorful wildflowers in the spring, a bounty of blue huckleberries in the fall, and sweeping views of the Foss River and Burn Creek Valleys year-round.

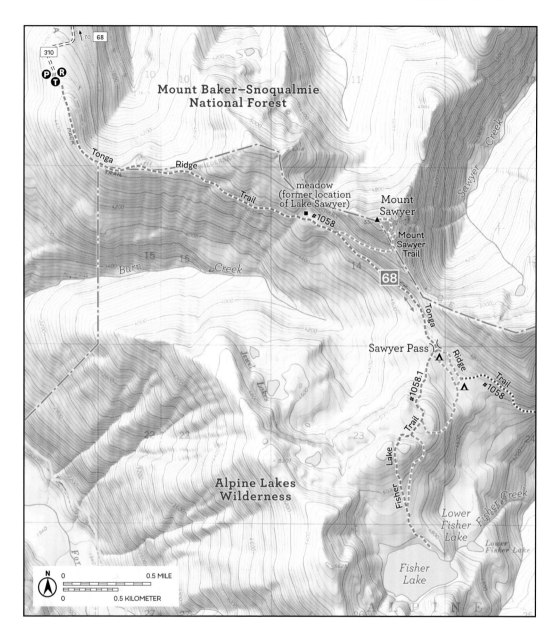

At 2.0 miles you reach a relatively large meadow that older maps mark as Lake Sawyer. Although the small lake is long gone, it is still a useful landmark for finding the unmarked trail to the summit of Mount Sawyer (see Going Farther). Continue to follow the ridgeline for another mile, reaching unassuming Sawyer Pass

at the 3.0-mile mark. There are a few campsites here among the heather, along with a sign pointing toward Deception Creek. Shortly beyond is another sign forbidding campfires above 4000 feet. This is Sawyer Pass, though it may not feel like much, as there was no dramatic climb to reach it and no broad vistas to take in.

Roam Tonga Ridge's subalpine meadows with views of the surrounding mountaintops.

From here, the Tonga Ridge Trail heads to the left, eventually connecting to the far reaches of FR 6830. Instead, veer right, onto the Fisher Lake Trail #1058.1. Note that there are a few unmarked junctions along the way, most of which are short loops that pass small campsites. These loops allow for a number of ways to navigate to the lake, and we recommend the simplest: always keep to the right. Find the first major junction at 3.5 miles, in a small meadow; the next is just ahead at 3.6 miles, and the last is at 4.1 miles. Each time, head right. All along the way the narrow, slightly brushy trail is easy to follow, climbing past small tarns and through grassy meadowlands while offering up a few glimpses of Glacier Peak and other snowy crags you can see so vividly from Mount Sawyer.

Not far past the last junction, the trail begins to angle down toward Fisher Lake's shores. The route veers south around the lake, passing a few access points before largely disappearing into the trees at 4.4 miles from the trailhead. For decades, a rough boot path continued from here out to the Ptarmigan Lakes, but the wilderness has largely reclaimed that approach, so a trek out to the lakes requires an adventurous soul as well as routefinding and bushwhacking skills; it's not recommended for most. Explore around Fisher Lake to reach the lake's outlet, Fisher Creek. Find a quiet spot on the water to enjoy the surrounding landscape and tuck in for a well-earned lunch.

While the Tonga Ridge Trail is an excellent choice for hikers of nearly all ages and skill levels, accessing Fisher Lake is a bit more challenging. It's not as approachable as the main trail, which tends to mean the crowds thin quite a bit beyond Sawyer Pass. It's a great trail for hikers looking for something a little more on the rough and wild side.

GOING FARTHER

The 1.5-mile round trip climb up to the top of Mount Sawyer is not to be missed as the lookout site provides views that make even the most jaded hiker want to linger and soak it all in. Find the boot path to the lookout at the 2.1-mile mark, just beyond the meadows of the onetime Lake Sawyer. Just after entering the trees, look for a small, steep track heading upward (sometimes a small cairn points the way). It's a short scramble and a few steep switchbacks to reach the top and a view of a vast expanse of mountaintops stretching out into the distance.

For a longer backpack, continue down the Tonga Ridge Trail to its end at FR 6830, where you can access the Deception Creek Trail (Hike 69) via spur trail #1059.1.

HISTORY

Back around the early 1900s, mining and timber companies were rolling through the valleys around Skykomish, harvesting trees and digging up ore at breakneck speed. Makeshift camps, overstoked locomotives, and the desire to move resources as quickly as possible inevitably led to forest fires that would threaten the very resources and camps that created the fires in the first place. The danger of forest fires led the Forest Service to build fire lookouts throughout the Skykomish Ranger District to get ahead of outbreaks before they grew out of control. Lookout sites included a fire lookout camp on Tonga Ridge that operated throughout the 1920s, likely established in response to a fire that stripped the trees off Mount Sawyer in 1914. A ranger named George Sawyer spent his life in the forests of the Skykomish District helping keep watch for those fires and, after his death in 1930, Mount Sawyer was named in honor of his service.

69 DECEPTION CREEK TO DECEPTION LAKES

DISTANCE: 16.6 miles
ELEVATION GAIN: 3100 feet
HIGH POINT: 5100 feet
DIFFICULTY: Moderate
HIKING TIME: 10 to 12 hours or overnight
BEST SEASON: Early spring to late fall

TRAIL TRAFFIC: Light foot traffic
PERMIT: Northwest Forest Pass
MAPS: USGS Scenic; Green Trails Stevens Pass
No. 176
TRAILHEAD GPS: 47.7121°N, 121.1937°W

GETTING THERE: Take Highway 2 to Forest Road 6088, also known as Deception Creek Road, near milepost 56 and the Deception Falls Interpretive Site. The poorly signed road can be easy to miss. Eastbound turn right; westbound turn left, following FR 6088 under the railroad trestle for about 0.5 mile to the trailhead.

Surprisingly, the Deception Creek Trail is among the least traveled in the Alpine Lakes Wilderness, despite lush old growth and the impressive cascades of Deception Creek. With relatively easy access to the trailhead and moderate elevation gain, this hike is approachable for almost anyone. And with so much to see and explore, the Deception Lakes are an ideal backpacking destination for an overnight or a base camp for further explorations.

Begin by following the Deception Creek Trail #1059 beneath the crackle of powerlines before plunging into a mature forest of fir, cedar, and hemlock. At 0.4 mile the trail crosses into the Alpine Lakes Wilderness and slips alongside Deception Creek. The somewhat narrow trail

Small falls along Deception Creek

crosses over streams large and small, usually with a bridge or boardwalk. Depending on the season, Deception Creek may have spilled over onto the trail, prompting you to find creative ways of getting across.

After crossing the log bridge over Deception Creek, the trail steepens, pulling you up the mountainside high above the creek. The first few miles climb slowly but steadily up the valley through huckleberry fields. Eventually the trail levels out and crosses Sawyer Creek. At roughly 3 miles, find a campsite well-suited for a break or a turnaround point.

When you're ready, continue onward to the junction with the Deception Creek Cutoff Trail #1059.1 at 4.8 miles, which follows Fisher Creek up to the Tonga Ridge Trail #1058. That's an adventure for another day. Keep left, following the Deception Creek Trail as it passes a campsite and crosses Deception Creek.

The next 2.2 miles from Fisher Creek is the toughest section of the trail; it traverses the ridge and rises far above Deception Creek, switchbacking steeply up forested slopes to reach the Deception Lakes Trail #1059.2 (signed "#1059B" at the trailhead) at 7.0 miles. The Deception Creek Trail continues straight ahead to Deception Pass, but the day's destination lies up and left along the Deception Lakes Trail.

Continue climbing, with the occasional view of the spreading valley below. In another 0.9 mile connect with the Pacific Crest Trail #2000 (PCT). The sign here helpfully points toward Deception Pass for those on a different adventure; for now heed the sign directing you toward Deception Lakes to the left, following the PCT for less than a half mile to reach Deception Lakes at 8.3 miles. There are some good campsites near the lake outlet;

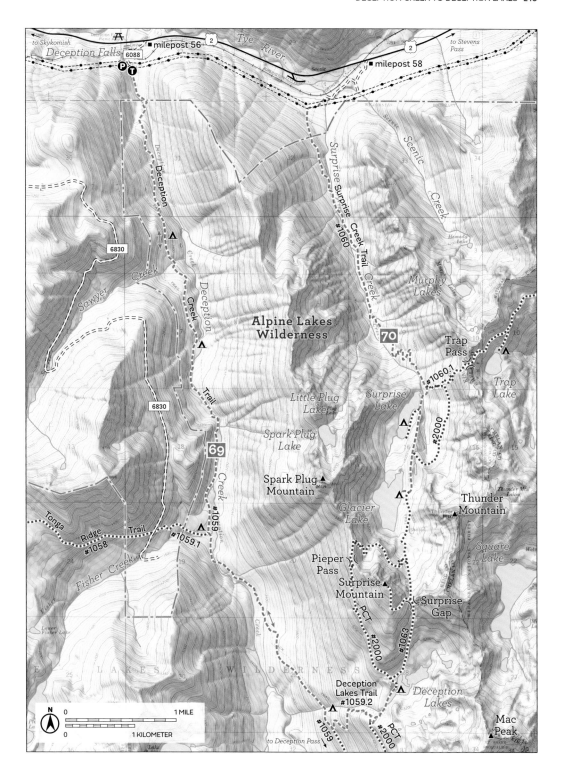

to Skykomish
Deception Falls
6088
milepost 56
Tye River
2
to Stevens Pass
milepost 58

6830

Deception Creek

Sawyer Creek

Deception Creek Trail

Surprise Surprise Creek Trail
#1060

Scenic Creek

Murphy Lakes

Alpine Lakes Wilderness

70

Trap Pass

#1060.1

Trap Lake

6830

Little Plug Lake

Spark Plug Lake

Surprise Lake

#2000

69

Spark Plug Mountain

Glacier Lake

Thunder Mountain

Square Lake

Tonga Ridge Trail
#1058

#1059

#1059.1

Fisher Creek

Pieper Pass

Surprise Mountain

PCT

#1063

Surprise Gap

#2000

Deception Lakes Trail
#1059.2

Deception Lakes

#1059

to Deception Pass

PCT
#2000

Mac Peak

N
0   1 MILE
0   1 KILOMETER

skip across the creek and claim one before continuing down the trail as it skirts the edge of the water.

Cupped in the bowl between Surprise Mountain, Thunder Mountain, and Mac Peak, Deception Lakes are deceivingly large, with waters hidden behind a long, wooded peninsula. Wander and explore, soaking up the wild alpine landscape. For the full experience, stay near the lakes, following boot paths and side trails snaking around the shores.

GOING FARTHER

Add a 1.3-mile trip up the Surprise Mountain Trail to the top of windswept Surprise Mountain, climbing roughly 1200 feet up to enormous views of the surrounding peaks. Or follow the PCT from Deception Lakes out to Deception Pass, which allows a loop back to the trailhead along the Deception Creek Trail #1059 or offers side trips up to Marmot Lake and Lake Clarice (Hike 58) or Tuck and Robin Lakes (Hike 57).

HISTORY

Quite a few geographical features in Washington have earned the name "Deception." Usually this is because the feature caused some sort of confusion upon discovery. Puget Sound's Deception Pass, for example, was named by Captain George Vancouver because it first appeared to be a narrow bay rather than a passageway. In 1893, the last spike of the Great Northern Railway was driven at Deception Creek near this hike's trailhead, connecting Seattle to St. Paul, Minnesota.

70 SURPRISE AND GLACIER LAKES

DISTANCE: 9.5 miles
ELEVATION GAIN: 2700 feet
HIGH POINT: 4900 feet
DIFFICULTY: Moderate
HIKING TIME: 6 to 7 hours
BEST SEASON: Late spring to early fall

TRAIL TRAFFIC: Moderate foot traffic
PERMIT: Northwest Forest Pass
MAPS: USGS Scenic; Green Trails Stevens Pass No. 176
TRAILHEAD GPS: 47.70813°N, 121.1564°W

GETTING THERE: Take Highway 2 to milepost 58 and an unmarked road east of the Iron Goat Interpretive Site. Turn onto this access road and follow it across the Tye River to the Burlington Northern Santa Fe railroad tracks. Cross the tracks and head to the right, paralleling the tracks for a short distance to a spur road heading into the trees. Follow this road a few tenths of a mile to the trailhead.

While this hike is a little long for a day trip, it's attainable for many hikers as most of the elevation gain is concentrated in one short section. Two gorgeous alpine lakes and some big views justify spending a day scouting this trail. There is also a lot to explore in this area, with more than enough to support a decent little backpacking weekend. Surprise Lake is popular in the summer, but few people make the trek in the winter, making it a good snowshoe option as well.

From the trailhead, the Surprise Creek Trail #1060 follows a service road as it crosses under a massive set of powerlines, after which the trail branches off the road and enters the trees, soon crossing into the Alpine Lakes Wilderness at 0.5 mile. Shortly thereafter, reach an impressive system of wooden boardwalks, stairs, and bridges. There is no visible trail along the lower reaches of this hike, as it's hidden beneath the boardwalks, which can be slippery in rain and snow.

Trek through the thick forest of cedar and hemlock, their giant trunks lining the route as you effortlessly cross creeks and glide past tumbling cascades. At 1.1 miles reach Surprise Creek and cross it on a narrow bridge using caution when the water is high. Beyond Surprise Creek the trail leaves the boardwalks behind and continues to gently climb up the valley for another mile before getting down to business. The trail abruptly steepens, climbing nearly 1000 feet in a series of tight switchbacks before leveling out among the thinning trees to reveal the valley below and your first glimpse of Thunder Mountain.

Just before you reach Surprise Lake, pass the Trap Pass Trail #1060.1 spur at the 3.8-mile mark. Continue on the main trail as it dips down to cross over Surprise Creek again before climbing up to the rocky shores of Surprise Lake, nestled at the base of Spark Plug Mountain 3.9 miles from the trailhead.

Some call it a day here, while others continue onward to Glacier Lake, connecting with the Pacific Crest Trail #2000 (PCT) at 4.3 miles at a junction with a sign pointing up the mountainside to Trap Lake (Hike 71). Continue up through thick trees that yield only a few tantalizing glimpses of the really big views of the nearby peaks before dropping down to Glacier Lake. At 4.8 miles, arrive the water's edge and take in the picture-perfect alpine landscape. Tucked in a bowl between Surprise Mountain and Spark Plug Mountain, boulder-lined Glacier Lake offers pristine views and more than one campsite for those looking to stay a little while.

GOING FARTHER

From Surprise Lake, the Trap Pass Trail climbs the steep valley walls in a nearly endless series of switchbacks up to Trap Lake (Hike 71) and continues out to Hope and Mig

Spark Plug Mountain above a frozen Glacier Lake

Lakes (Hike 72) via the PCT. Those thirsty for big views can continue past Glacier Lake to an unmaintained route up the slopes of Surprise Mountain, eventually following short scramble routes up to the summit.

HISTORY

One of two glacier-fed lakes in a depression tucked into a narrow valley between Spark

Plug Mountain and Thunder Mountain, Surprise Lake was named for the "surprise" that comes with finally reaching it after cresting the small ridge surrounding it. Along with nearby Glacier Lake, the duo is collectively known as Upper and Lower Scenic Lakes, named not just for their scenic beauty but also the nearby community of Scenic.

In the late 1880s when the Great Northern Railway was connecting Seattle to the Midwest, railroad workers enjoyed the natural hot springs found near the tracks. One of the first railroad stops on the west side of Stevens Pass was called Madison, but that name was quickly changed to Scenic when a hotel was built in 1904 to take advantage of the hot springs. The Scenic Hot Springs Hotel lasted until 1908, when it caught fire and burned to the ground. The undaunted owners rebuilt the hotel the next year, and it became nationally famous for its baths. A small settlement sprang up around the hot springs, becoming Washington's highest-elevation community west of the Cascades. The hotel was demolished in 1928 during the construction of Great Northern Railway's Cascade Tunnel.

71 TRAP LAKE

DISTANCE: 9.2 miles
ELEVATION GAIN: 2200 feet in; 400 feet out
HIGH POINT: 5400 feet
DIFFICULTY: Hard
HIKING TIME: 5 to 7 hours
BEST SEASON: Summer to early fall

TRAIL TRAFFIC: Light foot traffic
PERMIT: Northwest Forest Pass
MAPS: USGS Stevens Pass; Green Trails Stevens Pass No. 176
TRAILHEAD GPS: 47.71284°N, 121.1073°W

GETTING THERE: Because of barriers in the road, this hike is accessible only from the eastbound lanes of Highway 2. Take Highway 2 out past milepost 60. Just beyond the milepost, as the highway begins to turn sharply to the left, cross over Tunnel Creek and find an unmarked road on your right, shown as Forest Road 6095 on maps. Turn onto FR 6095 and follow it 1.2 miles to an intersection. Veer left for a few hundred feet to find the marked trailhead.

Not every alpine lake is set in a landscape as dramatic as Trap Lake, with towering exposed cliffs rising steeply from the edge of the water. Trek through deep forest on sturdy trail to reach the shores of this impressive yet often-overlooked lake.

Depart from the trailhead, following the Tunnel Creek Trail #1061 as it wastes no time entering the forest and beginning a climbing traverse up the mountainside. The forest is heavy, thick with hemlock and drooping cedar. Push upward, ever upward, alternating between tight switchbacks and longer climbs. Navigate sections of narrow and rocky trail that cross over small streams and creeks, talus fields and avalanche chutes. Breaks in the canopy offer pocket views of the creek valley below. Enter the Alpine Lakes Wilderness just before arriving at Hope Lake at 1.4 miles at a junction with the Pacific Crest Trail #2000 (PCT). To the left, the PCT heads past Hope Lake and to Mig Lake (Hike 72), while Trap Lake lies to the right.

Turn right down the trail toward Trap Lake, beginning a long traverse above

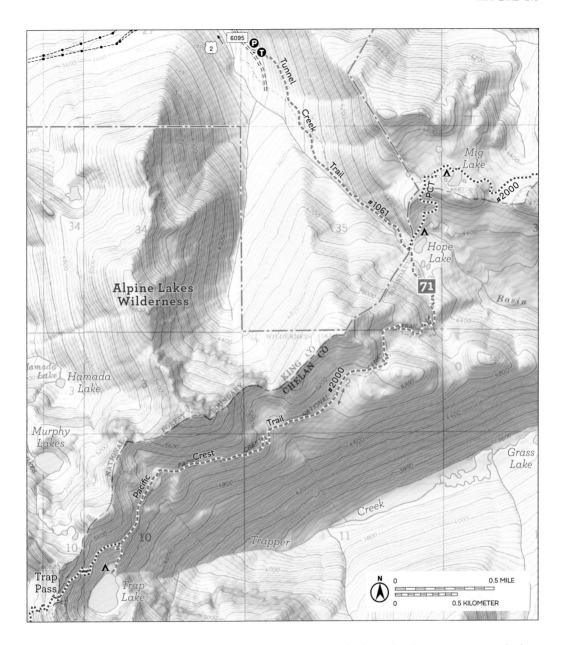

Trapper Creek. Alternate between stands of thick forest, lush rock gardens, and tranquil tarns. Views of the meadow-lined Trapper Creek Valley emerge, with Grass Lake drawing your eye and the tiptops of Nimbus Mountain and Slippery Slab Tower emerging up ahead.

Rugged alpine landscape passes underfoot as you progress toward the 4.4-mile mark. Here, reach an unsigned fork in the trail. To the right the PCT continues up to Trap Pass, following trail chipped in the exposed granite cliffs above Trap Lake. Veer left for the lake, quickly dropping 200 feet to Trap's shores at 4.6 miles. Boot

Hiking the Pacific Crest Trail on the way up to Trap Pass

paths wander around the lake, nestled in a deep bowl under the naked granite slopes of Slippery Slab Tower. Find campsites near the meadowy lake outlet, opposite talus-strewn shores. Find a sunny rock and soak up the tranquility.

GOING FARTHER

From the lake junction, the PCT climbs another 0.7 mile up open cliffs above Trap Lake to reach forested Trap Pass, though it does not offer views much better than those from the trail. Those still thirsty for adventure can drop steeply down to Surprise Lake (Hike 70).

HISTORY

Like so many other features in this area, Trap Lake was named by Forest Supervisor Albert H. Sylvester. The lake heads Trapper Creek, which flows out of the lake down through Grass Lake on its way to Icicle Creek. The creek bore the Trapper moniker long before the lake, and Sylvester chose the lake name to align with the creek. Backpackers, outdoor adventurers, and fishermen have long traipsed up this valley, with Grass Lake getting its name from fishermen who noted the grassy, reed-lined shores.

72 HOPE AND MIG LAKES

DISTANCE: 4.2 miles
ELEVATION GAIN: 1500 feet
HIGH POINT: 4700 feet
DIFFICULTY: Moderate
HIKING TIME: 2 to 4 hours
BEST SEASON: Late spring to early fall

TRAIL TRAFFIC: Light to moderate foot traffic
PERMIT: Northwest Forest Pass
MAPS: USGS Stevens Pass; Green Trails Stevens Pass No. 176
TRAILHEAD GPS: 47.71284°N, 121.1073°W

GETTING THERE: Because of barriers in the road, this hike is accessible only from the eastbound lanes of Highway 2. Take Highway 2 out past milepost 60. Just beyond the milepost, as the highway begins to turn sharply to the left, cross over Tunnel Creek and find an unmarked road on your right, shown as Forest Road 6095 on maps. Turn onto FR 6095 and follow it 1.2 miles to an intersection. Veer left for a few hundred feet to find the marked trailhead.

While Hope and Mig Lakes are not quite as stunning as some of their nearby lake brethren, they still make for a more-than-pleasant destination. The Tunnel Creek Trail is a little off the beaten path. Although the trail is being improved, some rough and steep sections still keep the crowds away from this approach. Though you are unlikely to share the trail up to Hope Lake, the lakes themselves are more frequently visited by those hiking the Pacific Crest Trail. Short and steep, this hike is a great option for those looking for something a little different or a quick conditioning hike.

From the trailhead, the Tunnel Creek Trail #1061 climbs up onto the shoulders of the mountainside into a mature forest of fir, hemlock, and cedar. Until you reach Hope Lake, the climbing never really stops, alternating between switchbacks and traversing ever upward. Some sections

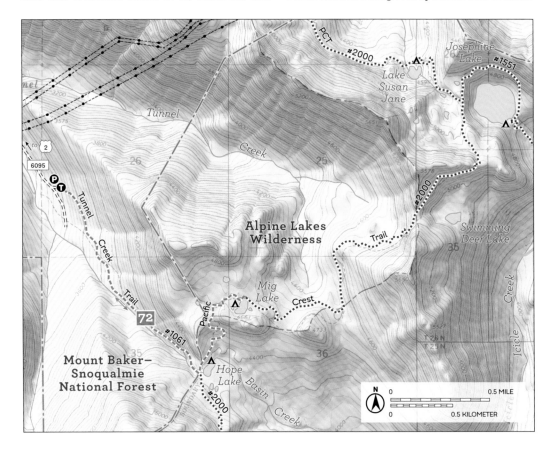

Mig Lake on a summer afternoon

of trail have been improved, but much of the route is rocky, narrow, and steep. As you press onward, talus fields offer occasional glimpses of the surrounding landscape and the valley below, while small streams cut across your path, adding a little variety to your ascent.

After 1.4 miles, the trail levels out and ends, delivering you to the Pacific Crest Trail #2000 (PCT) and the Alpine Lakes Wilderness near the edge of Hope Lake. Before pressing onward, explore the boot paths that snake around the lake, leading through the meadowlands to campsites and picnic spots.

From Hope Lake, head left along the PCT, quickly leaving dense forest behind. Here the trees thin and yield to expanding meadows. If you're heading up in the late spring or early summer, expect to see this area brimming with wildflowers and buzzing with bees. Later in the season, you'll find plenty of huckleberries

within easy reach. In 0.7 mile find yourself at pretty little Mig Lake, quietly nestled at the base of a small prominence. The lakeshores are lined with an alluring mixture of grassy meadows and clusters of evergreens. Find a comfortable spot to enjoy this idyllic alpine scene.

GOING FARTHER

For those looking for a longer day, continue farther down the PCT past Mig Lake to pass above Swimming Deer Lake in a little over 2 miles. Beyond that Josephine Lake beckons at 5.2 miles from the trailhead.

HISTORY

Tunnel Creek was named for the nearby Burlington Northern Cascade Tunnel that was first drilled beneath Stevens Pass between 1897 and 1900. It was replaced by a more modern tunnel in 1929.

73 JOSEPHINE LAKE

DISTANCE: 10.4 miles
ELEVATION GAIN: 1500 feet in; 800 feet out
HIGH POINT: 5100 feet
DIFFICULTY: Moderate
HIKING TIME: 5 to 6 hours
BEST SEASON: Late spring to early fall

TRAIL TRAFFIC: Moderate foot traffic
PERMIT: Northwest Forest Pass
MAPS: USGS Stevens Pass; Green Trails Stevens
Pass No. 176
TRAILHEAD GPS: 47.7460°N, 121.0865°W

GETTING THERE: Take Highway 2 to the Stevens Pass ski area. Park on the south side of the highway in the parking lot farthest from the main ski lodge. Find the PCT Trailhead to the east of this parking area. Privy available.

From ski slopes to wilderness in a matter of hours, a hike to Josephine Lake is a lesson in just how close these wild places are to civilization. It is a popular access point for those looking to connect with the Pacific Crest Trail from Highway 2, so you can expect some friendly faces as you make your way out to this sparking alpine gem. A popular hike during the summer months, this trail is all but deserted in the early fall. As an added bonus, the season paints the ski slopes in vibrant reds and oranges, making your trek past powerlines and ski resort outbuildings a little more visually appealing. While there is a moderate amount of elevation gain on this hike, the well-maintained trail makes it approachable for most hikers.

The hike begins from the Stevens Pass ski area parking lot, picking up the Pacific Crest Trail #2000 (PCT) as it winds up through the brushy ski slopes. The well-trodden trail offers glimpses of the surrounding landscape as it meanders under the occasional ski lift.

After 2.0 miles of traversing the slopes, you crest the first rocky ridge to find Mill Valley spread out before you, as well as the Jupiter Express ski lift. From this vantage point, you can see Mount Stuart and the rest of the Stuart Range looming large to the southwest. Note the large forested bowl almost directly across Mill Valley from you. Nestled within that bowl is Lake Susan Jane, and just over that ridge is Josephine Lake, your destination. You'll need to traverse the entire valley to get there, so enjoy the view for a few moments before heading down the mountainside.

The trail down to Mill Creek is largely exposed, affording big views of the valley.

Follow the trail as it gently guides you downward through talus fields and the occasional clump of evergreens. Ignore the powerlines and ski lifts and push onward, eventually rounding the bowl and beginning your climb out of the valley. At 3.4 miles, shortly after you enter a quiet forest of hemlock and fir, cross the Alpine Lakes Wilderness boundary and leave the ski slopes behind.

Continue to climb, passing a small tarn and, just beyond it, Lake Susan Jane, 4.0 miles down the trail. Several campsites here invite you to stay longer, and the lake is a decent destination if you're short on time or are not up for the final climb to the pass.

To reach Josephine Lake, continue upward for another 0.5 mile to a forested plateau and the junction with the Icicle Creek Trail #1551. Peer down at glimmering Josephine a few hundred feet below. Head left, trading the PCT for the Icicle Creek Trail, and continue to climb,

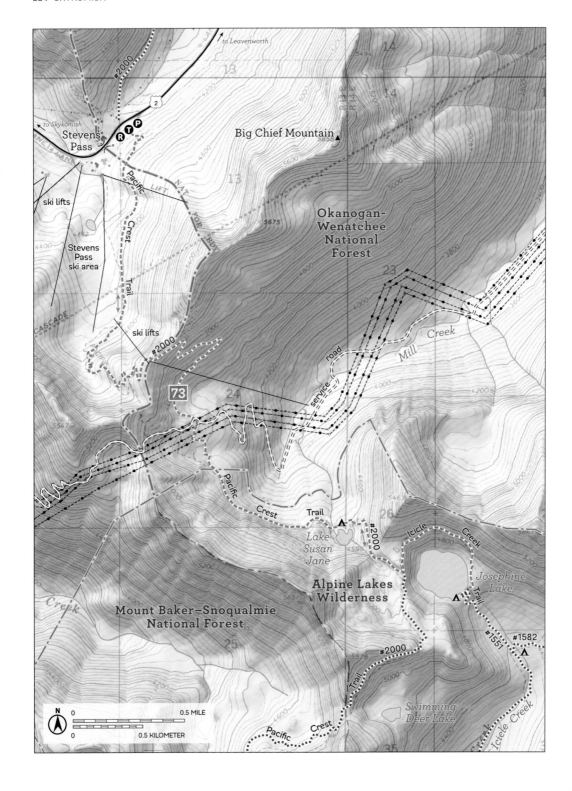

to Leavenworth

Ridge

13

1A

14

#2000

2

to Skykomish

Stevens
Pass

R T P

Big Chief Mountain ▲

Okanogan-
Wenatchee
National
Forest

ski lifts

Stevens
Pass
ski area

Pacific

Crest

Trail

CASCADE

ski lifts

#2000

73

24

23

service road

Mill

Creek

Pacific

Crest

Trail

Lake
Susan
Jane

#2000

26

Icicle

Creek

Josephine
Lake

Alpine Lakes
Wilderness

#1551

#1582

Creek

Mount Baker–Snoqualmie
National Forest

25

#2000

Trail

Swimming
Deer Lake

Icicle Creek

35

Pacific

Crest

Trail

N

0   0.5 MILE

0   0.5 KILOMETER

Josephine Lake from the Pacific Crest Trail

passing several tarns as you work your way around the lake high above the shore. The trail here is somewhat rockier and rougher than the PCT, but easily navigable.

Eventually the trail dips sharply down to Josephine Lake, depositing you at the edge of Icicle Creek near several established campsites 5.2 miles from the trailhead. Take a few minutes to explore the lakeshore and stake out a place to take in Josephine's crystal-clear waters. Follow the rushing sound of Icicle Creek for glimpses of Icicle Valley and the Stuart Range beyond. Find a spot, break out lunch, and enjoy this little slice of wilderness.

GOING FARTHER

For those looking for more, you can push farther down the PCT past Swimming Deer Lake to reach Hope and Mig Lakes (Hike 72). Or continue down the Icicle Creek Trail toward the French Ridge area or the ever-popular Chain Lakes region (Hike 74).

HISTORY

Back around the early 1900s, Albert H. Sylvester was a forest supervisor in the Snoqualmie Ranger District; he would later supervise the Wenatchee Ranger District. During his career he explored, mapped, and named thousands of features, including Josephine Lake, named after Josephine Williams, the wife of one of the rangers in his district. Often referred to as A. H. Sylvester, he began the tradition of naming lakes after women, a legacy that is now splashed across maps of the Cascades. (See Hike 87 for more detail.)

74 CHAIN LAKES AND DOELLE LAKES

DISTANCE: 22.2 miles
ELEVATION GAIN: 3900 feet in; 2200 feet out
HIGH POINT: 6200 feet
DIFFICULTY: Hard
HIKING TIME: Overnight
BEST SEASON: Early summer to early fall

TRAIL TRAFFIC: Light to moderate foot traffic
PERMIT: Northwest Forest Pass
MAPS: USGS Stevens Pass; Green Trails Stevens Pass No. 176
TRAILHEAD GPS: 47.7460°N, 121.0865°W

GETTING THERE: Take Highway 2 to the Stevens Pass ski area. Park on the south side of the highway in the parking lot farthest from the main ski lodge. Find the PCT Trailhead to the east of this parking area. Privy available.

Resting at the bottom of a deep trough beneath a distinctive granite finger known as the Bulls Tooth, the Chain Lakes share a kinship with the Enchantment Lakes Basin: both feature remote, high-elevation lakes hidden in boulder-strewn glacial troughs. Yet there is no need to secure special permitting to spend a night beside the dazzling Chain Lakes, nor should you expect much in the way of company along the way. And much like the Enchantments, there's often another set of lakes just over the next pass. Here, that's little Doelle Lakes—quiet, peaceful, and just waiting to be visited.

Begin your trek by heading out to Josephine Lake (Hike 73) and connecting with the Icicle Creek Trail #1551 just as you reach the lake. The well-loved trail circles the lake to its outlet, Icicle Creek. Descend and follow the water as it tumbles down into the creek valley. Follow the creek as it leads you through mature forest, past a few marshy meadows as well as the junction with the White Pine Creek Trail #1582 (Hike 75) at 5.7 miles. Continue 1.9 miles to reach the Chain Lakes Trail #1569 and turn left onto it, immediately trading smooth trail for a rougher ride.

The trail climbs relentlessly, tightly switchbacking up a steep forested ridge before cresting a rocky rib and entering the Chain Creek Valley. Traverse the valley walls, steadily climbing through hemlock and fir until the forest falls away near the first of the Chain Lakes, after 1.9 miles of climbing. Here are your first glimpses of the towering granite cliffs above, topped by a jumble of protruding slabs and boulders.

Serene waters lap against shores of rock and moss, and the trail beckons you deeper into the basin.

The landscape unfolds as you continue through alpine woodland, more meadows, and small stands of shrubby trees. Without much canopy to cloud your view, take in the alternating swaths of gray boulder fields and vibrant greenbelts of shrubs, each dotted with a few determined trees. Reach the second lake and ideal campsites (and backcountry toilets) at the 9.7-mile mark. Set up camp and marvel at your accommodations. Explore your surroundings to find the local vantage point for viewing the lakes, though your best perspective is farther down the trail.

From the second Chain Lake, the trail continues upward, passing an access trail out to the shallow third Chain Lake, which covers much of the cirque, nearly surrounding a large, tree-covered prominence. This meadow-lined wonderland is more than worth exploring

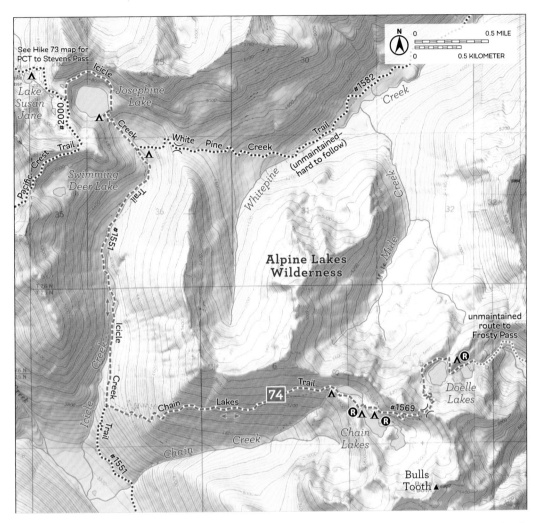

before you begin the climb up toward a saddle on the flanks of the Bulls Tooth. Largely confined to a vast talus field, the trail zigzags up the mountainside, offering lovely views of some (but never all) of the Chain Lakes before cresting the ridge above Doelle Lakes. Enjoy the sea of rolling green ridges spreading out before you, as well as the shimmering lakes filling the bowl below. Pick your way down through talus and heather to the lakes, finding a couple of established campsites near their shores. Marvel up at the rocky slopes you came down and relish the deep quiet of the Doelles.

This overnight through fairy-tale landscapes is a treat. From icy alpine lakes to dramatic rocky spires along fairly well-maintained trail, there is very little this hike does not deliver on. Unless you're feeling adventurous and want to attempt the loop sketched out below, camp near Chain Lakes and save Doelle Lakes for a day trip, which spares you the added effort of lugging your tent over the ridge and back.

GOING FARTHER

For the adventurous and prepared, it is possible to (mostly) follow a faded boot track from Doelle Lakes to Frosty Pass. Find Doughgod

The last of the Chain Lakes lies at the base of Bulls Tooth as seen from the trail up to Doelle Lakes.

Creek as it flows out of the lower of the two Doelles, and follow a brushy path alongside the creek down into a small valley. The trail crosses the creek and vanishes, leaving hikers to find their own way down toward a large meadow. Avoid crossing the meadow, and instead find a path skirting the edge of the grass and leading into the trees. The route turns away from the creek and climbs up to a ridge of exposed rock and meadows, following it, more or less, to Table Camp and then down to Frosty Pass. At Frosty Pass, take the Frosty Creek Trail #1582 back down to the Icicle Creek Trail and follow that path back to Stevens Pass via Josephine Lake.

HISTORY
Forest Supervisor Albert H. Sylvester is responsible for naming many of the features in the area. He named Doelle Lakes after William A. Doelle, an avid outdoorsman who was killed fighting a forest fire in the area in July 1929. Bulls Tooth got its name because Sylvester thought it appeared like a great fang on the jawbone of Icicle Ridge. He did not, however, name Chain Lakes. That was done by a USGS topographer who gave the chain of lakes a less than creative name.

75 WHITEPINE CREEK

DISTANCE: 12.0 miles
ELEVATION GAIN: 1100 feet
HIGH POINT: 3900 feet
DIFFICULTY: Hard due to trail conditions
HIKING TIME: 6 to 8 hours
BEST SEASON: Fall
TRAIL TRAFFIC: Very light foot traffic
PERMIT: Northwest Forest Pass
TRAILHEAD GPS: 47.7707°N, 120.9272°W

MAPS: USGS Mount Howard, USGS Chiwaukum Mountains, USGS Stevens Pass; Green Trails Wenatchee Lake No. 145, Green Trails Chiwaukum Mts. No. 177, Green Trails Stevens Pass No. 176
NOTES: This hike requires fording Whitepine Creek, which may be difficult during the spring melt. Portions are brushy and very overgrown, which may require some routefinding.

GETTING THERE: Take Highway 2 to the signed White Pine Road (Forest Road 6950) east of Stevens Pass, between milepost 78 and milepost 79. Turn onto White Pine Road and follow it 3.8 miles (its spelling changes to Whitepine Road) to the road end and the White Pine Trailhead.

Curious adventurers and avid explorers will enjoy this often-brushy romp up a long creek valley, following in the footsteps of long-gone sheepherders deep into the wild. Where creek fords and bushwhacking turn away the crowds, find lush valley views and dense mixed forest broken by creek crossings and mossy talus fields—all under the granite peaks of Arrowhead Mountain and Jim Hill Mountain.

Begin from the White Pine Trailhead, following the White Pine Creek Trail #1582 into dark and dense forest. Glide down the wide trail through second-growth forest still bearing signs of past clear-cuts. Whitepine Creek (note that while the creek's name is one word, the official names of the trailhead and trail use two words) makes the occasional appearance, and breaks in the trees offer glimpses of the surrounding valley walls. Climb gently, making short work of the 1.0 mile to the Alpine Lakes Wilderness boundary.

Cross creeks and talus fields as you work your way to the foot of Arrowhead Mountain. At 2.5 miles reach the junction with the Wildhorse Creek Trail #1592 (Hike 76), which leads up into the woods on the left. Veer right toward the sound of the creek, passing a campsite as you walk the few hundred feet to the edge of Whitepine Creek. The bridge that once spanned the water was swept away in 1990 and is unlikely to be rebuilt. Use caution fording when the water is high.

Once across the creek, the trail is immediately and markedly transformed. Gone is the wide, well-trodden trail. Instead, find a narrow old path cutting through encroaching vegetation. Stands of dark timber yield to crowding slide alder. Avalanche chutes, creek crossings, and talus fields offer glimpses of the peaks above and valley below.

Mile after mile, press ever onward, pushing brush aside and pausing when you break out of the thick undergrowth. Eventually, after hours of near-bushwhacking, reach the meadows of Mule Creek Camp at 6.0 miles. Quiet and secluded, this is a great turnaround point or camp for the night.

GOING FARTHER

From Mule Creek Camp, the White Pine Creek Trail continues deeper into the creek valley, eventually climbing up out of the drainage to connect with the Icicle Creek Trail #1551. Find a lovely meadow and camping here, 8.1 miles from the trailhead. Reach Josephine Lake (Hike 73), another 0.5 mile distant, by veering right and up the Icicle Creek Trail to the lakeshore. For a longer excursion, head left, following the Icicle Creek Trail 1.9 miles to reach the Chain Lakes Trail #1569 (Hike 74).

HISTORY

Back around the turn of the last century, livestock grazing was common in the river valleys and lake basins of what would become the Alpine Lakes Wilderness. At its height,

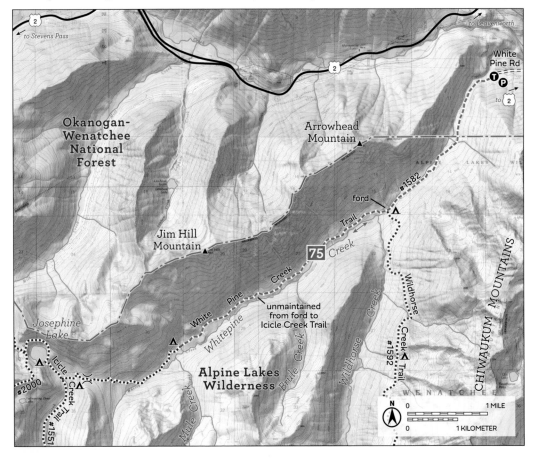

Boot drying after a wet slog down the brushy White Pine Trail

the Forest Service authorized eight separate sheep allotments, allowing sheepherders to drive more than nine thousand sheep into the forests, mostly in areas with recent burn that allowed for plentiful grasses and vegetation for grazing. Over time, the need for the allotments dwindled, and by the time the Alpine Lakes Wilderness was created in 1976, all that remained was the allotment in the Wildhorse-Whitepine drainages. While sheep grazing ended at that time, it's still possible to find evidence of those days—lingering artifacts are scattered around Mule Creek Camp's meadows, once a base camp for sheepherders.

Two features along the trail were named by Forest Supervisor Albert. H. Sylvester. The first, Arrowhead Mountain, he named for a talus field on the south slope that has the rough outline of an arrowhead. The other is Jim Hill Mountain, named for James J. Hill, the colorful chief executive of the Great Northern Railway who is famously credited with saying, "Give me enough Swedes and enough whiskey, and I'll build a railroad through hell!"

76 WILDHORSE CREEK

DISTANCE: 9.8 miles
ELEVATION GAIN: 2100 feet
HIGH POINT: 4900 feet
DIFFICULTY: Moderate

HIKING TIME: 5 to 7 hours
BEST SEASON: Early summer to late fall
TRAIL TRAFFIC: Moderate foot and equestrian traffic

Wildhorse Creek Valley and Chiwaukum Mountains near Frosty Pass

PERMIT: Northwest Forest Pass
TRAILHEAD GPS: 47.7707°N, 120.9272°W

MAPS: USGS Chiwaukum Mountains; Green Trails Chiwaukum Mts. No. 177, Green Trails Stevens Pass No. 176

GETTING THERE: Take Highway 2 to the signed White Pine Road (Forest Road 6950) east of Stevens Pass, between milepost 78 and milepost 79. Turn onto White Pine Road and follow it 3.8 miles (its spelling changes to Whitepine Road) to the road end and the White Pine Trailhead.

Explore a sprawling creek valley complete with thick forest, open country, countless streams, and rugged ridges sprouting granite peaks. Follow in the footsteps of sheepherders and stockmen of yore to find trailside perches presiding over tree-filled basins and long views of wild alpine landscape. Those pressing onward can discover hidden alpine lakes and windy mountain passes.

Starting from the White Pine Trailhead, dive into thick mixed forest along the White Pine Creek Trail #1582. The trail is wide and easy here, likely the remnants of a road used when this area was clear-cut decades ago. Whitepine Creek (officially one word, though White Pine Creek Trail is two) tumbles and chatters through the second-growth forest not

far from the trail as you climb gently up the creek valley. Enter the Alpine Lakes Wilderness at 1.0 mile.

Once you're in the wilderness, tree breaks become more frequent, allowing quick views of Arrowhead Mountain and the sloping valley walls. Pass through creek beds and talus fields as you march toward the junction with the Wildhorse Creek Trail #1592 at the 2.5-mile mark. Here the White Pine Creek Trail veers to the right past a campsite and down to Whitepine Creek (Hike 75) before continuing up the valley. Turn left to begin your trek down the Wildhorse Creek Trail.

Briefly follow Wildhorse Creek before a steep set of switchbacks lead you up the shoulders of the Chiwaukum Mountains to begin a long traverse above the valley. The trail starts shedding the forest here, with timber stands increasingly broken up by rocky creek beds and avalanche chutes, offering better and better valley views as well as glimpses of the boulder-strewn slopes above.

As you progress, note the campsites scattered along the trail; all come standard with private viewpoints and nearby creek access. Push onward to the 4.9-mile mark, to a particularly good set of campsites and the turnaround point for day hikers. Likely a former base camp for sheepherders, the camps are located at an unsigned junction. The well-worn side trail here leads up to Deadhorse Pass (see Going Farther).

Find views at the lower campsite by following a short path out to a broad opening in the trees. Spy Arrowhead Mountain and Jim Hill Mountain to the north, rising above the Whitepine Creek Valley. On good days, find snowy Glacier Peak farther north. Wildhorse Creek is far below, and above find Bulls Tooth jutting up sharply across the valley. To the south, the Chiwaukum Mountains' increasingly barren slopes eventually culminate in Snowgrass Mountain in the distance. Find your favorite vantage point to take in the wide-ranging views.

GOING FARTHER

Wildhorse Creek is often used as a jumping-off point for further adventuring, as the trail passes a few side trips just before it culminates at Frosty Pass. The trail to Deadhorse Pass offers a challenging approach that drops steeply down to Cup Lake and Larch Lake beyond (Hike 78). Backpackers can push farther along the Wildhorse Trail to an unsigned but well-loved trail

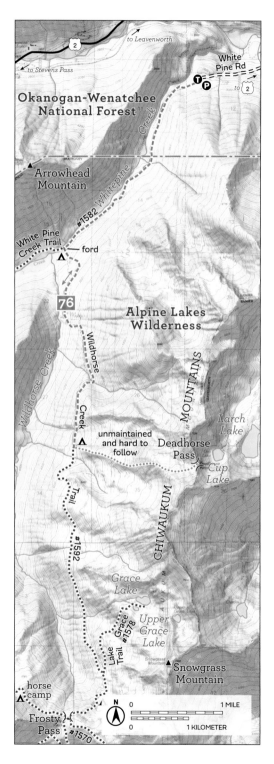

to Grace Lake at the 7.9-mile mark. The Lake Grace Trail #1578 is a steep 1.1-mile climb to a lovely alpine tarn complete with decent campsites and scramble routes up to Upper Grace Lake to explore.

Beyond the Grace Lake trail, the Wildhorse Trail ends at Frosty Pass, 8.8 miles from the trailhead. From the pass adventure awaits: Icicle Ridge Trail #1570, an unmaintained route to Chain Lakes and Doelle Lakes (Hike 74), and the Ladies Pass Lakes (Hike 98) are all worthy destinations.

HISTORY

Like Whitepine Creek, Wildhorse Creek was host to sheep allotments for decades, and sheep continued to graze the valley until the creation of the Alpine Lakes Wilderness in 1976. The creek was given its name by early herders who sighted wild horses in the area. In fact, most of the features in the valley were named by or in honor of the stockmen and sheep drivers who spent a great deal of time in the area. Snowgrass Peak was named for the vegetation prevalent on the mountain, which was preferred feed for sheep. Forest Supervisor Albert H. Sylvester named Deadhorse Pass after the long strings of packhorses and sheep that often did not fare well over this steep approach.

Sylvester is also responsible for naming Grace Lake, which—in the grand tradition of naming lakes for women in his life and the lives of his rangers—he named for the wife of Charles Haydon, who was accompanying him when he came across the lake. Sylvester named Frosty Pass on a 1909 excursion in which an early frost greeted him when he awoke in camp near the pass. Sylvester was also likely behind the naming of features bearing the *Chiwaukum* name, which means "many little creeks running into a big one" in the language of the Wenatchee Tribes (sometimes called Interior Salish).

77 LAKE ETHEL

DISTANCE: 9.1 miles
ELEVATION GAIN: 3300 feet in; 200 feet out
HIGH POINT: 5700 feet
DIFFICULTY: Hard
HIKING TIME: 6 to 7 hours
BEST SEASON: Late spring to early fall

TRAIL TRAFFIC: Moderate foot traffic
PERMIT: None
MAPS: USGS Lake Wenatchee, USGS Mount Howard; Green Trails Wenatchee Lake No. 145
TRAILHEAD GPS: 47.7729°N, 120.8324°W

GETTING THERE: Take Highway 2 to the well-signed Gill Creek Road (Forest Road 6940) east of Stevens Pass, between milepost 79 and milepost 80, noting the sign for the Lake Ethel Trail. Turn onto Gill Creek Road, almost immediately crossing Nason Creek. Keep left at the junction, crossing railroad tracks and again keeping left to follow the rough and bumpy road 1.4 miles to the Lake Ethel Trailhead. Parking is limited.

Climb through forest and denuded slopes to wildflower-filled meadows and a splendid alpine lake with access to high adventure beyond. Lake Ethel is the most popular gateway to the Scottish Lakes area, even though roughly a third of the hike works its way up through a mile-wide clear-cut, a section of private timberland standing between Highway 2 and the Alpine Lakes Wilderness. The felled forestland isn't pretty, but the abundant wildflowers lining the trail and the long views of Nason Creek Valley offer a welcome distraction.

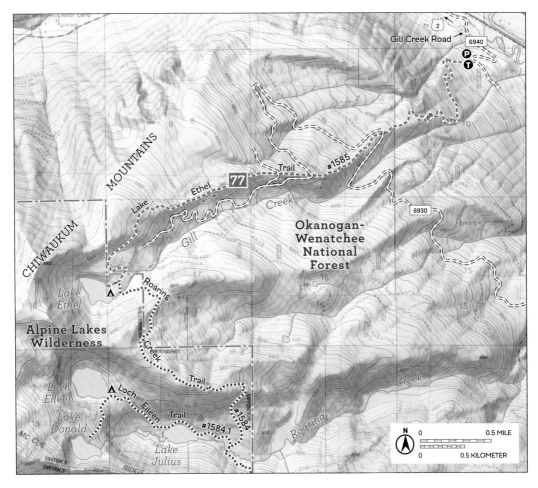

From the trailhead, the Lake Ethel Trail #1585 leaves the Gill Creek Road and heads into young forest on the crumbling remnants of an old logging track. Soon begin climbing steeply up the mountainside, alternating between tight switchbacks and longer traverses as you work to attain the ridgeline. Swing near Gill Creek, tumbling loudly near the trail largely out of sight but accessible if needed. Breaks in the trees and short sections of talus offer tastes of views to come—Nason Creek Valley, Nason Ridge, and Highway 2 below.

After 1.5 miles reach the top of the ridge and soon emerge on the edge of the clear-cut at a logging road. The trail stays on the ridgeline, cutting across the winding forest road twice more

before returning to the forest. Low shrubs and wildflowers line the trail as you climb through stump fields and past burn piles. Views of Nason Ridge, Mastiff Mountain, and the tops of the Chiwaukum Mountains abound, and watch for Glacier Peak to the north just before you reach the trees.

Once back in the woods continue your climb, traversing the valley walls above Gill Creek, then starting the descent toward the lake. Ignore the older trail here that marks a pre-clear-cut, now-abandoned approach to Lake Ethel. Stay on the main trail.

Pass through meadowlands bursting with wildflowers to reach the Alpine Lakes Wilderness at 4.4 miles. Just beyond, at 4.5 miles,

A healthy portion of the hike to Lake Ethel climbs through this wildflower-filled clear cut.

reach the junction with the Roaring Creek Trail #1584 with access to the other Scottish Lakes. For now, keep right and continue to Lake Ethel and a large camping area. Follow boot paths to more campsites. Find a spot on the shore and take in the view.

Lake Ethel is set in a glacial cirque, a bowl scooped out of the end of the Chiwaukum Mountains. Half the lakeshore is forested, the other half, boulder-strewn slopes, jutting granite cliffs, and brush. During the spring and early summer, snowmelt tumbles down the slopes to the lake, adding even more charm to this Scottish beauty.

GOING FARTHER

Those planning a longer day or an overnight can continue along the Roaring Creek Trail to the junction with the Loch Eileen Trail #1584.1. It's 2.7 miles out to Lake Julius from Lake Ethel, though you'll enjoy big views of the Roaring Creek Valley along the way. Beyond Lake Julius, Loch Eileen and Lake Donald await; a full tour of the Scottish Lakes takes you 3.7 miles from Lake Ethel, 8.2 miles from the trailhead.

HISTORY

Long-logged, the Gill Creek drainage has been a source of timber since the Great Northern Railway opened over Stevens Pass in 1890. Most of the features in the area were explored and named by Forest Supervisor Albert H. Sylvester. He named Lake Ethel in honor of Ethel Lenzie, wife of Forest Service Ranger Frank Lenzie. The rest of the Scottish Lakes have similar stories. Gill Creek he named for Justus Gill, a homesteader at the mouth of the creek. Sylvester is also responsible for Mastiff Mountain's name, which he thought resembled the head of a mastiff when it's seen from Lake Wenatchee.

78 LARCH LAKE AND CHIWAUKUM LAKE

DISTANCE: 23.8 miles
ELEVATION GAIN: 4300 feet in; 100 feet out
HIGH POINT: 6100 feet
DIFFICULTY: Moderate
HIKING TIME: 2 nights
BEST SEASON: Late summer to late fall

TRAIL TRAFFIC: Light foot and equestrian traffic
PERMIT: Northwest Forest Pass
MAPS: USGS Big Jim Mountain, USGS Chiwaukum
Mountains; Green Trails Leavenworth
No. 178, Green Trails Chiwaukum Mts. No. 177
TRAILHEAD GPS: 47.689°N, 120.7405°W

GETTING THERE: Take Highway 2 to Chiwaukum Creek Road (Forest Road 7908) between milepost 89 and milepost 90. Turn onto FR 7908 and follow it 0.2 mile to the parking area and trailhead. Privy available.

Stunning at any time of year, Larch Lake shows its colors during the fall season when the larches that line the lakeshore light up in bright yellow and orange. While the lake is well beyond the range of most day hikers, this secluded spot is entirely worth devoting a weekend to. Hikers can easily lose hours along these alpine shores, just staring at the rugged beauty.

Chiwaukum Creek Trail #1571 begins by following a logging road through privately owned property. Chiwaukum Creek chatters not far below, bubbling along and keeping you company as you plod to the beginning of the trail at 1.2 miles.

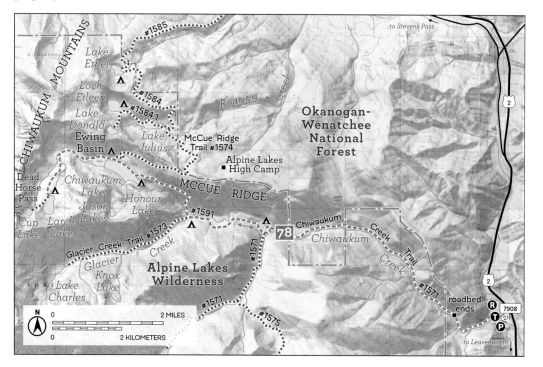

Golden larches surround Larch Lake in the fall.

From the end of the road, the trail climbs above the residences, switchbacking a bit and soon entering the Alpine Lakes Wilderness at 1.4 miles. Here are the beginnings of a major 2014 burn, blackened tree trunks and the vague smell of smoke still lingering. Wildflowers have already returned, adding color to the fire-thinned landscape.

The creek is never out of earshot as you push deeper into the valley, making good time down the sometimes-rocky but largely flat trail. Eventually after a short climb up a rocky prominence, veer across the creek on a large log at about 5.8 miles. This is a common turnaround point for day hikers. Just beyond the creek, reach the junction with North Fork Chiwaukum Creek Trail #1591 at 5.9 miles. Head to the right toward Chiwaukum Lake.

From the junction, the hike changes dramatically. Leave the charred forestlands behind, trading it for thick old growth. Left behind too is the flat grade and easy trail. Climb through mossy boulder fields and dense forest, eventually crossing Glacier Creek. Here at 7.6 miles, find ample camping and the junction with the Glacier Creek Trail #1573. Hikers spending multiple nights in the area might consider camping here, as the next section of trail is particularly challenging.

Continue straight ahead on the North Fork Chiwaukum Creek Trail. From this point, it is 1.8 miles to Chiwaukum Lake, and most of that stretch is a hard slog through a brush-filled boulder field. While there is no danger of losing the trail, brush and undergrowth may need to be pushed aside to gain passage in some sections. The trail is occasionally brushed out, but if it is not, be prepared for the steep climb to the ridges above the lake to take twice as long as your normal pace. Where the brush allows, catch views of the valley below and the granite tops of the Chiwaukum Mountains.

The trail eventually delivers you to the lake basin, high above the water on the shoulders of

McCue Ridge. Shortly after your first glimpse of Chiwaukum Lake's sparkling waters, arrive at a trailside campsite with excellent views, at 9.4 miles. The peaks of Chiwaukum Mountain are in their full glory here, cutting a dramatic profile above the tree-lined lake. Find more camps farther down the trail and closer to the lake, but none with comparable front porch views.

After a well-deserved break, continue down the trail, dropping elevation and soon hitting the junction with the McCue Ridge Trail #1574, leading up to the Scottish Lakes, at the 9.9-mile mark. Find a few good campsites here. Push onward and upward along the main trail toward Larch Lake, rounding the end of Chiwaukum Lake and soon leaving the trees to emerge into lovely Ewing Basin. This wide glacial trough is aglow with wildflowers in the spring and afire with color in the fall. It's an enjoyable 2.0-mile hike through heady alpine country to Larch Lake Basin.

Reach Larch Lake at 11.9 miles and savor the splendor. The larches hug shores that are more granite than grass and, wherever they can, find footholds in the terraces above the shimmering waters. In the fall, their yellows and oranges are nearly blinding against the stark landscape. The massive wall of rock that is the Chiwaukum Mountains rises above the lake, jagged cliffs and exposed peaks serrating the sky. Waters tumble down the boulder-strewn slopes from Cup Lake above. Here is the epitome of alpine. Explore. Find the perfect spot to drop your gear and bask in the landscape.

GOING FARTHER

Cup Lake is set in a ledge above Larch Lake, easily visible from Larch. Follow a well-worn boot path on the east side of Larch Lake up through talus to reach Cup Lake. The climb has some steep sections but never really becomes a scramble. The adventurous can continue up around Cup Lake to Deadhorse Pass for views of Wildhorse Valley (Hike 76).

For a longer excursion, follow the McCue Ridge Trail up to the Scottish Lakes area, touring Lake Julius, Loch Eileen, and Lake Donald. Through-hikers can then continue onward to Lake Ethel (Hike 77) and exit via the Lake Ethel Trailhead, 10.0 miles down Highway 2 from the Chiwaukum Creek Trailhead.

HISTORY

Larch Lake was named for obvious reasons, while Cup Lake got its name from Forest Supervisor Albert H. Sylvester, who thought the cirque it sits in resembles a cup. In 2014 a lightning strike started the Chiwaukum Creek Fire, which grew to burn nearly 14,000 acres, causing evacuations in Leavenworth and temporarily closing Highway 2.

79 LAKE AUGUSTA

DISTANCE: 14.8 miles
ELEVATION GAIN: 4000 feet
HIGH POINT: 6800 feet
DIFFICULTY: Hard
HIKING TIME: Overnight
BEST SEASON: Early summer to late fall

TRAIL TRAFFIC: Light foot traffic
PERMIT: Northwest Forest Pass
MAPS: USGS Big Jim Mountain; Green Trails Chiwaukum Mts. No. 177
TRAILHEAD GPS: 47.6714°N, 120.7555°W

GETTING THERE: Take Highway 2 to Hatchery Creek Road (Forest Road 7905) between milepost 90 and milepost 91, opposite Tumwater Campground. Turn onto FR 7905 and follow it past a few houses, keeping right at junctions at 1.7 miles and again at 2.3 miles. At 2.6 miles, turn right and arrive at the Hatchery Creek Trailhead.

Climb through the remains of burns and open forest along dusty trail to reach a splendid alpine lake filling a glacial cirque at the head of Cabin Creek. Lake Augusta's shores of meadow, wildflowers, and talus are more than enough to draw hikers up the valley to wander the parklands and sweeping slopes of Big Jim Mountain that rise above the water.

Your quest begins along the Hatchery Creek Trail #1577, which leaves the logging road and passes through a stand of second growth before breaking into open country on slopes scoured clean by 2014 wildfires. Cross into the Alpine Lakes Wilderness at 0.7 mile as you switchback steeply through wildflowers and charred snags, alternating between dusty trail and exposed rock.

Climb and climb, then climb farther still, eventually cresting the cliffs above Hatchery Creek. Views of the Wenatchee River Valley, Hatchery Creek, and a vast rolling expanse of mountaintops can be found here, your line of sight unencumbered by forest canopy. Continue your march through burnlands to reach

the junction with the Badlands Trail #1576 at the 2.9-mile mark. Keep left and press onward along the main trail.

The ups and downs continue, giving you some respite to enjoy the panoramas as you progress. Wildflowers liven a fire-blackened landscape as the trail rolls through grassland and talus fields, passing small groups of green-clad trees that managed to escape the fire. Eventually the greenery increases as you exit the burn, rejoin the forest, and then begin a short ascent up a ridge.

At 5.7 miles, attain the ridgetop and reach the junction with the Icicle Ridge Trail #1570 (Hike 80). Join this trail, turning right and dropping down into the meadow-filled Cabin

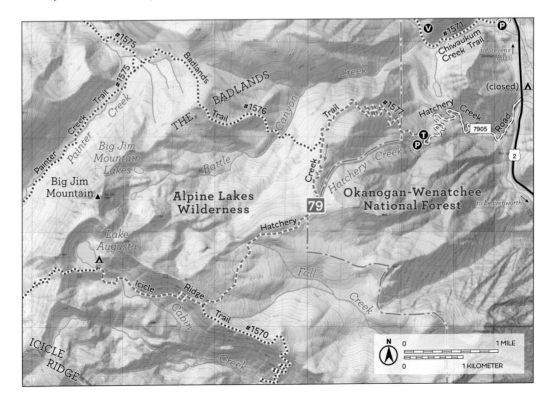

Lake Augusta from the heights of Big Jim Mountain

Creek Valley, soon trading the shade of the trees for open alpine country. Cross great slabs of rock and the exposed flanks of the valley wall to round a prominence and catch sight of the heights of Big Jim Mountain and the headwall that holds back Lake Augusta's waters. One final push leads to the edge of the lake and the lake outlet, 7.4 miles from the trailhead.

Campsites away from the shore are easily found, as are front-row seats to this sparkling and enchanting lake basin. The greens and grays of the meadowlands and cliffs reflected in Augusta's deep blue waters create a landscape that seems almost manicured. Listen for marmots and pikas while scanning the skies for raptors riding the thermals. Follow the boot paths and budget time to linger at the lakeside; you're going to need it.

GOING FARTHER

The Icicle Ridge Trail continues past Lake Augusta to a saddle on one of the arms of Big Jim Mountain, where climbers are well rewarded with big views of Painter Creek Valley below and the Chiwaukum Mountains in the distance. Climbing up to nearby boulder-strewn high points reveals even better views of Icicle Ridge to the south and the Stuart Range beyond. On good days, Mount Rainier and Glacier Peak both make an appearance.

Beyond the saddle, the Icicle Ridge Trail connects with many more trails and many more adventures. For a loop, drop down from the saddle to the Painter Creek Trail #1575 near Carter Lake, then follow the creek down to the Badlands Trail #1576 as it leads back to the Hatchery Creek Trail.

HISTORY

This area was a favorite of Forest Supervisor Albert H. Sylvester, who often led excursions into the wilderness, following creeks to lakes and tarns. In 1909 Sylvester stumbled onto Lake Augusta, naming it for his mother and the mountain above for James J. Hill of Great Northern Railway fame. Sylvester also named another nearby prominence Jim Hill Mountain for James J. Hill, though it is unclear which one he named first or why Big Jim needed two mountaintops named in his honor.

Other features predate Sylvester's tours. The prospectors' cabins that once lined Cabin Creek in the 1890s gave rise to its name. The Badlands are named for the predominance of talus and lack of good feed in the area for the sheep that were once herded through the creek valleys. Hatchery Creek has a less storied name—a hatchery at the mouth of the creek was abandoned around 1907.

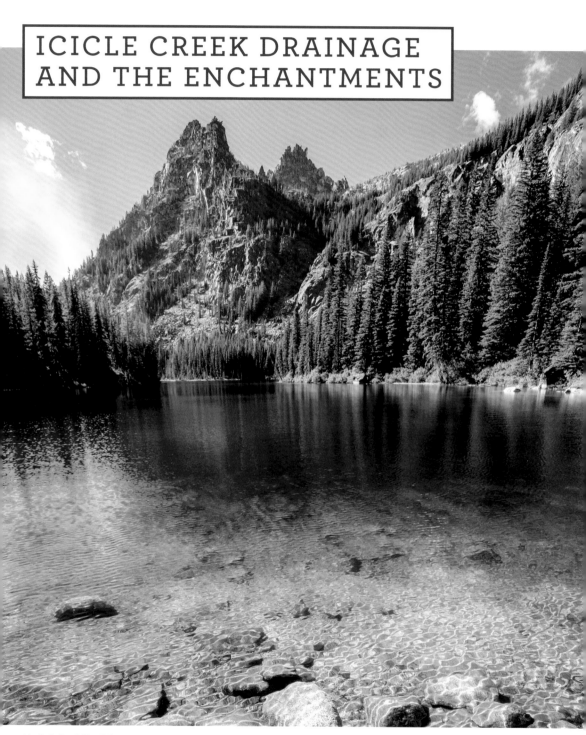

ICICLE CREEK DRAINAGE AND THE ENCHANTMENTS

Nada Lake (Hike 81)

80 ICICLE RIDGE

DISTANCE: 4.6 miles
ELEVATION GAIN: 1800 feet
HIGH POINT: 3000 feet
DIFFICULTY: Moderate
HIKING TIME: 3 to 4 hours
BEST SEASON: Late spring to late fall

TRAIL TRAFFIC: Heavy foot traffic
PERMIT: None
MAPS: USGS Leavenworth; Green Trails
Leavenworth No. 178
TRAILHEAD GPS: 47.5686°N, 120.6809°W

GETTING THERE: Take Highway 2 to Icicle Creek Road (Forest Road 76) just west of Leavenworth. Turn onto Icicle Creek Road and continue 1.4 miles to the Icicle Ridge Trailhead sign on the right. Turn right and then make an almost immediate left to the small trailhead parking area.

Pass abundant wildflowers as you climb to the top of Icicle Ridge for big views of the surrounding landscape on this popular hike. Located just outside Leavenworth, Icicle Ridge is part of the sprawling mountainous structure that makes up the northern wall of the Icicle Creek Valley. Just minutes from bustling downtown Leavenworth and easily accessible, the first section of the Icicle Ridge Trail is crowded on summer weekends, so be prepared to share it.

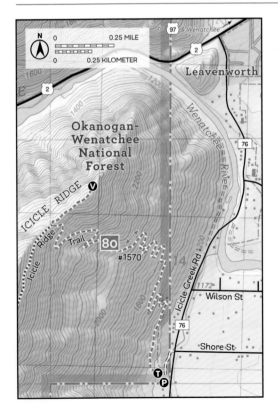

From the trailhead, the Icicle Ridge Trail #1570 begins, with little ceremony, a long series of switchbacks that relentlessly climb up the shoulders of the ridge, offering no reprieve until you reach the ridgeline. Early sections of the trail pass behind a few houses before zigzagging through thin forest and patches of wildflowers. Here too is the only water on the hike before you press upward toward the dusty reaches of the trail. As you climb, clusters of trees offer welcome shade, while breaks in the tree cover provide a window into Icicle Creek Valley in the distance.

The trail crests the ridge in a welcome clearing, complete with several logs to rest on, at 2.1 miles. Here you can peer down the other side of the ridge for your first peek at the Wenatchee River. If it's early enough in the season, you may be able to see the waters of Dumas Falls tumbling down the exposed cliffs to the north.

While this clearing is a tempting place to stop, veer to the right and continue down the trail to the 2.3-mile mark to find the biggest views. Leavenworth is spread out below, with

Wildflowers abound on fire-seared Icicle Ridge.

the Wenatchee River sparkling and shimmering in the sun. Note the charred remains of the trees that once covered this viewpoint, a reminder of the fires that made this panorama possible.

With abundant wildflowers and a spectacular view, the Icicle Ridge Trail has a lot to offer. At the same time, climbing 1800 feet in less than 2.5 miles makes this short trail a little challenging, especially on a hot day, so remember to pack sufficient water for the climb. This trail is also crowded on summer weekends, so be prepared to share it. As always, yield to the hikers who are climbing up.

GOING FARTHER
For those looking for more trail to explore, the Icicle Ridge Trail continues up the ridge from the clearing, passing Fourth of July Creek Trail at 9.0 miles before pressing into the Alpine Lakes Wilderness, eventually reaching Frosty Pass at the end of the 29.6-mile trail.

81 SNOW LAKES AND NADA LAKE

DISTANCE: 13.6 miles
ELEVATION GAIN: 4200 feet
HIGH POINT: 5500 feet
DIFFICULTY: Hard
HIKING TIME: 9 to 12 hours or overnight
BEST SEASON: Late spring to early fall

TRAIL TRAFFIC: Moderate foot traffic
PERMITS: Northwest Forest Pass; Snow Zone Enchantments permit for overnight stay
MAPS: USGS Leavenworth, USGS Blewett; Green Trails The Enchantments No. 209S
TRAILHEAD GPS: 47.54434°N, 120.7096°W

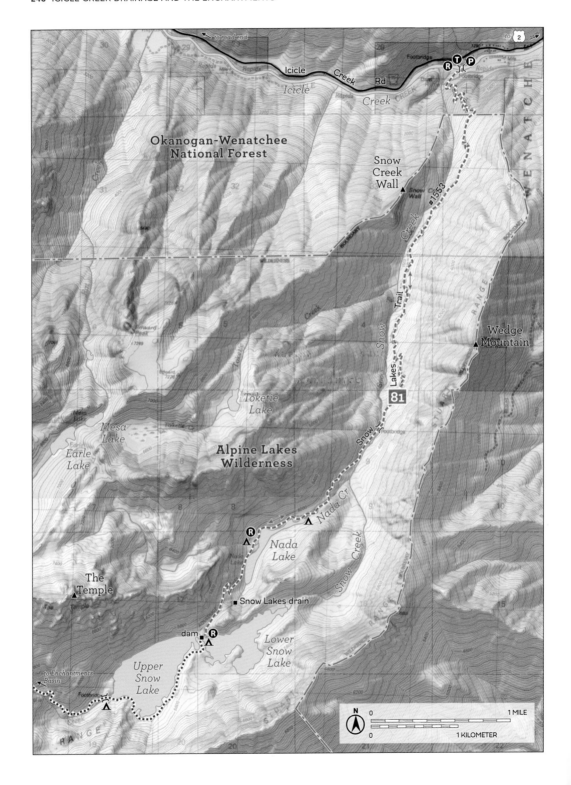

NOTES: Permit required to overnight in Enchantments area between May 15 and Oct. 31; reservation system changes often; for details visit www .fs.usda.gov/detail/okawen/passes-permits /recreation.

GETTING THERE: Take Highway 2 to Icicle Creek Road (Forest Road 76) just west of Leavenworth. Turn onto Icicle Creek Road and continue for 4.2 miles to the Snow Lakes Trailhead parking area on the left. Privy available.

The traditional—and some argue best—approach to the fabled Enchantments begins from the Snow Lakes Trailhead. Instead of leaping straight to dessert via Aasgard Pass, the Snow Lakes route delays the magic for as long as possible. The debate is as old as the trails themselves, and there is no right answer, though hikers should try both: they are very different experiences.

Snow Lakes is a challenging but attainable day hike and a decent backpacking destination unto itself, though most folks undertaking the dusty trek intend to push upward into the Enchantments Basin. Because permits to overnight in the core Enchantments zone can be hard to come by, the Snow Lakes—which are outside that special-permit zone—make a perfect base camp for day hiking the area by using the more easily obtained Snow Lakes overnight permit. After all, by the time you've made the long grind up to Snow Lakes, it seems a shame to be so close to the Enchantments Basin and not climb up for a visit.

From the road, the Snow Lakes Trail #1553 begins a slow switchback up into the sloping canyon. As you climb, evidence of the fires that ravaged the area in 1994 can still be seen. The skeletons of charred trees line the trail, though after a few decades the underbrush has obscured much of the damage. However, the underbrush has yet to grow up enough to provide much in the way of shade, so this first section of the hike has a lot of sun exposure, making it hot and dusty during the summer.

Cross into the Alpine Lakes Wilderness at 1.2 miles. As you leave the burn area and the faint smell of ash behind, the trail enters a pine forest and bends closer to Snow Creek, providing access to occasional creekside rest stops. At about 2.0 miles the trail meanders past the large cliff faces of Snow Creek Wall, looming across the creek, and frequented by rock climbers. From here the trail soon begins to veer up the rocky canyon slopes.

Continue another 2.0 miles through talus fields, scattered sections of forest, and brushlined portions of trail to the sturdy footbridge crossing Snow Creek. Soon find yourself sharing the trail with Nada Creek as you push up to the marshy end of Nada Lake at 5.4 miles. While most hikers press onward to Snow Lakes on their quest to reach the Enchantments Basin, some overnight in the quiet solitude of Nada Lake. Several campsites line the lower section of the lake. If nothing else, the shores of Nada Lake are an excellent resting point to recharge for the final push to Snow Lakes, 1.5 miles up the trail.

Continuing onward, the trail quickly and steeply rises up the slopes above Nada Lake, passing campsites along the way. If water is being released from Snow Lakes, you'll see the spray gushing from the cliffs above the lake. As you get closer, at a switchback in the trail at 6.3 miles, a boot path leads out to the tunnel and the control valves for the drainage system. Push upward through rocky terrain to the shady forests that surround Snow Lakes.

Reach Snow Lakes after 6.8 long miles, following the trail as it leads across the small dam that controls the water level between the lakes. Depending on the time of year, Upper Snow Lake may be quite low, exposing sandy shores

Common throughout the Cascades, American pika are often heard in talus fields.

covered in the bleached wood of fallen trees. The craggy heights of McClellan Peak and The Temple rise dramatically above Upper Snow Lake, a scene that captures the essence of the Alpine Lakes Wilderness. Find ample camping around both lakes.

GOING FARTHER

Continue beyond Snow Lakes to the Enchantments Basin, a challenging journey over exposed rock, up steep scrambles, and past a dozen ever more amazing alpine lakes all the way up to Aasgard Pass itself (see Hikes 82 and 83).

HISTORY

In the 1930s the construction of Grand Coulee Dam had an immediate impact on salmon runs. The US Bureau of Reclamation dealt with the issue through fish hatcheries, one of which was built on Icicle Creek to release into the Wenatchee River below the dam. Unfortunately, the bureau quickly realized that fluctuations in the water levels of Icicle Creek would cause problems for a sustainable hatchery. The problem was a lack of cold water; the solution was to tap the nearby Snow Lakes 7.0 miles upstream.

In 1938 the Forest Service cut a trail up to Nada Lake and the Snow Lakes and established a base camp on Nada Lake. From 1939 to 1942 crews carved a 9-foot-wide, 2250-foot-long tunnel through solid granite under Lower Snow Lake to the bottom of Upper Snow Lake. At the same time, a small dam was constructed to regulate the water levels between the upper and lower lakes.

Today, water drains from the bottom of 150-foot-deep Upper Snow Lake to a bulkhead where it is funneled into a pipe and shot out toward Nada Lake. A series of valves controls the amount of water discharged. Typically, the system is in operation around seventy-seven days a year, usually between July and October, releasing an average of 3700 acre-feet of water annually.

82 THE ENCHANTMENTS

DISTANCE: 25.2 miles
ELEVATION GAIN: 6500 feet
HIGH POINT: 7800 feet
DIFFICULTY: Hard
HIKING TIME: 2 nights
BEST SEASON: Late summer to fall
TRAIL TRAFFIC: Moderate foot traffic
TRAILHEAD GPS: 47.54434°N, 120.7096°W
MAPS: USGS Leavenworth, USGS Blewett, USGS Enchantment Lakes; Green Trails The Enchantments No. 209S

PERMITS: Northwest Forest Pass; Enchantments permit for overnight stay
NOTES: Permit required to overnight in Enchantments area between May 15 and Oct. 31; reservation system changes often; for details visit www .fs.usda.gov/detail/okawen/passes-permits /recreation. For reasons explained below, many features in this area are commonly referred to by more than one name. To avoid confusion, the official USGS name is used, followed by the alternate in parentheses.

GETTING THERE: Take Highway 2 to Icicle Creek Road (Forest Road 76) just west of Leavenworth. Turn onto Icicle Creek Road and continue 4.2 miles to the Snow Lakes Trailhead parking area on the left. Privy available.

The crown jewel of the Alpine Lakes Wilderness, the Enchantment Lakes Basin is a sprawling fairyland of high lakes, alpine meadows, snow-scoured boulders, and sawtooth ridges. A trip to these fabled highlands is nothing short of magnificent. The Enchantment Lakes Basin can be reached from one of two approaches: from Snow Lakes (Hike 81) or from Colchuck Lake via Aasgard Pass (Hike 83). The Snow Lakes approach is outlined here, as it is somewhat more accessible for most hikers. The price of entry is high, but once you reach this jaw-dropping landscape, you too will believe that the long, tough climb is a small price to pay.

Follow the Snow Lakes Trail #1553 for 6.8 miles to the dam between the two Snow Lakes (Hike 81). Continue on the trail as it contours the upper lake, passing campsites and views of the Temple's sharp peak and McClellan Peak's glacial crown. The Snow Lakes are an irrigation reservoir, so the water may have retreated far from the lakeshore, revealing fields of jumbled logs and stumps. Reach the bridge over Snow Creek and good camping at 8.1 miles. From here the trail becomes significantly more challenging, so tighten your pack straps and take one last look at Snow Lakes before starting the climb.

As you work your way up trail chipped into the rock, the trees increasingly yield to ever-larger slabs of granite. Snow Creek rushes noisily nearby, often becoming a tumbling cascade as it hurtles down the mountainside—a welcome distraction from the steep ascent. Trudging switchbacks leads to a barren headwall, the first lip of the Enchantments Basin. Scramble up massive boulders and slabs, finding footholds in rebar driven into the stone or chipped into the rock. After much effort, reach the top of the headwall and the shores of Lake Viviane at 9.4 miles. Temple Lake (Naiad Lake) is here too, hidden behind the granite knoll near the lake outlet just above the trail.

Cross Snow Creek as it rushes out of Lake Viviane and work your way up and around a hill of granite to reach the end of Leprechaun Lake at 9.7 miles. Find excellent campsites here, as well as a backcountry toilet. From the campsites, find rocky prominences that offer long views of the Snow Creek Valley and Snow Lakes below.

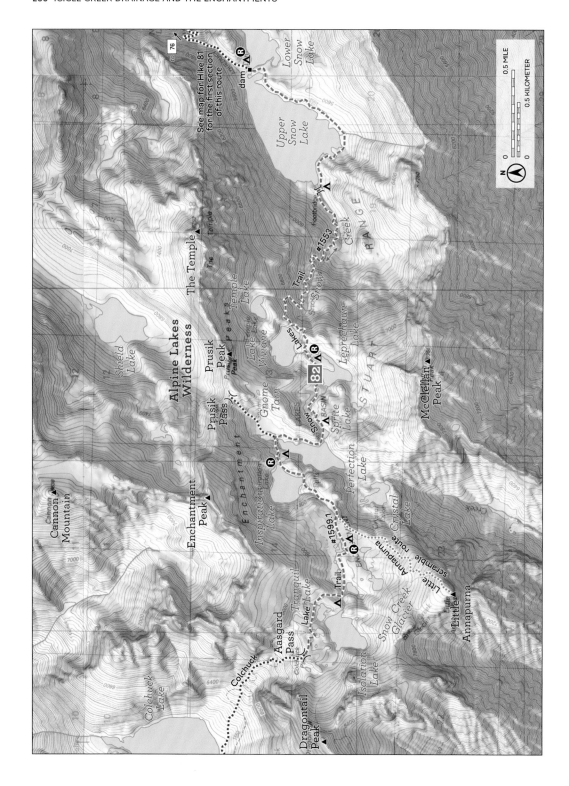

Larch-lined Leprechaun Lake in bright fall color

Push onward under the sharp spires of Prusik Peak, clambering over boulders and skirting jutting ribs of rock to little Sprite Lake and its campsites. The trail hugs the lakeside and rounds a rocky bluff to reveal Perfection Lake (Rune Lake) at 10.4 miles as it dumps water into Sprite Lake in a tiny cascade. Continue beside Perfection Lake toward a sprawling larch-filled meadow and the junction with the Prusik Pass Trail #6714 at 10.7 miles. The trail leads up to Prusik Pass and on to Shield Lake—as well as one of the best viewpoints in the entire Enchantments Basin. From the rubble-strewn shoulders of Prusik Peak, you can take in the full parade of lakes from Lake Viviane all the way up to Little Annapurna and the top of Dragontail Peak. The junction with the Prusik Pass trail also marks the end of the Lower Enchantment Basin. There are several comfortable campsites here for those who would prefer to day trip to the upper basin.

A short climb delivers you to Inspiration Lake (Talisman Lake) at 10.9 miles. From here the trail angles upward to climb into true alpine tundra where it is windier, colder, and a little less hospitable. Push your way up a boulder-filled creek gully to reach a vast meadowland riddled with ponds and streams. Some call this area the Brisingamen Lakelets; you will simply call it enchanting. This is a popular area to drop your pack and set up camp, as there are established camps and a backcountry toilet.

Continue pushing onward and find an unsigned but well-trodden scramble route at 11.4 miles, leading out and up to the top of Little Annapurna. You'll also find sweeping views of the Lower Enchantment Basin, including Crystal Lake tucked into a cirque between McClellan Peak and Little Annapurna.

Beyond the meadows, the trail enters a gray moonscape of talus, rock, and glacial till, contrasting with the stark white of the Snow Creek Glacier and the icy blue of the lakes and tarns. At the 12.2-mile mark the trail cuts between Tranquil Lake (Lake Freya) and a view of the largest lake in the Upper Enchantment Basin, Isolation Lake (Brynhild Lake). From here, it's a short 0.4-mile hike through a boulder field to reach windblown Aasgard Pass (officially Colchuck Pass, though no one seems interested in using that name). From the pass, look down the broad talus-covered slope to the turquoise waters of Colchuck Lake and out toward Mountaineer Creek Valley. From here, wander back down into the basin where water cascades over rock, snow and glaciers cling to mountain slopes, and countless stepping stones invite exploring.

GOING FARTHER

A climb up to the meadowy summit of Little Annapurna requires some routefinding, but the cairn-marked trail involves almost no scrambling, and the views from the summit are commanding and vast. Alternatively, through-hikers can drop down Aasgard Pass, navigating rubble and scree to Colchuck Lake (Hike 83), then leaving the boulders to arrive at good camping at 1.6 miles from the pass.

HISTORY

Around the early 1900s, Forest Supervisor Albert H. Sylvester spent the night near Snow Lakes, then known as Twin Lakes. He trekked up Snow Creek to find a series of unnamed alpine lakes he found "enchanting" and promptly named the group Enchantment Lakes. Sylvester's discovery brought more visitors, who gave local names to the lakes and prominences they found, though not in any official or systematic way.

That changed in 1959 when Bill and Peggy Stark first visited the region. Their experience was life-changing. They became tireless advocates for the Enchantments Basin, returning every year for the next thirty-five years, naming features along the way. The couple ended up drawing a topographical map labeling those features in 1967, and the names they chose proved to be incredibly popular with hikers, climbers, and other outdoor adventurers who visited the area.

Over time the US Board on Geographic Names officially adopted many, but not all, of the Starks' names. Despite that choice, many a hiker and hiking guide prefer the Norse and Arthurian names chosen by the Starks, and references to those names can confuse the uninitiated. For that reason, we've included both the official and the Starks' names here.

83 COLCHUCK LAKE

DISTANCE: 8.8 miles
ELEVATION GAIN: 2300 feet
HIGH POINT: 5600 feet
DIFFICULTY: Moderate
HIKING TIME: 6 to 8 hours
BEST SEASON: Late spring to late fall

TRAIL TRAFFIC: Moderate to heavy foot traffic
PERMITS: Northwest Forest Pass; Colchuck Zone Enchantments permit for overnight stay
MAPS: USGS Cashmere Mountain, USGS Enchantment Lakes; Green Trails The Enchantments No. 209S

TRAILHEAD GPS: 47.52774°N, 120.8208°W
NOTES: Permit required to overnight in Enchantments area between May 15 and Oct. 31; reservation system changes often; for details visit www.fs.usda.gov/detail/okawen/passes-permits/recreation.

GETTING THERE: Take Highway 2 to Icicle Creek Road (Forest Road 76) just west of Leavenworth. Turn onto Icicle Creek Road and continue 8.4 miles to Eightmile Road (FR 7601). Turn left and follow gravel FR 7601 over Icicle Creek about 4 miles to the road end and parking area for Colchuck Lake and Lake Stuart Trailhead, at the far end of the lot. Privy available.

Nestled in a rocky cirque surrounded by sharp, craggy mountains, Colchuck Lake and its aquamarine waters host multitudes of hikers every year. Dragontail and Colchuck Peaks steal the show, while a far-flung rocky spine of the Enchantment Peaks guards the eastern shore. The setting is so enticing that visitors happily overlook the steep ascent and rougher portions of the trail for their chance to visit this alpine beauty.

Colchuck Peak reflected in Colchuck Lake's dazzling waters

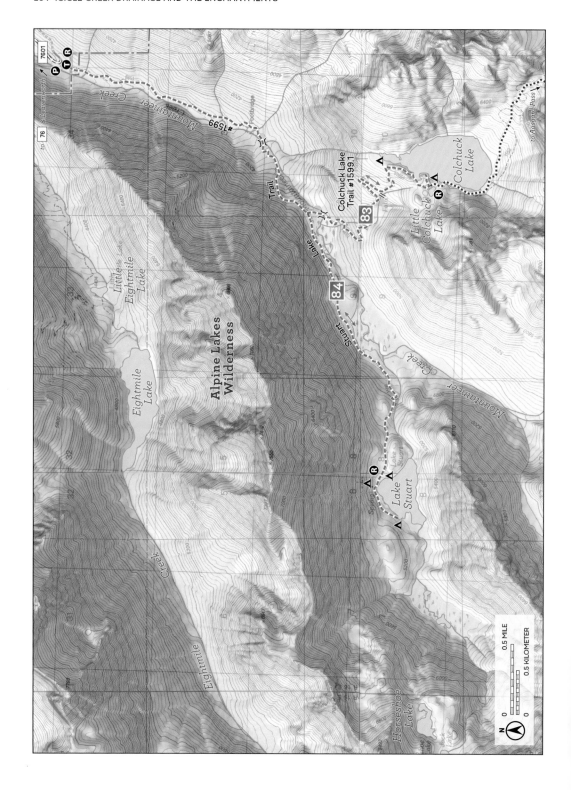

The Stuart Lake Trail #1599 begins by following Mountaineer Creek into a mixed forest of alder and pine. At 0.3 mile, the gentle trail crosses into the Alpine Lakes Wilderness, and the canopy slowly opens as you pass through talus fields and cross log bridges. The rushing sounds of the creek remain a fairly constant companion as you steadily gain elevation along the hardpacked trail increasingly lined with lodgepole and ponderosa pines. You'll cross Mountaineer Creek on a large log bridge around the 1.5-mile mark and soon arrive at the junction with the Colchuck Lake Trail #1599.1 (sometimes referred to as #1599A). The 2.2 miles you've gone so far have been relatively easy—that is about to change as you head left to push up toward Colchuck Lake.

From the junction, the once-friendly trail becomes steep, rocky, and difficult, with roots and rocks dominating the trail bed and tight switchbacks becoming common. As you navigate tricky sections of trail, keep an eye out for reasons to stop and catch your breath. Before long cross the rushing creek again on a sturdy bridge and, soon after, find a pocket view of Colchuck Peak rising in the distance. Beyond, splashing waterfalls and broad vistas beg for a moment's pause. As you near your destination, cross exposed granite faces and find yourself inexplicably descending dozens of feet of hard-earned elevation before beginning the final set of switchbacks up to the lakeshore.

At the 3.9-mile mark, the trail spills out onto granite bluffs high above the north end of Colchuck Lake, showcasing the rocky spires that surround the blue-green water. Across the lake, Aasgard Pass beckons from the saddle between Dragontail Peak and a low shoulder of a long ridgeline known as the Enchantment Peaks. Farther on, Colchuck Glacier clings to the north side of Colchuck Peak, slowly feeding the lake below. Press onward along the lakeshore to find access to the water or a suitable campsite. There is a designated day-use area next to Little Colchuck Lake 0.5 mile down the trail.

It's no surprise that this eye-popping alpine lake is incredibly popular. If the stunning lake color set against a dramatic backdrop of mountaintops is not enough, the quick "backdoor" approach the Enchantment Lakes Basin provides more than enough enticement to backpackers. The rough and rocky route can be difficult and will challenge some hikers. At the same time, this trail makes for a great backpacking destination or training hike.

GOING FARTHER

The Colchuck Lake Trail continues around the lake to snake up Aasgard Pass (Colchuck Pass on some maps) and into the realm of the gods: the Upper Enchantment Lakes Basin (Hike 82). Explore an otherworldly landscape of lakes and tarns or take a trek up to the top of Little Annapurna. Use caution on this approach, as the route is steep and mostly built on top of boulders and scree, making it treacherous under certain conditions. Avoid an ascent in the snow unless you have the equipment and training to undertake it.

HISTORY

In Chinook Jargon, *Colchuck* means "very cold water" or "ice water," an apt name for this glacier-fed lake, which is an irrigation reservoir for nearby farmers and residents. In 1926, a severe drought highlighted the need to supply water to Leavenworth and the surrounding areas during dry spells. Within a few years, the Icicle and Peshastin Irrigation District came together with a plan to dam alpine lakes to act as reservoirs. Four lakes were chosen to supplement seasonal water flows: Colchuck, Eightmile, Klonaqua, and Square Lakes (in addition to Nada and the Snow Lakes, which were already in use as reservoirs). By 1930 a dam was constructed at Colchuck Lake, and today's trail likely follows a route blazed for the construction of that dam.

In 2005 the dam began to fail, causing the lake level to fall dramatically. Repairs the following year returned the lake to its familiar reservoir levels. Today, Colchuck Lake is part of an irrigation system that includes 60 miles of canals supplying water to over 8000 acres of farmland and orchards.

84 LAKE STUART

DISTANCE: 9.0 miles
ELEVATION GAIN: 1600 feet
HIGH POINT: 5100 feet
DIFFICULTY: Moderate
HIKING TIME: 5 to 7 hours
BEST SEASON: Late spring to early fall
TRAIL TRAFFIC: Moderate to heavy foot traffic
PERMITS: Northwest Forest Pass; Stuart Zone Enchantments permit for overnight stay

MAPS: USGS Cashmere Mountain, USGS Enchantment Lakes, USGS Mount Stuart; Green Trails The Enchantments No. 209S
TRAILHEAD GPS: 47.52774°N, 120.8208°W
NOTES: Permit required to overnight in Enchantments area between May 15 and Oct. 31; reservation system changes often; for details visit www.fs.usda.gov/detail/okawen/passes-permits/recreation.

GETTING THERE: Take Highway 2 to Icicle Creek Road (Forest Road 76) just west of Leavenworth. Turn onto Icicle Creek Road and continue 8.4 miles to Eightmile Road (FR 7601). Turn left and follow gravel FR 7601 over Icicle Creek for about 4 miles to the road end and parking area for Colchuck Lake and Lake Stuart Trailhead, at the far end of the lot. Privy available.

On the trail to Lake Stuart, hiking through meadows with views of Argonaut Peak, Sherpa Peak, and Mount Stuart

Set at the feet of mighty Mount Stuart and fed by the glaciers clinging to the crags above, Lake Stuart invites hikers and backpackers to enjoy its wooded shores in a spectacular setting. While the lake draws fewer hikers than nearby Colchuck Lake, thousands visit these wild sparkling waters each summer. Lake Stuart's popularity is unsurprising, given the relative ease with which hikers can reach this rugged alpine lake. While some prefer a more lonesome destination, there is more than enough lake and rocky terrain for everyone. To minimize your company along the trail, visit in late fall—you risk encountering snow, but if your timing is right, you'll catch the Enchantments' famous golden larches.

From the trailhead, follow the Stuart Lake Trail #1599 into a mixed forest alongside the rushing waters of Mountaineer Creek, a sound that keeps you company for most of your hike. At 0.3 mile enter the Alpine Lakes Wilderness and begin your climb. Breaks in the pines allow glimpses of the rocky spires above as you navigate talus fields and sets of rocky switchbacks before crossing a sturdy log bridge spanning Mountaineer Creek at 1.5 miles.

After climbing 2.2 miles reach the well-marked junction with the Colchuck Lake Trail #1599.1 (sometimes referred to as #1599A); continue straight ahead toward Lake Stuart. With most of the elevation out of the way, the remaining 2.0 miles to the lake disappear beneath your boots with only a few ups and downs as you venture deeper into the creek valley.

As you near the lake, the trail skirts a large meadow, revealing the heights of Mount Stuart and Jack Ridge before returning to the trees. You finally reach the lakeside at 4.2 miles. The trail continues another 0.3 mile along the shore to the far end of the lake, passing a number of excellent campsites along the way. Find a spot to settle in and take in this picturesque setting.

GOING FARTHER
Beyond Lake Stuart, a boot path continues up to Horseshoe Lake. The route is marked by blazes carved into the trees, but blowdowns and brush can make for rough going. Climb for 0.75 mile to a large, swampy meadow and work your way toward the end of the valley, keeping the meadow on your left until you reach a tree with a horseshoe nailed to it. This is your sign to head straight uphill. Use caution as you work your way up the steep, treacherous, rocky mountainside to reach Horseshoe Lake.

HISTORY
George B. McClellan named Mount Stuart in 1853 after his longtime friend Jimmie Stuart, a soldier who was killed a few years earlier in a skirmish with American Indians. Lake Stuart inherited its name from the mountain it sits below. Horseshoe Lake was named for its vaguely horseshoe shape.

85 EIGHTMILE LAKE

DISTANCE: 7.8 miles
ELEVATION GAIN: 1400 feet
HIGH POINT: 4700 feet
DIFFICULTY: Moderate
HIKING TIME: 4 to 6 hours
BEST SEASON: Late spring to late fall

TRAIL TRAFFIC: Moderate to heavy foot traffic
PERMITS: Northwest Forest Pass; Eightmile/Caroline Zone Enchantments permit for overnight stay
MAPS: USGS Cashmere Mountain; Green Trails The Enchantments No. 209S

TRAILHEAD GPS: 47.5361°N, 120.8138°W
NOTES: Permit required to overnight in
Enchantments area between May 15 and Oct. 31;

reservation system changes often; for details visit
www.fs.usda.gov/detail/okawen/passes-permits
/recreation.

GETTING THERE: Take Highway 2 to Icicle Creek Road (Forest Road 76) just west of Leavenworth. Turn
onto Icicle Creek Road and continue 8.4 miles to Eightmile Road (FR 7601). Turn left and follow the gravel
road over Icicle Creek for about 2.9 miles to the Eightmile Lake Trailhead. Privy available.

---

*A perennial favorite, the Eightmile Lake Trail offers relatively easy access to a few alpine lakes
tucked into a section of the Enchantments' signature rugged terrain. In recent years fires have
ravaged the forests around the trail, leaving enormous swaths of charred lonely sentinels. On
the plus side, the fires cleared underbrush and removed the forest canopy, making way for a
wonderland of wildflowers in the spring and early summer. While a popular day hike, Eightmile
Lake is also a decent backpacking destination, though one that requires an Enchantments permit for overnight stays during the permit season.*

The hike begins along the Eightmile Lake Trail
#1552 as it follows Eightmile Creek, quickly
serving up impressive views of towering Dragontail Peak and Colchuck Peak. The dusty path

crosses multiple streams as you push deeper
into the creek valley. After about 0.4 mile of
mild elevation gain, note the abandoned logging roadbed that parallels the trail and keep

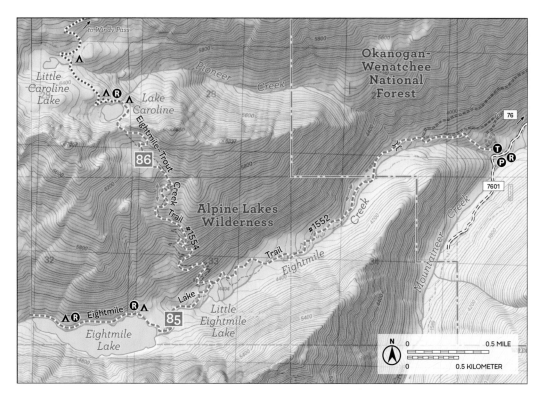

Little Eightmile Lake and the fire-damaged valley wall

left, continuing to push ahead to a wooden bridge spanning Pioneer Creek at 0.8 mile.

Soon after, at the 1.1-mile mark, enter the Alpine Lakes Wilderness while passing what remains of the ponderosa pines that once lined the trail. Within the wilderness, the trail begins to climb in earnest, switchbacking in places and crossing talus fields.

At 2.5 miles reach Little Eightmile Lake, which, as its name suggests, is tiny—depending on the time of year, it can appear to be little more than a deep marsh. Find the junction with the Eightmile–Trout Creek Trail #1554 here, which leads up to Lake Caroline (Hike 86), Windy Pass, and Trout Lake. Stay to the left, pushing onward to Eightmile Lake.

In another 0.5 mile reach Eightmile Lake, tucked quietly in a bowl at the base of Eightmile Mountain, which rises grandly at the far end of the lake. Other sharp ridges surround the pristine waters, adding further mystique to this wild and stunning setting. The trail continues to the far end of the lake, 3.9 miles from the trailhead, giving you plenty of space to find a quiet spot along the shore to enjoy the lake or set up camp if you're planning a longer stay.

Gorgeous and approachable for hikers of all skill levels, Eightmile Lake is the primary access trail for exploring this section of the Enchantments. Despite the smell of ash and smoke that will linger for years to come, this trail still manages to showcase the beauty of this area.

GOING FARTHER

A scramble route to the summit of Eightmile Mountain is fairly easy to follow from the lake. The Eightmile–Trout Creek Trail #1554 provides a quick (but very steep) side trip up to Lake Caroline (Hike 86).

HISTORY

Eightmile Creek got its name from the location where it flows into Icicle Creek: river mile eight. The lakes were then named for the creek that drains them.

Eightmile Lake is one of six alpine lakes that act as reservoirs for the Icicle and Peshastin Irrigation District. Easily seen from the trail at the lake's outlet, the Eightmile Lake Dam was built in 1929, but over the years ice and snow have significantly damaged the structure. While it's still partially functional, the damage has limited the irrigation district's ability to regulate the lake. Plans are in the works to upgrade and restore the system and dam. Opponents, however, object to further human intrustions into this protected wilderness, making the project's future uncertain.

Anyone hiking the Eightmile Creek Valley cannot help but notice that the area has seen more than its fair share of fires in the last few decades. Fires raged through the valley in 1994, and in 2010 the Eightmile Lake Fire made a lasting impression. But it was the 2012 Cashmere Mountain Fire that did most of the damage seen along the trail today.

86 LAKE CAROLINE

DISTANCE: 9.6 miles
ELEVATION GAIN: 2500 feet in; 100 feet out
HIGH POINT: 6300 feet
DIFFICULTY: Hard
HIKING TIME: 5 to 6 hours
BEST SEASON: Late spring to fall
TRAIL TRAFFIC: Moderate foot traffic
MAPS: USGS Cashmere Mountain; Green Trails The Enchantments No. 209S

PERMITS: Northwest Forest Pass; Eightmile/Caroline Zone Enchantments permit for overnight stay
TRAILHEAD GPS: 47.5361°N, 120.8138°W
NOTES: Permit required to overnight in Enchantments area between May 15 and Oct. 31; reservation system changes often; for details visit www .fs.usda.gov/detail/okawen/passes-permits /recreation.

GETTING THERE: Take Highway 2 to Icicle Creek Road (Forest Road 76) just west of Leavenworth. Turn onto Icicle Creek Road and continue 8.4 miles to Eightmile Road (FR 7601). Turn left and follow the gravel road over Icicle Creek for about 2.9 miles to the Eightmile Lake Trailhead. Privy available.

With so much attention focused on the Enchantment Lakes Basin, hikers often overlook nearby trips. And when a trail is dry, dusty, and difficult like this one to Lake Caroline, that is doubly the case. Yet the rough, steep, and challenging hike up to this demure alpine lake offers more than sparkling waters and a tranquil setting: the views are absolutely spectacular.

Start from the trailhead, following the Eightmile Lake Trail #1552 as it traces a path alongside Eightmile Creek. Note the rugged crags of Dragontail Peak and Colchuck Peak as you progress—you'll be getting better views of them soon. Push deeper into the creek valley, crossing the occasional stream and passing more than a few burnt trees along the way. Keep left when you encounter an abandoned logging road at the 0.4-mile mark, and cross the log bridge spanning Pioneer Creek soon after at 0.8 mile. Beyond lies the Alpine Lakes Wilderness boundary at 1.1 miles.

From here, start a steeper climb. Navigate your way up a few mild switchbacks and through

The trail up to Lake Caroline weaves through wildfire-charred forest.

a couple of talus fields to reach Little Eightmile Lake at 2.5 miles. Quite small even in the spring, this lake can seem more like a marsh in the high summer. Here too is the signed junction for the Eightmile–Trout Creek Trail #1554. Eight-mile Lake and good campsites are just another 0.5 mile farther along the main trail, but to reach Lake Caroline, the work has only just begun.

Veer right at the junction to begin a steep ascent on the brushy and exposed trail. Before fires denuded the mountainside, this early stretch threaded through the trees and enjoyed some shelter from the summer sun. Today hikers will find little respite from the heat as they climb through the charred remains of the forest. The rocky trail switchbacks relentlessly up from the valley, offering ever-increasing views of Little Eightmile Lake, Eightmile Lake, and Dragontail Peak, eventually entering meadows and parklands at heights that put large swaths of the Enchantment Peaks on prominent display.

After more than 2.0 miles of climbing, the trail levels out as you approach Lake Caroline, ultimately cresting the ridge that rims the wooded bowl the lake sits in. Eightmile Mountain rises some distance to the west, while Cashmere Mountain looms just to the north; behind you to the south find the heights of Mount Stuart rising above the surrounding crags, reaching toward the heavens. Continue down to reach the lakeshore, 4.8 miles from the trailhead. Find a quiet spot to enjoy a solitude that is sometimes difficult to come by in the Enchantments. There are sites around Caroline, but if you're camping, you may want to look for better sites by continuing onward and upward to the meadows around Little Caroline Lake 0.5 mile farther down the trail.

Rough, steep and challenging, the approach to Lake Caroline sees far fewer boot soles than a typical trail in the Enchantments. Although fewer visitors means you're likely to have Lake Caroline largely to yourself, the lack of traffic also means you can expect some sections of the underused trail to be a little overgrown. For those seeking to capture the essence of the Enchantments in all its rugged glory without having to share the experience with dozens of other hikers, there are few better options than the trek up to this sweet and unassuming alpine lake.

GOING FARTHER

If you've already made the hard trek up to Lake Caroline, the short journey up to Little Caroline Lake takes little effort and is well worth the tour through grassy alpine meadows. Beyond, the trail continues another 2.0 miles up through fields of wildflowers and tree-dotted meadows to windswept Windy Pass, offering panoramic views of the surrounding sea of mountaintops. For through-hikers, the trail continues down to Trout Creek Trail #1555 and eventually leads out to the Jack Trout Trailhead.

HISTORY

The fire damage along the Eightmile Lake Trail and the approach to Lake Caroline is the result of recent fires. In 1994 fires scarred much of the area below the lake. And while the 2010 Eightmile Lake Fire added to the destruction, the massive 2012 Cashmere Mountain Fire did the lion's share of the damage found along the trail today.

87 LAKE EDNA AND CAPE HORN

DISTANCE: 11.2 miles
ELEVATION GAIN: 4500 feet in; 400 feet out
HIGH POINT: 6750 feet
DIFFICULTY: Hard
HIKING TIME: 8 to 9 hours
BEST SEASON: Summer to early fall
TRAIL TRAFFIC: Light foot traffic

PERMIT: Northwest Forest Pass
MAPS: USGS Chiwaukum Mountains, USGS Jack Ridge; Green Trails Chiwaukum Mts. No. 177
TRAILHEAD GPS: 47.6087°N, 120.8821°W
NOTE: Camping is prohibited within 200 feet of Lake Edna.

GETTING THERE: Take Highway 2 to Icicle Creek Road (Forest Road 76) just west of Leavenworth. Turn onto Icicle Creek Road and continue as the pavement turns to gravel at 12.5 miles, then keep right at the Y just beyond. At 14.9 miles, turn right into the parking area for the Chatter Creek Trailhead just before reaching the Chatter Creek guard station.

Explore boulder-strewn creek basins, stands of alpine forest, and lonely lakesides on this sometimes-challenging trek up to Lake Edna. This is the high country—more rock slabs and alpine tundra than meadows and forest. Remote and pristine, the clear waters of Lake Edna invite quiet contemplation. This serene setting is within reach, but it is not an easy reach.

From the Chatter Creek Trailhead, follow the Chatter Creek Trail #1580 through the pines, switchbacking steadily upward through the trees and talus. The trail here is fairly new, cut less than twenty years ago, making for an easy hike up the mountainside. Reach Chatter Creek after about 1.0 mile, crossing it on a solid bridge and connecting with the tread of older trail on the other side. You will immediately notice the difference. Gone is the wide and hardpacked trail, replaced instead by a narrow, crumbling rut angling steeply up into the creek valley.

Soon after the bridge, enter the Alpine Lakes Wilderness at 1.2 miles, where the hard climbing begins. Unless the trail has been recently brushed out, expect undergrowth to increasingly crowd the trail as you press upward. The trail is easy to follow, if hard to see in sections.

The trees begin to thin, and talus fields and brushy slopes move in as you pass a good

Winter is coming to Lake Edna and Ladies Pass on a late summer day.

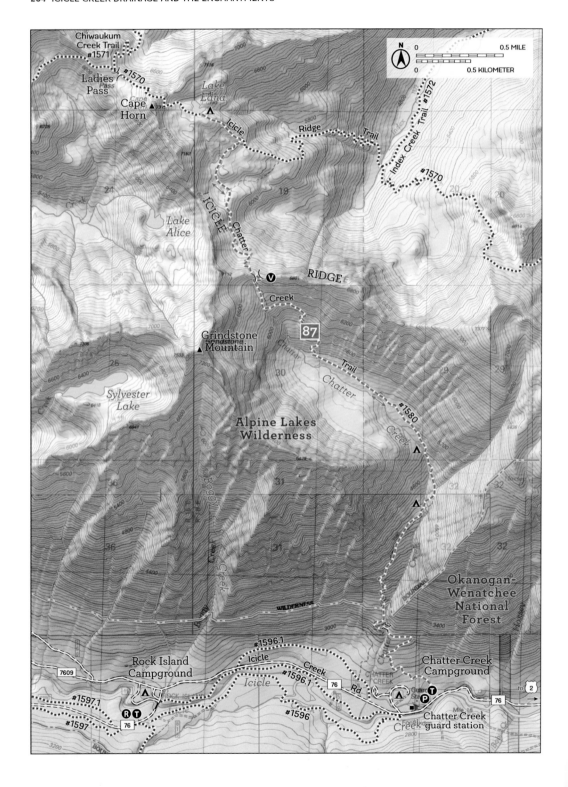

campsite at 1.9 miles, just before crossing Chatter Creek again. The trail continues its steep climb, becoming rockier until you round a shoulder of Grindstone Mountain and enter a broad basin. The grade slackens here, allowing you to catch your breath and marvel at the headwaters of Chatter Creek.

Reach an excellent campsite at 2.5 miles, with views of the valley below and the tips of Cashmere Mountain and Eightmile Mountain peeking out over the ridges across the valley. Press deeper into the basin under the watchful gaze of granite-faced Grindstone Mountain. Chatter Creek tumbles and bumbles nearby as you make your way toward the basin's headwall. Your destination is a low, nearly barren saddle on the ridgeline, easily spotted on your approach by the ribbon of trail cut through the boulders and scree below it.

Slowly but surely, climb the long, rocky switchbacks up the slopes of Icicle Ridge to the saddle and some excellent views. Some call it a day here at 4.2 miles from the trailhead, and it is no wonder—peaks and valley fan out in all directions from this vantage point. Find Bootjack Mountain (Hike 90), Jack Ridge, and the Trout Creek Valley (Hike 88) to the south, along with much more of Cashmere Mountain and Eightmile Mountain, as well as Mount Stuart in the distance. To the north are Index Creek Valley, Snowgrass Mountain, and Cape Horn.

From the saddle, the trail drops sharply into the rubble-filled bowl below, wasting little time shuttling you down among the thin larches. Work your way across the valley bottom through patches of greenery clinging to the rocks near snowmelt-driven streams. Skip across a stream or two before climbing once again. Reach a bench dotted with trees and a patch of meadow. Keep to the most well-worn trail here, avoiding thinner boot paths that will lead you astray. Climb along a rushing creek to the junction with the Icicle Ridge Trail #1570 at the 5.3-mile mark, and veer left onto it.

The trail heads straight up 0.3 mile to little Lake Edna. In high summer, when the snow briefly retreats for a few weeks, Lake Edna's heather-lined shores dazzle with pinpoints of pink and purple. Above, the jagged cleft top of Cape Horn draws the eye, its snow-patched slopes scrubbed of greenery. In the fall, the larches scattered above the shores light up the rock-covered, glacier-carved lake basin. After 5.6 miles of tough trail, find a comfortable rock, break out your lunch, and enjoy the rugged landscape before exploring the lakeshore.

GOING FARTHER

From Lake Edna, the Icicle Ridge Trail continues up over Ladies Pass and follows the ridge above creek drainages and cirques filled with alpine lakes. Not far over the pass, the trail reaches a junction with the Chiwaukum Creek Trail #1571, which leads down to Lake Brigham and Lake Flora. Beyond, the Icicle Ridge Trail passes above Upper Florence Lake, then Lake Mary and Lake Margaret, before ending at Frosty Pass. From Frosty Pass, backpackers can drop down into the Wildhorse Creek Valley via the Wildhorse Creek Trail #1592 (Hike 76) or make a loop by following the Frosty–Wildhorse Trail #1592 back down to Icicle Creek (Hike 98).

HISTORY

In 1909, Forest Supervisor Albert H. Sylvester led a tour through the Icicle Creek watershed with one of his rangers, Burne Canby. On that tour, they camped at Frosty Pass, naming it for the early frost that they awoke to in the morning. As they continued their tour, they stumbled upon lake after lake in rapid succession—first Margaret, then Mary, Florence, and Alice, followed by Edna, Ida, and finally Augusta. They even spied Lake Victoria across the creek valley, hiding in a deep cirque on the slopes of Cashmere Mountain. Each was named in honor of a woman in their lives—Edna was a girlfriend of Burne Canby—and it began a naming convention that continued for years to come.

As Sylvester put it in a speech he made years later in 1943, "It marked the beginning of a practice we followed on the forest for years. There are approximately 150 lakes and ponds in the forest, some of the smaller ones not yet named. The numbers of ladies' lakes grew until practically all rangers' and other Forest Service men's wives, sisters, sweethearts, mothers, and daughters had lakes named for them."

The pass above Edna was named Ladies Pass for all the lakes bearing women's names. After all these "Ladies Lakes" became better known, a lake that Sylvester had overlooked on his 1909 tour was named Lake Brigham by Jack Gonser, a game commissioner and outdoor enthusiast. This lake, surrounded by lakes named for women, was named for the Mormon leader Brigham Young, in reference to the practice of polygamy associated with the early Mormon church. As a result, this group of lakes is sometimes referred to as the "Mormon Ladies Lakes."

Other features in the area named by Sylvester include Cape Horn, which refers to the sharpness of the peak, as well as Grindstone Creek, named for a small grindstone that Sylvester and Ranger John Bender lost in the creek. The name was later given to the mountain the creek runs down. Chatter Creek he named for the "chattering" sound of the water. This last was not his most inventive name, but after days of christening lakes, mountains, and streams, his creativity may have understandably been running a little low.

88 TROUT LAKE

DISTANCE: 12.4 miles
ELEVATION GAIN: 2000 feet
HIGH POINT: 4800 feet
DIFFICULTY: Moderate
HIKING TIME: 7 to 8 hours
BEST SEASON: Late spring to late fall

TRAIL TRAFFIC: Moderate foot traffic
PERMIT: Northwest Forest Pass
MAPS: USGS Jack Ridge; Green Trails Chiwaukum Mts. No. 177
TRAILHEAD GPS: 47.6058°N, 120.9168°W

GETTING THERE: Take Highway 2 to Icicle Creek Road (Forest Road 76) just west of Leavenworth. Turn onto Icicle Creek Road and continue as the pavement turns to gravel at 12.5 miles, then keep right at the Y just beyond. At 16.7 miles reach Rock Island Campground and turn left across the bridge spanning Icicle Creek. In 0.1 mile turn left onto spur road 615 (FR 7600-615). Continue a little over 0.1 mile to the Jack Trout Trailhead on the right. Privy available.

Hike out to a wooded lake thick with moss and lined with grass—no alpine tundra or barren moonscapes here. Instead, find a welcoming lakeshore with plenty of room to explore the lake basin, tie up a hammock in the trees, or throw a line in the water.

From the Jack Trout Trailhead, head into the trees along the Jack Creek Trail #1558. Pass the Jack-Pine Tie Trail #1597 (signed "Jackpine Trail") on your right, a wide equestrian highway leading out to the Blackpine Horse Camp. The well-maintained Jack Creek Trail wanders under needles of pine and larch, soon crossing Jack Creek on a sturdy steel bridge. Beyond, enter the Alpine Lakes Wilderness at 0.6 mile.

Soon climb through the trees, veering away from the creek and reaching a junction with the Trout Creek Trail #1555 at 1.4 miles. Ahead that trail follows Jack Creek deep into the wild, reaching Cradle Lake (Hike 89) and beyond, a journey for another day. Instead, head left and up, continuing to climb the valley wall.

After 2.0 miles of switchbacks up the ridge, round the ridge at a rocky vista offering sweeping views of the Icicle Creek Valley before dropping onto the back side of Jack Ridge above Trout Creek. From here the trail skirts the wilderness boundary and soon exits the shelter of spruce and pine for a broad swath of clear-cut, logged in the 1980s by the Pack River Lumber Company. Skim along the top of the brutal mile-long cut, traversing a field of silvered stumps and snags, the trail increasingly obscured by new growth. Along the way take advantage of the missing canopy to admire the rugged ridges and cliffs of Cashmere Mountain rising across the valley.

Cut through a stand of trees spared the chain saw before returning to another long stretch of recovering mountainside. Reach the wild forest once again, angling down toward the valley bottom and crossing a few bubbling streams before reaching the 5.6-mile mark and the junction with the Eightmile–Trout Creek Trail #1554, which leads up to Windy Pass and Lake Caroline (Hike 86). Push past the junction along the main trail; the lake is a little over 0.5 mile ahead.

Pass the junction with the Jack Ridge Trail #1557 just before cutting through marshlands to reach Trout Lake at the 6.2-mile mark, with waters green from algae and aquatic plants. Grass spills over the lakeshore and out into the lake, blurring the shoreline. In the distance Eightmile Mountain rises above the valley, its sharp peaks flecked with snow. Find campsites tucked into the shore and ample tranquility just about everywhere.

GOING FARTHER

Bushwhackers and adventurers can continue past the lake deeper into the basin, picking their way toward the base of Eightmile Mountain. Your reward is ever-increasing views of Eightmile's rugged profile and a small tarn. Those looking for a loop, follow the unmaintained Jack Ridge Trail, which rockets straight up over Jack Ridge and drops down the other side to Jack Creek and the Jack Creek Trail.

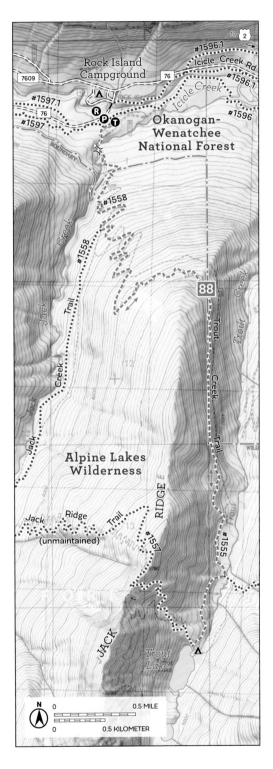

Eightmile Mountain from the marshy shores of Trout Lake

Follow it back to the Trout Creek Trail junction to close the loop. Backpackers have the option of tackling the steep Eightmile–Trout Creek Trail up to Windy Pass to eventually reach Lake Caroline (Hike 86).

HISTORY

Cashmere Mountain, which features prominently on this hike, was named by Judge James Harvey Chase, an early settler and booster in the nearby town of Mission. In 1904 the town decided to change its name, and Chase suggested Cashmere, inspired by the poem "Lalla Rookh" by Sir Thomas Moore, which highlights the beauty of the mountains of Kashmir in India.

Trout Creek and Trout Lake were named for the fish found in their waters.

89 CRADLE LAKE

DISTANCE: 17.8 miles
ELEVATION GAIN: 3400 feet in; 100 feet out
HIGH POINT: 6200 feet
DIFFICULTY: Hard
HIKING TIME: Overnight
BEST SEASON: Summer to fall

TRAIL TRAFFIC: Light foot and equestrian traffic
PERMIT: Northwest Forest Pass
MAPS: USGS Jack Ridge, USGS Chiwaukum Mountains, USGS The Cradle; Green Trails Chiwaukum Mts. No. 177, Green Trails Stevens Pass No. 176

TRAILHEAD GPS: 47.6058°N, 120.9168°W
NOTES: Hike requires a ford of Jack Creek and Meadow Creek; use caution and do not attempt during spring melt or when water levels are high. Camping is prohibited within 200 feet of Cradle Lake.

GETTING THERE: Take Highway 2 to Icicle Creek Road (Forest Road 76) just west of Leavenworth. Turn onto Icicle Creek Road and continue as the pavement turns to gravel at 12.5 miles, then keep right at the Y just beyond. At 16.7 miles reach Rock Island Campground and turn left across the bridge spanning Icicle Creek. In 0.1 mile turn left onto spur road 615 (FR 7600-615). Continue a little over 0.1 mile to the Jack Trout Trailhead on the right. Privy available.

Part forested river walk and part steep switchbacking ascent, this approach to Cradle Lake stores up all the hard climbing for one 2.6-mile burst up the steep valley wall to a wide lake bowl. The wild, isolated lake does not see too many visitors, and when night falls the open slopes are a front-row seat to a vast star show above.

The hike begins from the Jack Trout Trailhead, following the Jack Creek Trail #1558 as it crosses the Jack-Pine Tie Trail #1597 (signed "Jackpine Trail") that leads out to the Blackpine Horse Camp. Head into the forest of pine, fir, and larch on well-maintained trail. Soon cross Jack Creek on a hefty wooden bridge and enter the Alpine Lakes Wilderness at 0.6 mile.

From here the trail climbs briefly, temporarily leaving the creek and soon passing the junction with the Trout Creek Trail #1555 (Hike 88) at 1.4 miles. Beyond the junction, the trail veers back down toward the creek. Wind your way beneath the trees, Jack Creek never too far from your side. To the tune of rushing snowmelt and tumbling riverstone, these first few miles breeze by, punctuated by the occasional climb over a bluff or outcropping before dropping back toward the creek again.

Pass the unmaintained Jack Ridge Trail #1557 at 3.4 miles. As you press deeper along huckleberry-lined trail, blowdowns become increasingly common, as do stream crossings. Hop across stones to keep your feet dry as you continue down this lonely stretch of trail, passing a number of nice creekside camps along the way.

At 5.0 miles reach the junction with the Meadow Creek Trail #1559, where the Jack Creek Trail continues straight up the valley.

Turn right onto the Meadow Creek Trail, which drops down to Jack Creek. Depending on the water levels, the time of year, and a little bit of luck, there may be stones or logs to guide you across the water. If not, ford the creek and continue onward, but don't change footwear just yet, as you need to ford Meadow Creek a few thousand feet down the trail. As always, do not attempt to ford these creeks during the spring melt or when water levels are high. When in doubt, turn around and adventure another day.

Once you're across Meadow Creek, work your way through the trees alongside the creek. At 6.3 miles reach the junction with the Snowall–Cradle Lake Trail #1560 and a big horse-pounded campsite. If you're on a two-night excursion, consider bedding down here and saving the next leg of the journey for the morning, as it's a heart-pounding uphill battle from here to the lakeshore. It is a labor best tackled in the dew of morning rather than the heat of the day.

When you're ready begin your climb, take the Snowall–Cradle Lake Trail up, switchbacking tightly and seemingly endlessly up the mountainside, alternating between thin forest, the occasional burnt snag, and sections of exposed rock. Eventually find blessed relief from the switchbacks when you attain a ridge at 7.7 miles.

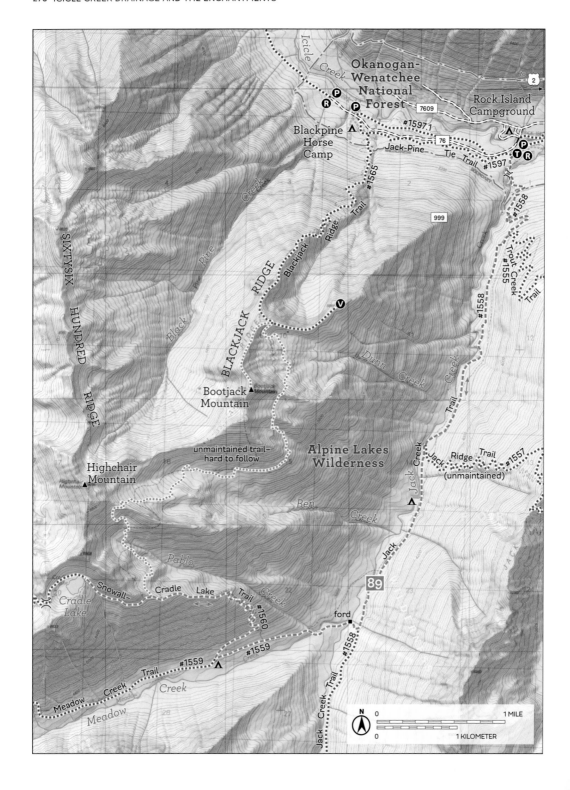

Continue climbing along the back of this ridge toward the lake. Views begin to open here, with the top of Highchair Mountain coming into view, along with nearby Harding Mountain and long views down the Jack Creek Valley and Blackjack Ridge. At 8.4 miles pass the junction with an abandoned section of trail that leads out along Blackjack Ridge to Bootjack Mountain (Hike 90).

From here the trail drops off the ridge and traverses toward Cradle Lake, with some ups and downs along the way, reaching the lake outlet at 8.9 miles from the trailhead. Step out toward the lakeshore's lovely alpine scene: iron-rich orange boulders lie at the bottom of a pointed ridge. Grassy meadows burst with wildflowers during the summer, and a backdrop of rugged peaks including Harding Mountain rounds out the horizon. Nestled between the long arms of the Cradle and Highchair Mountain, the shallow lake sparkles in the sun. Boot paths lead around the lake, offering a multitude of vantage points to enjoy this remote landscape. If you're spending the night, note that camping is prohibited within 200 feet of the lake, and campsites are hard to come by.

GOING FARTHER

The Snowall–Cradle Lake Trail continues around Cradle Lake and up the ridge to a

Harding Mountain from the trail below Cradle Lake

saddle. Any stay at Cradle Lake all but requires a trip up here for close views of Harding Mountain and the Cradle, as well as the Snowall Creek Valley. Those on longer excursions can continue on the trail over the saddle and down along Snowall Creek, following it to the Icicle Creek Trail (Hike 91) and FR 76. Alternatively, adventurers can follow the unmaintained trail between Cradle Lake and Bootjack Mountain (Hike 90), which also leads back to FR 76.

HISTORY

The Cradle was named for the distinct shape of its two-pointed summit. A wide, smooth scoop separates the two points, looking a little like a cradle. That name set the theme for the area: Highchair Mountain and Nursery Mountain are both part of a circle of ridges surrounded by Icicle Creek to the north, French Creek to the west, Meadow Creek to the south, and Jack Creek to the east.

90 BOOTJACK MOUNTAIN

DISTANCE: 7.0 miles
ELEVATION GAIN: 3900 feet
HIGH POINT: 6789 feet
DIFFICULTY: Hard
HIKING TIME: 6 to 7 hours
BEST SEASON: Summer to early fall

TRAIL TRAFFIC: Very light foot traffic
PERMIT: Northwest Forest Pass
MAPS: USGS Jack Ridge; Green Trails
Chiwaukum Mts. No. 177
TRAILHEAD GPS: 47.6100°N, 120.9450°W

GETTING THERE: Take Highway 2 to Icicle Creek Road (Forest Road 76) just west of Leavenworth. Turn onto Icicle Creek Road and continue as the pavement turns to gravel at 12.5 miles, then keep right at the Y just beyond. At 16.7 miles reach Rock Island Campground. Turn left, crossing a bridge over Icicle Creek, and continue another 1.4 miles to a large pullout on the right for the Blackpine Trailhead, 18.1 miles from Highway 2.

Blackjack Ridge rises between Black Pine Creek and Jack Creek, a rugged jut of rock that culminates in Bootjack Mountain. The views from the summit are spectacular, but the hike to the top is grueling. It's dry, dusty, and relentlessly steep, making it among the least hiked trails in the Alpine Lakes Wilderness.

From Blackpine Trailhead, cross FR 76 and enter the trees, following an access trail that soon reaches the Jack-Pine Tie Trail #1597 (signed "Jackpine Trail"), a wide and dusty horse highway that connects the Jack Trout Trailhead with the Blackpine Horse Camp. The camp is to the right. Veer left and continue for 0.1 mile to the junction with the Blackjack Ridge Trail #1565. Here the Jack-Pine Tie Trail continues out along Icicle Creek. Turn right onto the Blackjack Ridge Trail #1565.

Work through some encroaching underbrush that soon gives way to a solid, hard-packed trail lined with salal and fern as your ascent begins in earnest. And make no mistake, "ascent" is nearly an understatement, as you slog your way up through dense forest, zigzagging up switchback after switchback after switchback, crossing into the Alpine Lakes Wilderness at 0.3 mile.

There aren't any views to break up this workout, though on this steep climb, you will likely be focused on putting one boot in front of the other anyway. Pause often as the trail rockets 3000 feet up the mountainside in a little more than 2.0 miles. Eventually the trees thin and the brush thickens, soon yielding to a grassy meadowland and silver snags, a legacy of a long-ago burn. Here are the first hints of the panorama to come. In the spring and summer, wildflowers thrive here, painting the mountainside with pinks, yellows, and purples. Across the Jack Creek Valley, spy Cashmere Mountain and Jack Ridge, the closest prominences in an expanding sea of trees and snowy mountaintops. It's tempting to pull up a log and get lost in the vista, and it's a fine place to pause, but bigger views lie ahead.

Continue through the parklands, traversing the shoulders of the mountainside to attain the ridge at 2.8 miles. Pause here and avoid the temptation to continue following the trail, which descends through meadows and boulder fields toward the Jack Creek Valley. Instead, head left and downridge on a short path leading to a large, boot-pounded viewpoint on a rocky knob. The views are grand at this picnic point, with Grindstone Mountain to the north and the choppy prominences of Jack Ridge just across the valley, as well as Cashmere Mountain and Eightmile Mountain rising behind. This is the end of the trail for many hikers, but still better views await those who don't mind a little scrambling.

Return to the main trail and head straight up the ridgeline—a boot path is hard to find here, but you will run into it very soon. Views continue to broaden as you follow the knife's edge of the ridge 0.7 mile, crossing increasingly large sections of talus along the way. The boot path is well-worn and fairly easily followed to the summit block, where you can pick your way up the last few hundred feet through the boulders to the windswept summit

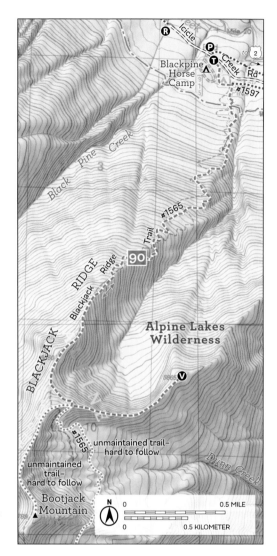

of Bootjack Mountain. The 360-degree views are vast.

Start taking peak attendance: Mount Rainier, Glacier Peak, Mount Baker, Mount Ingalls, Mount Stuart, and the rest of the Enchantment Peaks are all present. Nearer afield find Snowgrass Mountain, Grindstone Mountain, Highchair Mountain, and Harding Mountain. Black Pine Creek drainage is immediately below to the northwest, with Sixtysix Hundred Ridge

Icicle Ridge fills the horizon from the high meadows of Bootjack Mountain.

buttressing the opposite side of the valley. To the southeast are Jack Creek and Jack Ridge. Break out the map and see how many more you can pick out, then pull up a rock, tuck into lunch, and enjoy the view.

GOING FARTHER

The Blackjack Ridge Trail continues beyond the Bootjack summit boot path junction, dropping to a shelf below Bootjack and the rocky ridge and working through old burn, meadows, marshes, and forest to the Snowall–Cradle Lake Trail #1560, approximately 8.0 miles from the trailhead. This section of trail is all but abandoned, however, with the trail becoming indistinct at times.

HISTORY

Blackjack Ridge was named for its location between Black Pine Creek and Jack Creek.

91 ICICLE CREEK TRAIL

DISTANCE: 10.0 miles
ELEVATION GAIN: 500 feet
HIGH POINT: 3200 feet
DIFFICULTY: Easy

HIKING TIME: 5 to 6 hours
BEST SEASON: Late spring to fall
TRAIL TRAFFIC: Moderate foot traffic; light equestrian traffic

PERMIT: Northwest Forest Pass
MAPS: USGS Jack Ridge, USGS Chiwaukum
Mountains, USGS Stevens Pass; Green Trails

Chiwaukum Mts. No. 177, Green Trails Stevens
Pass No. 176
TRAILHEAD GPS: 47.6123°N, 120.9497°W

GETTING THERE: Take Highway 2 to Icicle Creek Road (Forest Road 76) just west of Leavenworth. Turn onto Icicle Creek Road and continue as the pavement turns to gravel at 12.5 miles, then keep right at the Y just beyond. At 16.7 miles reach Rock Island Campground. Turn left, crossing a bridge over Icicle Creek, and continue another 1.8 miles to the Icicle Creek Trailhead, 18.5 miles from Highway 2. Privy available.

As creekside walks go, this meander along the banks of Icicle Creek is hard to beat. The nearly flat trail is cooled by the creek's rushing waters and the sheltering pines, while openings in the canopy allow for pleasant views of forested valley walls and boulder-filled avalanche chutes. While this tour gives hikers a good sense of the Icicle Creek Valley, it covers less than a quarter of its length, which stretches out to Josephine Lake (Hike 73) and the Pacific Crest Trail, passing a half dozen trail junctions along the way.

From the trailhead, follow the Icicle Creek Trail #1551 into the old growth, soon coming within earshot of the tumbling creek and entering the Alpine Lakes Wilderness at 0.3 mile. Wide, flat, and dusty, the trail traverses the valley above the creek, skipping across a number of melt-driven streams as it winds its way through the trees. Breeze along hard-packed tread, quickly putting trail behind you and reaching French Creek Camp at 1.5 miles, complete with a backcountry toilet. This popular and well-established camp works as a stopping point for first-time backpackers or those on a longer journey.

Continue past the camp to a footbridge spanning French Creek, taking a moment to peer up at the rugged heights of Grindstone Mountain across the valley. Just beyond the bridge, reach the junction with the French Creek Trail #1595 at 1.7 miles. The French Creek Valley tempts, beckoning you toward the Snowall drainage (Hike 98) and Klonaqua Lakes (Hike 92). Resist the temptation and continue following Icicle Creek as it rounds the end of French Ridge.

At the 2.1-mile mark, find the junction with the French Ridge Trail #1564 leading up to a former lookout site, far-reaching views, and a brushy boot path out to Turquoise Lake. Stay

Icicle Creek rushes down its densely forested banks.

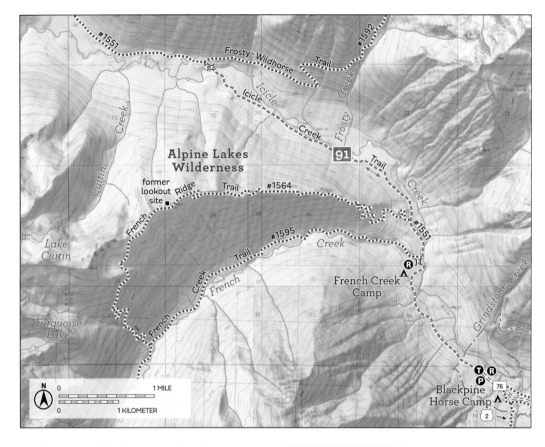

on the main trail and stick to the valley bottom, eventually rounding the ridge into a long view of the valley with the Bulls Tooth rising in the distance.

Wander deeper into the trees as Icicle Creek flows through broad meadows and over logjams. Pass pleasant camps and placid swimming holes, enjoying the valley views along the way. After a little over 2.9 miles that melt nearly effortlessly beneath your boots, reach a sturdy bridge crossing over Icicle Creek, and just beyond reach the junction with the Frosty–Wildhorse Trail #1592, a good turnaround point for day hikers. Find a cool place to picnic and soak your feet in the creek, or continue up the Icicle Creek Trail a few dozen feet to marshy meadows offering views of French Ridge and the hanging valley carved into it that holds Lake Cuitin.

GOING FARTHER

The Icicle Creek Trail is one of the main arterials through the Alpine Lakes Wilderness. From this well-connected trail, backpackers can adventure up to Frosty Pass and Ladies Lakes country via the Frosty–Wildhorse Trail (Hike 98), visit Lake Leland along the Lake Leland Trail #1566, climb up to Chain Lakes (Hike 74), or trek out to the end of the trail at Josephine Lake (Hike 73).

HISTORY

The Icicle Creek Valley was a favorite stomping ground of Forest Supervisor and prolific place-namer Albert H. Sylvester. He named Icicle Creek, using a derivation of the Wenatchee Indian word *na'sik-elt* meaning "narrow-bottom canyon or gorge." The way the word is pronounced, if the first and last letters are dropped, a'sik-el sounds a lot like "icicle." Sylvester also gave Lake Cuitin and Cuitin Creek their names. *Cuitan* or *ku-i-tan* is Chinook Jargon for "horse," a reference to the small amount of horse grazing available at the mouth of the creek.

French Creek begins its long journey to Icicle Creek from Sprite Lake near Paddy-Go-Easy Pass (Hike 52). The creek and the ridge were named for a prospector and homesteader who held claims along the waters. French Ridge was also home to a fire lookout, an L-5 cabin built in 1934 that was used until it was removed in 1970. The lookout site and its big views can be reached via the French Ridge Trail (Hike 92).

92 KLONAQUA LAKES

DISTANCE: 18.2 miles
ELEVATION GAIN: 2300 feet
HIGH POINT: 5100 feet
DIFFICULTY: Moderate
HIKING TIME: Overnight
BEST SEASON: Summer to fall

TRAIL TRAFFIC: Light foot traffic
PERMIT: Northwest Forest Pass
MAPS: USGS The Cradle, USGS Chiwaukum Mountains; Green Trails Stevens Pass No. 176
TRAILHEAD GPS: 47.6123°N, 120.9497°W

GETTING THERE: Take Highway 2 to Icicle Creek Road (Forest Road 76) just west of Leavenworth. Turn onto Icicle Creek Road and continue as the pavement turns to gravel at 12.5 miles, then keep right at the Y just beyond. At 16.7 miles reach Rock Island Campground. Turn left, crossing a bridge over Icicle Creek, and continue another 1.8 miles to the Icicle Creek Trailhead, 18.5 miles from Highway 2. Privy available.

Pristine, difficult to reach, and often overlooked, the Klonaqua Lakes make for an excellent overnight destination or a very challenging day hike. Travel through old-growth forest alongside three different creeks as you make your way up to a set of three alpine lakes nestled beneath Granite Mountain. Yes, three. While most maps of the area leave the impression that there are only two Klonaqua Lakes, there is a third tucked high up on Granite's slopes, often left unlabeled and visited by only the most ardent of lake baggers.

From the Icicle Creek Trailhead, follow the Icicle Creek Trail #1551 as it enters a mature forest filled with the rushing sounds of nearby Icicle Creek. Cross into the Alpine Lakes Wilderness at 0.3 mile. The trail bed is flat and well-traveled, allowing you to glide alongside the creek for 1.5 miles to French Creek Camp. Soon cross French Creek, and just beyond arrive at the French Creek Trail #1595 junction at 1.7 miles.

Veer left onto the French Creek Trail and trade smooth trail for a steady climb through the trees, weaving beneath the canopy and never straying far from the sounds of the water. After 0.5 mile, the grade tapers somewhat under the shadow of French Ridge. Continue working your way up the French Creek Valley, enjoying brief glimpses of the surrounding landscape through breaks in the canopy and the cheerful companionship of the creek, splashing merrily as you climb. The forest is lovely, but the miles soon pile up with only the occasional creek cutting across the trail to break things up.

At 5.2 miles, reach the junction with the French Ridge Trail #1564, which scales the heights of French Ridge in a long series of tight

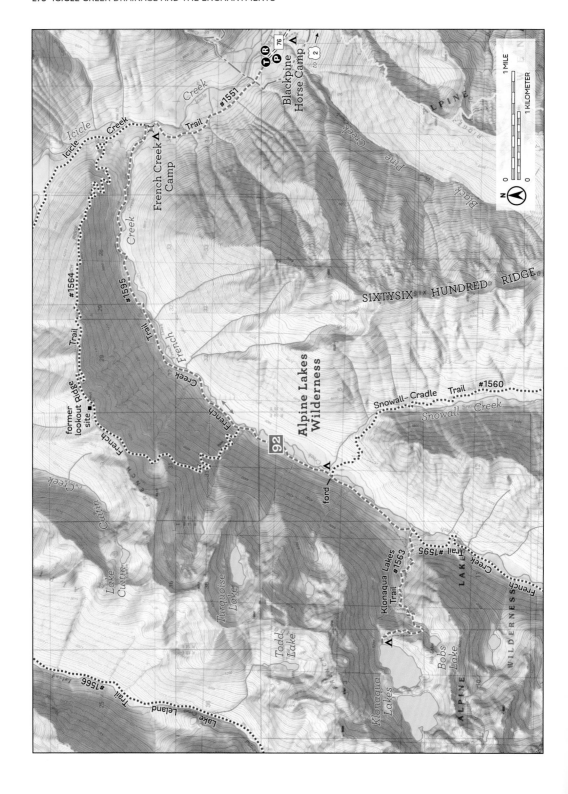

Lower Klonaqua Lake and snowcapped Granite Mountain

and extremely steep switchbacks before heading back along the ridgeline toward Icicle Creek. Push past this junction for another 1.0 mile to the next junction, with the Snowall–Cradle Lake Trail #1560, a rough trail leading up through the Snowall Creek Valley between Sixtysix Hundred Ridge and the Cradle. Campsites here serve as a good base camp for exploring Snowall Creek, which requires a creek ford. Ignore the temptation to drop your pack here in favor of Snowall Creek, and continue working your way down the French Creek Trail.

In another mile you finally reach the junction with the Klonaqua Lakes Trail #1563, 7.2 miles from the trailhead. Turn uphill to leave French Creek behind and begin the steep climb to the lower Klonaqua Lake, navigating the rough, blowdown-prone trail as it steadily switchbacks up the mountainside. Push onward and ever upward for nearly 2.0 miles to reach the lakes.

As you approach the lower lake, note a large cairn next to a steep boot path at the 8.6-mile mark. This is the most defined approach to the upper Klonaqua Lake (see Going Farther). For now, continue on the main trail to reach the sheltered edge of the lower Klonaqua Lake at 9.1 miles. A few campsites are scattered among the trees as the lake comes into view, and there is space for several tents in a large clearing near the water. Pick your way out along the remnants of the Klonaqua Dam to get the best view of craggy Granite Mountain overshadowing the lake and the tree-lined shore.

GOING FARTHER

With no official trail leading to it, the upper Klonaqua Lake sees even fewer visitors than its lower neighbor. From the cairn at 8.6 miles, follow the steep boot path up past Bobs Lake to the shore of the upper lake. Wilder, rockier, and untouched by irrigation projects, this Klonaqua

Lake is well worth the extra effort and route-finding. This is the end of the trail for most hikers, but climbers and mountaineers have been known to follow scramble routes up and around Granite Mountain to reach Robin Lakes (Hike 57) on the other side.

HISTORY

Sometime in the 1910s, that famed USGS surveyor turned Forest Supervisor Albert H. Sylvester explored the area around Klonaqua Lakes. He found a system of three lakes and dubbed them Klonaqua, as the number three is *klone* in Chinook Jargon, and *qua* means water in the Wenatchee tongue. Sylvester mixed the two languages to come up with the name.

The lakes are part of the historic Icicle Creek Irrigation District, which has had a variety of names over the years and is currently known as the Icicle and Peshastin Irrigation District. In 1927 the district was granted water rights to a number of lakes, including the Klonaqua Lakes, in order to bring water to thirsty orchards and residents. In 1933 the district built a dam at the outlet of Klonaqua Lakes to manage the water levels. The dam operated for decades before falling into disrepair. Today hikers arriving at the end of the main Klonaqua Lakes Trail will find a rusting gate actuator near the lakeshore and the crumbling remains of the dam among the logjam at the lake outlet.

However, this familiar scene may change soon. Proposals are in the works to expand the alpine lake storage capacity of the irrigation district, and one part of that plan includes replacing the Klonaqua Dam. The project is being spearheaded by the Icicle Work Group, a consortium of governmental, tribal, and agricultural stakeholders. Early versions of the plan proposed tapping into the upper lake as well, by boring a tunnel similar to the Snow Lakes system or installing a pump system, though this more ambitious proposal has been dropped. Wilderness advocates are working to delay, reduce, or block the plan, which has yet to be approved. In the coming years, hikers may find a new landscape—or still be greeted by scenery unchanged over the last eighty-five years.

OPPOSITE: *Rainbow Lake reflecting talus-sloped Pratt Mountain (Hike 94)*

EXTENDED BACKPACKS

This vast wilderness area is filled with countless sawtooth ridges, glacier-carved cirques, and pointed peaks reaching for the sky, all bejeweled with sparkling alpine lakes and tarns. To reach much of its interior, you must stuff your backpack with gear and head out into the wilderness for multiple nights. At the same time, the network of trails often offers so many ways of approaching a particular destination that putting together an itinerary can be challenging.

Backpackers attempting to piece together extended trips through the Alpine Lakes Wilderness can consult many resources, though statewide backpacking guides tend to limit trips to one or two options. For any of the hikes on the Pacific Crest Trail, *Hiking the Pacific Crest Trail: Washington* by Tami Asars is an excellent resource (see the Bibliography). But in some sources, depending on your destination, there is little or no information on whether a particular route is a good approach or whether another alternative might offer something more. Our own experience of trying to string together day-hike descriptions from multiple guidebooks and maps when planning backpacking trips showed us the need for a better resource for creating longer backpacking routes in the Alpine Lakes Wilderness.

With that in mind, the extended backpack trips in this section have a different format than the other hikes in this book. They are designed as an itinerary, broken down by day, with shorter descriptions of the route and what hikers can expect along the trail, including both elevation gain and loss. Each hiking day is an easily digestible snapshot that not only sketches out the route, but can also be used as a building block for creating your own routes. For example, you want to do the Trail Creek and Deep Lake Loop (Hike 96) but also want to add a few days to visit Spectacle Lake? No problem, simply review Days 2 and 3 of Hike 95 to get an idea of what to expect.

93 DUTCH MILLER GAP AND WILLIAMS LAKE

DISTANCE: 34.3 miles
ELEVATION GAIN: 4800 feet
HIGH POINT: 5900 feet
DIFFICULTY: Moderate
HIKING TIME: Allow 4 days
BEST SEASON: Summer to early fall
TRAIL TRAFFIC: Moderate foot traffic near Goldmyer Hot Springs; light foot traffic beyond
PERMIT: Northwest Forest Pass
TRAILHEAD GPS: 47.5173°N, 121.4542°W

MAPS: USGS Snoqualmie Lake, USGS Snoqualmie Pass, USGS Big Snow Mountain, USGS Mount Daniel; Green Trails Alpine Lakes West–Stevens Pass No. 176S
NOTES: The first day may involve fording Burnboot Creek. Middle Fork Trail #1003 is open to mountain bikes on odd-numbered days June through October. Before you go, reserve a campsite at Goldmyer Hot Springs for the third night; visit www.goldmyer.org for details.

GETTING THERE: Take I-90 to Exit 34 near North Bend. At 468th Avenue just off the freeway, eastbound turn left, westbound turn right. Follow the road past the truck stop for about a half mile until you reach SE Middle Fork Road (Forest Road 56). Turn right and follow this road for a few twists and turns, keeping left when the road splits. After 2.2 miles reach SE Lake Dorothy Road. Turn left and continue 12 miles, crossing the Taylor River Bridge. After the bridge, keep right on FR 56, sometimes labeled FR 5620 or Dingford Creek Road at this point. Continue for about 5 miles to the Dingford Creek Trailhead. Privy available.

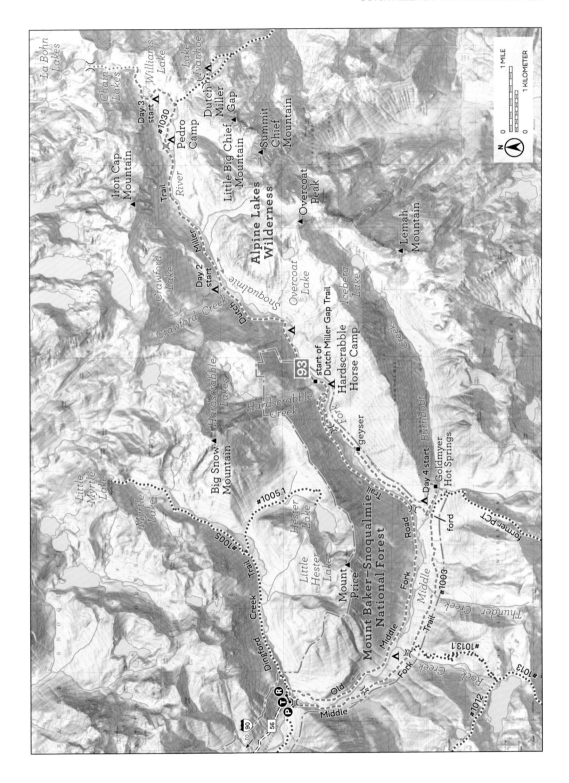

A backpacker crosses Burnboot Creek to reach Goldmyer Hot Springs.

Trek deep into the heart of the Alpine Lake Wilderness on this backpack to the beginnings of the Middle Fork Snoqualmie River. Follow in the footsteps of long-gone prospectors and pack mules out to Williams Lake and Dutch Miller Gap, climbing past rushing waterfalls and through lush meadows to reach captivating vistas, abandoned mines, and alpine tarns.

DAY 1:
Dingford Creek Trailhead to Crawford Creek Camp

11.5 miles, 1900 feet elevation gain

From Dingford Creek Trailhead, head down to the Middle Fork Snoqualmie River, crossing on the Dingford Creek Bridge and veering left onto the Middle Fork Trail #1003 at 0.2 mile. Head out toward Goldmyer Hot Springs (Hike 15), crossing bridged Wildcat Creek at 1.6 miles and passing the junction

with the Rock Creek Trail #1013.1 (Hike 14) at 2.8 miles.

A mile beyond, reach bridgeless Thunder Creek, at 3.8 miles. It's only challenging during the spring melt, so ford or hop across on stones, continuing to the 5.1-mile mark and Burnboot Creek (aka Burntboot or Burnt Boot). Cross the creek on logs (or ford it if they've washed away), and enter the Goldmyer property just beyond. Pass the caretaker cabin and note the campsites—you'll be staying here on night three. Follow the trail out of the camping area to the Middle Fork Snoqualmie and a bridge at 5.6 miles. Don't cross the bridge—turn right to stay on the Middle Fork Trail #1003. Pass soaking pools, bubbling hot springs, and a makeshift warm shower some Good Samaritan built 7.1 miles from the trailhead.

Reach another bridge and cross the river on it, then climb the slopes to reach solid forest road, sometimes called the Old Middle Fork Road Trail, at 8.7 miles. Turn right and uphill, reaching the Hardscrabble Horse Camp and the Dutch Miller Gap Trailhead in 0.3 mile. Camping pads are here if you're ready to call it quits for the day, but the Alpine Lakes Wilderness boundary is just 0.6 mile down the Dutch Miller Gap Trail #1030, and a couple easy miles beyond that, find Crawford Creek and decent campsites at the 11.5-mile mark.

DAY 2:
Crawford Creek Camp to Chain Lakes

7.2 miles, 2600 feet elevation gain; 1300 feet lost

From Crawford Creek, continue on the Dutch Miller Gap Trail through old-growth forest with gaps in the canopy offering increasingly better valley views, eventually crossing a sturdy bridge to reach a large meadow in the middle of a river oxbow at 2.8 miles. This is Pedro Camp, with excellent camping and magnificent views of the surrounding crags of Summit Chief, Little Big Chief, and Bears Breast Mountains. Push onward through swaths of huckleberry and underbrush to the 3.6-mile mark and the junction with the Williams Lake Trail #1030.1. Turn left onto it, wandering through parklands to reach lovely Williams Lake at 4.2 miles, surrounded by talus-covered slopes and jutting peaks. Find a campsite and set up camp, preparing for a day hike up to Chain Lakes.

Follow the boot path around the east side of the lake. Curious hikers can find an old adit and rusting tracks in this area. Climb up through boulder fields to reach the Chain Lakes basin at 5.2 miles. Spend some time in this barren, ice-carved landscape looking for mine shafts

and abandoned piles of ore. Work your way up the far end of the basin to reach a saddle near La Bohn Lakes for spectacular views of this alpine landscape, 5.7 miles from Crawford Creek Camp. Get your fill before returning to camp at Williams Lake.

DAY 3:
Williams Lake to Goldmyer Hot Springs

10.6 miles, 300 feet elevation gain; 2800 feet lost

Retrace your route from Williams Lake to the junction with the Dutch Miller Gap Trail #1030. Consider whether you want to climb 1.0 mile to Dutch Miller Gap for a view of Lake Ivanhoe (Hike 50) before heading back to Hardscrabble Horse Camp and then the junction with the Middle Fork Trail #1003 at 7.0 miles. Instead of dropping down to the river here, continue on the Old Middle Fork Road Trail to the 9.5-mile mark and a road junction. Head down to the Middle Fork Snoqualmie to find the bridge you passed on Day 1. Cross the river and arrive at the Goldmyer Property at 10.0 miles. Set up camp and hike a short 0.3 mile up to the hot springs for a soak.

DAY 4:
Goldmyer Hot Springs to Dingford Creek Trailhead

5.0 miles, negligible elevation gain; 400 feet lost

From Goldmyer, it is more or less 5.0 miles back to the Dingford Creek Trailhead. You can rehike the Middle Fork Trail #1003 if you prefer the trees, but this route returns to the Old Middle Fork Road Trail to shave off some time and wander down a different path. To close the loop, hike the 0.5 mile back to the Old Middle Fork Road Trail across the river, veer left, and glide back down an unexciting 4.5 miles above the river that returns you to the Dingford Creek Trailhead in record time.

94 I-90 LAKES TOUR

DISTANCE: 23.8 miles
ELEVATION GAIN: 5300 feet
HIGH POINT: 5584 feet
DIFFICULTY: Moderate
HIKING TIME: Allow 3 to 4 days
BEST SEASON: Late spring to late fall
TRAIL TRAFFIC: Heavy foot traffic to Melakwa
Lakes and Mason Lake; light foot traffic to Granite
Creek Trailhead
PERMITS: Northwest Forest Pass, Discover Pass

MAPS: USGS Snoqualmie Pass, USGS Bandera,
USGS Lake Philippa; Green Trails Snoqualmie
Pass Gateway No. 207S, Green Trails Mt. Si No.
206S
TRAILHEAD GPS: 47.41525°N, 121.4433°W
NOTE: This through-hike requires two cars. Park
one at the Granite Creek Trailhead (Hike 1) and
drive to the Denny Creek Trailhead (Hike 28) to
begin the hike.

GETTING THERE: For the shuttle vehicle, take I-90 to Exit 34 near North Bend. At 468th Avenue just off the freeway, eastbound turn left, westbound turn right. Follow the road past the truck stop for about a half mile to SE Middle Fork Road (Forest Road 56). Turn right and follow this road for a few twists and turns, keeping left when the road splits. After 2.2 miles reach SE Lake Dorothy Road. Turn left, and continue 3.6 miles to the Granite Creek Trailhead on the right just before crossing the Middle Fork Snoqualmie River. Privy available.

From I-90 between North Bend and Snoqualmie Pass, take Exit 47. Eastbound, turn left to cross over the freeway to a signed T intersection; westbound, turn right to this T intersection. At the T, turn right, heading under the freeway for 0.25 mile to Forest Road 58. Turn left on FR 58 and follow it for 2.5 miles to Denny Creek Campground. Just past the entrance to the campground, turn left onto FR 5830 for 0.25 mile to the road-end trailhead and parking. Privy available.

Depending on how you count them, there are about twenty named alpine lakes between the Pratt River Valley and the Middle Fork Snoqualmie River Valley. Some are frequently visited, others rarely. This cross-country backpack and through-hike skirts the shores of nearly all of them. A lake-bagger's dream, this tour travels through rugged landscapes, climbing mountainsides to mammoth vistas before dropping into sheltering lake bowls.

DAY 1:
Denny Creek Trailhead to Pratt Lake

7.5 miles, 2300 feet elevation gain; 1100 feet lost

From the Denny Creek Trailhead, follow the Denny Creek Trail #1014 (Hike 28) as it winds under I-90 at 0.5 mile before reaching the Alpine Lakes Wilderness at 0.9 mile. Not far beyond, at 1.1 miles, find the Denny Creek Waterslide. Clock Keekwulee Falls at the 1.7-mile mark before beginning a stiff climb up to Hemlock Pass. Switchback up through talus and thin forest to reach the pass at 3.8 miles. Find the junction with the Melakwa Lake Trail #1011 in the trees near the pass.

Keep right onto the Melakwa Lake Trail to head up and into the narrow granite trough holding Melakwa Lake at 4.2 miles. Wander the cirque, clambering over logjams of silvered snags and marveling at the jagged points of Chair, Bryant, and Kaleetan Peaks. Find Upper Melakwa Lake at 4.4 miles from the trailhead.

After a long climb, you may enjoy a dip in Melakwa Lake as much as these pups.

Settle in for a lunch break before returning to the Melakwa Lake–Denny Creek junction.

Stay right on the Melakwa Lake Trail, which drops steeply down into the Pratt River Basin to Lower Tuscohatchie Lake at 6.9 miles, along with the junction for the Kaleetan Lake Trail #1010. Push past both to reach Pratt Lake and the end of the Melakwa Lake Trail at the 7.5-mile mark. Find a campsite and enjoy the quiet solitude of Pratt Lake.

Option: Those wishing to add another day can camp at Lower Tuscohatchie Lake and climb up to Windy Lake and Kaleetan Lake, a 7.0-mile roundtrip journey.

DAY 2:
Pratt Lake to Thompson Lake

9.6 miles, 2400 feet elevation gain; 2200 feet lost

From Pratt Lake, follow the Pratt Lake Trail #1007 (Hike 26) as it works its way around the lake and up the shoulders of Pratt Mountain for 1.8 miles to reach Pratt Lake Saddle above Olallie Lake (Hike 25) and the junction with the Mount Defiance Trail #1009. Turn right, following the Mount Defiance Trail along the ridge before dropping off and switchbacking up the flanks of Pratt Mountain, with Talapus Lake (Hike 25) coming into view below. Drop down through boulder fields to a trail junction at 3.1 miles. Head left for a quick 0.3-mile side trip down to Island Lake (Hike 24), passing a few tarns before dropping down to an idyllic lakeshore, complete with signature islands.

Return to the Mount Defiance Trail, trekking through meadows to pass Rainbow Lake at 4.0 miles, then the spur to Lake Kulla Kulla at 4.5 miles. Kulla Kulla is a bit challenging to see and even more challenging to access. You can catch it sparkling through the trees, but the better view is from the top of Mount Defiance. At 4.9 miles, reach the junction with the Ira Spring (Mason Lake) Trail #1038 (Hike 22).

Option: Popular Mason Lake is to the left, with viewpoints and lakeshore access about 0.1 mile down the trail, along with the multitudes of day-trippers.

Stay on the Mount Defiance Trail and push up the shoulder of Mount Defiance (Hike 22) on a ridge between Little Mason Lake and Lake Kulla Kulla. Vistas open in wildflower meadows with big views of the Snoqualmie Valley. At 6.1 miles reach an unsigned junction with a well-worn boot path zigzagging up the mountain. Follow it 0.3 mile out to the summit of Mount Defiance for jaw-dropping views of the lakelands below.

Return to the Mount Defiance Trail and traverse the bowl above Spider Lake and below Web Mountain, eventually dropping down to the shores of Thompson Lake (Hike 1). Find the junction with the Thompson Lake Spur Trail #1009.3 at 9.3 miles and push past it around the lake to find campsites near the lake outlet at 9.6 miles.

DAY 3:
Thompson Lake to Granite Creek Trailhead

6.7 miles, 600 feet elevation gain; 3200 feet lost

From Thompson Lake, head back to the Thompson Lake Spur Trail #1009.3, following it as it climbs out of the lake bowl. Crest the ridge at 0.7 mile and reach forest road at the 1.2-mile mark. Descend on wide roads, keeping right and continuing downhill at a junction at 1.8 miles and continuing straight at the next junction 0.1 mile beyond. At 2.3 miles reach another road junction. Veer left and downhill to traverse above Lower Granite Lake and reach Upper Granite Lake in 0.6 mile. Dirty Harry's Peak sits above.

Retrace your steps and head down the decommissioned logging road alongside the crashing sounds of Granite Creek as it descends into the Middle Fork Snoqualmie Valley. At 5.7 miles find the Granite Creek Connector Trail. Keep to the main trail and reach the trailhead and end of the tour at 6.7 miles.

95 PACIFIC CREST TRAIL–DUTCH MILLER GAP LOOP

DISTANCE: 57.6 miles
ELEVATION GAIN: 11,400 feet
HIGH POINT: 5980 feet
DIFFICULTY: Hard
HIKING TIME: Allow 5 to 7 days
BEST SEASON: Summer to early fall
TRAIL TRAFFIC: Moderate to light on Middle Fork and PCT; heavy on Snow Lake Trail
PERMIT: Northwest Forest Pass

TRAILHEAD GPS: 47.4454°N, 121.4235°W
MAPS: USGS Snoqualmie Pass, USGS Chikamin Peak, USGS Big Snow Mountain, USGS Mount Daniel; Green Trails Snoqualmie Pass No. 207, Green Trails Alpine Lakes West–Stevens Pass No. 176S
NOTE: You may have to ford Burnboot Creek if there are not logs across it. Before you go, reserve a campsite at Goldmyer Hot Springs for the fourth night; visit www.goldmyer.org for details.

GETTING THERE: Take I-90 to Snoqualmie Pass. Eastbound take Exit 52 and turn left onto Alpental Road for about 2 miles to a large gravel parking lot. Westbound take Exit 53, turning left under the freeway and soon reaching a T intersection. Turn right onto State Route 906, following the sign pointing toward Alpental. Continue 2.7 miles through the ski area to the parking area. Privy available.

This wide loop climbs though some of the most rugged country within the Alpine Lakes Wilderness. Traverse talus slopes under glacier-clad mountains, camp at lonely creeksides, and spend hours marveling at sparkling alpine lake waters. Wild sections of trail lead to remote lakes, while numerous lakeside camps tempt you to spend yet another night under the stars. This adventure follows the modern Pacific Crest Trail (PCT) out to the vicinity of Waptus Lake, where it trades the new for old, following trail that was once known as the Cascade Crest Trail, the predecessor of the PCT, back to Snoqualmie Pass. For more details about each segment of the route, see the hikes described earlier in this book.

DAY 1:
Snoqualmie Pass to Ridge and Gravel Lakes

8.6 miles, 2400 feet elevation gain; 100 feet lost

Begin by hiking 1.3 miles back down Alpental Road to the Pacific Crest Trail North–Snoqualmie Pass Trailhead. Head down the Pacific Crest Trail #2000 (PCT) toward Kendall Peak and Kendall Katwalk (Hike 34), passing the junction with the Commonwealth Basin Trail #1033 at 3.9 miles. Continue through wildflower-filled meadows and pika-packed talus fields

and ever-better views of Commonwealth Basin. At 6.8 miles reach a boot path that scrambles up to the top of Kendall Peak, a short but worthy side trip up to sweeping views of surrounding mountaintops.

Push deeper into the wilderness, crossing the granite-carved Kendall Katwalk at 7.6 miles. From here follow the ridgetop through talus fields to reach Ridge and Gravel Lakes, 8.6 miles from the trailhead. Follow boot paths around both lakes to find good campsites. Ridge Lake offers views of Alaska Lake below and Alta Mountain, but whether you camp there or not, be sure to take in the views of the Middle Fork Snoqualmie Valley and

Looking out over the Waptus River Valley toward Waptus Lake from high up on Dutch Miller Gap Trail

Mount Price, which stands above Goldmyer Hot Springs (where you will stay on Day 4).

DAY 2:
Ridge and Gravel Lakes to Lemah Creek Camp

12.2 miles, 1800 feet elevation gain; 3800 feet lost

Begin your day by pressing down the PCT, passing a tempting path leading up to Bumble Bee Pass, which provides impressive views of Mount Thompson and Edds Lake below. Continue around the top of Alaska Mountain, revealing Joe Lake below as you crest the ridgetop, then drop down the mountainside to a narrow rib between Edds Lake and Joe Lake. Traverse the open meadows on the slopes of Huckleberry Mountain, enjoying the views from these parklands as the trail rounds the end of the mountain and begins a long climb up the flanks of Chikamin Peak. From these heights, the trail angles slightly downward, continuing to traverse the high country over rocks and boulders beneath Four Brothers.

Eventually climb your way over the top of Chikamin Ridge to find Park Lakes tucked into the basin below. Reach the junction with the Mineral Creek Trail #1331, with access to the Park Lakes, at 7.2 miles.

Option: Excellent camping can be found here for those looking to spend another night in the wild.

Continue to push down the PCT to the 9.6-mile mark to reach the access trail to Spectacle Lake and take this short 0.3-mile climb to an alpine beauty and another tempting place to set up camp. The loop returns you to the PCT, which drops to cross Delate Creek and reach Delate Meadow. Pass the junction with the Pete Lake Trail #1323 at 11.0 miles, staying on the PCT to reach Lemah Creek. If the bridge is still out, ford Lemah Creek to find a campsite at 12.2 miles.

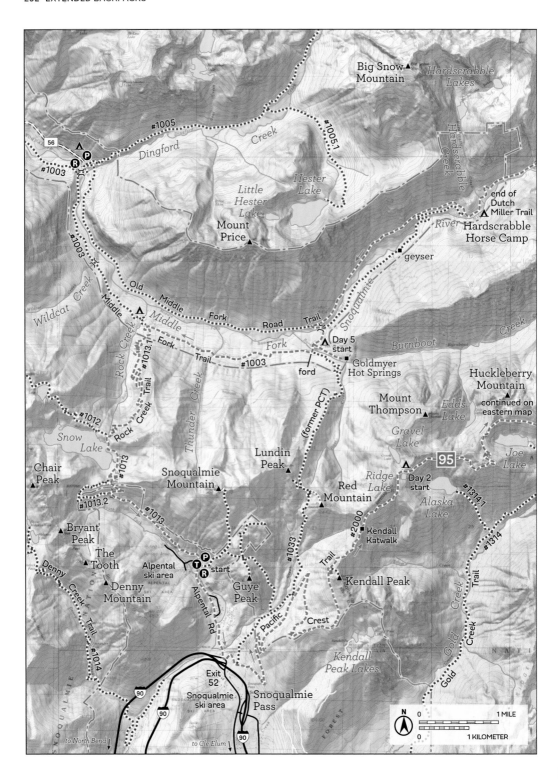

DAY 3:
Lemah Creek Camp to Chief Creek Camp

**13.6 miles, 2400 feet elevation gain;
2500 feet lost**

Continue down the PCT, passing the junction with the Lemah Meadow Trail #1323.2 at 1.3 miles. Stay on the PCT to begin the day's toil, a long switchbacking climb up a forested arm of Summit Chief Mountain. After many switchbacks, climb past the timberline and into old burn, and finally attain the ridgeline at 6.9 miles. Continue over granite outcroppings through a group of tarns above Escondido Lake, and below Summit Chief Mountain. Round the bowl above Escondidio Lake, and pass the junction with the Waptus Burn Trail #1329.3 at 9.3 miles, before dropping down into the Waptus Lake Basin. Switchback down to the junction with the Dutch Miller Gap Trail #1362 at 13.6 miles, turning left to leave the PCT and find campsites near Chief Creek to bed down for the night.

DAY 4:
Chief Creek Camp to Goldmyer Hot Springs

13.9 miles, 1900 feet elevation gain

Follow the Dutch Miller Gap Trail toward Lake Ivanhoe (Hike 50) as it fords Chief Creek, then begins a long, switchbacking climb up forested slopes, crossing creeks and entering boulder country. Cross Ivanhoe's outlet creek near the remains of the bridge at 2.4 miles. The trail splits around the lake near here, with either path leading up to Dutch Miller Gap. Opting for the eastern side of the lake rewards you with a tumbling terraced waterfall at 2.9 miles. Climb up to Dutch Miller Gap, reaching it at 3.1 miles and savoring the views from the top: sparkling Ivanhoe below, Waptus in the distance.

Continue through the meadowy gap, dropping into the Middle Fork Snoqualmie Valley and passing the junction with the Williams Lake Trail #1030.1, at 3.9 miles (campsites at that lake are 0.6 mile distant). Stay on the Dutch Miller Gap Trail #1030 (Hike 93) as it descends the river valley and soon pass Pedro Camp at 4.7 miles to eventually arrive at Hardscrabble Horse Camp at 10.0 miles. From here, follow the Old Middle Fork Road Trail, a largely decommissioned forest road, passing the junction with the Middle Fork Trail #1003 in 0.3 mile and reaching a road junction at 12.8 miles. Veer left and down to the Middle Fork Snoqualmie River, crossing a bridge and reaching the Goldmyer property after 13.3 miles of hiking. Check in and end the day by walking up 0.3 mile to soak in the hot springs.

DAY 5:
Goldmyer Hot Springs to Snow Lake Trailhead

**9.3 miles, 2900 feet elevation gain;
1500 feet lost**

Leave Goldmyer by heading out to Burnboot Creek (aka Burntboot or Burnt Boot), crossing it on logs, or by fording the creek if they've washed away, to reach the Middle Fork Trail #1003. Follow the river down toward the trailhead, tiptoeing across bridgeless Thunder Creek to reach the Rock Creek Trail #1013.1 (Hike 14) at the 2.5-mile mark.

Turn left and up, beginning a tough climb up the Rock Creek Valley, switchbacking first through forest, then talus, past Rock Creek Falls and up to the trail's end, where it connects with the High Lakes Trail #1012 (Hike 30) to the right and the Snow Lake Trail #1013 (Hike 29) to the left at 3.5 miles. Veer left, hugging the shore of Snow Lake for 0.5 mile to the short spur trail down to the remains of a cabin. Push upward from the lake, attaining a saddle at the 6.8-mile mark. From here, descend steeply toward the Snow Lake Trailhead, zigzagging past the junctions with the Source Lake Trail #1013.2 and reaching the parking area 9.3 miles from Goldmyer.

96 TRAIL CREEK AND DEEP LAKE LOOP

DISTANCE: 31.5 miles
ELEVATION GAIN: 5800 feet
HIGH POINT: 5600 feet
DIFFICULTY: Moderate
HIKING TIME: Allow 4 to 6 days
BEST SEASON: Late spring to early fall
TRAIL TRAFFIC: Moderate foot traffic
PERMIT: Northwest Forest Pass

MAPS: USGS The Cradle, USGS Mount Daniel, USGS Polallie Ridge, USGS Davis Peak; Green Trails Alpine Lakes West–Stevens Pass No. 176S
TRAILHEAD GPS: 47.54348°N, 121.0968°W
NOTES: Parking is scarce on summer weekends. Route requires multiple river fords, so do this backpack when water is low and be prepared to get your boots wet.

GETTING THERE: Take I-90 to Roslyn, Exit 80. Eastbound turn left; westbound turn right, following Bullfrog Road 2.8 miles to the traffic circle junction with State Route 903. Follow SR 903 toward Roslyn for 16.6 miles through the town and along Cle Elum Lake to just beyond the Salmon La Sac guard station, where the road splits. Keep right, continuing toward Tucquala Lake along FR 4330 (aka Fish Lake Road or Cle Elum Valley Road) on dirt and gravel for 12.3 miles to the Cathedral Pass Trailhead. Privy available.

Filled with big alpine lakes, snowcapped peaks, and long views, this loop is a nice mix of well-trodden pathways and lesser-known destinations. The route also intersects many other trails, making it easy to add more lakes and mountaintops to your tour.

DAY 1:
Cathedral Pass Trailhead to Lake Michael

8.5 miles, 2500 feet elevation gain; 800 feet lost

From the trailhead, follow the Cathedral Pass Trail #1345, crossing into the Alpine Lakes Wilderness at 0.4 mile and ascending to the junction with the Trail Creek Trail #1322 at 2.0 miles. Veer left to follow the Trail Creek Trail as it angles down through thick forest to the junction with the Lake Michael Trail #1336 (Hike 53), 4.7 miles from the trailhead. Turn left and head uphill, climbing over creek beds along a brushy traverse to reach Lake Michael at 8.5 miles. Tucked beneath Goat Mountain, this is a lovely and often overlooked lake. Campsites can be found on either side of the lake outlet.

Option: For even more seclusion, continue another 1.6 miles down increasingly brushy and hard-to-follow trail to climb another 500 feet up to lonely Lake Terence and its solitary campsite.

DAY 2:
Lake Michael to Waptus Lake

8.9 miles, 500 feet elevation gain; 2600 feet lost

From Lake Michael, retrace your route 3.8 miles back to Trail Creek Trail. Turn left to descend to a sprawling horse camp and the Waptus River at 6.2 miles. Ford the river to reach the Waptus River Trail #1310 (Hike 48). Keep in mind that you'll be fording the river again in about a mile. Turn right on the Waptus River Trail and follow it to the Waptus Pass Trail #1329 and a few campsites at 7.1 miles. Keep right to reach the well-signed Waptus Horse Ford Trail #1329.1 in 0.1 mile, fording the wide river again. Continue toward Waptus Lake, rejoining the Waptus

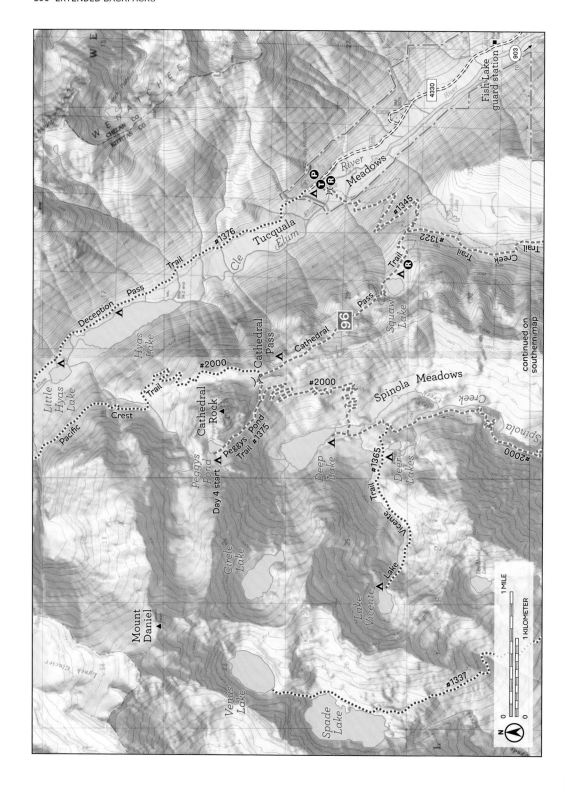

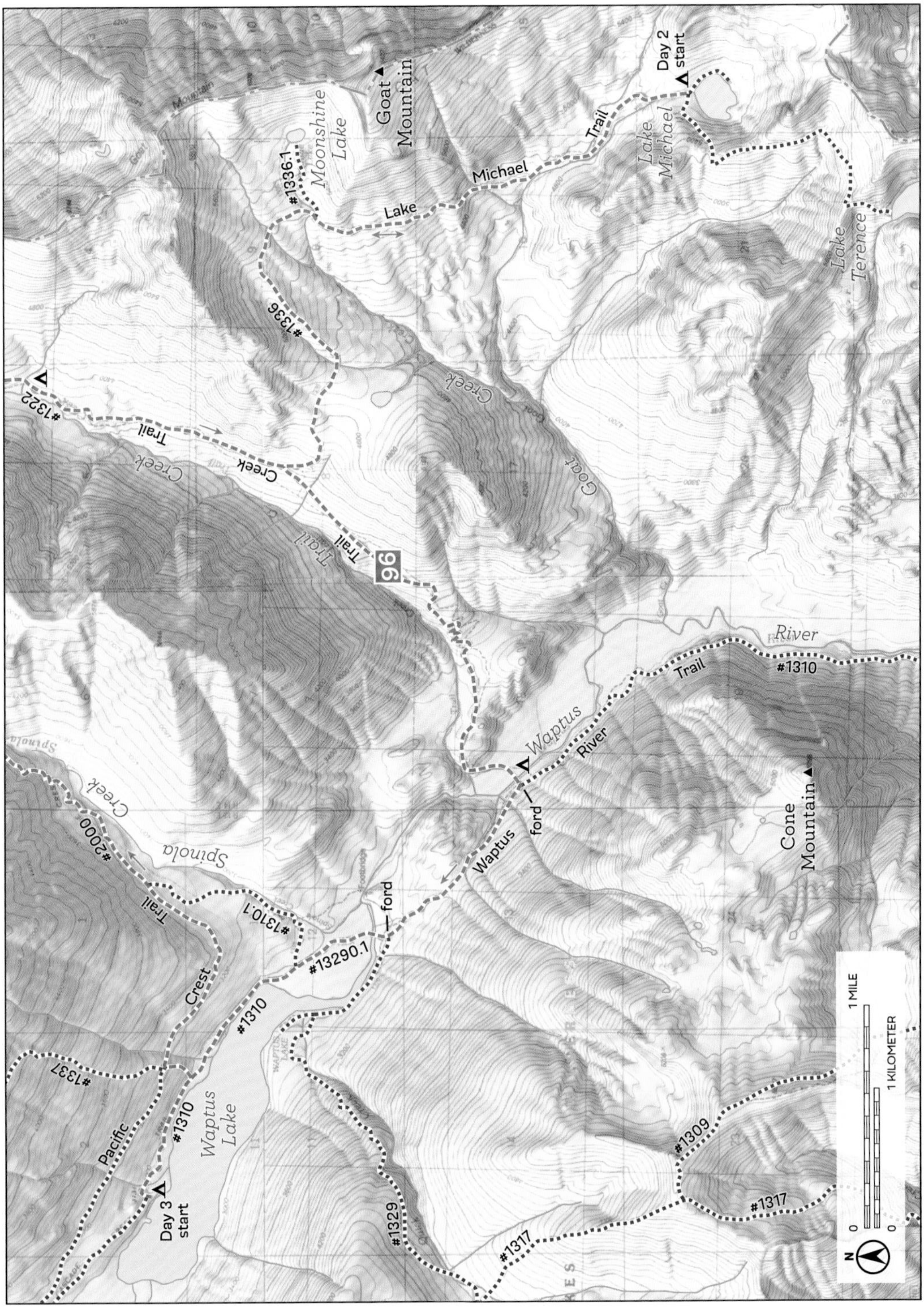

Goat
Mountain ▲

Moonshine
Lake

Lake

Michael

Trail

Day 2
start

Lake
Michael

Lake
Terence

#1336.1

#1336

#1322

Creek
Trail

Creek

Trail

Trail

Goat Creek

Creek

96

River

Trail

#1310

Waptus

River

▲
ford

Waptus River

Cone
Mountain ▲

ford

Waptus

Spinola

Creek

#2000

Spinola Creek

#1310.1

#13290.1

#1309

Trail

Crest

#1310

#1337

Pacific

#1310

Waptus
Lake

Day 3
start

#1329

#1317

#1317

1 MILE

1 KILOMETER

0

0

N

Cathedral Rock soars above golden meadows near the shores of Deep Lake.

River Trail at 7.7 miles. Soon after, reach the lake and the first campsites.

Camp here or keep following the trail, passing a few campsites on your way to the junction with the Spade Lake Trail #1337 at the 8.3-mile mark. Note this trail, as you'll be taking it on the next leg of your journey. There is an excellent campsite a little farther down the trail, set on a rocky bluff overlooking the lake. Find it just beyond a designated horse camp at 8.9 miles. Look for a faint boot path leading off the trail toward the water. For the adventurous, there is also access here to a small rocky island camp, easily reached when the water is low.

Option: Some may want to spend more time near Waptus, as it is easy to add destinations like Lake Ivanhoe (Hike 50) or Spade and Venus Lakes (Hike 49).

DAY 3:
Waptus Lake to Peggys Pond

9.1 miles, 2600 feet elevation gain

From the bluff camp, retrace your steps back to the Spade Lake Trail #1337, 0.6 mile distant. Turn left and up for 0.2 mile to reach the Pacific Crest Trail #2000 (PCT). Turn right and head up on good tread under a canopy of old growth. Pass the junction with the Spinola Creek Trail #1310.1 at 2.0 miles and continue on the PCT as you climb up the Spinola Creek Valley.

Climb around rocky outcroppings, through talus fields, and over tumbling creeks, passing the Lake Vicente Trail #1365 (Hike 55) at 5.2 miles. The meadows surrounding Deep Lake are just beyond, with a spur trail leading out to good campsites at the 5.6-mile mark. Follow this spur out to marvel at Cathedral Rock and Mount Daniel towering over this tranquil alpine lake. Wander out to the campsites for a better look, or if you're planning a longer trip, set up camp for the night.

From the junction leave the meadows and climb up the mountainside, switchbacking through open country, to reach the junction with the Peggys Pond Trail #1375 at 8.5 miles near Cathedral Pass. Follow the rough and rocky trail 0.6 mile to Peggys Pond and serene camping against the backdrop of Mount Daniel to end your 9.1-mile day.

DAY 4:
Peggys Pond to Cathedral Pass Trailhead

5.0 miles, 200 feet elevation gain; 2400 feet lost

Leave Peggys Pond behind, heading back toward the PCT. Turn left on the PCT and reach Cathedral Pass at 0.7 mile. Drop down to connect with the Cathedral Pass Trail #1345 at 0.8 mile and begin your descent on it back to the Cathedral Pass Trailhead. Pass Squaw Lake (Hike 54) at 2.3 miles and reach the junction with the Trail Creek Trail #1322 at 3.0 miles, closing the loop. Finish out your journey by dropping another 2.0 miles back to the trailhead.

97 INGALLS CREEK TO LAKE INGALLS

DISTANCE: 31.0 miles
ELEVATION GAIN: 4600 feet
HIGH POINT: 6500 feet
DIFFICULTY: Moderate
HIKING TIME: Allow 4 days
BEST SEASON: Summer to early fall
PERMIT: Northwest Forest Pass

TRAIL TRAFFIC: Moderate foot and equestrian traffic below Fourth Creek; light foot traffic beyond
MAPS: USGS Blewett, USGS Enchantment Lakes, USGS Mount Stuart; Green Trails Alpine Lakes East–Stuart Range No. 208SX
TRAILHEAD GPS: 47.4629°N, 120.6733°W

GETTING THERE: Take I-90 to Exit 85, following signs to State Route 970. Merge onto SR 970 and continue 37.9 miles, as SR 970 turns into Highway 97, to Ingalls Creek Road on the left. Turn onto the road, cross the bridge, and keep left at the fork, continuing 1.2 miles to the road end and trailhead. Privy available.

This long out-and-back connects to a half dozen trails as it follows Ingalls Creek beneath the Stuart Range out to Lake Ingalls and Stuart Pass. The farther reaches of this trail are less traveled and sometimes a bit brushy, but the increasingly wild landscape, snowy peaks, and tumbling waters are more than enough to compensate for some overgrown sections. Cap the adventure with a night in Headlight Basin near otherworldly Lake Ingalls.

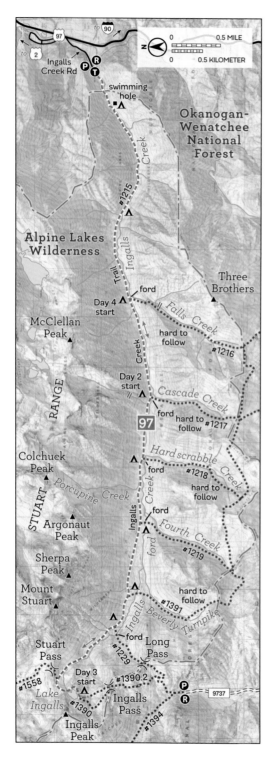

DAY 1:
Ingalls Creek Trailhead to
Hardscrabble Creek

8.1 miles, 2000 feet elevation gain

Start your journey by following the Ingalls
Creek Trail #1215 (Hike 62) as it sets off into
the creek valley, following rumbling Ingalls
Creek and crossing into the Alpine Lakes Wilderness at 0.3 mile. Pass a swimming hole, then
the first campsites under rugged landscape at
1.0 mile. Soon round the edge of the Stuart
Range and press deeper into the valley proper.
Enjoy wildflowers and an easy grade to the day
hikers' turnaround point at a campsite at the
3.0-mile mark.

Note Three Brothers looming above as you
continue on rougher trail, passing increasingly
tempting campsites at 4.0 and 4.9 miles. Reach
Falls Creek at 5.4 miles, finding an excellent
camp and access to a hard-to-follow trail across
a ford of Ingalls Creek that leads up the Falls
Creek drainage. There's also a lone grave here,
resting place of a cabin owner who died in an
avalanche.

Continue onward, passing more camps and
the signed junction with the Cascade Creek
Trail #1217 at 7.2 miles, another hard-to-follow
trail reached by fording Ingalls Creek. From
here, the Ingalls Creek Trail enters old wildfire burn. Reach two campsites 0.4 mile before
Hardscrabble Creek and set up camp at 8.1
miles from the trailhead.

DAY 2:
Hardscrabble Creek to Lake Ingalls

7.4 miles, 2600 feet elevation gain

Continue farther into the wilderness, climbing steadily. Pass Hardscrabble Creek and
access to the Hardscrabble Creek Trail #1218
at 0.4 mile. This is another of those overgrown
trails that work their way up the slopes across
Ingalls Creek, each with a campsite and all
requiring a ford to reach. There's more up

Wilderness camps at lower elevations lack dazzling lakes and broad vistas, but campfires are allowed in these areas.

ahead. Press ever onward, navigating brushy trail and blowdowns as you work your way through forest and open talus, passing Fourth Creek Trail #1219 at 2.0 miles, followed by Beverly Turnpike Trail #1391 at 3.6 miles and finally the Longs Pass Trail #1229 at 4.3 miles. From here the trail is increasingly rocky and steep as it crosses the base of Mount Stuart, steadily closing in on the valley's headwall. Climb the largely open slope to reach a junction just below Stuart Pass at 4.2 miles.

Before heading left to Lake Ingalls, consider climbing the 0.2 mile up to Stuart Pass for impressive views of Jack Valley, Ingalls Peak, and Mount Stuart as well as Mount Daniel and Glacier Peak in the distance. From here, the Jack Creek Trail #1558 drops down into the Jack Creek drainage. Take a long look down the valley you've just climbed up, then head back down the junction.

From the junction, head left (right if you went up to Stuart Pass) and climb a rocky ridge to reach Lake Ingalls. Rest on stone shores next to this icy lake at the foot of Ingalls Peak. To find a campsite, work your way around the south shore to scree-lined Ingalls Way Trail (Hike 60), which leads down into Headlight Basin at the 6.9-mile mark. Soon reach the junction with Ingalls Way Alternate #1390.2. Good campsites can be found down this path at 7.4 miles.

DAY 3:
Lake Ingalls to Falls Creek Camp

10.1 miles, negligible elevation gain; 3100 feet lost

From Headlight Basin, retrace your steps 0.5 mile back to Lake Ingalls, then drop to the junction below Stuart Pass to rejoin the Ingalls Creek Trail and your old trailside companion Ingalls Creek. Switchback down the headwall, again passing Longs Pass Trail, at 3.1 miles, followed by the Beverly Turnpike Trail at the 3.8-mile mark, leaving the last shoulder of Mount Stuart behind. Pass Fourth Creek Trail at 5.4 miles followed by the Hardscrabble Creek Trail at 7.0 miles where the trail reenters the burnlands. Hike through the campsites from Day 1, resisting the temptation to spend another night here. Instead press downward, passing the Cascade Creek Trail at 8.3 miles before reaching an excellent camp at the junction with the Falls Creek Trail at 10.1 miles.

DAY 4:
Falls Creek Camp to Ingalls Creek Trailhead

5.4 miles, negligible elevation change

From Falls Creek, it's a quick 5.4-mile descent along Ingalls Creek back to the trailhead, passing several campsites on wildflower-lined trail. Linger before reluctantly leaving the wilderness and returning to the parking area.

98 LADIES LAKES LOOP

DISTANCE: 21.8 miles
ELEVATION GAIN: 5600 feet
HIGH POINT: 7100 feet
DIFFICULTY: Hard
HIKING TIME: Allow 3 days
BEST SEASON: Summer to fall
TRAIL TRAFFIC: Moderate foot traffic; light equestrian traffic
PERMIT: Northwest Forest Pass

MAPS: USGS Jack Ridge, USGS Chiwaukum Mountains; Green Trails Alpine Lakes East–Stuart Range No. 208SX
TRAILHEAD GPS: 47.6123°N, 120.9497°W
NOTE: The 3.6-mile gap between the trailheads requires either walking along the road, arranging for a ride, or parking a second vehicle at the endpoint trailhead.

GETTING THERE: Take Highway 2 to Icicle Creek Road (Forest Road 76) just west of Leavenworth. Turn onto Icicle Creek Road and continue as the pavement turns to gravel at 12.5 miles, and then keep right at the Y just beyond. If you're bringing an extra vehicle to shuttle between the trailheads, the Chatter Creek Trailhead is on the right at 14.9 miles, just before the Chatter Creek guard station. At 16.7 miles reach Rock Island Campground. Turn left, crossing Icicle Creek on a bridge, and continue another 1.8 miles to the Icicle Creek Trailhead, 18.5 miles from Highway 2. Privy available.

This loop explores the rugged tundra and windswept passes of the Chiwaukum Mountains, fabled highland of alpine lakes. Challenging to reach, this land of snow and stone has a harsh and captivating beauty. The route outlined here suggests three days, but hikers could spend much more time exploring these lake basins.

A storm closing in on Frosty Pass

DAY 1:
Icicle Creek Trailhead to Lake Margaret

9.1 miles, 2600 feet elevation gain

From the Icicle Creek Trailhead, follow the Icicle Creek Trail #1551 (Hike 91) into the trees, crossing the Alpine Lakes Wilderness Boundary at 0.3 mile. Glide down easy trail, passing French Creek Camp at 1.5 miles and the junction with the French Creek Trail #1595 0.2 mile beyond. Press onward, passing the French Ridge Trail #1564 at 2.1 miles. At the 5.0-mile mark reach the junction with the Frosty–Wildhorse Trail #1592 and turn up onto it, beginning the first of many steep climbs on this route.

Switchback your way up the mountainside, crossing Doughgod Creek, to reach Frosty Creek's hanging valley. Soon the trail tucks in alongside the creek, cutting through alternating sections of forest and brush before climbing the headwall of the cirque and delivering you to the ledge above Lake Margaret at 9.1 miles. Find camps near the lake outlet and enjoy the greenery of this pretty lake bowl at the base of Snowgrass Mountain on the edge of the high country.

DAY 2:
Lake Margaret to Lake Flora

4.9 miles, 1600 feet elevation gain; 1300 feet lost

From Lake Margaret, continue your climb up the headwall to Frosty Pass, reaching it at 0.5 mile.

Option: From the pass you can drop into the Wildhorse Creek Valley (Hike 76), continuing

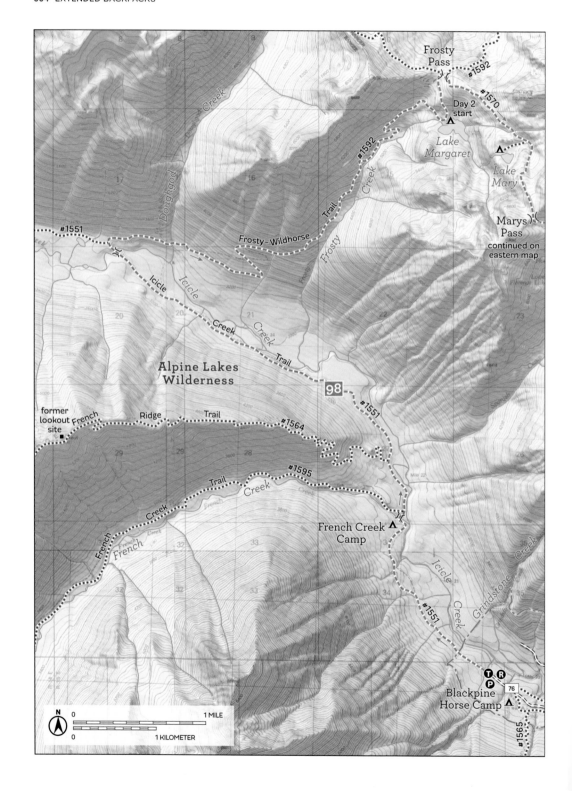

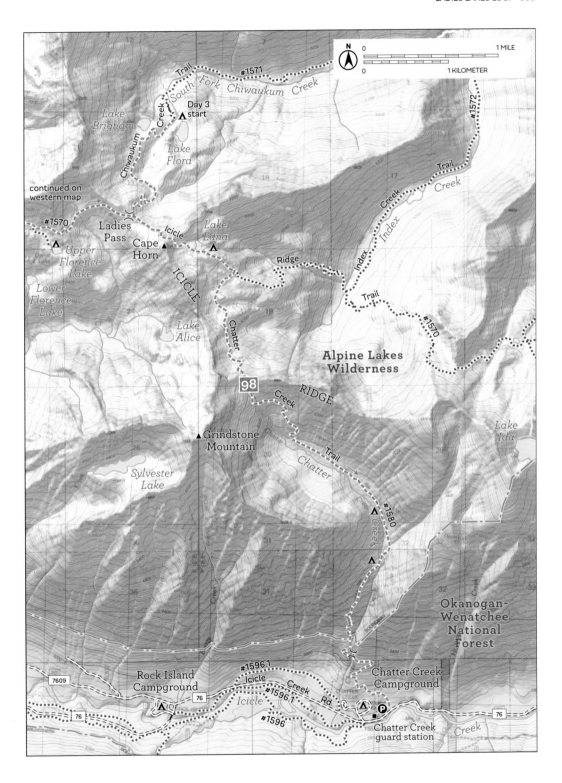

down #1592, known as the Wildhorse Creek Trail on this side of Frosty Pass. Trek out to the well-signed Lake Grace Trail #1578, and then follow it as it climbs sharply up 1300 feet to Lake Grace. It's 2.0 miles from the pass to the lake, but if you pursue this option, consider being leisurely and spending the night. Grace Lake makes for a tranquil night's sleep, and there's enough to explore in the lake basin to fill up another day.

From Frosty Pass, follow the Icicle Ridge Trail #1570 as it leaves the timberline and traverses a high, open shoulder of Snowgrass Mountain. Enjoy big views of the Icicle Creek Valley and the snow-covered peaks rising in the distance. Mount Rainier makes a showing on a good day. After 1.2 miles, reach a spur trail leading down to Lake Mary. Consider taking the short 0.2-mile trek down to the lakeshore for a better look and some exploration before continuing onward.

Back on the main trail, climb up and around a hefty ridge and cross over Marys Pass to the south face of Snowgrass Mountain and Upper Florence Lake tucked below the next ridge. Find a junction at 2.6 miles where a side trail heads south to Upper Florence Lake. If you want to see it, switchback down to a broad bench and out 0.4 mile to the water's edge. Quiet campsites await by that lakeshore for those who want to linger.

Continue the tour by climbing over another of Snowgrass's ridges to traverse a bowl above Spanish Camp Creek, then climb the flanks of a ridge to reach Ladies Pass and the junction with the Chiwaukum Creek Trail #1571 at 3.4 miles. Veer left and switchback steeply down to reach Lake Flora, with long views of the Chiwaukum Creek Valley, and camp 4.9 miles from Frosty Pass.

DAY 3:
Lake Flora to Chatter Creek Trailhead

7.8 miles, 1400 feet elevation gain; 4500 feet lost

From Lake Flora, climb 1.5 miles back up to the junction at Ladies Pass, veering left onto the Icicle Ridge Trail and climbing up the shoulders of Cape Horn to attain the ridgeline above Lake Edna (Hike 87) at 1.9 miles. Drop steeply for 0.3 mile through snow-scrubbed moonscape to the granite shores of Lake Edna. Linger here and enjoy Edna's cold beauty before descending a rocky gully another 0.3 mile to the junction with the Chatter Creek Trail #1580.

Bear right, working your way through marshy meadows, then a boulder-filled basin. Climb up, up, and over Icicle Ridge to switchback down through talus fields and finally reach brushy Chatter Creek Basin. It's a long, slightly overgrown, somewhat rough slog down toward the trailhead, with scattered campsites along the way. You'll find relief shortly after you exit the Alpine Lakes Wilderness at the 6.6-mile mark, not much more than a mile from the end. Cross Chatter Creek on a study bridge and follow well-built trail for the remainder of the day's 7.8-mile hike.

99 THE CRADLE LOOP

DISTANCE: 33.3 miles
ELEVATION GAIN: 6400 feet
HIGH POINT: 6400 feet
DIFFICULTY: Hard
HIKING TIME: Allow 4 to 5 days
BEST SEASON: Late spring to fall

TRAIL TRAFFIC: Moderate foot traffic; light equestrian traffic
MAPS: USGS Chiwaukum Mountains, USGS The Cradle, USGS Jack Ridge; Green Trails Alpine Lakes East–Stuart Range No. 208SX, Green Trails Alpine Lakes West–Stevens Pass No. 176S

The Cradle and the wildflower-laden meadows of Snowall Creek Valley

PERMIT: Northwest Forest Pass
TRAILHEAD GPS: 47.6123°N, 120.9497°W

NOTE: Camping prohibited within 200 feet of Cradle Lake.

GETTING THERE: Take Highway 2 to Icicle Creek Road (Forest Road 76) just west of Leavenworth. Turn onto Icicle Creek Road and continue as the pavement turns to gravel at 12.5 miles. Keep right at the Y just beyond. At 16.7 miles reach Rock Island Campground. Turn left, crossing over Icicle Creek on a bridge, and continue another 1.8 miles to the Icicle Creek Trailhead, 18.5 miles from Highway 2. Privy available.

This loop visits less-traveled lakes that some rank among the most beautiful in the Alpine Lakes Wilderness. Long, lonely stretches of creekside trail offer solitude, and the ever-constant presence of the Cradle is welcome company on the sometimes-difficult journey.

DAY 1:
Icicle Creek Trailhead to Klonaqua Lakes

9.1 miles, 2300 feet elevation gain

Start by following the Icicle Creek Trail #1551 (Hike 91) into the trees, entering the Alpine Lakes Wilderness in 0.3 mile and making quick work of the wide and nearly flat trail to reach French Creek Camp at 1.5 miles. Cross the bridge spanning French Creek and reach the French Creek Trail #1595 at the 1.7-mile mark. Turn left onto it to climb up the creek valley through alternating sections of forest and open slope, passing the French Ridge Trail #1564 at 5.2 miles and the junction with the

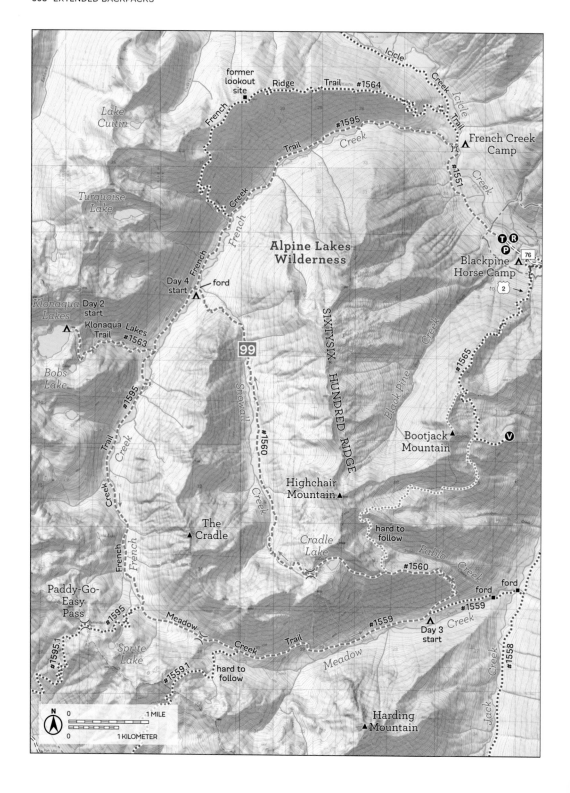

Snowall–Cradle Lake Trail #1560 at 6.2 miles. Note the campsite at this junction: you will be calling it home at the end of Day 3.

Press onward to the 7.2-mile mark to reach the Klonaqua Lakes Trail #1563 (Hike 92), turning right onto it to climb a very steep set of switchbacks. At 8.6 miles note a cairn-marked junction with a rough boot path that leads up past Bobs Lake to one of the upper and arguably prettier Klonaqua Lakes. Beyond the junction, reach steep-shored lower Klonaqua Lake and good campsites, resting at the base of Granite Mountain at 9.1 miles.

DAY 2:
Klonaqua Lakes to Meadow Creek Camp

9.6 miles, 1700 feet elevation gain; 2800 feet lost

From Klonaqua Lakes, drop 1.9 zigzagging miles down to rejoin the French Creek Trail. Head right, continuing your trek deeper into the creek valley. At 5.6 miles reach the junction with the Meadow Creek Trail #1559. Here, the French Creek Trail continues up to Sprite Lake (Hike 52); instead veer left onto the Meadow Creek Trail, following the sometimes-faint pathway through meadows and forest.

Climb up to a saddle between the French Creek and Meadow Creek Valleys at 6.4 miles, soon dropping down through talus fields to reach spur trail #1559.1, which leads up the slope to the top of the divide to connect with the North Scatter Creek Trail #1328.1 at 7.0 miles. Stay on the main trail, pushing another 2.6 miles, to reach the junction with the Snowall–Cradle Lake Trail #1560 and the end of a 9.6-mile day. Camps here make a good stopping point to rest up before the steep climb up to Cradle Lake.

DAY 3:
Meadow Creek Camp to Snowall Creek Camp

8.4 miles, 2400 feet elevation gain; 3000 feet lost

Begin your day with a long climbing traverse through the trees to a set of tight switchbacks along the Snowall–Cradle Lake Trail. Ping-pong up the mountainside to attain a ridge, following it to the junction with the largely abandoned trail leading out toward Blackjack Ridge and Bootjack Mountain (Hike 90) at 2.1 miles. Stay on the main trail for another 0.5 mile, rounding a rocky rib, then climbing through parklands to arrive at gorgeous Cradle Lake, surrounded by wildflower meadows, orange-hued boulders, and the rounded peak of Highchair Mountain. Spend some time exploring these shores before going around the lake and climbing up and out of this lovely alpine basin.

Reach the top lip of the basin at 3.1 miles, tipping into wildflower meadows and rock gardens as you descend. The trail is sometimes indistinct and may require occasional routefinding as you work your way down to the valley floor and Snowall Creek. Push down through this long glacier-carved trench, following Snowall Creek as it passes between the Cradle and Highchair Mountain, rushing to meet French Creek at the 8.4-mile mark. Ford or find a bridge across French Creek to reach the Snowall Creek camp you passed on Day 1.

DAY 4:
Snowall Creek Camp to Icicle Creek Trailhead

6.2 miles, 500 feet lost

From the Snowall Creek camp, retrace your path back to the trailhead, passing the French Ridge Trail at 1.0 mile and reconnecting with the Icicle Creek Trail at the 4.5-mile mark. Veer right, crossing the bridge over French Creek and then passing French Camp at 4.7 miles. The last stretch of trail quickly disappears beneath your boots, and you soon find yourself emerging from the trees at the Icicle Creek Trailhead, ending your adventure a short 6.2 miles from camp.

100 PCT THROUGH-HIKE

DISTANCE: 67.6 miles
ELEVATION GAIN: 14,200 feet
HIGH POINT: 5980 feet
DIFFICULTY: Hard
HIKING TIME: Allow 6 to 8 days
BEST SEASON: Summer to early fall
TRAIL TRAFFIC: Moderate foot traffic
PERMIT: Northwest Forest Pass
TRAILHEAD GPS: 47.42787°N, 121.4134°W

MAPS: USGS Snoqualmie Pass, USGS Chikamin Peak, USGS Big Snow Mountain, USGS Mount Daniel; Green Trails Snoqualmie Pass No. 207, Green Trails Alpine Lakes West–Stevens Pass No. 176S
NOTES: This hike requires a second vehicle, coordination with friends, or a shuttle service. You can find shuttles for hire that cater to PCT through-hikers with a little research online.

GETTING THERE: Take I-90 to Snoqualmie Pass. Eastbound take Exit 52 and turn left under the freeway toward Alpental, and in a few thousand feet turn right onto a small spur road marked "Pacific Crest Trail." Westbound take Exit 53, turning left under the freeway, soon reaching a T intersection. Turn right onto State Route 906, following the sign pointing toward Alpental. Continue 0.7 mile through the ski area to a small spur road marked "Pacific Crest Trail." Follow the spur road to two large parking areas. The first is reserved for stock; hikers should continue to the farther parking lot and trailhead. Privy available.

The grand tour of the Alpine Lake Wilderness—a stretch of the Pacific Crest Trail that many consider to be among the best the trail has to offer. This jaw-dropping wilderness romp from Snoqualmie Pass to Stevens Pass encounters lake after alpine lake, offers endless vistas of sharp peaks and glaciated mountainsides, and wanders through wildflower-flecked tundra and meadowlands. If you want to experience the essence of the Alpine Lakes Wilderness in a single backpacking trip, this is it. This route moves at breakneck speed, so consider adding an intervening day or two to help smooth the journey.

DAY 1:
Snoqualmie Pass to Ridge and Gravel Lakes

7.1 miles, 2400 feet elevation gain; 100 feet lost

From the trailhead, follow the Pacific Crest Trail #2000 (PCT) toward Kendall Peak and Katwalk (Hike 34), reaching the junction with the Commonwealth Basin Trail #1033 (Hike 33) at 2.4 miles. Continue past it, rolling through boulder-covered slopes, skipping over creeks, and enjoying the wildflowers. Find the scramble route up to the summit of Kendall Peak at 5.3 miles, a side trip worth the effort for the commanding 360-degree views from the top. Cross Kendall Katwalk at 6.1 miles and continue along a rocky ridgetop through talus fields to reach Ridge and Gravel Lakes, 7.1 miles from the trailhead. Both lakes have good camping and even better vistas.

DAY 2:
Ridge and Gravel Lakes to Lemah Creek Camp

12.2 miles, 1800 feet elevation gain; 3800 feet lost

From Ridge and Gravel Lakes, continue on the PCT down past a side trail leading up to

Trap Lake from the Pacific Crest Trail below Trap Pass

Bumble Bee Pass, another quick climb that offers impressive views of towering Mount Thompson and Edds Lake below. Climb upward, across the flanks of Alaska Mountain, revealing Joe Lake below as you climb around a ridge, then drop down the mountainside to a narrow rib between Edds Lake and Joe Lake. Traverse Huckleberry Mountain's open slopes, crossing alpine meadows and enjoying the stunning views. Round one of Huckleberry Mountain's ridges to begin a long climb up toward the craggy heights of Chikamin Peak.

From this high point, the trail descends slightly, traversing vast fields of rocks and boulders beneath Four Brothers. Follow the trail as it climbs over the top of Chikamin Ridge and discover Park Lakes tucked into the basin below. Push on to the junction with the Mineral Creek Trail #1331 (Hike 45) to the right at 7.2 miles, with access to the Park Lakes and good camping.

The PCT continues to drop, switchbacking down to reach the access trail to Spectacle Lake at 9.6 miles. Take this short 0.3-mile loop trail to climb to a gorgeous alpine lake and a good stopping point for those looking to spend another night in the wilderness. Where the Spectacle Lake loop trail rejoins the PCT, descend steeply to cross Delate Creek and reach Delate Meadow and sections of old burn. Pass the Pete Lake Trail #1323 (Hike 46) junction at 11.0 miles, continuing onward until you reach Lemah Creek. Find a way across Lemah Creek, fording if you must. On the other side, choose a campsite to end your day after a long 12.2 miles of hiking.

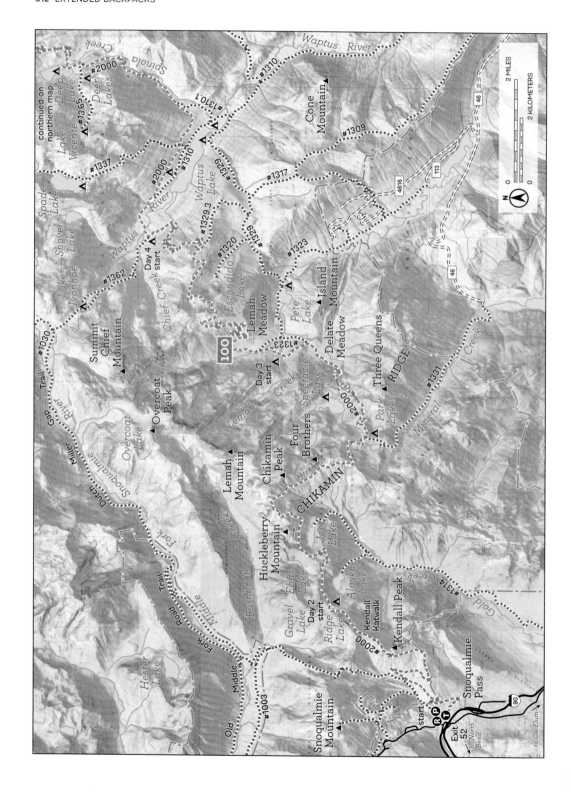

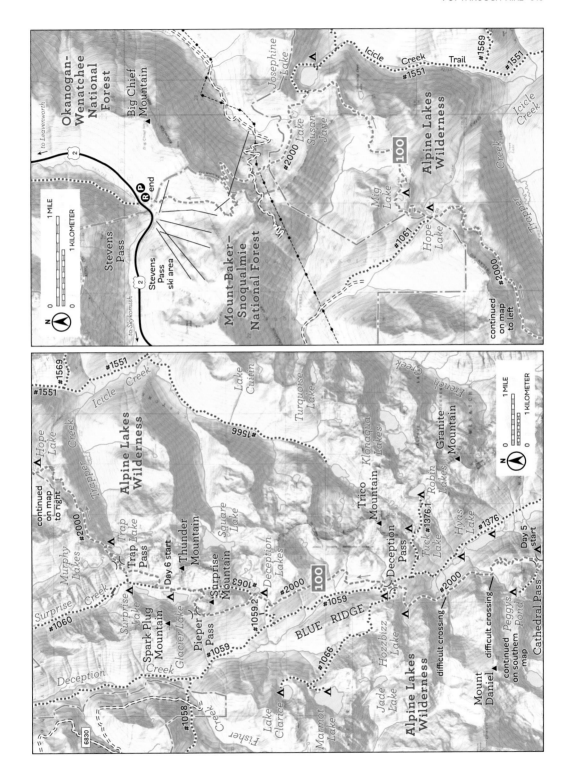

DAY 3:
Lemah Creek Camp to Chief Creek Camp

13.6 miles, 2400 feet elevation gain; 2500 feet lost

From Lemah Creek, push onward along the PCT, passing the junction with the Lemah Meadow Trail #1323.2 at 1.3 miles. From here, begin a long, steep climb up one of Summit Chief Mountain's many ridges, switchbacking over and over again. Eventually push out of the trees and enter another old burn, continuing to climb and crest the ridge at 6.9 miles. Continue over granite country, winding between the Escondido Tarns above Escondido Lake in the shadow of Summit Chief Mountain.

Continue to contour around the slopes above Escondido Lake, reaching the Waptus Burn Trail #1329.3 junction at the 9.3-mile mark. Stick with the PCT, following it into the Waptus Lake Basin, switchbacking steeply down to meet the Dutch Miller Gap Trail #1362 at 13.6 miles. Here, head left for a short jaunt off the PCT to find campsites near Chief Creek to set up camp for the night. Those willing to put in a little more distance can trek down to Waptus Lake (Hike 48) for lakeside camping.

DAY 4:
Chief Creek Camp to Cathedral Pass Tarn

10.4 miles, 2600 feet elevation gain

From Chief Creek Camp, proceed down the PCT, passing the junction with the Waptus River Trail #1310 at 0.9 mile, staying high above Waptus Lake. Continue through the trees, crossing the Spade Lake Trail #1337 at 2.2 miles. Stay under the canopy of old growth, passing yet another junction, this time with the Spinola Creek Trail #1310.1 at the 3.4-mile mark. Continue up the Spinola Creek Valley, climbing around rocky outcroppings, through talus fields, and over tumbling creeks, passing the Lake Vicente Trail #1365 at 6.6 miles. The meadows surrounding Deep Lake (Hike 55)

are just beyond, with a spur trail leading out to good campsites at 7.0 miles. Take a moment to marvel at Cathedral Rock and Mount Daniel towering over this tranquil alpine lake. Wander out to the campsites for a better look, or if planning a longer trip, set up camp for the night.

From the junction, press upward, leaving the meadows and climbing the mountainside, switchbacking through open country to pass the junction with the Peggys Pond Trail #1375 at 9.9 miles. Continue up and over Cathedral Pass to reach the Cathedral Pass Trail #1345 (Hike 59). Leave the PCT here to find camping at a lovely alpine tarn just down the Cathedral Pass Trail at 10.4 miles.

DAY 5:
Cathedral Pass Tarn to Glacier Lake

12.3 miles, 2100 feet elevation gain; 2800 feet lost

From the tarn, return to the PCT and head out toward Deception Pass (Hike 59), cutting through a broad ledge of parkland, passing tarns and enjoying views of the Hyas Lakes as you progress. Drop down through the trees to two difficult creek crossings, the first at 2.0 miles, the next at 3.2 miles. Use caution when waters are high. From the second creek crossing, the trail angles up, climbing to Deception Pass after 4.9 miles of hiking. In this broad hollow find a number of trails, including the Deception Pass Trail #1376 (Hike 59), the Marmot Lake Trail #1066 (Hike 58), and the Deception Creek Trail #1059 (Hike 69). There's a lot of potential for adventure in this area, but for now, stay on the PCT.

Climb higher on the valley wall above Deception Creek, then begin a long traverse out to Deception Lakes (Hike 69), passing the Deception Lakes Trail #1059.2 junction at 8.2 miles, just below the lakes. Climb up to Deception Lakes, skirting the lakeshore and reaching the junction with the Surprise Mountain Trail #1063 at the 8.8-mile mark. Stay left on the PCT, pushing up the flanks of Surprise

Mountain to arrive at Pieper Pass at 9.8 miles. Find enormous views of dazzling Glacier Lake and Surprise Lake (Hike 70) below, the snowy crowns of Mount Daniel and Mount Hinman and countless others. Spend some time up here enjoying the panorama before switchbacking down through the talus to Glacier Lake and your camp for the night at 12.3 miles.

DAY 6:
Glacier Lake to Stevens Pass

13.1 miles, 2900 feet of elevation gain; 3300 feet lost

From Glacier Lake, continue your journey along the PCT. Pass the Surprise Lake Trail #1060 junction at 0.4 mile, keeping right on the PCT. Climb up the boulder-strewn slopes toward Trap Pass, switchbacking steeply, gaining the pass at 1.9 miles. Drop into a basin high above shimmering Trap Lake (Hike 71), traversing open slopes down to a spur trail at 3.1 miles leading down to the shores of Trap Lake. Stick to the main trail, and spend the next 2.6 miles trekking across a long ridge just at the edge of the tree line, crossing alpine meadows and enjoying long views of the surrounding landscape.

Eventually round a ridge and drop down to Hope Lake (Hike 72) and the junction with Tunnel Creek Trail #1061 at 5.6 miles. Pressing onward, reach Mig Lake 0.7 mile distant. Either of these lakes would make for a decent stopping point if you'd like to add a day. Another excellent stopping point is Josephine Lake (Hike 73), reached at the 8.8-mile mark. Here too is the Icicle Creek Trail #1551 (Hike 91). Continue down the PCT, passing Lake Susan Jane at 9.3 miles and crossing the bowl above Mill Creek. Climb your last climb, up to the ridge above Mill Creek, reaching the top at 11.1 miles. From here, drop down through the Stevens Pass ski area to the trailhead and odyssey's end, at 13.1 miles for the day, and clocking in at 67.6 miles of trail.

ACKNOWLEDGMENTS

This book would not have been possible without the tireless support of our families, our friends, and the hikingwithmybrother.com community. Our friends and family have tolerated years of us gallivanting off on yet another extended backpack into the Alpine Lakes Wilderness and listening to us talk incessantly about this book. The journey of writing this book has been so long that, along the way, we both got married and a child was born. That little girl, who has never known a day when her father wasn't working on this guidebook, will be four by the time this book hits the shelves.

We cannot thank everyone enough for the love and support that made this effort possible, but we would like to thank a few folks who went above and beyond: Alysha Yagoda for her invaluable editing skills, Meg Manthos for her tireless cheerleading, Hillary Witte for her tolerance of our endless talking, Kolbe Kegel for his willingness to repeatedly accompany us on backpacking trips for this guide, and Myrna Barnes, Nathan's daughter, who grudgingly forgave Daddy for being gone so often.

And finally, to our mother, Diane Barnes: thank you for setting us down this trail.

OPPOSITE: *Steep cliffs hem in the shores of Rainy Lake (Hike 4).*

LAND MANAGERS' CONTACT INFORMATION

Mount Baker–Snoqualmie National Forest
www.fs.usda.gov/main/mbs/home

Skykomish Ranger District
74920 NE Stevens Pass Hwy.
P.O. Box 305
Skykomish, WA 98288
(360) 677-2414

Snoqualmie Ranger District
902 SE North Bend Way, Bldg. 1
North Bend, WA 98045
(425) 888-1421

Okanogan-Wenatchee National Forest
www.fs.usda.gov/main/okawen/home

Cle Elum Ranger District
803 W. Second St.
Cle Elum, WA 98922
(509) 852-1100

Wenatchee River Ranger District
600 Sherbourne St.
Leavenworth, WA 98826
(509) 548-2550

**Washington State Department of
Natural Resources**
www.dnr.wa.gov/DiscoverPass

Natural Resources Building Headquarters
1111 Washington St. SE
Olympia, WA 98504
(360) 902-1000

OPPOSITE: *A snow-driven creek tumbles down the cliffs of Stuart Range on its way to Ingalls Creek (Hike 97).*

GUIDE TO PLACE NAMES

The Alpine Lakes Wilderness is filled with captivating geographical features that must have begged to be named. Early prospectors and trappers started the name-game, followed by loggers, sportsmen, and lovers of the outdoors. Standing above them all is Albert H. Sylvester, a surveyor and then forest supervisor who was a prolific place-namer, christening hundreds of ridges, creeks, mountains, and lakes across what would become the Alpine Lakes Wilderness. By no means comprehensive, the following list is a handy reference to features mentioned in this guidebook and a quick way for the curious to find out the reason behind a name.

Alice Lake Named in 1909 by Albert H. Sylvester in honor of his wife, Alice.

Arrowhead Mountain Named by Albert H. Sylvester in reference to a talus field on the south slope that has the rough outline of an arrowhead.

Augusta, Lake Named in 1909 by Albert H. Sylvester in honor of his mother.

Badlands, the Named by sheepherders for the lack of good food for their sheep and the predominance of talus.

Big Jim Mountain Named by Albert H. Sylvester in honor of James J. Hill, the chief executive officer of the Great Northern Railway.

Blackjack Ridge Named for the ridge's location between the Black Pine Creek and Jack Creek drainages.

Box Canyon Named for the way Rampart Ridge and Keechelus Ridge "boxed" travelers in and prevented passage across the Cascades.

Brigham, Lake Named for Brigham Young, an early leader in the Mormon church, due to the lake's close proximity to seven lakes named after different women. The name refers to the practice of polygamy associated with the Mormon faith; the group of lakes that includes Alice, Augusta, Edna, Flora, Grace, Ida, and Margaret is sometimes referred to as the Mormon Ladies Lakes.

Bryant Peak Named in 1924 in honor of Mountaineer Sidney Bryant, who passed away that year. Bryant was the first chairman of The Mountaineers Lodge Committee, who helped make the construction of the club's Snoqualmie Lodge a reality.

Bulls Tooth Named by Albert H. Sylvester for its resemblance to a tooth on the "jawbone" of Icicle Ridge.

Cabin Creek Named for the prospectors' cabins that populated the creek drainage in the 1890s.

Cape Horn A rocky prominence near Ladies Pass named by Albert H. Sylvester in 1909 for its sharp peak.

Cashmere Mountain Named by Judge James Harvey Chase in reference to the poem "Lalla Rookh" by Sir Thomas Moore, which highlights the beauty of the mountains of Kashmir in India.

Chain Lakes Named by a USGS topographer because the lakes form a chain.

Chatter Creek Named by Albert H. Sylvester in reference to the "chattering" noise made by swiftly flowing water.

Chiwaukum: Lake, Mountains, Creek *Chiwaukum* means "many little creeks running into a big one" in the Wenatchee Tribe's language, sometimes called Interior Salish.

Colchuck Lake *Colchuck* means "very cold water" or "ice water" in Chinook Jargon.

Cuitin: Lake, Creek *Cuitan* or *ku-i-tan* is Chinook Jargon for "horse." Named by Albert H. Sylvester in reference to the lack of good horse grazing at the mouth of the creek.

Cup Lake Named by Albert H. Sylvester for the cuplike depression the lake sits in.

Davis Peak Named in 1926 by Grover Burch, a Cle Elum District ranger and one of the first rangers in the Forest Service, in honor of Louie Davis, a lookout worker who had recently died.

Deadhorse Pass Considered the only pass suitable for crossing the Chiwaukum Mountains on horseback, the pass was named by Albert H. Sylvester for the long packhorse strings (and herds of sheep) that sheepherders and stockmen used when crossing the pass. Not all the horses made it over the pass.

Deep Lake The name refers to the unexpected depth of the lake.

Denny Creek Named for David T. Denny, brother of Arthur Denny, who had claims along the creek in 1890.

Doelle Lakes Named by Albert H. Sylvester in honor of William A. Doelle, an outdoorsman and friend of Sylvester's who died fighting a forest fire in the area.

Donald, Lake Named by Albert H. Sylvester for the son of Jason Williams, a ranger in Sylvester's district. Nearby Loch Eileen is named for Williams's daughter.

Dutch Miller Gap Named for Andrew Jackson "Dutch" Miller, who located the Dutch Miller Mine nearby in the La Bohn Gap area.

Edna, Lake Named in 1909 by Albert H. Sylvester for the girlfriend of his camping companion Ranger Burne Canby.

Eightmile: Creek, Lake Named for the location where the creek flows into Icicle Creek: river mile eight. The lake is named after the creek.

Eileen, Loch Named by Albert H. Sylvester for the daughter of Jason Williams, a ranger in Sylvester's district. Nearby Lake Donald is named for Williams's son.

Emerald Lake The second of the Necklace Valley Lakes, sometimes called Necklace Valley Lake Number 2. Necklace Valley refers to the way Jade, Emerald, and Opal Lakes appear to be strung together like a necklace strung with streams.

Enchantment Lakes Named by Albert H. Sylvester, who stumbled upon them and found them to be enchanting.

Ethel, Lake Named by Albert H. Sylvester in honor of Ethel Lenzie, the wife of Frank Lenzie, one of the rangers in Sylvester's district.

Flora, Lake Named in 1909 by Albert H. Sylvester in honor of Flora Green, the wife of one of the rangers in Sylvester's district.

Florence, Lake Named in 1909 by Albert H. Sylvester in reference to nearby Margaret and Mary Lakes. Margaret and Mary were sisters of Burne Canby, a ranger who was camping with Sylvester at the time, and two lakes were named in their honor. The sisters had a mutual friend named Florence, and because of the close proximity of the lakes, Sylvester named the lake after their close friend.

French: Creek, Ridge Named for a local prospector and homesteader who had claims along the creek.

Frosty: Creek, Pass Named in 1909 by Albert H. Sylvester in reference to the cold and frosty morning when he first explored it.

Gill Creek Named by Albert H. Sylvester for Justus Gill, who owned a homestead at the head of the creek.

Gold Creek Named for the gold and other precious metals found by miners prospecting the Gold Creek area.

Goldmyer Hot Springs Named for William Goldmyer, who purchased the land around the hot springs and built a lodge for local lumberjacks and miners around 1900.

Grace Lake Named by Albert H. Sylvester for the wife of Charles Haydon, who was with him when he came upon the lake.

Grass Lake Named by fishermen for the grassy, reed-covered shoreline.

Grindstone: Creek, Mountain Named by Albert H. Sylvester and Ranger John Bender for a grindstone that was lost while crossing the creek. The mountain was named in reference to the creek.

Guye Peak Named for F. M. Guye, who staked a number of mining claims in the area.

Harding Mountain Named by Albert H. Sylvester in honor of President Warren Harding.

Hatchery Creek Named for the hatchery built at the mouth of the creek that closed in 1907.

Hibox Sometimes called High Box; the high point on Box Ridge was named by forest officers.

Hinman, Mount Named in 1934 in honor of Dr. Harry B. Hinman, a member of The Mountaineers and founder of the organization's Everett chapter.

Horseshoe Lake Named for the horseshoe-like shape of the lakeshore.

Hyas Lake *Hyas* is Chinook Jargon for "big" or "great." Over the years the lake has often been referred to as simply "Big Lake," though that name never appears on official maps of the area.

Icicle Creek Derivation of *na'sik-elt*, meaning "narrow bottom canyon or gorge."

Ida, Lake Named in 1909 by Albert H. Sylvester in honor of his wife's sister, Ida.

Ilswoot, Lake A corruption of *itswoot*, Chinook Jargon for "black bear."

Ingalls: Lake, Pass, Creek, Peak Named for Captain Benjamin Ingalls, who led a survey of the area in 1855 and is credited as the first person to discover gold in the region.

Island Lake Named for the small islands that populate its waters.

Island Mountain Named for its isolation from nearby ridges, created in part by the creeks that surround it: Lemah Creek to the north and Delate Creek to the south.

Ivanhoe, Lake Named after Wilfred of Ivanhoe, from Sir Walter Scott's book *Ivanhoe.*

Nearby Lake Rebecca and Lake Rowena are also nods to the story.

Jade Lake The first of the Necklace Valley Lakes, and as a result is sometimes called First Lake. Necklace Valley refers to the way Jade, Emerald, and Opal Lakes appear to be strung together like a necklace strung with streams.

Jade Lake Near Marmot Lake. Named for the unusual color of the lake's waters, a deep, almost milky green created by glacial silt.

Jim Hill Mountain Named by Albert H. Sylvester in honor of Great Northern Railway chief executive James J. Hill.

Josephine Lake Named by Albert H. Sylvester in honor of Josephine Williams, the wife of a ranger under Sylvester's supervision.

Julius Lake Named by Albert H. Sylvester for Julius Kummel, a member of the Forest Service who accompanied Sylvester on his first trip to the lake.

Keekwulee Falls *Keekwulee* is Chinook Jargon meaning "to fall down" or "low-below." The member of The Mountaineers who named the falls intended the "to fall down" meaning, but the "low" or "below" meaning works as well, since Keekwulee Falls are the lowest falls on Denny Creek.

Klonaqua Lakes A set of three lakes named by Albert H. Sylvester during his tenure as the first forest manager of the Wenatchee National Forest between 1908 and 1931. Sylvester took the Chinook Jargon word for "three," *klone*, and combined it with the Wenatchee word for "water," *qua*, to make Klonaqua.

Larch Lake Name refers to the predominance of larch trees in the lake basin.

Little Annapurna Named by the Sherpa Climbing Club of Ellensburg for its resemblance to the Annapurna of Himalayan fame.

Little Big Chief Mountain Named by The Mountaineers for L. A. "Shorty" Nelson, a mountaineer and hiker who had a reputation for out-hiking and outclassing everyone in his climbing party.

Margaret Lake Named in 1909 by Albert H. Sylvester for one of the sisters of Burne Canby, a ranger he was camping with.

Marmot Lake Named for the abundance of marmots in the area.

Marten Lake Named by early visitors to the lake for the pine martens that were once prevalent in the area.

Mary Lake Named in 1909 by Albert H. Sylvester for one of the sisters of Burne Canby, a ranger he was camping with.

Mastiff Mountain Named by Albert H. Sylvester for the mountain's resemblance to the head of a mastiff when viewed from Lake Wenatchee.

Melakwa Lake *Melakwa* is Chinook Jargon for "mosquito."

Myrtle Lake Named by Albert H. Sylvester around 1918, likely following his convention of naming lakes for women in his life or the lives of his forest rangers.

Nordrum: Lake, Lookout Named for Martin Nordrum, a homesteader who had a claim near Quartz Creek beginning in 1902. Nordrum worked for the US Forest Service from 1910 to 1929 doing maintenance and fire patrol while maintaining a cabin on the Taylor River Road just past Quartz Creek. He was friendly and well known, befriending many of the hunters, fishermen, and backpackers who came through the area.

Olallie Lake *Olallie* means "berry" in Chinook Jargon.

Opal Lake The third of the Necklace Valley Lakes, sometimes called Necklace Valley Lake Number 3. Necklace Valley refers to the way Jade, Emerald, and Opal Lakes appear to be strung together like a necklace strung with streams.

Otter Falls Also known as Otter Slide Falls or Otter Creek Falls. Named for the granite slide that the falls tumble down, which one imagines an otter might enjoy playing on.

Overcoat Peak Named by Albert H. Sylvester in 1897 when he ascended the peak and built a cairn to mark the achievement. For fun, he buttoned his too-small overcoat around the cairn and left it behind, giving the mountain its name.

Paddy-Go-Easy Pass Named for a miner's burro named Paddy, whose owner would tell the animal to "go easy" over rough portions of the trail.

Pete Lake Named in honor of a Forest Service packhorse named Pete that spent a great deal of time on the trail to the lake.

Polallie Ridge *Polallie* means "dust" or "sand" in Chinook Jargon. Albert H. Sylvester named the ridge in reference to the sandstone that makes up much of the ridge.

Pratt Lake Named by The Mountaineers to honor one of their members, John W. Pratt.

Pratt River Named for George A. Pratt, a prospector with mining claims in Middle Fork Snoqualmie Basin near Chair Creek. Instead of following a more established route along the Middle Fork Snoqualmie and Taylor Rivers, Pratt approached his claims via what is now known as the Pratt River Valley and helped establish the first Pratt River Trail.

Putrid Pete's Peak Named in honor of Pete Schoening, a Seattle-area mountaineer and outdoorsman who is most famous for his belay on K2 on August 10, 1953, often known simply as "the Belay" in the climbing community.

Rainy: Lake, Creek Named for the high levels of precipitation that fall in the area around the lake.

Sawyer, Mount Named in honor of George Sawyer, a long-serving firewatcher for the Skykomish District, after his death in 1930.

Scenic Lakes The collective name for Glacier Lake and Surprise Lake, named by The Mountaineers in 1916 for their close proximity to Scenic, a small railroad community. Originally Upper and Lower Scenic Lakes.

Shovel Lake Named for the lake's outline, which looks something like a shovel. Likely named at the same time as nearby Spade Lake.

Snowgrass Mountain Named by sheepherders for the grass that was commonly found on the slopes, a preferred forage for their sheep.

Spade Lake Named for the shape of the lake, which was likened to a flat garden spade, likely at the same time as nearby Shovel Lake.

Stegosaurus Butte One of many names for a small but distinctive ridge near the confluence of the Taylor River and the Middle Fork Snoqualmie River, for its resemblance to a slumbering stegosaurus when viewed from afar; a name popularized by Harvey Manning and The Mountaineers. Also known as Choirboy or Taylor Knob.

Stuart: Mount, Lake Named by George B. McClellan in 1853 to honor his longtime friend Jimmie Stuart, a soldier who was killed a few years earlier in a skirmish with American Indians. Lake Stuart inherited its name from the mountain it sits below.

Surprise Lake Named for the "surprise" that comes with finally reaching this lake in a small depression after cresting the small ridge that surrounds it.

Talapus Lake *Talapus* means "coyote" in Chinook Jargon.

Thorp, Mountain Named for Fielden Mortimer Thorp, a famed Yakima Valley pioneer who is often credited as being the first settler in that area, in 1960.

Tin Cup Joe: Falls, Creek Named in the 1890s by miners for another prospector. The creek is now known as Cripple Creek.

Trap Lake Named by Forest Supervisor Albert H. Sylvester to harmonize with Trapper Creek, which drains Trap Lake.

Trout: Lake, Creek Named for the fish that inhabits the waters.

Tunnel Creek Named for the nearby Burlington Northern Tunnel that was drilled beneath Stevens Pass.

Vicente: Creek, Lake Named by Albert H. Sylvester in honor of a Spanish sheepherder Sylvester worked with.

Victoria: Lake, Creek Named in 1909 by Albert H. Sylvester in honor of Queen Victoria of England.

Waptus Lake *Wáptas* is a Sahaptin word meaning "feather."

Wildhorse Creek A very old name given by early stockmen, who sighted bands of wild horses in the area.

Wright Mountain Named by The Mountaineers in 1924 in honor of member George Wright, who passed away in 1923.

BIBLIOGRAPHY

Asars, Tami. *Hiking the Pacific Crest Trail: Washington: Section Hiking from the Columbia River to Manning Park.* Seattle: Mountaineers Books, 2016.

Bentley, Judy. *Hiking Washington's History.* Seattle: University of Washington Press, 2010.

Egan, Michael. "Visions of Arcadia: Wilderness and the Ecology of Trail Construction in the Costal Pacific Northwest." Master's thesis, Simon Fraser University, 2000. Library and Arhives Canada, www.collectionscanada.gc.ca/obj/s4/f2/dsk1/tape4/PQDD_0014/MQ61425.pdf.

Hitchman, Robert. *Place Names of Washington.* Tacoma: Washington State Historical Society, 1985.

Knibb, David. *Backyard Wilderness: The Alpine Lakes Story.* Seattle: Mountaineers Books, 1982.

Manning, Harvey, Ira Spring, and Vicki Spring. *100 Hikes in Washington's Alpine Lakes,* 3rd ed. Seattle: Mountaineers Books, 2000.

Sylvester, Albert H. "Place-Naming in the Northwest." *American Speech* 18, no. 4 (Dec. 1943): 241–252.

OPPOSITE: *Subalpine daisy in the avalanche fields on the route up to Hibox Mountain (Hike 43)*

INDEX

Note: **Bold** page numbers indicate primary references.

Nathan and Jeremy on the summit of Little Annapurna (Hike 82)

ABOUT THE AUTHORS

The Barnes brothers were always on the right path to be dedicated hikers—they just didn't know it until early 2008. Born and raised in the Pacific Northwest, they were piled into the car at a young age for family trips to the Columbia River Gorge, Mount Rainier, Mount St. Helens, and really any campground with towering trees and a creek that could be reached in a day's drive. Nathan and Jeremy loved mucking about in the forest, but even after leaving boyhood behind, they weren't much for long hikes.

Nonetheless, in an excess of high spirits not long after college, they thought it would be a good idea to tackle Mount Rainier. After eight months of trail conditioning in the form of many, many hikes, Nathan and Jeremy attained Columbia Crest on September 7, 2008. It seemed a shame to let all that hard-won hiking stamina go to waste, so they resolved to keep up the training regimen of weekly hikes to stay in shape. Idle trail talk led them to set a goal:

Explore all the hikes in Harvey Manning and Ira Spring's *55 Hikes Around Snoqualmie Pass* (Mountaineers Books, 2001). Before long, they decided it would be fun to track their progress, and hikingwithmybrother.com was born.

Along the way Nathan and Jeremy have met a lot of hikers and outdoors lovers and have partnered with *Backpacker Magazine*, the *Seattle Times*, Washington State Parks, and the Washington Trails Association, as well as The Mountaineers. Their first book, *Hiking through History Washington: Exploring the Evergreen State's Past by Trail*, was published in 2014. Today they continue to hike as often as they can, but they no longer do it simply for the exercise. They also do it for everyone who follows hikingwithmybrother.com and enjoys up-to-date trail reports, out-of-the-way destinations, and adventuresome hikes.

Feel free to drop them a line sometime at hikingwithmybrother@gmail.com.

OTHER TITLES YOU MIGHT ENJOY FROM MOUNTAINEERS BOOKS

100 CLASSIC HIKES: WASHINGTON
3rd edition
Craig Romano
Enjoy the best, most challenging,
and most beloved hikes across
Washington state.

HIKING WASHINGTON'S FIRE LOOKOUTS
Amber Casali
Hike to 44 still-standing lookouts
in the Cascades and Olympics.

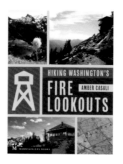

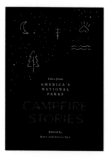

CAMPFIRE STORIES
Tales from America's National Parks
Edited by Dave and Ilyssa Kyu
Soak up stories about six of
America's iconic national parks.

DIRTY GOURMET
Food for Your Outdoor Adventures
Mai-Yan Kwan, Emily Nielson, and Aimee Trudeau
Choose from more than 120
deliciously modern recipes for day trips,
car camping, and backcountry treks.

DAY HIKING SERIES
Get out on the trail. The second edition of *Snoqualmie Region* covers 136 hikes in the Cascade foothills, Interstate 90 corridor, and Alpine Lakes. *Central Cascades* covers 125 hikes around Stevens Pass, Alpine Lakes, and Lake Wenatchee.

www.mountaineersbooks.org

recreation · lifestyle · conservation

MOUNTAINEERS BOOKS is a leading publisher of mountaineering literature and guides—including our flagship title, *Mountaineering: The Freedom of the Hills*—as well as adventure narratives, natural history, and general outdoor recreation. Through our two imprints, Skipstone and Braided River, we also publish titles on sustainability and conservation. We are committed to supporting the environmental and educational goals of our organization by providing expert information on human-powered adventure, sustainable practices at home and on the trail, and preservation of wilderness.

The Mountaineers, founded in 1906, is a 501(c)(3) nonprofit outdoor recreation and conservation organization whose mission is to enrich lives and communities by helping people "explore, conserve, learn about, and enjoy the lands and waters of the Pacific Northwest and beyond." One of the largest such organizations in the United States, it sponsors classes and year-round outdoor activities throughout the Pacific Northwest, including climbing, hiking, backcountry skiing, snowshoeing, camping, kayaking, sailing, and more. The Mountaineers also supports its mission through its publishing division, Mountaineers Books, and promotes environmental education and citizen engagement. For more information, visit The Mountaineers Program Center, 7700 Sand Point Way NE, Seattle, WA 98115-3996; phone 206-521-6001; www.mountaineers.org; or email info@mountaineers.org.

Our publications are made possible through the generosity of donors and through sales of more than 800 titles on outdoor recreation, sustainable lifestyle, and conservation. To donate, purchase books, or learn more, visit us online:

MOUNTAINEERS BOOKS
1001 SW Klickitat Way, Suite 201 • Seattle, WA 98134
800-553-4453 • mbooks@mountaineersbooks.org • www.mountaineersbooks.org

An independent nonprofit publisher since 1960

Mountaineers Books is proud to support the Leave No Trace Center for Outdoor Ethics, whose mission is to promote and inspire responsible outdoor recreation through education, research, and partnerships. The Leave No Trace program is focused specifically on human-powered (nonmotorized) recreation. For more information, visit www.lnt.org.